Dearest Sweetheart

Letters from a GI to his wife during World War II

by Jeanne Walser Price

TURNER PUBLISHING COMPANY

Turner Publishing Company

Turner Publishing Company Staff:
Editor: Herbert C. Banks II
Designer: Heather R. Warren

Library of Congress Catalog
Card No: 99-61090
ISBN: 978-1-68162-246-0

Table of Contents

Dedication

Dedicated to the GI's, the men and women
who gave their lives in this terrible war, so
we might live in peace. God bless them all.

Introduction

Jack and I had both come from families who had great regard for saving family records and letters. We each had ancestors who had fought in every war, for causes they believed in, beginning with our own American Revolution

The Price family had settled in Virginia and later in Brazeau, Missouri, on the Mississippi River. My mother's family had also settled in Virginia and later in Mississippi and Alabama. My grandfather, John Hatfield, was a confederate veteran. Both Jack's and my grandparents lived with us so we have their letters and papers, also.

As soon as Jack received that Draft Notice we realized we were now a part of history, whether we liked it or not. I wrote to Jack each day, with every detail of the baby's and my life. He wrote to me every day, since he was a clerk at Camp Fannin and then in England. Understandably, he was not able to save my letters. Naturally, the daily letters ended when he went into combat. Even so, he did remarkably well.

His letters are a day by day account of the life of an ordinary GI missing his home and family. They are sad, happy, humorous, touching, and sometimes very profound.

When the war was over and Jack returned to civilian life he was very fortunate. He had a position waiting for him with J.J. Newberry Company (retail stores) as assistant manager. He was in the retail business all of his working life. He was transferred constantly as manager.

We had three more children and where Daddy went, we went! In 1976, after moving to Texas, Jack's company (W.E. Walker Stores, Inc.) transferred him to Tyler, Texas as Supervisor. It was something we had never imagined and brought a flood of memories. The next few years were happy indeed.

We had always planned to assemble Jack's war letters and papers and pictures in a notebook for our children. We began reading some of the letters and the papers which had been carefully kept in boxes. We had kept everything, including his full uniform with all the insignia (on a hanger.) It all went where we went!

Sadly, Jack became ill shortly after our project began. He died February 12, 1984, in Tyler. He was buried with full Military Honors in Hunt Japonica Cemetery near Kerrville.

We had expected to retire in Kerrville, since our children are all in that area. After my move there in 1988, having my own house, I made a work place for myself in a dormer room. I learned to use a computer, and began our book in earnest. The dining room table downstairs became a World War II War Room for the duration!.

Jack and I had always planned to go to Europe, to all the places he had been. However, we wanted to wait until he retired so we could spend more time there. That was a mistake!

I became determined to finish what we had started. There were a thousand questions I wished I had asked him. I simply had to see the places he had been. Therefore, in September, 1994, 1 set out for Europe with my niece, Phyllis Fletcher, of Santa Barbara, California. We visited Tidworth, England, then to the Ardennes where we rented a car and drove to Stavelot, Belgium. It was the 50th anniversary of their liberation by the Americans on September 12, 1944, and in the Battle of the Bulge, December, 1944. We then went into Germany where Jack had been wounded. The book was complete except, Part III Combat. When I returned I finished writing it. I had to be certain the events and places were historically correct in every detail.

This is a love story of World War II. Every word is true, every person Is real, and every place is real. I pray that it may remind those who read it, what enormous sacrifices were made for us. I hope you enjoy the book.

Acknowledgments

Since I first began writing this book I have been constantly amazed at the interest and help from so many people. I may not be able to thank everyone, but I shall surely try.

Tyler, Texas: Carnegie Library, Sally Harper, for helping when I started my research. Carnegie Museum, Alice Gilbert, for presenting Jack's letters to the museum. Gordon Nielson, for writing our "love story" in his book, Camp Fannin, Texas. Zelda Boucher, for publishing Jack's letters in The Chronicles of Smith County, Texas, Winter 1993. Mary Jane McNamara, many thanks for old pictures of the Blackstone Hotel and Smith County Courthouse. Betty Smith, for loving England and reading about it as fast as I could write. Viola Errett, for her hospitality at the reunions, the fun of selling things, and our talking all night. Kay and Paul Lockhart, for just being there, close neighbors, close friends.

England: Jack Sweet, Yoevil, Somerset, many thanks for books, information, histories and especially the photographs of Yeovil in this book and for visiting us. The Pickernell family, Ken and Gwen, Tony and Julie, Tidworth, Hamshire, for being family to Phyllis and me. On our first visit to Tidworth, we were shown through all parts of that very strict militllary post. On our 1994 visit, Tony obtained special permission to take us inside Tidworth House, where he brought out the guest book which now contains the signatures of both Queen Elizabeth...and Jeanne Price! The Pickernells have visited us in California and then in Texas. We have shared many happy times; have exchanged gifts, including a tankard which had been in the Pickernell family for generations; and will be treasured by our family, also. We have made memories that will last a lifetime.

Combat, Bulge, and Germany: Madeleine and Joseph Dejardin, Stavelot Belgium, for their gracious hospitality when Phyllis and I visited in September, 1994, and for their delightful correspondence since. Veterans of the Battle of the Bulge, Inc. (of which I am a member), for queries in the Bulge Bugle regarding Jack's records. John D. Bowen, VBOB, for much helpful information in searching for Jack's lost records. Frank Towers, 30th Division, for books and insignia. Grover Twiner, 30th Division, for his help. One special thank you to the wonderful army doctors and nurses who gave so much and truly cared. God bless them every one.

Kerrville, Texas: The entire staff at Butt-Holdsworth Memorial Library, for the display of Jack's uniform and memorabilia and for all of their assistance. There was no end to their help, from reference to inter-library loans. Kerrville Daily Times newspaper for the splendid front page article on Sunday July 30, 1995, about the books I was writing. Radio station KERV, for such beautiful music 24 hours a day, including our old wartime favorites -- just what I needed when writing at

I worked one night each week at the Red Cross making bandages. We wore as white uniform and this headband, with a hairnet. We could not wear lipstick or nail polish. everything had to be completely sterile. We all knew that our own loved one might need the bandage we made.

2 A.M. So Fast Printing, Wally and the whole staff, for their help, the extra things, the perfect work, and a fun place to be. Lupe Lopez, who does my hair at the Hair Pen where I have written many rough drafts while under the dryer. My friend Donna Steichen who listened to every word I wrote, Sunday after Sunday, driving to St. John's Anglican Church in Boerne, Texas. That is a friend. John Henry Key, USMC retired. Boerne, for books and researching records. Major James Kerr Chapter NSDAR, for our members' support and interest and their accepting "Footsteps" in the DAR Library in Washington, D.C. Captain Charles Schreiner Chapter UDC, for our members' encouragement And, special thanks to Clarabelle Snodgrass, who told Mr. Turner about my book. Now, special thanksto my dear and oldest friend, Maryellen Walker Maclin, of Searcy, Arkansas and her husband John, for my lovely visits there, always reading what I wrote, and for being so encouraging.

And, my family: The children -- our daughter Peggy and her husband Bill Braun and our grandson Will Braun; our son Bill Price and our granddaughter Rachael Jeanne Price; our daughter Judi and her husband Rob Walts; and our son John Price, for all the holiday meals eaten on TV trays because the dining room table was being used as a "war room." Unpack the china! And, my "California chick," Phyllis Fletcher, "Little Phillie", who traveled with me and cheered me on when I was convinced I would never finish. Without Peggy and Phyllis there would be no book!

Preface

Aug 21 1943
The President of the United States,

To <u>John Kenrick Price</u>,
Order No <u>1026</u>

GREETING:
You are hereby notified .....

The dreaded message had finally arrived, the order to report for induction! Jack and I had married on November 22, 1940. We were high school sweethearts and the first in our class to marry. The following spring we moved to Houston, Texas.

On December 10, our first baby, a little boy, was born and died. It was three days after Pearl Harbor.

We grieved for the loss of our baby but soon rejoiced when we found I was expecting again. We had been transferred to Birmingham, Alabama, in March, 1942. This was indeed a happy time. It was well that we did not know what was ahead of us.

We had a small house in Green Acres. It was a newly built section, probably one of the first FHA (Federal Housing Administration) developments in Birmingham, Alabama. FHA was a federal program for low cost housing and financing. The houses were almost exactly alike, the big decision being what color roof and shutters. Of course, Jack chose blue.

We had lived in the Tutwiler Hotel for a month, there in Birmingham, Alabama, so our first sandwich on a card table in the little dining room was a feast. We had only a stove and refrigerator, so we decided that I should go to Pizitz Department Store, which was across the street from Jack's office, and buy only the minimum of furniture. That was a mistake!

I bought a maple bed and chest of drawers, and they gave me a little cricket rocker as was the custom. I also bought a small maple dinette set and one lovely big, soft lounge chair for Jack, but something impelled me to go upstairs and just look at carpets. Of course, they were having a sale, a big sale. I knew we had to have that beautiful rose-colored Wilton carpet. For the first, and only one of a few times, Jack was really upset because I had not discussed buying that carpet. However, when winter came and we sat on it before the fire, cozy and warm, all was forgiven. We laughed about it many times later.

Birmingham, Alabama, was a very important city. It was one of the largest steel, iron, and coal centers in the United States. It would have been a prime target if we had been attacked, which did not seem totally impossible at that time. The city had a well-organized civil defense plan. Jack, with several other men, had volunteered to be Air Raid Wardens for Green Acres. It was treated very seriously. He had a vest, a white helmet (with insignia), and a whistle; and when the air-raid siren sounded, there was to be a blackout of the entire city.

One night the siren sounded. Even knowing it was practice, it was an eerie feeling standing in the backyard talking over the fence to my neighbor, in total darkness. Suddenly Jack came rushing across our yard blowing his whistle frantically — guess who had a light showing! I had totally forgotten a low fire in the fireplace. He had seen it two blocks away. It stood out like a spotlight through the front window.

About this time <u>rationing</u> began. Due to the war effort, a number of items were in short supply. Everyone went to the elementary school nearby and registered with the OPA (Office of Price Administration). We received ration books for each member of the household, even for infants! There were ration stamps for sugar, meat, shoes, and some other items. No one we knew complained about it. It was all for our <u>boys</u>. Tires and gasoline were also rationed; however, one had to prove that it was needed for the war effort.

That winter the war had been going on for a year, but it seemed so far away. Most of our neighbors had small children, and the men were in war work, so had not been called. Many of us were knitting olive drab socks, scarves and gloves for the Red Cross, but they were just for any soldier so far. I also knitted pink and blue baby things that winter for the baby we were expecting.

On July 29, 1943, we were overjoyed at the birth of a beautiful baby girl whom we named Margaret Jeanne and called Peggy. Jack had been reclassified 1A which was the highest classification of the draft law) six months before; however, my doctor had been able to get him a deferment due to the circumstances. We had prayed that the unthinkable would not happen, but it did; and we found that the "President" had been thinking of him all along! I wept bitterly, but to no avail.

Our country was fighting for its very life. It had been nineteen months since the bombing of Pearl Harbor in Hawaii on December 7, 1941. Young men were fighting and dying on all fronts, but until this time the war had not touched our family.

Jack was twenty-four years old. I had told myself they were only taking eighteen to twenty-one-year-olds, and they weren't taking fathers yet. I was wrong. They were, and they did, and our lives were changed forever.

Now came the sad task of selling most of our furniture, disposing of all but two of the registered Cocker Spaniels we were raising, and leav-

Houston, 1941 Classified 3A (expecting baby)

7

ing our little house and the nursery we had so lovingly prepared. We had an automobile, but had to get a special permit for gas and tires, which of course were rationed, to get to the induction center which in Jack's case was Jefferson Barracks in St. Louis, Missouri. His parents lived in Webster Groves, a suburb of St. Louis.

August 27, the day of our departure, was a sad leave-taking from our friends and neighbors. Little did we then know how much more precarious our country's situation would become and that the families who were bidding us farewell would soon be torn apart. It was dreadfully hot in Alabama in August so we left in the evening and drove all night while it was a little cooler. We had sent the furniture we were keeping ahead on a van; however, we had the car packed beyond capacity with the bassinet, clothing, and all the things we needed in those days for one little baby, plus two dogs, ourselves and the baby.

The trip was a disaster. We had one flat tire just before we got to Tupelo, in northern Mississippi. We had to unpack the trunk to get to the spare. Jack changed it in the dark on the highway only to have another as soon as we left Tupelo. These were brand new wartime tires! In addition we had a poor little baby suffering from prickly heat, a formula which didn't agree, and a distraught Mother. Thank Heaven for a strong, solid, imperturbable Daddy. We drove the rest of the night without mishap, arriving in the morning at my parents house in Kirkwood, Missouri, (where the baby and I were to stay for the duration of the war). When we arrived, my wonderful mother immediately took over.

My parents had always had someone living with them. First my grandparents, and at the present time my mother's brother Robert Hatfield and my sister Phyllis Hills' daughter Little Phillie, who was eight years old. She would stay until spring, then go to her mother who was doing war work in Washington, D.C. Now the baby and I had come, but who could know how long the duration would last?

The next morning we went to Jack's parents' house in Webster Groves, Missouri, about a twenty minute drive. We proudly presented their first grandchild. Jack had been an only child so this was a special blessing, especially for his mother, since Peggy was the image of her. We stayed with them until it was time for Jack to go.

Jack reported to his draft board as directed at 6:45 A.M., Thursday September 2, 1943. He and the other draftees were then taken by bus to Jefferson Barracks in St. Louis. As any soldier knows, the Army does not tell you what is going to happen to you until it happens. We had all kissed him an emotional goodbye that morning as though he were going to war at that moment. That evening to our amazement he came home on the bus. The next day the same sad leave-taking and then his return. The third day he came home and said he had been inducted, but did not have to report for active duty until Saturday, September 25, 1943. Of course we were overjoyed, but it was a long ten days for him. He went then, as scheduled.

On Sunday September 5, 1943, both families went to see him. What a shock! Besides the usual G I haircut, he had the most ill-fitting uniform they could find — as did all the others. After the well-tailored clothes Jack had always worn, it was hard not to laugh, except it was not a laughing time. At our leave-taking that day, we clung together overcome with dread, as we knew he would be leaving the next day, destination unknown. Leaving his wife and baby was a heart-wrenching thing for him, beyond description. He was going into a new life filled with danger. The separation seemed unbearable and the future bleak seemed bleak for us.

It turned out less bleak than we had at first feared, however, as several days later we received a letter telling us he had arrived safely at Camp Fannin in Tyler, Texas, an overnight ride on the train. My mother's cousin Carrol Mosby Cox lived there, and it was in the South, so it was not the end of the world.

Jack with Litle Audry (Houston, Texas).

November 1941 - Two weeks later World War II.

Our first house. 1308 Montview Road. Birmingham, Alabama.

Car bought from a friend for the trip to report to draft board and to move the baby and me to parents house.

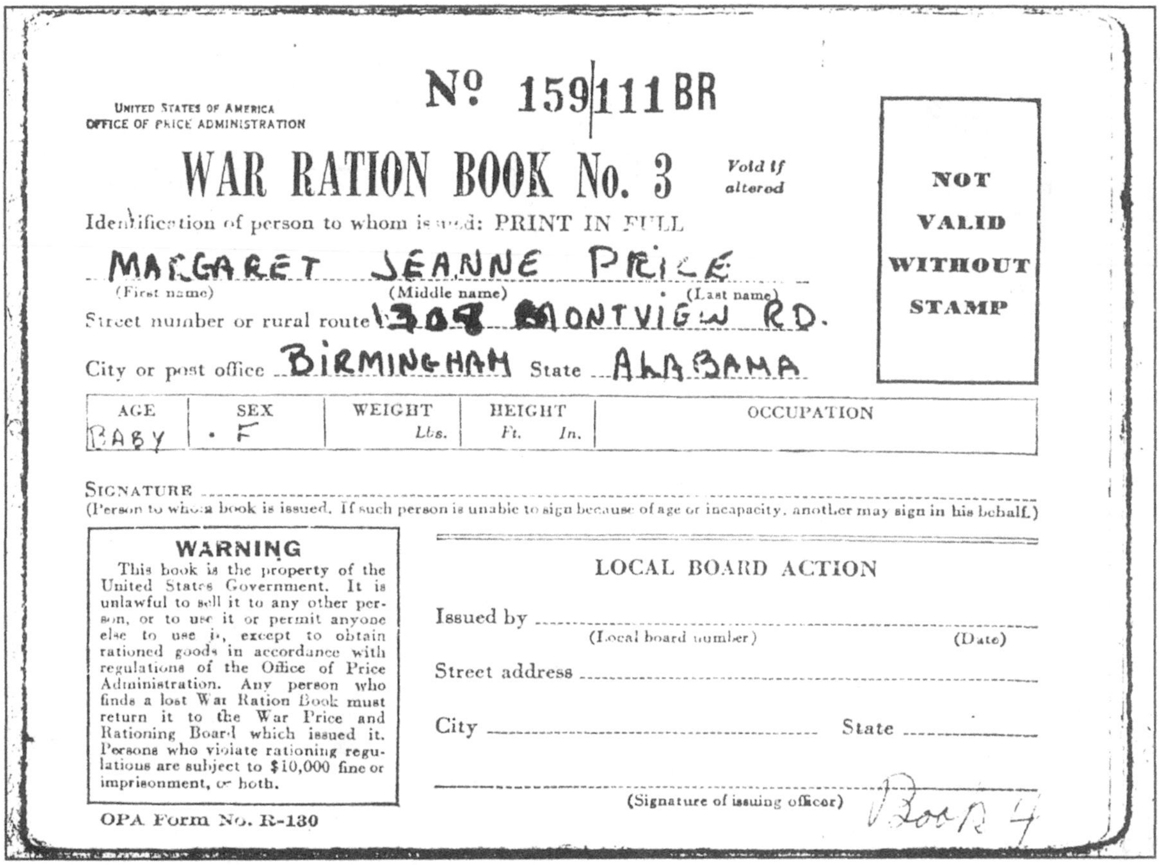

N⁰ 159|111 BR

UNITED STATES OF AMERICA
OFFICE OF PRICE ADMINISTRATION

WAR RATION BOOK No. 3   *Void if altered*

NOT VALID WITHOUT STAMP

Identification of person to whom issued: PRINT IN FULL

MARGARET   JEANNE   PRICE
(First name)   (Middle name)   (Last name)

Street number or rural route 1308 MONTVIEW RD.

City or post office BIRMINGHAM State ALABAMA

AGE	SEX	WEIGHT Lbs.	HEIGHT Ft. In.	OCCUPATION
BABY	F			

SIGNATURE _____
(Person to whom book is issued. If such person is unable to sign because of age or incapacity, another may sign in his behalf.)

WARNING
This book is the property of the United States Government. It is unlawful to sell it to any other person, or to use it or permit anyone else to use it, except to obtain rationed goods in accordance with regulations of the Office of Price Administration. Any person who finds a lost War Ration Book must return it to the War Price and Rationing Board which issued it. Persons who violate rationing regulations are subject to $10,000 fine or imprisonment, or both.

LOCAL BOARD ACTION

Issued by _____
(Local board number)   (Date)

Street address _____

City _____ State _____

(Signature of issuing officer) *Book 4*

OPA Form No. R-130

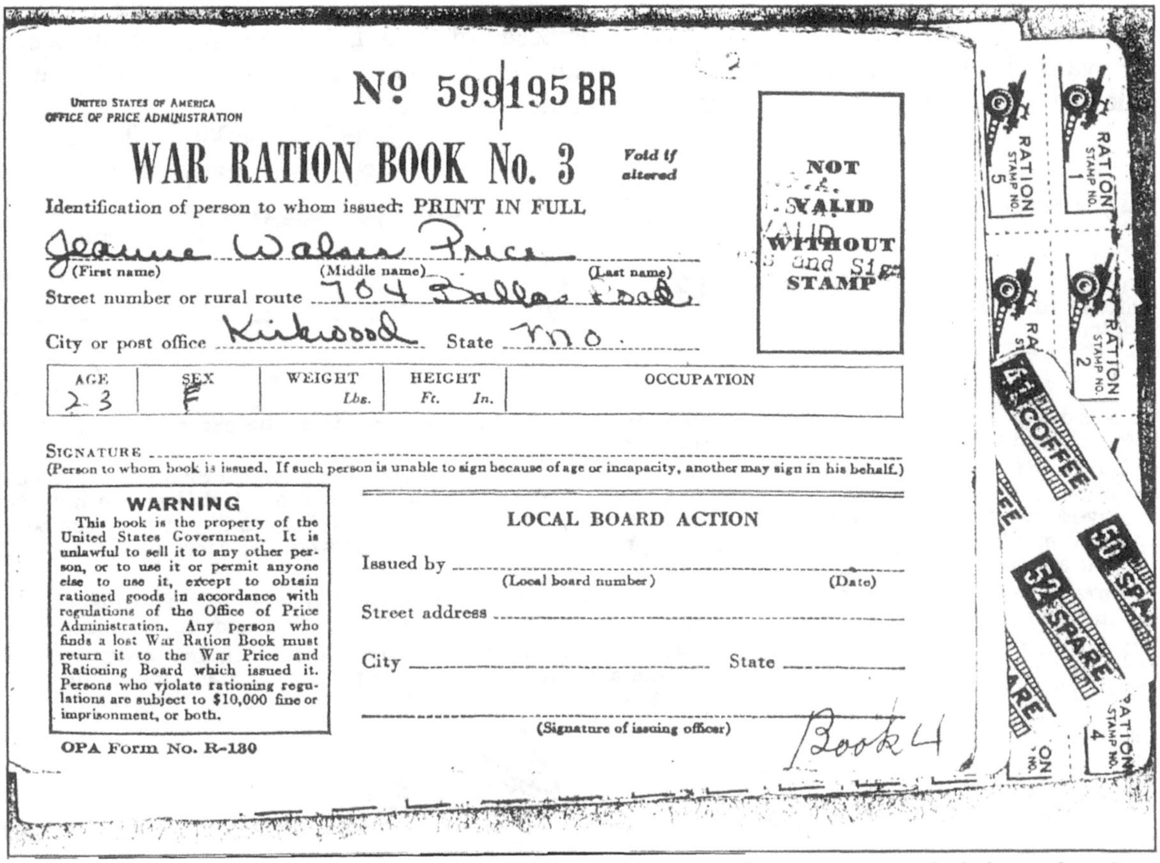

N⁰ 599|195 BR

UNITED STATES OF AMERICA
OFFICE OF PRICE ADMINISTRATION

WAR RATION BOOK No. 3   *Void if altered*

NOT VALID WITHOUT STAMP

Identification of person to whom issued: PRINT IN FULL

Jeanne   Walker   Price
(First name)   (Middle name)   (Last name)

Street number or rural route 704 Dallas Road

City or post office Kirkwood State Mo.

AGE	SEX	WEIGHT Lbs.	HEIGHT Ft. In.	OCCUPATION
23	F			

SIGNATURE _____
(Person to whom book is issued. If such person is unable to sign because of age or incapacity, another may sign in his behalf.)

WARNING
This book is the property of the United States Government. It is unlawful to sell it to any other person, or to use it or permit anyone else to use it, except to obtain rationed goods in accordance with regulations of the Office of Price Administration. Any person who finds a lost War Ration Book must return it to the War Price and Rationing Board which issued it. Persons who violate rationing regulations are subject to $10,000 fine or imprisonment, or both.

LOCAL BOARD ACTION

Issued by _____
(Local board number)   (Date)

Street address _____

City _____ State _____

(Signature of issuing officer) *Book 4*

OPA Form No. R-130

Many things were rationed for which we had to use coupons. Things such as sugar, coffee, meat, margerine, lard, shoes and gasoline.

AUG 2 1 1943
_____
(Date of mailing)

ORDER TO REPORT FOR INDUCTION

The President of the United States,

To _____ John _____ Kendrick _____ Price _____
    (First name)   (Middle name)   (Last name)

Order No. _____ 1026 _____

GREETING:

Having submitted yourself to a local board composed of your neighbors for the purpose of determining your availability for training and service in the land or naval forces of the United States, you are hereby notified that you have now been selected for training and service therein.

Selective Service Board #8
St. Louis County, Missouri

You will, therefore, report to the local board named above at ~~34 N. Gore, Webster Groves, Mo~~
                                                                    (Place of reporting)

at _____ 6:45 A. m., on the _____ SEP 2 1943 _____ day of _____, 19__
(Hour of reporting)

This local board will furnish transportation to an induction station. You will there be examined, and, if accepted for training and service, you will then be inducted into the land or naval forces.

Persons reporting to the induction station in some instances may be rejected for physical or other reasons. It is well to keep this in mind in arranging your affairs, to prevent any undue hardship if you are rejected at the induction station. If you are employed, you should advise your employer of this notice and of the possibility that you may not be accepted at the induction station. Your employer can then be prepared to replace you if you are accepted, or to continue your employment if you are rejected.

Willful failure to report promptly to this local board at the hour and on the day named in this notice is a violation of the Selective Training and Service Act of 1940, as amended, and subjects the violator to fine and imprisonment.

If you are so far removed from your own local board that reporting in compliance with this order will be a serious hardship and you desire to report to a local board in the area of which you are now located, go immediately to that local board and make written request for transfer of your delivery for induction, taking this order with you.

B H Miller
Member or clerk of the local board.

D. S. S. Form 150
(Revised 1-15-43)

U. S. GOVERNMENT PRINTING OFFICE   16—18271—5

Draft Notice

Birmingham, Alabama, 1943 Classified 1A (Ordered to report for induction.)

4 September 1943

SPECIAL ORDER)

NUMBER ....211)

E X T R A C T

* * * * * *

6. The following named privates indctd into the AUS this date are reld fr AD and trfd to the ERC and WP their Local Board of origin:

Local Board #6, State Nat'l Life Bldg, St Louis, Mo

Melvin R Wingo   Colored   37623718

Local Board #7, 1801A Chouteau Ave, St Louis, Missouri

Thomas W Cox   37623711

Local Board #13B, Am Ex Natl Bank Bldg, St Louis, Mo

Aloysius H Wiese   37623701

Local Board #15, 2232 South Grand, St Louis, Missouri

Max Mudrovich   37623703
Charles F Moses **   37623705
Harold J Cuddy, Jr.   6831165

Local Board of Transfer, 1801A Chouteau, St Louis, Mo

George Lawrence, Jr.   Colored   37623719

Local Board #8, 34 North Gore Ave, Webster Groves, Mo

John K Price   37623699

Local Board #1, Kennett, Dunklin County, Missouri

William A Cruse   37623700
Wilborn S Parker   **   37623708

Effective 25 September 1943 the above named EM are called to AD and will proceed to Recp Cen, Jefferson Barracks, Mo, rptg to the CO for duty. Should any of the above Enl Reservists be found physically disqual upon rptg for AD after a post induction inactive status or upon recall to AD nec steps will be taken to insure disch under provisions Sec 2, AR 615-360, as amended. Under no circumstances will physically disqual persons be trfd back to the inactive ERC. TO will furn nec T. TDN 1-5070 P 431-02 A 0425-24.

* * * *

By order of Captain SIMON:

HAROLD R PHELPS
2nd Lt, AUS
Adjutant

OFFICIAL: *Harold R Phelps*
HAROLD R PHELPS
2nd Lt, AUS
Adjutant

DISTRIBUTION: A

** In Charge

11

Co C, 117th

IMMUNIZATION REGISTER[1]

LAST NAME	FIRST NAME	ARMY SERIAL NO.
Price, John K		37623699

GRADE	COMPANY	REGT. OR STAFF CORPS[3]	AGE	RACE
Pvt	A		24	W

SMALLPOX VACCINE

DATE	TYPE OF REACTION[6]	MED. OFFICER[2]
10-16-43	Vaccina (Fannin)	L.J.P.

TRIPLE TYPHOID VACCINE

SERIES	1ST DOSE	2D DOSE	3D DOSE	MED. OFFICER[3]
1st	SEP 27 1943			JAR
2d	10-16	10-23	4/6	
3d	(Fannin)			

TETANUS TOXOID

INITIAL VACCINATION		STIMULATING DOSES		
DATE	MED. OFF.[3]		DATE	MED. OFF.[3]
1st dose SEP 27 1943	JAR	1cc		J.A.M.
2d dose 10-16	J.J.P.	(Fannin)		
3d dose 11/6/43	J.P.	BLOOD GROUP AB		

YELLOW FEVER VACCINE

DATE	LOT No.	AMOUNT	MED. OFF.[3]

OTHER VACCINES

TYPE OF VACCINE	DATE	MFR'S. LOT NO.	AMOUNT	MED. OFF.[3]
TYPHUS	5/23/44	(Fannin)	1.cc	
TYPHUS	5/31/44	(camp)	1.cc	
TYPHUS	6-6-44	Shanks	1.cc	

LOUIS J. POLIMENI, Capt., M.C., M.C., U.S. Army.

16-20202-1 To 170 PAR 3

WCP H/ (Bulge) 12/17/44

IMMUNIZATION REGISTER
AND OTHER MEDICAL DATA
(SEE AR 40-210)

1039

NAME (LAST, FIRST, MID. INITIAL)	ASN
PRICE, JOHN K	37 623 699

DATE OF BIRTH	RACE	BLOOD GROUP	MED. OFF.
9-May-19	W	AB	

SMALLPOX VACCINE

DATE	TYPE OF REACTION	MED. OFF.
16 Oct 43	Vcc (Fannin)	

TRIPLE TYPHOID VACCINE		TYPHUS VACCINE	
DATES EACH DOSE	MED. OFF.	DATES EACH DOSE	MED. OFF.
6-Nov-43		6-June 44 (Shanks)	
11-Jan 45		11-Jan 45 (Bulge)	

TETANUS TOXOID		CHOLERA VACCINE	
DATES EACH DOSE	MED. OFF.	DATES EACH DOSE	MED. OFF.
6-Nov-43	(Fannin)		
17-Apr-44	(Fannin)		

YELLOW FEVER VACCINE

DATE	LOT NO.	MED. OFF.

W. D., A. G. O.
FORM 8-117
15 AUGUST 1944

THIS FORM SUPERSEDES M. D. FORM 81, 23 SEPTEMBER 1942, WHICH WILL NOT BE USED AFTER RECEIPT OF THIS REVISION.

16-43404-1

PART I: BASIC TRAINING
CAMP FANNIN
Tyler, Texas

Camp Fannin was named for Colonel James Walker Fannin, the hero of Goliad. It was a very new camp (Jack mentioned that they were having them make lawns.) It covered 15,000 acres of rolling, hilly country nine miles north of Tyler. It was activated in the Spring of 1943, was opened to the public to see on May 16, 1943, and by August had troops in training. It was strictly an Infantry Replacement Training Center.

The men were trained for combat and sent directly overseas. It was the second largest training center in the country. Fort Benning, Georgia, was the largest. Every four months 35 to 40 thousand men were trained. These were infantry soldiers who were trained only, to replace killed, wounded, and troops being rotated at various battle fronts. There was also a detachment of WAC's (Women's Auxilliary Corps).

The camp had, in addition, one area containing 1200 German prisoners of war who had been captured in the North African Campaign from Rommel's Tank Division.

Tyler had been a gentle southern town of 30,000 people. It was changed overnight, as can well be imagined. The regular permanent officers and men fared well; the people of Tyler opened their hearts and homes to them. The infantry replacements, however, did not have as much opportunity to become involved with the activities and entertainments. They came and went fast and trained long and hard.

Jack arrived on October 3, 1943. His first letter to me was the typical longing of a lonely man away from his home and family for the first time in his life. His letters are a day by day account of the life and training of an ordinary infantry rifleman headed for combat in seventeen short weeks.

THE LETTERS

To:
Mrs. John K. Price
704 Ballas Road
Kirkwood, 22, Mo.

From:
Pvt. John K. Price
ASN 37623699
Co.C 81st Tng.Bn.
Bks2
Camp Fannin, Texas

Oct. 3, 1943

(Sunday)
Dearest Sweetheart:

Well, we arrived here ok about noon today and it is really lousy. We are about 10 miles from Tyler, however, and it is a real nice town. Don't you have relatives down here? Let me know. If you do maybe you could come down. I miss you and the baby so much I hardly know what to do, dearest, it will really be wonderful when we can be together again. I would have wired you but they have no facilities for that here as far as I have been able to find out. I am sending this airmail special though so you will get it as soon as possible.

I don't mind telling you that if there were any way for me to get out of it I sure would. All I can think about is you and the baby and how much I would love to see you. Please send me a good picture of you and one of the baby in your next letter. It doesn't have to be a new one, just anything you have that is good.

Well, we will be here for about six months and then be eligible for overseas unless we get some special duty. The way I feel now I'd rather be overseas right now than where I am. Of course after I am able to get to town once in a while and can get out of these barracks I might feel better. We had a real nice trip down. We traveled pullman and were very comfortable. I'm not writing Mom tonight so you call her and give her my address and tell her to write.

Well, sweetheart, I'd better close now as I have some work to do before I turn in. Give the baby a big kiss for me and say hello to everyone for me.

All the love in the world to my little sweethearts.

Jack

Pvt. John K. Price
Co.C- 71 Bn. 15th Tng.Regt. I.R.T.C.
Camp Fannin, Texas.

Oct. 5th, 1943
(Tuesday)

Dearest Sweetheart:

Well, hon, another day is over, thank goodness. They are really working us and it really hasn't started yet. I haven't received a letter yet but I guess I will in the next day or so.

I am hoping you will say you have some relatives in Tyler that you can visit cause if you do, I can get off all week-end and 2 or three nights a week to stay with you and Peggy.

By the way, if by any chance an emergency arises and you need me at home, first notify the Red Cross and then wire me and in the wire say that you have notified them. That will enable me to get away faster.

We will be finished about March or April and at that time we will be ready to be shipped overseas. There will be approximately 3 out of ten who will be shipped. We got another haircut today. I now have a small top knot about a half inch long. - (Diagram > me). Ain't that sumpthin, tho.

I guess this army isn't so bad after you get used to it except for being away from you. We really have a fine bunch of fellows in our barracks and every one clicks off fine which helps a whole lot.

I had better close now as I have a lot of equipment to get ready for tomorrow. All my love to the sweetest wife and baby in the world.

Your Sweetheart,
Jack

Oct. 9th, 1943
(Saturday)

Dearest Sweetheart:

Just a note to let you know I am thinking about you. I haven't much time so it will have to be short.

I have been assigned my regular Battalion and Company but am in the same Regiment and Camp. My address is Pvt.John K. Price, Co. D, 81st Trng Bn., 15th Regt., I.R.T.C. Camp Fannin, Texas. In case you would like to know what it means it is Company D, 81st Training Battalion, 15th Regiment, Infantry Replacement Training Center. It is also a good idea for you to know my serial number which is 37623699.

Whoops- I had to stop to wash the windows and have forgotten what I was saying. That is about all the necessary stuff you need to know. I have had to buy quite a bit of stuff. They don't furnish everything. We got our guns today and had to buy a cleaner kit for them, with rod, etc., which set me back a few bucks.

I am sure disappointed in leaving my old Bn & Co, as we were really whipping it in to a swell outfit. Now I'll have to get acquainted all over again.

How is Peggy, honey, is she growing any? Has she gotten over fretting so much and is she starting to notice things? Don't forget the pictures. I guess I had better close now, while I still have time. Love me and remember how much I love you.

All my love,
Your Sweetheart
Jack

Sunday,
Oct. 10th, 1943

Dearest Sweetheart:

Well, this has been the most lonesome and blue Sunday I have ever spent. I received the first 2 letters from you today, one from Mom and one from Pop. It was swell to hear, even tho it did make me bluer than ever.

We got some good news last night. We were transferred up here for specialist school. So instead of 19 to 22 weeks basic cycle we will only have 5 weeks then to school. Sounds good doesn't it? I am no longer in a regiment so from now on write me as follows: C0. D. 81st Trng. Bn.

You see, when you are preparing for specialist school you are no longer assigned to a regiment because you won't be shipped until you finish school. Then you are attached to a new Bn, Regt, and Co.

I miss you so much. It will be wonderful when this mess is all over and we can come home. You don't realize how much you really have as a civilian in the way of freedom, etc., until you get in the army. We have been restricted to Co. Area until I was transferred here which means we couldn't leave our barracks. Now we can go to the P.X. and show but not out of the camp. Although there isn't anything in Tyler it will be nice to be able to go there on Sunday and act like a civilian again. You know, go to church, then have dinner and feel free to do what you want.

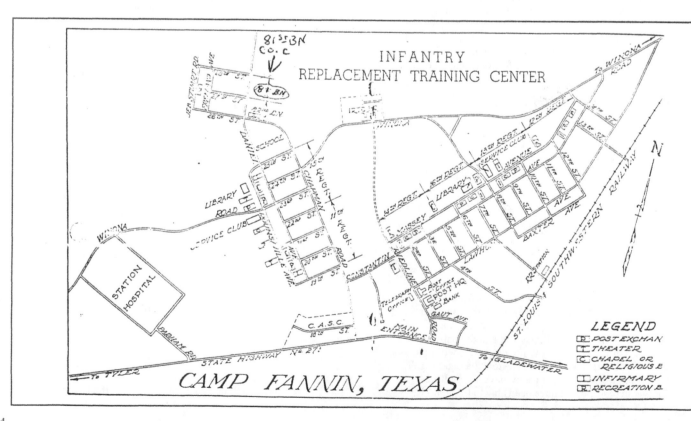

INFANTRY REPLACEMENT TRAINING CENTER

CAMP FANNIN, TEXAS

LEGEND
PE POST EXCHAN
T THEATER
C CHAPEL OR RELIGIOUS B
I INFIRMARY
R RECREATION B

New Testament
Psalms

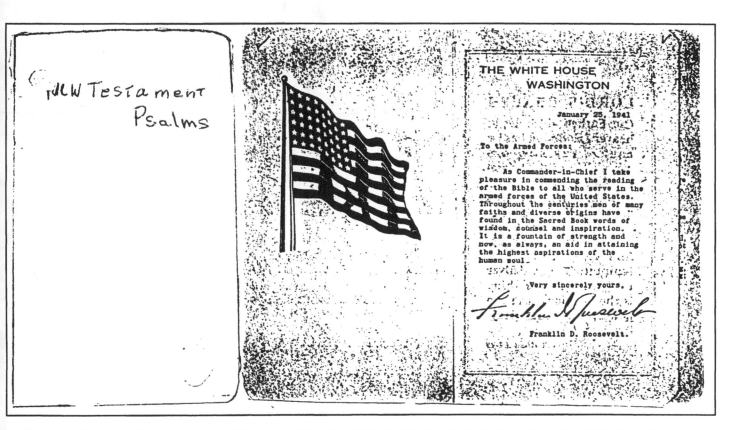

THE WHITE HOUSE
WASHINGTON

January 25, 1941

To the Armed Forces:

As Commander-in-Chief I take
pleasure in commending the reading
of the Bible to all who serve in the
armed forces of the United States.
Throughout the centuries men of many
faiths and diverse origins have
found in the Sacred Book words of
wisdom, counsel and inspiration.
It is a fountain of strength and
now, as always, an aid in attaining
the highest aspirations of the
human soul.

Very sincerely yours,

Franklin D. Roosevelt.

Your Chaplain

Look up your chaplain at the first opportunity. Your welfare is his first concern, and you will find him friendly and helpful at all times. His counsel and advice will guide you in avoiding or overcoming difficulties. In many ways you can help him in his services for others. A close friendship between a chaplain and his men preserves and promotes a fine spirit in any service unit.

—The GIDEONS

Attention

By special request of the U. S. Military and Naval Authorities you are instructed to place your NAME ONLY on the fly leaf, *nothing more*. On no account name your organization, post, ship or station at any place in this book. To do so might afford valuable information to the enemy.

A Sacred Token

To_____

_____

From_____

_____

_____

_____

_____

_____

Date

Small Brown Bible presented to Soldiers by the Gideons Society.

I believe we'll be able to go out by next Sunday. Give me the relatives name in Tyler so I can get in touch with them. Love me and miss me and kiss Peggy for me and write all the time. You don't know what your letters do for me.

I have $1 left so if you can- send me a couple.

All my love,
Your sweetheart,
Jack

A big one for you   A baby size one for Peggy
    (X)   (x)

Tuesday
11/2

Dearest Sweetheart:

While I'm waiting for chow I decided to write a letter. I got a letter today and I'll try to tell you what you want but I don't know how far I'll get.

I got up yesterday morning, for instance, at 5:45, I got dressed, put my leggins on, made my bed - chow - I'm back now and feel better. Now where was I? Gotta go again-be back later. — Well, it's after dinner now so maybe I'll be able to finish this. They have a dance tonite so I thought I might go down and watch them a while this evening.

Now where was I - oh yes, after making my bed I run over if I have time and wash and fallout for chow about 6:15. After eating we come back and clean up the barracks and police the grounds, mop, sweep, and dust and polish shoes until 7:25. 7:25 to 7:30 we are assigned our work details for the day.

At 8:00 we go to work, usually making lawns and drainage ditches and various landscaping jobs until 11:30. At 11:30 we are off and come back to the barracks, have mail call, try to write a few lines, shine our shoes again and wash for chow. We eat at 12:15. Then we come back to the barracks and clean it up for afternoon inspection.

At 12:45 we fall out and are assigned back to work. We work until 4:30 or 4:45 then come back again, have mail call again, wash and dress in Class A uniforms to fall out for retreat at 5:30. At 5:45 we eat and then if we are lucky we are off for the evening.

Usually if we are off we wash clothes, darn socks, sew buttons, shine shoes, write letters, shower, shave and a million other things we have to get done. When we are in cycle we will be in the field during this time and then Lord knows when we will get all this done. At 9:45 lights are out, and we are plenty ready for bed, however, you don't have to be in bed until 11:00. At 11:00 they have bed check and if you aren't in bed you are marked A.W.O.L. That's about all, but we'll have a lot more to do when we're in our cycle.

Honey, I'll try to get a picture taken of me as soon as I can but I just don't have the money now. Have I gotten the compliments on that cap! It is really good looking. I am going to try to get by wearing it. I won't get in trouble, they will just tell me to take it off.

All my love to my two darlings and thanks for the kisses. Here is one for you - real too.

I love you,
Jack

November 15, 1943. Peggy, 3 1/2 months old, studying old Buff.

Thursday
11/4

Dearest:

I guess you will wonder how come this paper to write you on but I am out in the woods on a detail and this is all I have. We are supposed to be making a bayonet course but George and I decided to hunt for hickory trees and when we got out here decided to gold-brick a little.

The woods are beautiful through here. We didn't get to see any woods when we were in Houston but I was surprised to find that Texas has such swell woods. All the leaves are red and it is hard to describe just how pretty they are. I guess I'll have to give you a bawling out. I didn't get any mail yesterday and none today. Come on. Gosh I wish you were here with me. You'd really enjoy it. How is Peg? Keep me posted on everything she does. It tickles me the way you carry on about her. She must be cute. Course she was before.

Well, sweetheart, I'm going to stop now as the fellows want to move a little. I'll write you off and on all day. Bye for now, darling.

Well, here I am again. I'm going to close this now, honey, as I'm sending you a couple of roses which grow in the woods and everywhere here. As soon as I can afford it I'll send you a few dozen. Bye sweet, I love you. Give Peg a kiss for me. I'll write again this evening.

All my love,
Jack

P S Send me my candid camera & I'll take some pix.

Little Phillie 81/2, Peggy 61/2 months. February 1944.

Bye now
I love you

(Note: The camp had been built in the middle of rose fields. I received the roses he enclosed, pressed them, and they are still recognizable today! The letter was written on small note paper.)

Tuesday &
Wednesday
9th & 10th

Dearest Sweetheart:

Well, I've started this letter 6 or 8 times in the last few days and never got any farther than this. It's about 10:15 PM now and I'm in the latrine trying to get this written. I got a wonderful letter from you today. I'll try to answer some of your questions. I'll be able to take care of the camera ok, so please send it. I'll be able to send you some good pictures. I got the towels ok. The sox were swell. I don't want anything for Xmas.

I haven't started my basic yet, but I got all the dope today. We start Monday. We begin with a week and a half of dismounted drill and drill with rifles and full field packs. The next week and a half we have dry firing which is practicing positions for firing the rifle and aiming, etc. The next 4 days we fire live ammunition on the range and the next 2 days we fire for medals in marksmanship. The rest of the time we have hand grenade and bayonet. Then at the end of the five weeks we begin our 12 weeks of school. After we are finished with our cycle we will most likely learn to fire the Browning Automatic Rifle, we call it the B.A.R., Machine gun, Mortar, and Bazooka.

I am really tired. I have been in the woods from 7.00 this morning until 9.30 tonite. We have been making a truck obstacle course for training truck drivers. We have made over 7 miles of road through dense woods in the last two days cutting trees and making bridges, etc.

I must close and get to bed as I have a terrible hard day coming up. Goodnight sweetheart. Love me like I love you.

All my love always,
Jack

Sunday
11/14/43

Dearest Sweetheart:

How are you this evening? It's about 9:30 now and I just got off. I was called out this morning to finish up that truck course I was working on all week. If I keep up at the pace I've been working any longer it'll kill me. I missed today off and I have K.P. next Sunday and am on duty all next week with 2 hikes of about 8 or 10 miles scheduled so I won't have a whole lot of free time.

I sure hate to see this day come around. I always feel blue on Sunday. I'll give you an idea tho of what we will do tomorrow. Our schedule runs like this. From eight to nine we have Calesthenics(?) and Physical Ed. From nine to ten a class on Military Courtesy. From ten to eleven a class in Military Sanitation. Then off until 1:15 for lunch.

At 1:15 we fall out with blanket, towel, shaving brush, razor, a package of blades, soap, tooth powder, shaving stick, haversack, pack carrier, canteen, mess kit, pup tent, pole, rope 5 pegs, raincoat, shovel, bayonet, rifle, handkerchief, socks, underwear, Field Manual, and steel helmet. We are learning to make up a full field pack and all that stuff is what goes in it. That will take all afternoon. When we go on hikes that is what we carry with us. Altogether I'll weigh about 245 pounds including everything.

I still wish you could come down to Tyler. A bunch of the fellows from St. Louis have their wives here for a visit this weekend. We have won best area in camp Fannin for the second consecutive week. That is quite an honor as there are over 250 companies in the camp and we are the only company here or at Camp Robinson that has won it twice in a row. Ahem.

How is that wonderful daughter of ours? How I would love to see her and be with you both. I was looking forward to this part of her growing up more than anything else. They are sweeter and do cuter things from three months to a year than any other time. They are just learning everything then. Well, I guess when I come home we'll get busy on another one.

It's funny how you realize how much you love and need a person when you get away from them. You kind of take them for granted until something separates them. I must close as it's getting late and I have a pretty strenuous day ahead.

All my love-
Jack

P.S. I love you.
I love you both, you bestest tho-

Peggy February 1944. Seven months. Jack's favorite picture. Later he said she looked like the British babies in their pram's!

11/20/43
Sat.

Dearest Sweetheart:

Well honey, happy anniversary. I would give anything to be with you today of all days. I love you and miss you so much.

I just finished cleaning my rifle and as lights are out I am writing in the latrine again. I'll be able to finish tho, cause I don't have to get up in the morning till I feel like it. Your husband is an example (good one) to Co. C. (ahem). To explain - we had inspection this morning. Our Lt. inspected our rifles and general neatness, such as haircuts, shined shoes, etc. I am in the third squad of the second platoon and as there are 4 squads in a platoon I was near the last to be inspected. As he went down the line inspecting, each man would bring his rifle up to inspection arms, which is holding it in front of his chest, diagonally, with the bolt open. The Lt. would stand there in front of you and look you over and then, without any warning, would grab your rifle. Of course as soon as he touched your piece you should let go of it and come to attention as he inspected or if you didn't leave go you would be pulled over which would get you in trouble.

As he walked along inspecting the Sgt. followed and wrote down the names of the men who were gigged and why, for dirty rifles, etc. When he got to me I came to inspection arms (scared for fear I wouldn't pass) and he took my rifle inspected it and looked me over and handed my piece back and moved on to the next man. When he had passed me I closed my rifle and came to order arms which is the position of attention with the butt of the rifle on the ground. I no sooner had done this when he told the sgt. to get my name. The sgt. took my name and asked if it was for dirty rifle. He said no and didn't give a reason.

It took him about 15 minutes to finish the inspection. I stood scared silly wondering what I had done wrong. When he finished he walked up in the front of the platoon & Co. and read the names of those who had gigs. Then he said there is one man, Pvt. Price who excelled everyone for neatness and his performance of inspection arms. He asked me if I had any military training before, a lot of questions and wrote a lot in his notebook. He kept his eye on me the rest of the day, too. Was I relieved and proud. Maybe it will do some good.

Well, it's 11:30 and my eyes are closing so I'll finish this tomorrow. — Good morning honey, I'm going to close now and go eat. Happy anniversary,

I love you.
Jack

Monday
11/22/43

Dearest Honey:

I feel so bad today. I am ashamed for not getting you a little anniversary card or something. I got the cutest card from
you. I went to the dentist today and had three teeth filled. I was surprised that I only have 6 to fill and that is all. These dentists here are really rough. Before I forget, they announced today that trainees would no longer be allowed to wear the belts or caps. I'll keep my cap here to wear home when I come. I can't see any reason for it, but that's the way they are in the Army. I had a class tonight from 7 till 9 on first aid and military sanitation so it's late again and I haven't anything done for it tomorrow. We have a gas drill tomorrow and go thru real poisonous gas and tear gas. This is the final period on gas as we have covered it from one end to the other. We have had some hand grenade drills today. We have classes until 10:30 Wednesday night on interior guard duty. We start out with a 10 mile hike Wednesday morning with full field pack and then work until 10:30 that night, so don't expect a letter that day. You said they don't believe in loading us. Heck that was just the first week and the easiest of all. Just think we have to do in 7 weeks what every other Company has 17 weeks to do. It's a big job and requires a lot of hard work and lack of sleep.

One nice thing about the army is they furnish you with back scratches, this camp doesn't furnish sheets so we sleep on a mattress cover and under wool blankets so when my back itches I just turn over on my stomach and let the blanket do the rest. Honey, don't build your hopes up too high about this being over so soon . There is more going on than meets the eye. I'll tell you a secret. More than 50% of the men sent from this camp are sent to an embarkation port and directly overseas.. They get

17 weeks training here and 12 at the embarkation and they're ready. This thing is far from over. I'll be in the army for two years and maybe longer. We are seeing in our training just how strong Germany really is. You know, when a country can mass 150,000 men on one small front that is almost lost and at the same time operate on several other fronts she is far from whipped. I'll tell you one thing that will show you when Germany is on her last legs, when you read that she is using gas warfare. Yes, honey, both pair of glasses are silver rimmed. Of course, when I go out anywhere I'll wear my civies but the main reason for the G I's is because they'll fit under a gas mask and mine won't. If I put a mask on with my glasses on it would break them to pieces and also allow gas to leak in. Well it's late so I'd better close now.

Don't forget how much I love you and miss you. Pray hard for me and for this war to be over quick.

All my love always,
    Jack

11/25/43
Thursday

Dearest Sweetheart:
    Well, darling, happy thanksgiving. I had a real nice time today. I'll tell you the whole story starting from yesterday Morn. We got up at 5 AM. At 7 AM we started on a ten mile hike. We got back at about 10:30 and had extended orders until noon, which is the proper way to act in combat and consists of throwing yourself all over the ground learning to fall with a rifle properly. All afternoon we did the same thing and that night we had a night problem on interior guard. I got off about 10 o'clock and got to bed about 10:30. At 11:30 someone woke me up and said I had a long distance call at the orderly room. Naturally I tho't it was you so I jumped up and ran down. It was Edwin Mosby and he invited me to Carrol's for dinner. I couldn't accept the dinner as I had to work until 12:30 today and they were going to eat at 12:00 and go to a football game so I told them I would be down this evening. I got down there about 5 PM. Saw Edwin and Olive. They are just the same. They were very complimentary about Peg, which made me very proud. Carrol and Joyce are really fine. I had a swell time. We had cold turkey, etc for our evening meal and then sat around and gabbed. They brought me home about 9:45. It's about 10:30 now. Before I get into what we had for dinner, tell Mom & Pop that I got the box and I'll write them tomorrow.

    We had turkey, of course, which was very good and had as much as we wanted. Also had sweet and mashed potatoes, peas, asparagus, dressing, salad, pie, ice cream, fruit, nuts, and candy.

    Honey, I'm so lonesome and blue I don't know what to do. I wanted to be with you so much today I could hardly stand it. It will sure be a happy day when this is all over so I can come home. I was miserable all day long. I just couldn't get my mind off of what you all were doing. It makes me want to cry when I think of it. If you were only closer to me so I could see you just once in a while. I was going to answer the letter I got from you today, but I am in the day room and I left it in the barracks. I'm so tired I can hardly hold my eyes open. The best way for me to write now is if you ask a lot of questions

Daddy's big girl! March 1944, 8 months old.

in your letters. I don't have a lot of time and that fixes it so I don't have to figure what to write about. How is Peg? Keep me posted. It is swell the way you write all about her. It is almost like I can see just what she is doing. Honey, I'm going to close now. Goodnight again. All my love to my sweet Momma and gal.

    Their Pop

11/28/43
Sunday

Dearest Sweetheart:
    Well, honey, another Sunday is about over and I have finished my washing, rolling my full field pack, shining my shoes, playing three games of pinochle, taking a shower, shaving, going to church, and seeing a swell picture show, so I will finish this letter and get ready for bed and the day will be over. If you want to see a good picture, see Thousands Cheer. It is really swell. You'll see a little of the Infantry. The guys in my outfit act just about as crazy as the guys in that picture did.

    Well, we have a big day ahead of us. We have a nice long hike and make camp when we get there which consists of pitching our tents, etc., and then throw real live hand grenades what can kill. We eat lunch in the field and work all afternoon and then walk back. Then after we eat supper we are liable to be called out and have to work until late at night. Some fun. I guess altogether we will walk about 25 or 30 miles. Honey, I found out today that I won't be able to get home for Christmas. This is definite so don't even hope. They announced tonight that we will get Saturday and Sunday off as far as passes are concerned. In other words they will only issue a 2 day pass. Honey, wouldn't it be worth it to you to make the trip down for Christmas? Say to stay for about 4 or 5 days? What is the difference if it does cost a little. You could leave the baby for just those few days.

I could make reservations for you at the Blackstone Hotel here, however, I am sure that when Carrol learned of you being in town you would be invited to stay there. I just wonder if we will see combat? They keep throwing it up to us that as soon as we finish this basic 75% of us will be sent to a port of embarkation for duty overseas. I wonder. You know, they have gotten me to where I never look forward to anything except one day to the next, that is one reason why I want to see you Xmas. Co. A. which just finished their basic here in our Bn. were sent yesterday to Fort Meade, Md. which is an embarkation port, without a furlough. I was talking to a second Looey today about it, and he said that according to their shipping orders they won't receive a furlough.

I'll make reservations at the hotel next week for the week of 12/22 to 12/29 to be sure we have a place to stay. Don't forget how much I love you and miss you. If you love me you"ll find a way to get here Christmas. I know you love me anyway but if I have to be alone Christmas I'll flat die.

All my love always,
    Jack

Saturday
4 Dec. 1945
(Army style)

Dearest Sweetheart:
    Hooray, Hooray! I feel wonderful. The only trouble is the time from now till Christmas will drag something awful. Also I am worrying and hoping that I miss K.P. & Guard duty over Xmas. I believe I'll have two and maybe three whole days Christmas with you and 2 New Years that I won't have to report to camp.

I found out about the hotel. We will stay at the Tyler Hotel. It's the second best in town and is recommended by the U.S.O. The rooms are $2.00 without or $3.00 with bath. You do not reserve a room as they do not take reservations. They told me they have never turned anyone away, but to be on the safe side you had better get here Thursday if possible. I priced the Blackstone and they wanted $3.50 for just you and $5.00 for both. Isn't that terrible?

Honey, you have no idea how wonderful I feel. Gosh, just think, I'll see you in about 3 weeks. I haven't called Carrol yet but I will sometime this week and tell her you're coming. I'll be able to get to town about 6:30 and be with you until about 10 or 10:30 during the week and weekends from Saturday at 6:30 till Sunday at 10:00. That's not very long but at least I'll be with you then. I can hardly wait. All the fellows keep threatening to write you

and tell you not to come cause that's all they've been hearing all day. Don't be surprised if they do write. They're a bunch of nuts. You said it would have to be my Christmas present if you do come down. Can you think of a better present or one I want more than to see you? About the belt, I'll be able to wear one. It's just the caps they have banned.

I was out on a problem yesterday advancing on an enemy outpost, throwing myself on the ground every 10 or 15 feet and I landed on my watch and broke the devil out of it. It made me sick.

My hands are a mass of small cuts and bruises. They are really in bad shape. If I keep on I'll kill myself. I have noticed one thing, tho, this training is really whipping me into
shape. I have lost about 4 inches off my waistline and haven't lost a pound of weight. I'm in darn good shape right now.

Of course I'll get off every night. I won't be able to stay with you all night as I'll have to be back in camp in time for bed check at 11 PM but I'll at least be able to eat dinner with you and be with you in the evening. I'll most likely get all day off New Years and a half a day Friday, Sat. and Sunday. The same with Christmas. Our cycle will be almost over by then too, so I won't be as busy and as tired as I am now in the evenings.

I know you'll enjoy the trip, honey, as it is really a nice little town and there is plenty to see. The camp will interest you too. Oh, I cant wait. I want to see you so bad. Lord, it seems like I've been gone a hundred years and I've got another year or 2 before Christmas gets here. I was just thinking, it will be nice for you to get in early in the morning cause it will give you a chance to rest up after the trip as you'll be plenty tired, I know.

Well, dearest they are chasing me out of here. I'm in the day room and it's closing time, so I guess I'd better close and go to bed.

All my love to the sweetest wife in the world. I'll see you Christmas.

Bye now,
Love,
    Jack
P.S. I love you.

12/6/43
Monday

Dearest Sweetheart:
    Well, honey, this will have to be another short one as I am tired and I have a long day tomorrow. From 7:00 AM till 9:30 PM tomorrow in the field for chow and everything.

Got some good news. I got a reservation at the Blackstone for us from 24th to the 26th. They want 3:00 a night if I don't stay any later than 10 PM or 5:00 if I stay later. I can't figure out how they will know whether I am there or not tho. A friend of mine from St. Louis, had the reservation and found another room so he said I could use it. When you come in, you will have to register as Mrs. F.X. Meyers, but that's better than nothing.

Of course, it would be a good idea to try at the Tyler first to find out if they have any rooms and to see how they are before going to the Blackstone, but at least we are sure of a place to stay. Gosh, I can hardly wait. That's all I've been talking about for a week. If anything happens to keep you from coming, I think I'll die.

We had a conference this evening, all the clerks

I mean, with the executive officer and he told us that probably 50% of us will be sent overseas about 2 months after we complete our basic. A few will be kept in this camp and the rest of us will be scattered all over the country. So you see how important it is for you to come down Christmas. It might be the last one I'll be able to spend with you for some time.

How is Peg? Write and let me know all the new little things she is doing. I would sure love to have you bring her Christmas, but it would be much to hard on her. I'll bet she's getting
sweet. I guess I'd better close now and hit the hay. You won't know your husband when you get here. I go to bed early, I've lost my big bay window, and I am actually getting some muscles. We are having courses in hand to hand combat now and I'm getting to be able to take care of myself. Boy, I'm going to be a man when I get out of here.

Well, Darling, love me and dream of me. I love you and miss you and am really looking forward to Christmas.

All my love always,
Your sweetheart,
    Jack
P.S. I love you.

12/16/43
Thurs.

Dearest Sweetheart:
Well, dearest, I've kind of let you down on this writing business the last 2 days but I haven't even had my shoes off since Tuesday morning and it's Thursday nite now. Maybe I'll get some sleep tonight. I'm so darn tired I hardly know what I'm doing. I had guard duty Tuesday night and we camped out last night and I was on guard again. We have been firing our rifle since Monday and is it swell. I've done pretty fair so far. I had a score of 130 out of a possible 150 today which qualified me as an expert. However, that won't count on my record. We fire for record tomorrow and Saturday so the score I make then is what counts. Hold your thumbs for me cause I want to make a sharpshooter or Expert medal out of it. Expert is the highest. (He got Expert for rifle, Carbine, B.A.R., and Bayonet.) Just think, honey, only 7 more days. I can hardly wait. I found out today that a new K.P. Schedule has been made up. The new one calls for our company on the 24th and the 1st, New Years day. If I get it the 24th I won't get it the 1st but I'll be late in getting to town to meet you and if I don't get it the 24th I'll get it New Years day and it will cost me money so I guess it would be better to get it the 24th. If I am on K.P. I'll be late so don't worry. Just leave word at my orderly room where and what room number you're staying so I won't have to waste time.

I have three letters to answer, but changed my mind. I'm going to clean my rifle before lights go out then finish this. That rifle of mine has to be perfect tomorrow.

Well, Darling, a whole day has passed since I started this. Right after I stopped last night we were called out on a force march and walked 15 miles from 9 o'clock till midnight, so I missed writing you again. I'm afraid my letter writing will be very few and far between next week too. We are right at the end of our cycle and are getting our toughest work. It is all practical work. Next week we will

be on the combat range and will have small battles, with shells exploding around us and we are going through the infiltration course. That is where we crawl 50 yards on our bellies under live machine gun fire which is fired 30 inches off the ground, with mines and shells, etc., firing all around us. I hope I come thru alive. Hah!

To answer that letter you wrote Monday, when I said 50% were going overseas I meant as soon as we finish our basic which includes the specialist training. In other words, as soon as we finish 17 weeks training. If I am chosen to go, I'll receive a seven day furlough when I finish and then report to a port of embarkation for a few months training and then shipped. When I arrive at my destination I'll receive about 6 months combat training before I see actual combat, so actually our training covers about a year.

Honey, there is a rule of the camp which keeps the C.O. from taking anyone off K.P. for any rea-

Blackstone Hotel, Tyler, Texas.

Smith County Courthouse. Tyler, Texas.

Jack and his buddies at studio on Courthouse Square. Top row: Louis Poelker (St. Louis, MO), George Preiner (St. Paul, MN). Bottom row: E.H. White (Louisana), John K. Price, Duane Perry (St. Paul, MN). Camp Fannin Tyler, Texas 1943.

son. If I get it, I'll have to take it and like it. We have been firing on the range for the last three days in zero weather. It was so cold no one could fire worth a darn. I wore my long underwear, a pair of O.D. pants, my fatigue pants, my long underwear shirt, my O.D. shirt, my fatigue shirt, my regular underwear, my leggins, 2 pair of socks, field jacket, overcoat, a little stocking cap, a helmet liner, a steel helmet, a combat pack, cartridge belt, canteen, bayonet, and rifle and gloves, and froze to death on top of it. I have never been so cold. It is warming up a little now and I hope it is real nice when you get here. I got the package from you yesterday. Silly, wrapping them like presents. Sure was glad to get all the stuff tho. Just think, Dearest, this time next week I'll be with you. I can hardly believe it. Give Peg a big kiss for me and say hello and Merry Christmas to the folks. Love me and dream of me. I'll see you next Friday. All my love forever and ever.

Your sweetheart,
    Jack

Dec. 19, 1943
Sunday

Dearest Sweetheart:

Only 5 more days and I'll be holding you and seeing you again. Gee, honey I don't see how I can wait. Things look like they are going to turn out ok. 13 men out of our company are going to have K.P. so the 1st Sarge said he would accept volunteers so every one else pitched in 25 cents to pay the 13 men who take it. It will give them close to 5.00 apiece.

Also I don't think I'll have any trouble getting a pass for Friday nite, Saturday, and Sunday. One thing I want to caution you about and that is to be sure to register as Mrs. F. X. Meyers and don't lose that reservation as rooms are almost impossible to get and all reservations have a waiting list. That is awful nice of Carrol (staying with her). Gosh, I hope you get here ok. Of course I understand about Peggy, sweet, I would love to see her but the trip would be too much for her.

That boy I was telling you about, (Joe Mathas) is an orphan living with some farm people and he has gotten very little mail since he has been here and I doubt he'll get many Christmas packages. About him being fresh he acts like he is afraid of being taken advantage of or something.

Well, we finished our range work yesterday. I qualified as rifle marksman and get a medal. It makes me feel kinda good. Another fellow and I were sitting here figuring how much we would weigh with all our equipment on. We came to the conclusion that we would carry all told about 85 pounds. Ain't that sumpin. I guess I'd better close now and hit the hay as we have to walk to the hand grenade course tomorrow. We throw live grenades. Love me and dream of me. Hurry down. All my love always.

Your Sweetheart,
    Jack
P.S. I love you.

Dec. 20, 1943
(Monday)

Dear Mom & Pop:

I have time to write you all a decent letter for a change. I believe I told you I got the box. The only trouble was, it didn't last over one evening. You have no idea how hungry a bunch of guys get for good stuff from home. I am now waiting expectantly for that fried chicken. I got a box from Sister the other day, too, with half a homemade fruit cake and candy. Boy, did it hit the spot. Last week we were firing on the rifle range. We fired for record Friday and Saturday and I won a rifle marksman medal. We are firing the bazooka this week. It's really fun. I guess you've seen them in newsreels. They look something like Bob Burns blow pipe. It's almost like firing a cannon while holding it on your shoulder.

We also threw real live hand grenades today. You would throw them and then duck behind a mud wall as they exploded. You could hear the fragments that do the dirty work whistling over your head. That rifle of ours is about the most wonderful gun I have ever handled. We fired at targets from 100 yds, 200 yds, 300 yds, and 500 yds rapid and slow fire. I did the best in rapid fire. We had to load a shell in the chamber, fire it and then load a clip of 8 shells and fire them, all in 51 seconds and every range I fired it from I made a score of 40 out of a possible 45. That in case you don't know is darn good shooting. I sure wish you all and the baby could come, but I guess you are as excited about keeping Peg as you would be about coming. I'll bet she's getting sweet tho. I sure wish I was home to watch her grow up. Just think, she won't even know me when I get home. Well, maybe this will help keep a decent place for her to grow up in, so I guess I don't have any room to gripe. Babe writes such cute letters about her and what she does. You would think we had a genius. Take good care of Peg for me and send Babe down in a hurry. All my love to the most wonderful Mom and Pop in the world. Hope you all have a really Merry Christmas. I'll be thinking of our swell times we used to have. Remember? All the arguments about the Christmas tree and all. Well, maybe we can have them again next year. Merry Christmas, Mom and Pop, and a Happy and prosperous New Year.

Your Son,
Jack

CHRISTMAS
1943

I almost did not get to Tyler for Christmas, 1943. I had come down with the flu on Sunday the 19th of December. Jack's parents came out and took Peggy home as they had planned to keep her while I was in Texas. On Monday I was worse. A great many doctors had gone to the war, but Dr. Luckey, our old family doctor who had planned to retire, took on an enormous load as did many other older doctors. A house call was out of the question so I dressed warmly and went on the bus to his office. The office was filled to capacity with very ill people. At last I got in to see him, and he gave me his own formula flu shot which he had done many times. The cure at first was worse than the disease, but I knew it always worked.

I left Dr. Luckey's office and stood on the corner, among the crush of Christmas shoppers, waiting for the bus. It was quite dark now, and had begun to snow. Two overloaded busses passed us by. I finally got on a bus, by now sick beyond belief. My mother had been frantically watching each bus which stopped at the corner of our yard. When I arrived she immediately took me upstairs, put me to bed and did all the things dear mothers do.

Jack's father had already written him that I would not be able to come, but I recovered. Fortunately, Jack received the telegram saying I was coming, before the letter saying I was not coming! I was very sick for the next few days. On Thursday morning I assured Mother I was much better. I was determined to go, no matter what.

Jack's father (the only one in the family with a car during the war) took me to Union Station in St. Louis. This was one of the most important railroad stations in the United States. Virtually everyone was required to change trains there, regardless of whether they were going north, south, east, or west. One would have to experience a railroad station during the war to believe the seething mass of people, almost entirely servicemen and women, with many wives, parents, and loved ones joyously meeting them, or sadly saying goodbye.

There was a time when those who were seeing you off went into the train with you to visit until the train was ready to leave, but the war changed all that forever. Jack's father left me at the gate with my suitcases. The age of Southern chivalry was still with us, and there were always a dozen soldiers helping ladies with their luggage and children, so I was quickly assisted and seated.

There was no such thing as a Pullman (a sleeping car) for ordinary mortals, of which I was one. It was a miracle just to have a seat. A nice girl about my age had the seat next to me. She also was bound for Camp Fannin, Texas. A few minutes after six o'clock the train pulled out and we were on our way. My companion was very friendly and we went to the diner together. However, she also had been sick, and we were both glad to be quiet and try to sleep sitting up. There were no extra seats. How we longed for a Pullman-bed!

Jack's parents had bought my ticket for our Christmas present. I was so overjoyed at just being able to go, the discomfort of the trip was incidental. There is something very pleasant about a night train trip, the rocking of the coach, the rhythm of the wheels, the ringing of the road-crossing bells and flashing lights. Then the occasional stops at small town stations, and the voices of people getting off band on. In the morning the other girl and I went to the diner for breakfast, and we were amazed to find that during the night we had both recovered from our illness. Oh, what love can do! I never saw her again but have thought of her often.

The train had traveled through snow all night. When we arrived at Troup, Texas, at 9:55 A.M. Christmas Eve morning (Friday), it was sleeting. Mother's cousin Carrol (Mrs. Thomas Cox) was at the train station to meet me. She had invited me to stay with her, and she had driven from Tyler, Texas, in freezing rain. It was terrible driving back with the ice-covered road with sleet-covered windshield; however, we finally arrived safely at her house.

I had not seen Joyce, her daughter, since she was a little girl about eight years old. now a lovely sixteen-year-old young lady, she greeted us warmly at the door. After lunch Carrol suggested I take a nap, which I gladly did, and I slept all afternoon!

When she awakened me, it was totally dark. The electricity was off all over town due to the ice storm, so they were using candles. She wanted me to go with them to deliver Christmas presents, which we did, stopping at all of their friends homes to leave gifts. We stopped at the beautiful Taylor home on Chilton Street (which is now the Caldwell Play School) to leave a gift. The front was covered with long icicles which hung from the balcony. It was absolutely beautiful.

When we went into the darkened house, Mr. Taylor and another gentleman were playing chess by candlelight. It was like another world. All of Tyler, Texas, looked like fairyland with the ice-covered trees and houses.

When we returned to Carrol's house, the electricity was back on. The beautiful Christmas tree, which nearly touched the ceiling, was breathtaking. We knew Jack would be there shortly. Carrol and Joyce thought it was so romantic for us to be seeing one another for the first time in four months, they had everything planned. We knew Jack could not get there before eight, so I had plenty of time to get ready. I wore a beautiful dark blue velvet dress, especially made for the occasion.

I stayed in the bedroom until I heard the doorbell before I made my "entrance." I thought I would surely die when I heard Jack's voice, but thank Heaven, I didn't.

Carrol and Joyce quietly disappeared. We were alone with the Christmas tree, the firelight, and the wonder of being together. We kissed and laughed and cried all at once. He was so lean and strong. He seemed so different, and yet, not changed at all, except for that awful G I haircut!

He had taken the bus in from camp, and he had walked from the bus station. Carrol's house was just four blocks from the square (505 So. Broadway). It was not far, but he was nearly frozen as he had no overcoat to wear. They had been lying out on the rifle range all day in the sleet and snow and his overcoat was soaked. After a little visit Carrol took us to the Blackstone Hotel where I registered as Mrs Felix X. Meyers as planned, and we checked into our room. Felix X. Meyers (Jack's friend) had reserved the room for his wife. She was unable to come, so I had to use her name, or lose the reservation.

We had planned to go out to the chapel at camp for the Christmas Eve service, but the weather was impossible so we met Carrol and Joyce and went to the beautiful Christmas Eve service at Christ Episcopal Church. After the service we walked through the snow back to the hotel. Our hearts were overflowing with love and one of our dearest memories would always be that Christmas Eve.

In the morning we enjoyed the novelty, for us, of staying in a hotel. For Jack it was the sheer luxury of sheets and warmth and a tub to bathe in instead of a shower in the barracks. We were so much in love we couldn't get over the joy of just being together.

The Blackstone was a beautiful hotel. It had wrought iron all across the front and side. It was a perfect setting for our little Christmas honeymoon. After we ate our breakfast in the dining room, Carrol took us to an eggnog party given by one of her friends. In the evening she had a buffet supper for us. Among the guests was the Commander of Camp Fannin. When Carrol introduced Jack, poor Private Price nearly fainted. The Colonel, however, was cordial and friendly. He soon put Jack at ease.

Sunday night we checked out of the hotel and went back to Carrol's. Jack had to catch the bus back to camp by ten o'clock. I spent all the next week with Carrol and Joyce, a delightful visit and wonderful rest for me, since I had not had a minute to myself since Peggy was born.

Jack was off every night while I was there. As soon as he got to

I sent Jack that hat and a belt when he first got there. Shortly after that they banned both.

Jack Price. Bivovac February 20-March 1, 1944.

Carrol's, we walked the few blocks to the Courthouse Square. It was bright and clear. I was also absolutely freezing, since we faced the north wind all the way. We went to the movie several nights, and Carrol was very thoughtful about letting us have her living room to ourselves.

On New Year's Eve I checked into the hotel in the afternoon as Mrs. Felix X. Meyers <u>again,</u> and Jack arrived shortly. We had the entire wonderful weekend ahead of us. New Year's Day we went out to the camp on the bus, and I got to take the tour. It was so nice to see his barracks and where he slept so I could imagine it when I got home.

Sunday night Carrol and Joyce took us to the bus station where the camp busses were lined up. It was parting time for most of the men. Christmas and New Year's were over for the men who had been allowed passes. Wives, sweethearts, and parents were going home. There were many clinging farewells. We had already had our sad parting at Carrol's, but it was so hard leaving. We knew it would be four long months before we would be together again. Then, we would have only ten short days before he left for overseas.

I had fond hopes that he could find an apartment so Peggy and I could be with him but in my heart I knew it was impossible. There simply were no apartments available, ever.

The camp bus left. He returned to camp. The next morning I returned home. Christmas and New Year's were over. So brief!!

THE LETTERS

1/9/44
Sunday

Dearest Sweetheart:
It's just about dinner time now, but I thought maybe I could get a few lines written before I go eat. I got up this morning about 9 o'clock and got all my laundry washed, took a shower and got dressed so now I'll write a bit. I got a wonderful letter this morning from my sweetheart. If you were only with me and I was with you and Peg all the time. Well, maybe it won't be much longer. I want you to come down so bad, but I don't know whether you should until I'm through with my basic or not. I think I would get along just as good if not better with you here, but I am thinking of you and the baby. Now, you decide what you are going to do and let me know. In the meantime I'll keep looking for a place. George just came in and said he was going to town today so maybe I'll go with him. I might not finish this till this evening.

Hi Honey, here I am again. It's about 9 oclock and I just got back from town. A little good news. I called Carrol and, this is not definite yet, so I'll let you know more about it later. She told me she had heard of a very wealthy man by the name of Mr. Fair who has a small cottage behind his house which he is thinking of fixing up to rent and she is going to get in touch with him tomorrow. He is just doing it as part of the war effort and Carrol believes the rent will be cheap. Also it is in the nicest part of town, so hold your thumbs. Honey, I'm so lonesome for you I hope we can get it.

I'm sending along a picture we had taken in town. We five fellows kinda bum around together all the time. The bottom row is E.H., Louisiana, White, Jack Price, & Duane Perry. In the top row is Louis Poelker, and George Preiner. Preiner & Perry are from St. Paul, Poelker is from St. Louis and you know where White hails from. I hope folding it won't hurt it much cause it is the only way I can mail it.

I didn't use the dollar you sent me to go to Kilgore. I used it to go to Tyler instead as I wanted to exhaust every possibility there first. I'd rather have you live in Tyler if possible cause it would be a whole lot nicer for you. If this cottage comes thru it will be too good to miss.

I'll bet you were worn out after that long trip, but I'll bet it felt swell to be home and see Peg again. I wish I could see her. Well, maybe. Let's hope. Gosh, I had a good time Christmas. It was so wonderful being with you. You know, I could hardly believe it when you walked into the living room. That's one time I was really at a loss for words. You were so beautiful. Don't worry about me studying cause I have to and you worry about me more in St. Louis than you would here. But you use your best judgement.

You tell (Little) Phillie I'll sure write her this week. Tell her I've been really busy but I'll sure get to it this week. It was sure cute. You tell her to write again real soon. Well, dearest I'd better close now and go to bed. I wishI could tell you in this letter how I feel. I love you so much. Sleep tight, sweet dreams and dream of me a little.

All my love,
Your sweetheart,
Jack

P.S. I love you. Here's a big kiss for you and a baby one for
Peg. X x

13/1/44
Thurs.

Dearest Sweetheart:

Well, honey, here I am back in that same old class again. I thought I'd better try to write you a few lines now as I have a class tonight and I might not get a lot of time to write after that. It is about 9:30 AM now and it is sleeting to beat the band. There is about an inch of sleet on the ground now and it is still going strong. Thank goodness I'm a clerk. I'd sure hate to be in the field on a day like this. How is the weather up there? Have you had any snow since you got back? Gosh, I wish I was with you. I think when I get out of the army I'm coming home and go to bed and stay there for a month. Just lay there and rest and sleep. How is Peg? Is she getting any teeth yet? How old do they have to be to sit by themselves? That's another thing I'm going to do when I get home and that is get acquainted with my daughter and play with her and everything. I'll bet I couldn't even change her diaper I've been away so long.

Here I am again, had to go to another class and then eat. As I was saying, I wish she would know me when I come home, but I know she won't. I guess you are at Sister's now. Hope you had a good time. Tell me everything you did and all. I sure would have liked to have been with you.

Honey, I'm not looking for a place any more but I sure hope one finds me cause I sure would like for you to be here with me. I miss you so much I don't know what to do.

I'm just about worn out. I haven't been to bed before midnight any night this or last week. I studied till after 11 o'clock last night cause we are hav-

ing a shorthand test and that is going to be tough. It is kind of hard for me anyway and takes a lot of studying. I guess I'd better quit for a while. I'll be back this evening so don't run off...... Here I am again. I forgot to send that shorthand paper to you. I'll put it in this letter.

The weeks are really going fast since we started this school. We are learning so much new stuff that it keeps us interested and makes the time go by. I'm at the classroom now. It's almost 7:30 and after I finish this I'm going to do some studying. You know if I would have studied like this while I was in school I'd have made straight A's. I'm trying to make good so I'll be assigned to this camp, as it is still fairly close to home, where if I was transferred, Lord knows where I would go. I stand a chance of being shipped to a camp near a larger town and closer to home, but on the other hand, at least if I stay here you can come down here to stay and that is more than you could do if I went to California or someplace equally as far.

As a clerk I have a good chance of not being shipped across and if I am shipped I'll have a nice job not too close to actual combat as I would be in charge of the records of the outfit which must be kept well behind the lines, or else I'd be with Headquarters which is always well behind the lines. Well, Dearest, it's time to get to work so I'd better close. Love me and miss me. I love you.

Your sweetheart,
Jack

Friday
14/1/44

Dearest Sweetheart:

Here I am again. That same old class again. Is it dry. Well, we are in the midst of the worst snow storm they have had here in 28 years. There is about 5 inches of snow on the ground now and it is sleeting. It has sleeted for the last 2 days and it snowed and sleeted all day today. It's been a long time since I've seen weather like this. Oh, oh, it's raining now. What a mess. I won't be able to write tonight as we are having a big inspection tomorrow and it will take me till midnight to get ready for it tonight.

Well, the class is over so I'll finish next hour....Here I am again. It's sleeting and snowing again. Boy will it be something tonight when this freezes.

How is Peg? How I'd love to be able to see her and hold her and play with her. I'm jealous of you, you know. Just think you get to see her every day, all the time. It just isn't fair to keep a guy away from his family like this. I just want to be with you all the time. Well, it can't be helped. I'll just be tickled silly when it's all over so I can come back home. Things look pretty favorable now as far as being assigned to Camp Fannin. If I am, by any chance, shipped to Fort Ord, California or Fort Meade, Maryland I'll be shipped about 2 weeks after I get back from my 7 day furlough. So if I come home on a furlough immediately after I finish my basic you will know that 2 weeks after I leave I'll be on my way to England, Australia, or one of the south sea Islands. Of course after I get to where they ship me I'll receive about 17 weeks more training and then I'll be a clerk which will be nicer than what the other guys get, so I haven't got any room to kick, I expect.

Well, I'd better close now and get busy. Bye for now, I miss you. Give Peg a big kiss for me.

All my love, always,
    Jack
P.S. I love you.

Sunday
Feb. 13, 1944

Dear Mom & Pop:
    Well, folks I finally found a minute to drop you a line. As we are going on bivouac next week, we have been kept darn busy finishing up our other work. March 12 I'll be all finished, thank goodness. I guess Babe has told you all about my grades and how this Lt. wants me to become assigned to his branch. It sure makes me feel good even tho I doubt that it will do me a lot of good. I have the highest average of the class so far. The trouble is, all general servicemen are slated for overseas duty. All they will keep in this camp now are limited servicemen and WACs. So I guess about a month or two after I finish here it will be overseas for me, but quick. We have a 30 mile hike tomorrow instead of the usual class work as there is a combat rifle range we have to fire on so this will have to be a little short as I have to get ready and get to bed early as we must get up at 4:30 so we can start at 5 o'clock. I sure dread it cause it's pouring downrain now and most likely will be tomorrow too. We had Red Skelton here today in person and I went down to see him. He was really good. He came in and the first thing he said was this must be part of the earth God forgot about. He didn't lie there. I can hardly wait for this to be over so I can get home. I don't give a darn what they do with me when I finish here just as long as I get those seven days at home. That is the only reason I hope I'm not assigned here cause if I am I won't get that furlough, and that is the most important thing to me right now.
    Well, I've got to stop and eat some ice cream a fellow brung me. I'll be back in a minute or two..... Please don't wait for me to write before you write me Mom. You don't know how swell it is to get those letters from you. Please write more often and have Pop write too.
    Good night folks, take good care of yourselves and say hello to everyone for me. Watch out for Babe and Peg too, till I get back home. All my love to my sweet Mom and swell Pop,

Your son,
    Jack
P.S. I leave on bivouac the 20th. Don't forget the packages of food. Some more chicken too. It was swell.

Bye now,
    Jack

Feb. 20, 1944
Sunday

Dear Sweetheart:
    Well, honey, we are all set up and ready to start work tomorrow so as tonight is the only night we are allowed to have lights, candles, I thought I could jot you a note. I brought some paper out with me but whether I'll be able to use it or not I don't know.

Honey, I'm so worn out I can hardly write let alone think. I've been on the go since 4 this morning and it's ten P M now. This is going to be plenty rough. If I get 10 hours sleep next week I'll be lucky and I'm not exaggerating a bit. Here is part of our schedule. Tomorrow (Mon.) we have a usual day of tactics. From 5 in the morning till midnight. The next day (Tues.) from 5 till 12 midnight we have tactics and then from 12 to about 5 we go on a 15 mile hike. The next day (Wed.) we start at 5 in the morning no sleep the night before and go till midnight. The next morning (Thurs.) we start at 5 and have tactics till noon. From noon till 8 o'clock we are on a hike, walking continuously with full field pack. (Friday) Morn at 2:30 we go out and go through the infiltration course in the dark. All day we have a problem of taking a village. They call it village fighting. Surprise targets, booby traps, mines and all. Everybody uses live ammunition and artillery shells going over our head and bombs, real ones, going off all around us. (Saturday) I don't know what we do but that will be the last day of our dangerous work. All next week we have problems in the work we have taken in school.
    Well I guess I'd better try to get some rest. I won't sleep worth a darn tonight anyway so I've got to get as much rest as I can.
    Love me and miss me. Give Peg a kiss for me. Goodnight, sweet, say a prayer for me.

Your sweetheart
    Jack

P.S. I Love You

Feb. 24, 1944
Thursday

Dearest Sweetheart:
    Maybe if you work real hard you can read this. I am writing standing up.
    I would give anything if I had my camera here to get a picture of me. I have a beard about 1/4 inch long. I'm going to let it grow till I get back and then save the mustache. Today is Thursday and is the first day since we've been here that it isn't raining. We are knee deep in Mud. I am really surprised tho at the ease in which we are going thru this. You know, after a day or two you can get used to anything. The only bad thing is being so dirty.
    Of course we have been working like hell. We haven't been to bed before 1 o'clock in the norming since we've been out, and we are up every morning at 5. Everything we do is tactical and I'll bet we walk 50 miles a day. Then all we get to eat is rations. I have a dinner, breakfast and supper ration that I'll bring home to show you. I can't write too much honey about what we are doing because I don't have the time. I'll tell you about it when I come home.
    I got a box from you and one from Mom all ready. It sure was swell. Keep the letters coming too, honey, cause you have no idea how I look forward to them. I won't get many chances like this to write you but I'll drop you a line every time I get a chance. Don't worry about me as although it's plenty tough and sometimes a little dangerous I am plenty tough now and can take it and I've been trained well enough to where I can take care of myself. The dangerous work will be over Saturday anyway. So far we only had 1 fellow hurt. We were going cross

country last night on a patrol and we came across a supply dump which we had to charge. This fellow started running in and hooked his lip and face on a piece of barbed wire stretched between 2 trees and ripped half his lip off. Had 5 stitches to put it back together. He is ok tho and is still with us.

It's cloudying up now so I guess it will start raining again, damn. Well, darling, I've got to quit now as I'm supposed to be cleaning my rifle and I must get busy on it. Bye sweet, love me and miss me. Say a prayer for me every night and don't worry. I feel swell. All my love forever and always.

Your sweetheart,
Jack

Feb. 25, 1944
(Friday)
Feb. 27, 1944
(Sunday)

Dearest Sweetheart:

Well, believe it or not I have a few minutes to write a little. We are on the battle firing ranges today. Well, we have had one day so far that it hasn't rained. It's raining now. It sure makes it miserable. Thank goodness we only have one more day of field work. Next week we have practical problems covering what we learned in school. Gotta go now. Be back in a little while. Here I am again for a minute or two. I am covered from head to foot with thick sticky mud. I sure feel horrible. We got up about 4 o'clock this morning and hiked 15 miles to get out here. We go thru the infiltration course again, both day and night, and close combat and village fighting. Well, gotta go again. Be back.

(Sunday) Well, honey, here I am agin two days later. It's Sunday now and all our tough work is over with. It's still raining. Friday nite we got in about 12 midnight after a horrible day in the rain and the sky had cleared up and we all thought the rain had finally stopped. We went to bed and about 3 o'clock we awoke with what sounded like machine gun fire on our tents to find we were in the middle of one of Texas' cloudbursts. No need to say much more. It rained buckets full for 3 hours. Everything was washed out. The rain beat on our tents so hard it drove right through and all our blankets and everything we have was drenched. Yesterday it cleared up a little and we got everything dried out but I mean we were miserable. To top it all off about 6 o'clock Saturday morn an artesian well or spring bubbled up right out of solid ground in the middle of our tent. It spouted up about 3 inches out of the ground and ran all day practically. We've got it stopped up now so we shouldn't have any trouble. We got a little time off yesterday, an hour, so we worked on our tent and got it all fixed up so last night when it started raining again we kept plenty dry and got a good nights rest for a change. We didn't get in till almost midnight but at least we were dry.

I've gotten all your and Mom's boxes honey. You'll never know how swell they were. You see, we pitched 2 tents together so four fellows are sleeping together (helps to keep warm) so every night we eat from someone's box that they got from home. Course, Perry, Poelker, Preiner and I are together.

By the way, George is covered from head to foot with poison oak. Is he ever a funny sight.

Honey, I don't think I'll be able to call you today cause it doesn't look like we'll go in although we need to plenty bad. Even if we did go in I doubt that I could reach you in time fore I had to come back out cause it's so hard to get a call through on Sunday afternoon but you positively must be down at the house early next Sunday cause we go in next Saturday and I'll call you about 7:30 or 8 o'clock Sunday Morning.

Don't throw the stick of wood away that I'm sending you, keep it. When it's dark outside take it out and look at it. This stuff is all over out here and looks real pretty at night. Just in case it has all worn off by the time it gets to you I'll tell you what it is.

Put. John K. Price,
377 23699,
C.C. 81st Inf. Bn. Rko?,
Camp Fannin, Tex

CAMP FANNIN, TEXAS
MAR 9
11 30 AM
1944

Mr. & Mrs. N. K. Price
874 Providence Ave,
Webster Groves, 19,
Mo.

Company C - 81st Battalion Camp Fannin - Tyler, Texas. March, 1944.

Infantry Replacement Training Center
Camp Fannin, Texas

Has awarded this Certificate to

Private John. K. Price

Company C , 81 Battalion, Regiment

For having completed the basic Infantry
course in the Army of the United States
Dedicated to the defense and preservation
of the United States of America

Clerk

Awarded this 11 day of March 1944.

K. C. Johnson
1st Lt.
Infantry.
Company Commander.

Russell P. Hartle,
Russell P. Hartle
Major General, U. S. Army,
Commanding.

It was covered with phosphorous and glows real bright. Even the bugs get coated with it and worms and everything glow real bright.

Well, sweet, I don't have anything else to write about so I guess I'll close. I will be seeing you and that wonderful daughter of mine in a couple of weeks. Love me and miss me and don't worry about me. I'm getting along fine. I'll say this much, this bivouac has made me as hard as nails. I'm really in good condition for the first time in about 4 years. Just think I've gone thru all that rain. Been soaking wet all day and slept that way all night and don't have a sign of a cold.

Well, hon, Church services are about to begin so I must go. Say a big prayer for me. I love you. Give Peg a kiss for me too. All my love always.

Your sweetheart
Jack

Feb. 29, 1944
Tuesday

Dearest Honey:

How are you today sweet? I have a few minutes extra today as we are getting paid and got off about a half hour early on our afternoon classes so tho't I'd write you a line or 2.

Man, if I tho't last weeks schedule was bad, I didn't know anything. Do you know we are working from 7 in the morning till 10:30 every night this week. It finally stopped raining last night and the temperature dropped to about 35. We about froze to death. The sun came out today tho for the first time since we have been out and it has turned real warm so maybe we'll have some decent weather.

Honey, please don't feel bad or blue about not getting any mail cause really every time I get a minute I write you. When we get off it's dark and we aren't allowed any lights. We can't even smoke after dark. We only have 1/2 hour to eat and that doesn't even give me time to wash my mess gear. Have patience with me, honey, I'll be able to write you every night after Saturday.

I got a V-letter from Joe Barnes that I'm sending you. I gotta go now, I'll finish later. Gotta go get paid. I'm standing

in line so maybe I can write a little before I get up to the pay table. I heard I only get $5.00 this month. I hope I get more. I hope that clears me up and I start drawing a full pay next payday.

Well, I don't have a lot to write about. We're working pretty hard, but it makes the time go by a little faster, pretty soon I'll be home. Gosh, those seven days will go like wildfire.

Listen, hon, save this letter from Joe for me will you? I'd kinda like to keep it. As soon as I get into camp I'll write him. Have you heard any more about Rusty? I guess not as I would have heard. Lord, I hope he is ok. I didn't get a letter from you Saturday or Sunday but I got 2 yesterday which made me feel a lot better. I've gotten all the food too. Hope I get anther box tonight cause I'm all out now. Did I tell you that Mom sent me some Velveeta cheese? Boy was it good. I liked the deviled ham too. I wish you all would have sent me some home-made cookies, too, but I'm not kicking cause I've had plenty to eat, thanks to you all.

Well, hon, I'm almost there so will stop for now. I'll try to finish this evening in class. Bye for now, I love you.

Well, surprise. I got $8.35 this month. That must clear me up, so next month I should get about $12.00, goodie goodie.

Had to go eat so here I am again. Got a few more minutes fore mail call so will try to finish this now. I'll admit it's not much of a letter, honey, but it is the best I can do out here. Tell everyone hello and tell Mom and Pop to write me and don't any of you worry as I am fine.

How is Peg? Gee, sweet, she sounds so cute, I can hardly wait to see her. Mom keeps raving in her letters what a sweet baby she is and how unspoiled, too. How she could help but not be spoiled is beyond me but it's swell she isn't. Something so sweet and cute as she must be, you just can't help but spoil a little.

Well, honey, I guess I'd better close now and go see about my letter from you. Give Peg a kiss for me. I love you and miss you more than anything in the world. Give Peg a kiss for me.

All my love always,
Your sweetheart
Jack

(Note: Joe Barnes was good friend in the Pacific Theatre; Rusty Chapman was Jack's cousin who was a prisoner of the Germans)

March 1, 1944
Wednesday

Dearest Sweetheart:

It's about 9 o'clock and I'm supposed to be working but I got 2 such wonderful letters today that I just had to stop and write my honey a letter.

Did you get the pictures? I got them in the evening and didn't have time to add anymore to the letter. One of the fellows wanted them enlarged so he is using the negatives but I'll get them from him before I come home as you might want to get some of them enlarged to regular size. I thought they were pretty good. (These were the bivouac pictures.)

We are sitting in a large tent working by candlelight. There are 4 groups working. It's interesting but awfully tiresome. We have to put in such long hours.

Gosh, honey, I can hardly wait to see Peg. She sounds so darn cute. Well, it might be more than 2 weeks before I get home cause I'm afraid I'll be delayed because I haven't gotten my glasses for my gas mask yet and I won't be able to leave till I do. However, it won't be too long before I'll be home.

Well, honey, I've got to stop now and get busy cause we'll be quitting soon and I have to clean up my papers, etc., fore I leave. I'll try to finish this tomorrow. Night, sleep tight, I love you more than anything in the world.

Good morning. It's Thursday morn so I decided to finish this fore I do anything else. Our platoon of Clerks got together last night after classes and presented Lt. Curtin with a traveling case, as he is leaving us this Saturday. We sure hate to see him go. He is a really fine man. We paid over $25.00 for the case. It's really a good one.

Well only today, Friday and Saturday and it will be over then our real work in getting ready to ship will begin. Next week will really be hectic with checking all our equipment and everything. You ought to see my moustache. I got into camp yesterday afternoon to see about my gas mask so I had time to shower and shave so I trimmed it up. It looks like this. (picture!) Pretty isn't it? I don't

Jack's parents, Gram and Grandaddy Price.

My parents, Mimi and Grandpa Walser.

like it but it's fun to fool with. Well, sweet, I'd better go now and get busy. I'll write you a nice long one when I get in.

By the way George is confined to quarters in camp from that poison oak he has. He has been all week. He was really in bad shape. Well, sweet, I must close now. Write me lots. By the way you can stop the packages now. All my love to my wonderful sweet little wife and gal.

Your Sweetheart
Jack

Sunday
3/5/44

Dearest Sweetheart:

I can't find a pencil so I'll have to write with ink. I hope I have enough to finish this.

Well, honey, I don't have much to write about. I was awfully busy today. I had to wash all my clothes and get them back in shape. About all I can think about is coming home. I'm so anxious and excited I hardly know what to do. It was so wonderful talking to you last night honey. You sounded so wonderful. I guess Perry thought I was an awful goose but I don't care. I was so choked up afterwards, I couldn't talk for a while.

We had gotten in about 5 o'clock yesterday and so Perry and I decided we were going to town and really go whole hog and be comfortable after 2 weeks of discomfort. So we had a big steak dinner and then went to look for a room which we couldn't find so we went to the late show and saw Destination Tokyo which was really swell. Then I called you and talked and Perry was calling his wife. When we finished talking to our honies we went over and bowled a little and then got back to camp about 2 AM. I got up about 10 AM this morning and worked till 2:30 then Perry and I went down to the camp show and saw See Here, Private Hargrove. Don't miss that. It comes closer to basic training than any other picture I have seen. In it the obstacle course and barracks and things they do are almost identical to what we have been doing. We got back about 5 PM and I got to work and just finished so I'll drop you a line and go to bed. I can't get over how Peg has grown. I can hardly realize she is 7 mos old. Honey, I can just hope and pray that this won't be the last time I see her. I want to help and watch her grow so much. It's a darn shame I have to miss all this. I'll be so happy when this mess is over & I can come home to stay.

You know, you don't appreciate your family and home and freedom till you can't have them. Then you realize just what the United States stands for and just how lucky we all are. I guess my life doesn't mean so much in comparison to our country. It's worth a little hardship and lonesomeness and blood to keep what we have. Well, honey, it's almost lights out so I must close. Love me and miss me. Give Peg a big kiss for me and say hello to everyone.

All my love and a million kisses,
Your sweetheart,
Jack

Tuesday
Mar. 7, 1944

Dearest Sweetheart:

Hey, how are you today? Well, honey it's Tuesday. Only 5 more days and I'll be all through with my cycle and waiting for my shipping orders.

We had our final" Physical" yesterday. What a joke that was. We all lined up and walked thru the dispensary. The doctor, a captain, sat at a desk and as each man passed he asked, "any complaints?" Then before you had a chance to say a word he would say next man and ok you for General Service. Course, after we get to where we are going and before going overseas we will get a very thorough exam. I'll pass that one the same as I have passed them all.

You know, seven days is an awfully short time. It'll take me longer than that to tell you how much I love you. Those days will go by so fast it will seem like only an hour or 2. But, I guess I'm lucky to get that much time at home. I am so anxious to get there I can hardly wait. Just cause I want to leave as soon as possible, I'll bet they hold me over 5 or 6 weeks. Darn, I hope not. I'm so anxious to see Peg. You know, I'm awfully proud of that big girl of mine. I'll bet she is the sweetest thing. She is cute as a bug. The only thing that worries me is I hope she doesn't look like me when she grows up. I want her to be beautiful like her mama and I guess she will be as sweet and lovable as her Mama too. You know, I've been thinking, and I've almost come to the conclusion that while I'm home we ought to get busy and have another one, a boy, just in case I don't get back, which is entirely possible. Whatcha think? I have tried to get in touch with Carrol and say goodbye, but we are restricted while waiting for our orders which means we must stay in the Company

Jack and Peggy and her cousins. Children of my sister Corinne and Oliver Taetz.

Our little family together at last!

A kiss from daddy.

area from Saturday at 5 PM until we leave this camp. The red tape we have to go through this next week is really something. No one knows what is going on. One minute it's one thing and not a minute later an order to do just the opposite. I don't think any of them know exactly what they are doing.

It's time to change classes. I'll finish later

I don't have a thing to write about. We are all doing what is absolutely necessary just trying to get this week over with so we can all get home. I am anxious to find out how I am going to be classified when we leave here. There are 3 different classes. Of course the higher the classification the better chance for a good job when we are assigned. I don't guess we'll find out anything much before we leave if they tell us anything at all. All I can think about is getting home. Those seven days with you will mean so much to me. I want to be able to hold you again and just be together like we used to be. Funny, how 1 week can mean so much now when a year ago it didn't mean a thing and didn't realize what every day being with you meant till I came here and was away from you. I guess every one wakes up and realizes that after what he has has been taken away from him.

Well, that's enough psychology (or however) for now. I wonder what's holding Peg's teeth up from coming in. You don't suppose she won't have any do you? Is she a little slow in getting started on the different things? I just wondered if at 7 mos she should be crawling and really getting around. Well sweet I'm going to close and get this off before noon. Bye, love me and miss me and give Peg a big kiss for me. Look for me, I'll be seeing you.

All my love,
Your sweetheart,
    Jack
P.S. I got a sweet wonderful letter from you this noon with the pictures (2) of you and the baby. Honey, I just can't get over how much she has grown. It is really amazing. She is so darn cute. I just can't wait till I get home again. I want to see you both so bad.

All my love to my two darlin's
    Jack

(Note: This baby had four doting grandparents, and one very protective mother. Every word of the "Better Homes and Gardens Baby Book" was followed to the letter!)

Thursday
March 9, 1944

Hello Dearest:
    Well, it won't be long now. 2 more days and we'll be finished and most likely our shipping orders will come through about Tuesday of next week. I also heard a rumor that just because I don't have my gas mask glasses doesn't mean I won't ship. They will ship me as soon as my orders come through regardless of glasses or no. I hope so. That might mean I'll be home next week some time. If I am shipped to another camp it would most likely be to Camp Hood, Texas which is near Temple, Texas. I would be shipped there to go to Cadre school which means after 3 weeks of schooling I would come out a Non-Commissioned officer and would most likely be assigned to a training Battalion there. They are starting a new IRTC training camp there and need men very badly. In fact, almost half

of the cadre, or NCO's that are here in our company are being shipped there.

That would be a very good deal, but it is improbable in my case as I don't believe I can qualify for cadre school. I didn't make too good a showing in the field as far as being able to take charge of men like that for training, but this is still the Army and Lord knows what might happen. Well, at any rate, we are all through training and I'll be doing something. At least it will be doing some one some good. If it is being shipped over I'll be helping the war along and if it is a training camp at least I'll be teaching someone else to fight.

I didn't hear from you at noon today but did hear from Mom and Dad. Mom sent me the clipping about Ty Leeper. That sure was a shame, but before this mess is over, a lot more of us will go the same way. I'll swear the way Mom talks, and Dad too, our daughter is nothing less than a genius. Well, an angel maybe would be a little more appropriate word. Mom says she thinks Peg is a little slower than other children in some things but that none can compare in how good she is and how smart she is. Honey, I can hardly wait to see her. I'll bet she's the sweetest thing in the world. It tickles me half to death about the shine she has taken to Dad. You know he was proud as a peacock about her anyway. It's a wonder she isn't spoiled as can be. At least she'll have some swell grandparents all the way round. I hope her old man will be around for long too, so he can help to spoil her. Well, Honey, I don't have time to write any more tonight as we are getting ready to fall out and go get shot at by the big stuff, artillery cannons to you. Say a prayer for me hon, that I get to come home real soon.

Bye now, be seeing you soon. All my love always,

Your sweetheart,
    Jack

Friday
March 10, 1944

Dearest:
    Well, I only have a few minutes so I doubt I'll get a lot of writing done.

Man, and all that stuff, am I in bad shape this morning. We had a company party last night and they had 600 bottles of beer, 200 cokes, sandwiches, candy, cigarettes, cookies, and pickles, olives, and Lord knows what all. I had 10 bottles of beer that I can remember. We didn't quit till about 1 o'clock. I've really got a hangover today.

Nothing new has happened yet. No news about shipping or anything yet. I wish they would hurry up. I want to get going. I've gotten to where I can't see any further than the end of my nose. All I can think about is the 7 days and I should be thinking about what will come after those 7 days are over. It is definitely overseas for us and there's no way of getting out of it. O well. You know, the trouble with typing a letter to you is that I can't tell you I love you because everyone that walks by reads a little of the letter, but you know how much I do anyway. It looks like I'll have to quit. Yep, they found some work for me to do. I'll see you later...........

I'll have to finish this in pencil. It is now Sunday (12th) and have I ever been busy. They are getting us all ready for shipment. Yesterday 113 men got their orders and leave for Fort Ord, Cal. Thursday. That leaves only about 40 men who are eligible for shipment left, they got all the clerks except 6 of us. I don't know what they plan to do with us. Guess I'll know in a day or so. They took everybody in the Clerks alphabetically till they got to George. Then they skipped Preiner & Price, our names follow each other, and started up on the alphabet again. Darn, if I was on it I would be seeing you next Friday. Now, Lord knows how long it will be. Honey, I want to see you and the baby so bad. That's all I can think about and I haven't gotten a letter from you in 3 days. Sunday is a bad day for me.

How is Peg? You know, I just can't realize that I have a daughter that big at home, she was so darn little when I left. They sure grow fast don't they? I just sit here and look at those pictures over and over again but I just can't believe it. She is so cute, honey. I can't get over that smile of hers. She must be a little doll. The hardest part of this army is sitting here waiting. Perry got his orders, by the way, and I was kinda hoping we could stick together. Well, that's about all, so I'll close.

I love you like anything,
P.S. XXX etc.

Your sweetheart,
real ones, too.
Jack

Thursday
March 16, 1944

Dearest Sweetheart:

Well, I am very much ashamed of myself. I'm talking about not writing for such a long time. I feel so bad tonight. All the fellows left tonight. It sure made me feel bad. Perry left, too, you know. Gosh, I wish I was leaving with them. We only have 36 fellows left out of over 200. I made some darn swell friends too. That is the bad part of this army, breaking up a bunch of swell fellows like that. I hope my orders come thru soon cause they are working me half to death. I have been on K.P. twice this week and have worked in the supply room every night checking in equipment after I get off K.P. Tomorrow I am on a detail on a firing range all day and have guard duty tomorrow night. The two limited Service men out of clerk school who were assigned in our Company have gotten Corporal stripes already. The guys who aren't physically fit and don't go to fight get the ratings. Sometimes I don't get it. Maybe it's just because I'm so down in the dumps and blue tonight. Honey, I want to see you so bad I guess that's why I wanted to be shipped right away. At least I have a chance of going to Meade instead of Ord and if everything goes right I should get about 8 or 9 days at home. How is Peg? Any teeth coming in yet? I can hardly stand it I want to see her so bad. I am an awful lucky guy to have such a wonderful wife and daughter. We've always had such wonderful times together and gotten along so well and loved each other so much. You know we are a very unusual family. There aren't many people who love each other so much. It'll be so wonderful when the war is over and we can get our family going again. I can hardly believe it will really be. I've been away so long it's hard to remember how it was to be able to live like you want to and be with the ones you love. Let's hope it won't be too far off. I am sending a picture of our Company marching in a parade

Jack and Wallace Decker at Zimmerman's Hungaria Restaurant, New York City, June 4, 1944.

we had last week and also my diploma they issued after completing our basic training. Save all these things will you, hon, as they might be nice to have later on, after this is over.

Have you heard any more about Rusty? I would like to write him if it is possible. Do prisoners of war receive mail from home? I want you to make the plans to do anything you want to do while I'm home. It would kind of be fun to go to dinner, a show, and dancing somewhere some evening. Maybe with Dot and Tommy too. I guess I'd better close I have a busy day ahead of me. Love me and miss me.

Your sweetheart,
P.S. I Love You.
Jack

3 /17/ 44
Friday

Dearest Honey:

I finally got a letter and I'm sorry you've been sick, honey. Are you sure you're all right now? I'm so mad, 17 more fellows got shipping orders today and I'm still here. I believe I'll buy my own ticket when I get my orders so I can get right home. I imagine I'll get mine about next Friday. I heard something good today, anyway. All the rest of us are supposed to be going to Ft. Meade. Then from there overseas. I don't have a thing to write about, sweet. We are doing all the dirty details they can find. Lord, with all the time we have wasted fooling around and with all the red tape we could have really done something toward winning the war. Well, it won't be much longer before I'll be home with my wonderful family. The days are dragging so, though, I can hardly stand it. Let's hope and pray that the war will be over soon enough so that it won't be another 6 months fore I see you again or that I will see you again at all.

I forgot to tell you. My civilian glasses broke today. I hope I can get it fixed when I get home cause these G.I. glasses look terrible on me and I want to look particularly nice with such a beautiful wife and daughter being with me. I'm so darn lucky to have such a wonderful sweet wife loving me and waiting for me. I'm lucky to have such a wonderful daughter too. I don't know how you are, but every time I think of you and Peg and home I get all choked up in side to where it hurts and I feel like finding a dark corner somewhere by my self and having a good cry. That would just make me feel worse, so I don't. Well, Maybe it won't be forever and some day we'll all be together again. It's getting late and I must close. All my love to my sweet lil Momma and gal,

Your sweetheart,
Jack
P.S. I Love You

3/19/44
Sunday

Dearest Darlin':

Well, honey, another week is gone and I'm still waiting. I sure feel terrible today, too. I'm so down in the dumps and blue and lonesome. If those orders don't come through soon I don't know what I'll do. I've just gotta get home for a while anyway. Those 7 or 8 days are going to be like heaven to me. Be back in a minute....... Here I am again. I was so lonesome I decided the best thing to do was get busy so I sorted all the mail and made mail call for Company B and Company C. By the way, I am no longer in Co. C. They changed the companies around so now write me to Co.B. instead of C. Well, it's just about time for lunch so I'll finish this evening. I guess I'll go to a show this afternoon. I'll see youa little later...... Here I am again, I went to the show, saw Cover Girl. It was real good. I did something I shouldn't have today but it was a good deal so I guess I did ok. You know I tore my field jacket all to pieces on bivouac so I salvaged it but won't get my new one till I get to my new camp so I bought one today from a trainee here who was short of money. The darn jackets cost $12.50 on a statement of charges when you buy one from the Government if you lose yours so I got this one for 6.00. I used six bucks of my furlough money but I'm glad I did. It is brand new as the trainee has only been in the army 2 weeks and it is my exact size. He will have to buy a new one now and will have 12.50 deducted from his next months pay but he wanted the dough so I guess he is happy. I know I am.

How is Peg? Are her teeth coming in yet? Honey, I want to see her so bad. I can hardly wait till I walk up the driveway of old 874 again. Honey, I know I'm silly but I would kinda like to come home on the streetcar and surprise you all. Would you mind too much if you didn't get to meet me? It would be just like when I walked into Carrol's that night. It was so thrilling. You were so beautiful and wonderful I just didn't know what to do or say. I just wanted to stand there and look at you. I just sit here and dream about it.

I believe the next orders will come thru for Thursday. I hope I'm on them cause that will mean I'll be home for the weekend. Love me and miss me. Give Peg a big kiss for me, I love you,

Yours, Jack
P.S. I Love You.

OVERSEAS FURLOUGH
At Home

Jack's orders finally came through on April 21st, 1944. For some reason he was held at Camp Fannin several weeks after the others shipped out. He went by train for the eleven hour overnight trip to St. Louis, Missouri. He then took a taxi from Union Station to my parents' house in the town of Kirkwood, Missouri.

No one ever came to our house in a taxi or came without calling as we lived so far out of town. Well, there was the taxi and there was Jack. He wanted to surprise me and he surely did. My joy knew no bounds. After all the delays I could not believe he was really there.

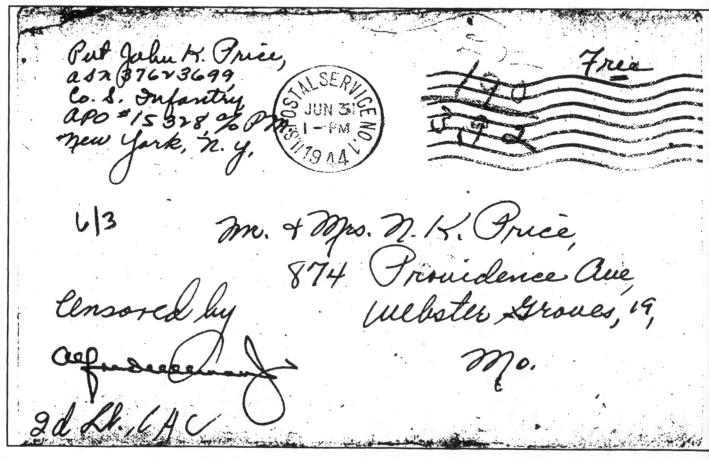

It was a Saturday afternoon, and all the family was there. Peggy was just waking from her nap. As we walked up the stairs to my room, Jack was so fearful the baby would reject him, but he didn't know that I was even more fearful. We did not need her rejection! Fortunately our fears were groundless. She studied him for a moment, and then she held her little arms out to him. He was totally overcome with emotion.

From the day he left I had Peggy kiss his picture every night and I talked constantly about Daddy. Maybe it was the uniform, maybe it was my hugging and kissing him, but for whatever reason there was not a moment strangeness between them. She was only nine months old, and he had only ten short days to get his little girl to love him. There was no way to know when he would see her again and always the unspoken thought - if ever.

Jack's parents drove out to our house that evening. We had a grand reunion, and we heard first hand all about Camp Fannin and his months of training. Jack's father had the only automobile in the family during World War II. With gas and tires so closely rationed he used it sparingly. Therefore, we packed it with the baby's and my things as though we were going to California instead of just to Webster Groves, Missouri, to spend his furlough with his parents!

A few days after Jack got home his Grandfather Evans died. He was quite old and ill, but Jack had been able to see him in the hospital for a few moments. The next few days were given over to the funeral. It had a good side, however, as all the relatives came, and we were able to visit with everyone at once. Some of the cousins were home on furlough also.

One evening we went out for dinner and dancing, as planned, with his cousin Dot and her husband Tom Gavin. Within a few months Tom was drafted into the service. They had two small children.

The war was beginning to take its toll on our family now. For the first five days of the furlough we did not want to think of its end; however, as the rest of the days passed so quickly, one by one the end of Jack's furlough was drawing closer. We tried not to let one another see our depression, but it was not easy.

We spent one of the days visiting my sister Corinne Taetz (Sissy) and their children, David, Anne, Philip and Kathy. They lived in Gray Summit, Missouri, about 30 miles distance. Her husband Oliver was doing war work in Hanford, Washington. (We later learned that it had to do with the atomic bomb.)

Jack loved their children very much, and they loved him. Philip, ten years old, was proudly wearing a tee shirt with U.S.Army printed on it in honor of Uncle Jack! We took pictures, of course!

One night we went to a movie by ourselves, but mostly we let Jack and Peggy grow as close as possible. We took her to the zoo, and we had picnics in Forest Park in St. Louis. One day took her down town shopping, and we had Jack's picture made at Stix Baer & Fuller, a department store.

Jack was so proud showing Peggy off, and I was so proud showing him off in his uniform. The Spring weather was perfect. Everything was blooming, and our world was beautiful at that moment. It is a wartime euphoria which is indescribable.

The ten day furlough, which was actually fourteen days counting the weekends, passed all too quickly. On Wednesday, May 3rd, 1944, we celebrated Jack's 25th birthday. The next day his mother and father and Peggy and I accompanied him to Union Station in St. Louis where he was to board the train for Fort Meade, Maryland, and then to a port of embarkation, "Somewhere on the East Coast."

It was a great relief to know that he would go to the European Theater and not the Pacific Theater. We could not know, however, that the invasion of Europe would take place the following month on June 6th, 1944. We also could not know that he would be at the Port of Embarkation on D-Day. If he had left Camp Fannin with the first group to ship out, he would have undoubtedly been in the initial landing of the invasion of Europe.

His parents and Peggy and I were not allowed to see him onto the train, so our sad parting was at the gate. We watched him walk down the platform to the coach with his barracks bag over his shoulder. He walked so straight, and he tried to look so brave it was almost unbearable. He turned once and waved when he reached the coach, but when Peggy waved her little hand at him, it was too much. He turned and ran the last few steps and boarded the train.

Privately we all had the same thought. Would we ever see him again? Would Peggy ever know her Daddy?

When the train pulled out of the station, we left with such heavy hearts we could hardly speak. Jack's father went to work at his office nearby. His mother and I had no heart to go home so we did what two sensible ladies should do. We spent the afternoon shopping for Peggy!

EMBARKATION
Fort Meade, Maryland
May, 1944

Jack arrived at Fort Meade, Maryland, on May 5th, 1944. Bob Medley, from Camp Fannin, was with him. They had traveled all day and all night, arriving in Washington D.C. at 8:30 A.M. They then rode a short distance by train to Fort Meade, which is located between Washington and Baltimore, Maryland.

The Fort was named for Major General George Gordon Meade, of Civil War fame. It had been at one time a rail-head for the Union Army, a military hospital, and had provided housing for servicemen during World War I. In 1917 the building project was completed and named Camp Meade. In February, 1929, it became, by Act of Congress, Fort George G. Meade.

By 1941 additional training areas were added which expanded the post to 13,500 acres. During World War II more than five million men passed through its gates, including Private John K. Price!

The first letter he wrote upon his arrival was filled with love for the baby and me, the loneliness of separation, and the feeling of dread that he would not come back. They had been issued all new clothing and all their overseas equipment.

Jack was at Fort Meade for several weeks. On May 12th (Friday), he and Bob Medley got a three-day pass. They went to Washington, and they had lunch with my sister Phyllis who worked at the Department of Labor. They went to a baseball game that night. The Washington Senators played the St. Louis Browns. The "Brownies" won!

The next day they rented a car and drove around the area. They had dinner that night at the 400 Club in Washington with Phyllis. They spent Sunday sightseeing, enjoying the beautiful buildings of the capitol. It was the first and only time Jack went to Washington, D.C.

His letter on the 15th of May, 1944, telling me about his trip was the last one I received from Fort Meade. He had also telephoned that night. It was wonderful to hear one another for even those few precious minutes. His family and I knew he would be leaving, but did not know exactly when he would leave, or where he would go, except it would be the port of embarkation.

THE LETTERS

Fort Meade
Saturday
May 6, 1944

Dearest Darling:
I wish I could tell you how I feel tonight, dearest. My heart aches so I don't know what to do. That sounds awfully silly I guess, but I love you so and am so lonely and miserable I hardly can stand it. I found out something that made me feel awful today. We won't be here over 7 days so it will be impossible for you to come up. We are definitely going to a Port of Embarkation from here and then overseas. You don't know what it would mean to me to be able to see you and hold you just once more before I go. I'll never forget how beautiful you were and sweet and lovely when I said goodbye at the station and how cute Peg was waving bye bye. She is so sweet, dearest. Take good care of her and keep her as sweet as she is and have her grow up as sweet and wonderful as her Mommy.

I guess this is awful mushy, honey, but I can't help it. It's just the way I feel and I gotta tell you. This is a terrible thing to say, sweet, but I am worried cause somehow I have a feeling that I'm not coming back and I want you to know just how much I really did love you and need you. That's enough of that kind of talk now or I'll be crying right here in front of God and everybody. Say a prayer for me every night.

Well we had a very wonderful trip. It was really beautiful. It is a wonderful train, streamliner and fast, and we arrived about 8:30 Friday morn in Wash. They had quite a few women on the train with young babies and between the soldiers and the stewardess they hardly saw their kids the whole evening. You would really have enjoyed it. I wish you could have come with me. You could have visited Phillie and had a real nice time.

Fort Meade is a very old camp and is very beautiful in parts. They have beautiful homes for the officers right on the post but so far I don't care as much for it as I did Fannin. Well, darling, it's late and I've been on K P from 5 o'clock yesterday till 2 this morning and from 4:30 this morn till 7 tonight so I'm plenty worn out so I am going to close for now. We haven't done anything yet but K P so I can't tell you anything about what we will do but I'll let you know. Oh yeah, We have been issued all new clothing and all our overseas equipment. Bye for now, honey, love me cause if you didn't or ever stopped I just wouldn't have anything to live for. You and Peg are my whole life. Pray that this terrible thing will be over soon. All my love,

Your Sweetheart,
    Jack

Morning, honey. I just got up and feel a lot better. I am going try to reach you on the phone.
    Bye, Me.
                    Fort Meade
                    Monday
                    May 15, 1944

Darling honey:

How are you this evening, darling? Now that was a silly question, I just finished talking to you. Gosh, honey, telephones are so wonderful. Just think, even tho I may not see you for a long while I can still hear your voice and that is so wonderful. It makes me feel so good.

Well, I'll give you a resume of every thing we did on our three day vacation. We left Friday morning and got into Washington about noon or a little before. The first thing we did was have breakfast, we had missed it here at camp, then I called Phillie and made a date for lunch. We walked around downtown till time to meet Phillie. It is a very beautiful city with beautiful buildings and parks and all, but it's terribly confusing. There are so many people bustling around you can hardly walk the streets. Well, then at noon we walked down to the Department of Labor and met Phillie and had lunch and made a date for Saturday. Friday afternoon we went to Philadelphia but we didn't have a whole lot of time cause we wanted to be back in Washington by 8:30 that night to go to the ball game. We walked around Phillie a while but didn't get to see any of the historical points. It's a nice city but nothing like Washington. We got back to Washington about

7:30 and went to see the Brownies play Washington Senators and win. The game was over about 11 o'clock and we went back to town and had a bite to eat and started to hunt for a place to sleep. The first hotel we came to, we got a room with a bath and twin beds for 6.60 a night which is reasonable here. It was about midnight then so we went to bed.

We got up about 9 o'clock and went down and had breakfast and then got a different room, $3.30, then went out to see the town. All morning we walked along Constitution Avenue looking in, and at all the Government buildings. That afternoon we rented a car and drove along the Potomac river on Riverside Drive. It is the most beautiful place. It is a parkway and on one side is the river and on the other are lagoons with all kinds of sailboats on it and everything. Then on either side of the road are bridle paths and bicycle paths and the road is completely covered with huge trees for the entire length of the drive and it's about 5 or 6 miles long. About 6 o'clock we took the car back and went over to a service center here and washed and shaved. Then we walked over and met Phillie and Art and went to dinner at the 400 Club (Ahem). When we had finished dinner we grabbed a cab out to their house and got their car, a 39 De Soto Coupe. We got to Baltimore about 9 o'clock. We went to the waterfront and saw all these big ships coming and going which was really interesting, then we started going in these waterfront dives, talk about fun, we really saw some sights. We got back to Washington about 2 A M a little woozy and worse for wear and after a cup of coffee went to bed.

We got up at about 10 o'clock (Sunday) had breakfast and started out to see the sights. First we went to the Washington Monument. I wish I could describe how beautifully that is laid out. It is in a line from the Capitol, with beautiful parks and all in between. We went up to the top and you can see all of Washington from there. From there we went to the Capitol and went all through it. We saw the Senate Chambers and the House of Representatives. You have no idea how impressive it is. The two houses were in session today and the gallery is open to Servicemen. I sure wish I could have gone to see that. After leaving the Capitol we went to the Jefferson Memorial which is on the order of that band stand in Forest Park only 50 times bigger with a huge statue in the middle. Then we ate and after lunch went to the Smithsonian. I wish I would have had more time to see that cause it would take you seven days to see everything in there. Dinosaurs skeletons and all kinds of Prehistoric animals. In fact they have a copy of everything there is in any line there is, from the oldest automobile to the smallest animal. It was really interesting.

We saw the Lincoln Memorial, Congressional Library, Arlington Cemetery, and the grave of the unknown soldier, the White House, Mount Vernon and a million other things. We got back to camp about 11 o'clock completely worn out. Definitely after this war is over we are coming back here as you must see this. Well, that's the extent of the trip. I'll write more about it later. Well, sweet, the way it looks I'll be living here tomorrow. It looks like I'm always the last to leave. I sure dread it. I can hardly stand being away from you and Peg.

By the way here is the schedule:
    Aunt Catherine — England,

Aunt Alice — India.
Aunt Stella — Italy,
Aunt Louise — Australia.
Buff & Cookie — South Pacific Islands.
Aunt Hilda — France or Germany.
Uncle Ralph — North Africa.
That about covers it, honey, I must close now. All my love to my darling and my big gal and a million kisses.

Your sweetheart,
Jack

P.S. Send the snapshots we took, but nothing of value. I've got to send all my civilian clothes home. Don't be surprised.

(The soldier with Jack was Bob Medley, who was also at Camp Fannin.)

EMBARKATION
Camp Shanks, New York
May 24 - June 9, 1944

On May 24th, 1944, Jack wrote that he was now at a camp "Somewhere on the East coast," and it was designated only as Co. S, Infantry, APO 15328 c/o Postmaster, New York. (It was Camp Shanks, New York). This was the port of embarkation. They had come from Fort Meade, Maryland, on a troop train. His letters were now censored. A military officer read their letters for security reasons and cut out any subject that could possibly "affect the war." It was hard for him to write since he could not tell anything he was doing at the camp.

Camp Shanks was located at Orangeburg, New York. The site was used during the Revolutionary War when large elements of General Washington's Continental Army camped there twice. It was named for General David Cary Shanks, who was Commander of the New York Port of Embarkation during World War I.

Camp Shanks was re-opened on January 4, 1943, and processed a total of 362,630 troops for overseas duty in World War II. Jack described it as "a fairly nice camp."

They were allowed passes into New York City (approximately 25 miles) when they were not on duty. Everything was very expensive, but they could get free passes from the USO (United Services Organizations). On the 31st they went to see the movie "Going My Way," with Bing Crosby and Barry Fitzgerald, free. Regular movie tickets were $1.40, standing room only.

On Sunday, June 4th, 1944, he and another soldier (Wallace Decker from Massachusetts) went to New York City again and got USO tickets for the show "New Moon." They had orchestra seats, right in front. After the show they went sightseeing. They took the Staten Island Ferry, saw the Statue of Liberty and other interesting sights. In the evening they ate at a well-known restaurant, Zimmerman's Hungaria, and had their picture taken.

We did not receive many letters from Jack at Camp Shanks. They were kept very busy. His last letter from there was written Friday, June 9th, 1944. He had just received the pictures we took while he was home. He was so happy to take them with him. I also sent him the words to the song, "I'll Be Seeing You," which he had requested. A sad song indeed! He had heard they were to be put on alert that evening which meant shipping out next week. They were now restricted to the barracks, except for ten minutes every hour, when they could go to the P X. (Post Exchange). He said the camp food was horrible. Any one who could, ate at the P X. He said a fellow at the P X would mail this letter so it would not be censored. It was a sad letter, filled with all the love his heart could hold. He said I would not hear from him for awhile. He didn't know when they would leave, or where they would go. He just wrote "DON'T WORRY - I'LL BE ALL RIGHT!!!"

When I did not hear again, I knew he was on his way. The invasion of Europe had begun on June 6th, 1944. We thanked God over and over that he was not in it.

THE LETTERS

Camp Shanks   Saturday
(Censored)   May 27

Dear Folks:
Just a few lines to let you know I am thinking about you all. How is everything at 874? I haven't heard from you since I left home so I haven't a darn thing to write about. I found out today that I won't get that Money order till sometime next week. Maybe I can borrow a few bucks and use the money order to pay it back. It seems that the wire is sent to the postmaster in New York under my APO number and he makes out a Postal Money order and mails it to me, so it delays it considerable. I sure appreciate you sending it to me, tho. I am having one last fling fore I leave. I have been to New York on pass and sure wasn't very impressed. It is definitely not a serviceman's town. Course there are quite a few things to see that are free but the time you can get in to see them you can't get off. Everything else is so expensive.

I prefer Washington all over New York. I really had a good time there. Course, I had a lot more time to spend there with that three day pass.

Well, Folks, I'll close now and hit the hay. Write soon and more often.

All my love and kisses to my two favorite parents.

Your Son,
Jack

                     Camp Shanks
(Censored)   Thursday
                     June 1, 1944

Dear Mom & Pop:
I got the $10 bucks yesterday. Thanks a lot. I haven't had it cashed yet. I went to town last night but didn't need any money. We went to the U.S.O. and got some free passes to Going My Way and also to a dance. It is a very wonderful picture. Whatever you do, don't miss it. This Barry Fitzgerald, who is in it, should get the academy award. It has been running 3 weeks on Broadway with standing room only at every performance at $1.40 per. I'll bet it runs 20 weeks. It was without a doubt the best picture I have seen in a long time. You know, I wish I had known about that U.S.O. sooner. We can get free passes to every show and any other type of entertainment they have. I would like to see a good stage show like Ziegfeld Follies before I leave. I have gotten very few letters lately. The mail is so mixed up. Guys have been getting 5 or 6 in one day and going 6 or 7 days without any mail so I guess mine will come all together. How is that big gal of mine? I'll bet she's getting cute. Darn I sure hate to miss this part of her life. They are so cute when they are first learning to walk and talk.

I still have a hard time writing a letter cause I'm not allowed to write about anything we are doing here at camp and other than my visits to New York that's about all there is to write about. I guess after you kind of get used to what they don't want you to write you'll get along ok. You try to be careful cause these censors have a pretty tough job and you want to do everything to make it a little easier on them. I wouldn't have their job for anything in the world

Well folks I'll close now. Write real soon and give me all the news. Give everyone my love.

All my love,
Your Son,
Jack

Camp Shanks
(Censored)
Monday
June 5th, 1944

Dearest Sweetheart:

Well, Honey, I'm going to have to make this a long one to make up for not writing the last two days. I received two letters and the birth announcement this morning which were the first letters I have received since Friday. That's swell about Cookie. As soon as you can, send me a picture of the litter. Are the pups cute? Are you planning on keeping any of them? I'm sure glad she came through so easy as she was so small. I got the program of the dog show this morning. I don't know whether you want it back but I have a picture and a few souvenirs to send home so I'll send it along.

We were in New York again Sunday and went to see "The New Moon." It was really wonderful. Had a very good cast. I'm sending the program as I thought maybe you would like to look through it. We got free passes for the show from the U.S.O. and had orchestra seats right down in front. After the show we decided to get on a subway and just ride. We rode all the way across town and when we got off we were at the Battery where the Staten Island ferry crosses, so we got on it. It was without a doubt the longest ride for a nickel I have ever taken on a boat. It passes right in front of the Statue of Liberty so I got a really good look at the Old Lady. It is really impressive.

After the boat trip we caught a subway back to town and went up in the Empire State Building. That is the tallest darn thing I have ever seen. I'll swear you stand at the front door and look up and it almost breaks your neck. Then we went up to the U.S.O. and found a place to eat. It was called Zimmerman's Hungaria. While you sit at the table a girl walks around with a camera taking pictures which is where we had the picture taken that I'm sending you. It is really a swell place, good food and nice entertainment and not too expensive. We really had an enjoyable day. The only thing to keep it from being a perfect day was that you weren't seeing it with me. I missed you an awful lot honey, and I guess Decker, the fellow with me, got awfully tired of hearing me say that all day. I believe the thing that made me more lonesome for you than anything was the beautiful music in The New Moon. I think that has some of the most wonderful music.

Honey, don't worry about when I leave or anything cause I'll be ok. It might be a little longer between letters but I'll write you every day and, too, when I get to my destination I believe the government sends you a card telling you I arrived safely. The best thing for you to do is just imagine I'm in some foreign country right now and forget all about me leaving or worrying about where I'm going. You know, if you knew it wouldn't help anyway, so please don't worry about me, darling, I'll be ok and I'll be back before you know it. About the puppies honey, just as soon as the eyes are open it wouldn't hurt to take them outside in a basket for awhile. Be careful at first about the bright sun, but by the time they are four weeks old they should be playing in the yard. About 5 weeks you must start to wean them, I guess you know. I imagine Cookie would be good with a litter. She has the best disposition. Will she let Buff near them?

It must be terribly warm up there or rather down there, having the baby outdoors and in a tub. Does she enjoy the water? I'll bet she's getting as brown as a little indian. When this is all over and I come back home we will have to take her swimming a lot and teach her to be a good swimmer. We are both pretty good at swimming so she should take after us that way (I hope).

I tried to reach you Sunday at the folks house but I guess it was too late, I imagine they were taking you home just about the time I called. I sure was disappointed, too, cause I was really counting talking to you. I love you and miss you so much, honey, and you have no idea how much it helps and how wonderful it makes me feel to be able to talk to you and hear your voice. I'll be so happy when we can be together again and have all the nice things we had before and have our own family together again. I think just thinking about that keeps me going more than anything else. I wonder how I'll feel the day they tell me I can go home for good and that it's all over. It's a wonderful thing to think about. Well, I guess I'll close. Goodnight, dearest, love me and miss me like I do you. Sleep tight and sweet dreams. Don't worry and take good care of yourself and Peg and give her a big kiss for me.

All my love, always,
Your Sweetheart,
Jack
P.S. I love you.

(The soldier with Jack, in New York, was Wallace Decker from Massachussets,)

Camp Shanks
June 9, 1944
Friday

Dearest Darling:

Well, sweet, I guess you are wondering about the wire for the $10 so I'll clear that up. I got a tip this morning that we were going to be put on the alert this evening which means shipping in the next week and which stops all mail. I was flat broke and need some money for the trip to keep me in cigarettes. We are restricted now to our barracks except for 10 minutes every hour when we are allowed to go to the PX. We have orders to have everything in readiness to leave. I met a fellow in the PX who is going to mail this for me in town to get by the censors so I could let you know I got the money. I, of course, don't know when we will leave or where we will go, but it won't be long. If my letters are irregular and kind a senseless you will be able to understand why. Also you may not hear from me for awhile.

I received three wonderful letters from my darling tonight. I got the pictures, too. They were really good. I'm keeping the one of Peg sitting by herself and the good one of all three of us. I'll swear, darling, that little gal of ours is the most beautiful, wonderful thing I have ever seen. I showed the pictures around the barracks and you should have heard the fellows rave. They are always talking about my very beautiful wife and cute little girl.

I heard about the strike the street cars had up

there. I'll bet it was terrible. What did your Dad do for transportation. They ought to send men like that to where I'm going. We are doing what we can for $50 a month. You would think they'd be willing to do their share for $100 a week and no risk. That sure burns me. I got the words to "I'll be seeing You" but that's the trickiest darn tune. I really love the song. Especially with Bing Crosby singing it. Honey, I'll tell you where I spend so much money since this letter isn't going to be censored. The food here is so terrible that I have eaten only one meal in the mess hall. There are only about 25% of our Company who eat there and most of them have been sick. It is really awful and I'm not exaggerating. I have been eating breakfast of eggs and bacon at the Service Club and sandwiches and milk at the PX.

Honey, when it's so hot I don't think it's good for Peg to lay and cry and I think you did the best thing the other night when you rocked her to sleep. After all, she will have a bad night once in a while and as long as it doesn't become a habit I see nothing wrong with it, in fact, I think you are doing the right thing.

The descriptions you write of the cute things Peg does are wonderful so keep them coming. I can almost see her doing the things. You tell about them so vividly. You know, we have a truly beautiful, remarkable and wonderful daughter. I can remember when I was at Fannin and you used to write me about Peg and tell me to just wait and I'd see that she was as wonderful as you said she was. I used to sit and try to imagine what she was like and whether she was as wonderful as you said. I was so proud when I saw her the day I got home, I could hardly believe she was really ours. She looked so sweet, laying in her little crib sleeping. I believe I would have cried from being so proud and everything that day if the family hadn't been there. As it was my eyes watered pretty bad. I was so afraid she wouldn't come to me or I would scare her and I felt so good when she held out her hands for me to take her. That day is one I'll never forget, honey, as long as I live. I was so relieved at being home and so much love for you and the baby was inside of me I thought I'd bust. You'll never be able to realize how I felt. I love you so much and need you so I don't know what to do. If I had hunted for a million years I could never have found a sweeter, more beautiful and wonderful person, and my love will never change except to become greater. I'm getting kind a poetic or something, honey, but that's the way I feel. Well, I must close as it is getting late and it's no telling when they might pull us out so I'll need all the rest I can get.

Goodnight , Darling, sleep tight and dream of me. Love me and miss me like I miss you. Give Peg a big kiss for me and say hello to all the folks. AND DON'T WORRY - I'LL BE ALL RIGHT !!!

All my love to my wonderful sweetheart,
   Jack
P.S. I love you.

PART 2: ENGLAND
1944

Jack could hardly have come to England at a better time, having arrived three weeks after D-Day. From early 1942 until the invasion of Europe over a million American soldiers landed in Britain. They would man the many U.S. bases and embark for other battle fronts. In late June, 1942, General Eisenhower arrived. He had been appointed Commander of the European Theater of Operations United States Army (ETOUSA). At that time only two barely trained Army Divisions and a handful of Air Force Detachments were there.

By Spring of 1944 all of southwestern England was one enormous staging area, preparing for the invasion of Europe from the channel ports (Southampton, Plymouth, Weymouth, and others). England became a giant arsenal.

It was jokingly said that the island would sink under the weight of men and equipment if it had not been for the hundreds of huge antiaircraft balloons floating overhead. In the hedge-bordered fields were parked camouflaged trucks, bulldozers, tanks, jeeps, and self-propelled guns. Airfields had planes lined up on runways in every area.

By 1944, there were twenty American infantry divisions, 600,000 men, 10,000 combat planes, 5,000 transport planes and gliders. The ports were jammed with ships and landing craft (including six battleships, twenty-two cruisers and hundreds of destroyers).

The towns and villages were thronged with American troops. Some English people referred to it as a "Yankee" invasion. The Americans courted the English girls and drank the pubs dry. Their pockets were overflowing with American money. An American private made three times more than a British private, and a British captain's pay was about equal to an American sergeant's pay. The British had a saying, "The trouble was, the Yanks were overpaid, oversexed, and over here!"

The American soldiers reflected The way they had been brought up. Some were rude and overbearing, while some were as courteous and gentlemanly as they would have been at home. Hardly an English town or village remained untouched. Most Britons, however, took it in stride, fortunately!

D-Day, June 6th, 1944, finally arrived and in one day 150,000 Allied troops landed on the beaches of Normandy. On June 12th, 1944, the third wave landed, and 326,000 Allied forces were now on French soil.

ATLANTIC CROSSING
June 9, 1944

We learned later that Jack had left Camp Shanks on a troop train which took them to the New York City Dock. Upon their arrival they were lined up alphabetically and marched up the gangplank of the ferry which took them out to their ship waiting in New York Harbor. As the ship headed out into the Atlantic Ocean, it was an entirely different feeling passing the Statue of Liberty this time. So final!

The ship was part of a large convoy which gave them a certain feeling of security. It was an old German troop ship which had been captured earlier in the war. When they were nearly half-way across, the rudder broke. The convoy had to go on, but left a destroyer to circle around them for protection. They were completely vulnerable, being one lone disabled ship in all that vastness. It was two days before the repairs were completed and they could go on.

Jack wrote that the trip was tiresome after a few days, but still very interesting. He said the crossing was calm, and they were lucky to have good weather for the whole trip. The only excitement was seeing big fish (submarines). After March, 1943, the submarine menace had been greatly reduced, due to the use of small aircraft carriers with fighter planes. The planes patrolled for submarines trying to break into convoys; however, they still had not been entirely eliminated.

He said he was not a bit seasick, in fact he felt better and his appetite was something to behold! The meals were delicious, in great quantities, and the food wasn't too bad. The only trouble was inactivity, nothing to do but lie around. Even so, it went fast. They sailed through the North Atlantic to Edinburgh, Scotland, where they debarked on June 27, 1944. They were then sent to a staging area where they were attached to the 70th Replacement Battalion. They went by train to "somewhere in England" (Yeovil, Somerset), arriving on June 28, 1944.

He was now no longer just in the Army — he was in the war, and only God knew when we would be together again.

YEOVIL
SOMERSET

Yeovil was located in Southern England. Just before D-Day the town had been brimming with United States troops and equipment. The last few weeks the streets were filled with vehicles of all sorts and description and the supporting troops, waiting to embark from Weymouth or other southwestern ports. Several military hospitals had been set up in the vicinity to deal with the casualties from the battle fronts.

On June 25th, 1944, one of the B 17 Bombers returning from a raid in France (completely shot up) crashed near Yeovil. Sadly there were no survivors. Later the people from the town put up a memorial stone. The German Air Force by 1944 was no longer a threat to the countryside, but the bombs they had dropped earlier in the war left many scars on the town.

On June 28th, 1944, Jack arrived in Yeovil, England. By this time most of the troops and equipment had already moved out. The 70th Battalion Headquarters where Jack worked (we learned much later) was Barwick House, a magnificent manor. It was used by both the British and the United States Armies. What had once been the Park, the beautiful area surrounding it, now had military buildings, Nissen huts, tents, and equipment stored all over. It also still had an anti-aircraft balloon floating above from a nearby field.

The buildings in this picturesque area were built mostly of the native stone. Many of the churches had the large towers for which Somerset is so famous. In the country-side numerous manor houses, in their beautiful settings, were built by notable families and go as far back as Tudor and Georgian times.

Barwick House had been built by the Messiter family during the early part of the 19th century. The family had lived there for one hundred years. There were four stone towers called "Follies," as they had no particular purpose except the work it gave to unemployed men to build them. They were constructed as ornaments and stood at the four points of the compass from the house. This was the stone tower Jack described in a letter.

In his first letter, on June 29, he remarked sadly about the train journey across England. He noticed as they passed through the cities how pale and undernourished the people looked, especially the children who crowded around whenever the train stopped. Where he was now, he wrote, it was so peaceful one would hardly know a war was going on — except for the large number of planes flying over to bomb Germany. He said the planes started out in the evening and for maybe an hour you heard a constant roar. They stretched out in the sky for miles in width. You think they will never stop.

Although Jack could not tell us exactly where he was, we were able to get a fair idea from his letter of the 30th through clues such as, "Too far from London to go there, you would know all about the place, and so would your family." From his description of its beauty, my Aunt Winnie who was from England felt sure he was in the southwestern part. He wrote that it was such beautiful country, the camp was surrounded by blue bells and holly, and he enclosed a bloom and leaf. The old farm houses were low and covered with ivy. Everything was laid out in neat patterns; they did not have planted fields, but grass land with cattle grazing.

When the war was over, he wanted us to come and stay a month and stop in the quaint little inns! He said it felt strange to realize there was 4,500 miles between him and home and to actually be in the war theater where the war was going on.

He could not tell me anything he was doing or how long he would be there, but he said not to worry about him. He had a beautiful prayer his dad had sent him, and he assured me he was wearing both his dad's and my medal, with his dog tags. His dad was Roman Catholic, and we were Episcopalians.

Being a clerk in the Headquarters Company, Jack worked in the manor house and did not have to drill like the others, as they were training. A Sergeant Carr was over him. They all ate in the mess hall, however, using their own mess gear. The mess hall was a Nissen hut. Also, he slept in the tent with the others (8 cots to a tent), and they used candles for light in the tents. It was cold, damp, and the days were long. It did not get dark until midnight and then got light again at 4:30 A.M. They were living under field conditions, but it was not too bad.

On July 17, he received his first mail, five letters from me, and he was beside himself with joy. He wrote that on Sunday (the night before) he and another soldier got a pass and walked into town. There was a gorgeous cathedral built in the time of the Romans. As they walked by it, a soloist was singing a lovely hymn. The church and the hymn were so beautiful he was very touched. While they were in town, they went to the Red Cross Canteen for coffee and doughnuts. The Guy Lombardo Show came on the American radio broadcast, and it made him think of Sunday afternoons in our little house. He felt so homesick.

Jack very much wanted some rank or a rating, which he would not get until he was assigned. He was up for assignment for three days; the adjutant had everything planned, the job and the rating, but Headquarters would not let him be assigned there. He was only to be there until his orders came for overseas. He was dreadfully disappointed to still be a replacement. Several weeks after they arrived, Bob Medley shipped out; and Jack thought he was doing some fighting in France. Bob was with Jack at Camp Fannin and when they came overseas.

In his letter of the 28th he said he got a pass and walked into town (Thursday) and happened to meet a WREN, an English sailorette. They compared pictures of their wife and husband and children and had a nice long talk. She took him to the YWCA (Young Women's Christian Association) for tea and crumpets, then he took her to the American Red Cross Canteen for coffee and doughnuts. He said it was so nice to talk to someone besides soldiers. She told him when the Yanks (which is what the English called the Americans) first came over, she thought they were rowdy, impolite, and crude, but later found them generous and friendly!

On August 7 he wrote that the day before, a Sunday, was the most beautiful day they had since he had been there. He got a pass for the whole day. He wrote, "I got a bicycle from the Red Cross and rode from about noon until about eleven o'clock and was I tired. I went by myself and did everything I wanted to and stopped whenever I felt like it and saw everything there was to see." He had wanted so badly to get Peggy a present for her first birthday but with all the shortages he did not know whether he could. On the night of the 7th, he and two other fellows had to take a trip of thirty miles about 9:30 P.M. and got lost in the English countryside. It was a lovely moonlit night and they saw some beautiful country. We learned later, they had taken a Colonel to a party in a big manor house! Returning they picked up three American soldiers and had a great time talking, as one was from Houston.

August 13th, 1944, Jack wrote that a lot of changes were being made. The Headquarters were leaving and a new one was coming in. He would be working for the new headquarters. He could not tell me that troops were shipping out, or that the devastating Battle of Mortain was going on in Northern France. On August 18th, 1944, they just received the news on the radio that Patton would be in Paris by morning. The Germans were in full retreat, and they thought that part of the war would not last much longer! That day, the outfit he came over with shipped out. The entire 70th Replacement Battalion went overseas, but Jack remained. For a time his mail went to France with them and was then sent back to England.

On August 20th, he wrote that it was a dreary, lonesome Sunday. He was answering my letter about Peggy's first little birthday party and feeling so bad. Not too bad, however, as someone brought him a can of grapefruit sections and he ate the whole thing! He had gotten friendly with the mess sergeant in the new battalion (the 107th) and mentioned he was not going to chow because they had corned beef hash which he detested. That evening the sergeant invited him over to his mess hall which was not feeding any troops and fried him four eggs and two big pieces of steak. He said, "Boy was it wonderful."

On August 22nd, 1944, Jack wrote that everything was in an uproar, but he could not tell me what was going on. He was writing hurriedly as he was on guard that night. He finished it at 11:30 P.M. That was the last letter from Yeovil. A pass issued to him dated 22 August 1944 was for the geographical area of Yeovil and shows his new organization: Hq. Det. 107th Repl. Bn. I did not hear from Jack again for eighteen days. They departed by truck on September 6, 1944, and moved in convoy to Tidworth Garrison near Andover, England.

THE LETTERS

To: From:
Mrs. John K. Price   Pvt. John K. Price
704 Ballas Rd.   37623699
Kirkwood, 22 Mo.   70th Replacement Battalion
U.S.A.   358th Replacement Company
                             Infantry Co. S, APO 15328
                             c/o Postmaster, New York,
                             N.Y.

                             Thursday
                             June 29th, 1944

Dearest Darling:
     Well, honey, it has been quite some time since I wrote you. After a rather awesome ocean voyage I'm now somewhere in England. Surprised? Although the trip was tiresome as the devil after we had been out a few days it was still very interesting. After the war, you and Peggy and I are going to take the same trip on some big luxury liner and see England. We were lucky as the devil and had good weather for the whole trip and without any unusual excitement except seeing big fish and I wasn't a darn bit seasick. It was really exciting and sort of thrilling. All I could think about though was you and how much you would have enjoyed it. England is pretty much like what you hear at home, however, the people aren't very friendly. It is awfully damp

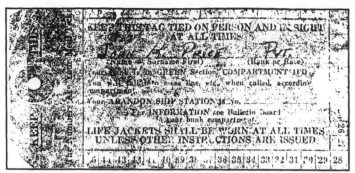

Green Identification Tag - kept on person at all times.

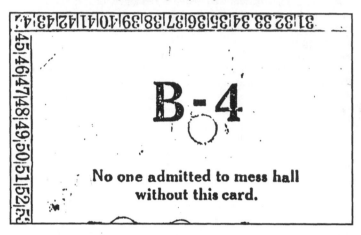

B-4

No one admitted to mess hall without this card.

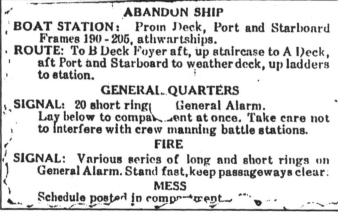

ABANDON SHIP
BOAT STATION: Prom Deck, Port and Starboard
  Frames 190 - 205, athwartships.
ROUTE: To B Deck Foyer aft, up staircase to A Deck,
  aft Port and Starboard to weather deck, up ladders
  to station.
GENERAL QUARTERS
SIGNAL: 20 short rings   General Alarm.
  Lay below to compartment at once. Take care not
  to interfere with crew manning battle stations.
FIRE
SIGNAL: Various series of long and short rings on
  General Alarm. Stand fast, keep passageways clear.
MESS
Schedule posted in compartment.

Mess Hall Card.

and kind of uncomfortable and I hope it isn't that way all the time. The cottages on the country side are really beautiful. Everything is laid out just so, in a neat pattern. Gosh, you would go crazy over the little towns and villages, but the big cities are terrible. Dirty and narrow streets. The children, in particular, look terribly undernourished. When the train pulled into a station hordes of kids would come swarming up begging for candy and cigarette and anything else they could get. I'll swear I never saw so many children in all my life and where they all appeared from, Lord knows. I can't describe much to you, Sweet, so how about you asking me about anything and I'll try to answer your letters and tell you all about it.

I haven't had a letter for a long time and I'm sure lonesome for one. Gosh, honey, I'm an awfully long way from home. By the way, when you write me, write air mail instead of V-Mail. I don't care for V-mail cause the letters are too short and impersonal.

How are you and Peggy getting along? Do you need anything? I'm going to make out a new allotment to you for a few dollars which you should start receiving the end of August. I guess Peggy is walk-

ing now and saying all kinds of things. Just think, a month from today she will be a year old. I am going to try to get a birthday present for her, honey, but course there is a chance, with all the shortages and all over here, that I won't be able to find anything and there also may be some restrictions regarding the mailing of anything like that. I'll have to find out about it. I hope I can cause its her first birthday and it would be nice to have something from England.

I won't be able to visit Mrs. Wills and would you tell Aunt Winnie just in case she might have written her that I might visit her.

This is really very beautiful over here honey and you would hardly know there is a war going on so closely except for the large amount of planes in the sky, but give me the U.S. You know I'll say this much. I don't believe I'll be as lonesome for you and homesick over here as I was back in the states cause here I know there isn't a chance of getting home and can adapt myself more readily to it while in the states that was all I could think about. Of course I still miss you terribly honey and would give anything I own to be home again but I'll just have to wait until we get this nasty job done.

Are you going to have a new picture taken of Peg at Stix at a year old? I hope you do and be sure to send me one. Have you taken any new snapshots lately? Be sure and send me prints of all the good ones. Peg is so cute now. I just can't imagine her growing up. Just think, when I get home she will be a regular little girl instead of a baby.

How are the puppies getting along? Have you sold any yet? You know, I guess, that they should be weaned at six weeks and can be sold any time after that.

I just found out that I will be able to send a present home for Peg so now the next thing is to find something. I'll do my best to send some little toy anyway. Did you get her that big teddy bear you were talking about. I want her to have everything we can possibly give her and I don't think it is money thrown away when you buy good toys for her.

Well, Darling, I believe I'll close now. I can't say goodnight any more cause you are just about to give the baby her morning bottle or whatever she had in the morning. By the way, does she still take her milk from the bottle or have you stopped that all together?

Love me and miss me. Take good care of Peg and give her a big kiss for me. Say hello to everyone at home for me.

All my love, darling, for always,
Your Sweetheart,
  Jack

Thursday
June 29th, 1944

Dear Mom & Dad:

I guess you all were rather worried about me after not hearing from me from such a long time but this is the first opportunity I have had to write as we have been doing quite a bit of sailing lately.

We had a swell trip as far as it being interesting. You can't imagine how it seems to see nothing but water around you for days. We had a very calm crossing and didn't have a bit of trouble, and believe it or not I wasn't the least bit seasick. The only trouble with the trip was the inactivity; we didn't have a darn thing to do but lie around. Even so the time really went by in a hurry. We traveled by train through England after we docked which gave us a

Map of England-Troop shop landed at Edinburgh, Scotland.

swell chance to see some of the country. It is very beautiful except for the cities which look worse than any of the most terrible slums we have at home, but the country was wonderful. Very neat and orderly. The weather is terrible, tho. It is very damp and miserable and cold as the duece and the days are so long. It gets light here about 4:30 and gets dark about 11:30 or 12 o'clock. Dad would have a terrible time cause he would lose an awful lot of sleep.

You know, it a funny thing, but I'm really not as homesick now as I was before I left the states. I guess have something close to 4500 miles between me and home and the realization that it is impossible to get there together with being in a theater of operations where the war is actually going on has remedied that.

Well, folks I guess I'll close for now but will try to write again tomorrow. Write real soon and often as I need to hear from home more now than ever before. Give my love to everyone and look out for Babe and Peggy for me.

All my love,
Your Son,
    Jack

P.S. Write me air mail from now on.

Friday
June 30, 1944
Somewhere in England

Dearest Honey:

Well, darling, another day closer to coming back home. I hope to Lord there aren't too many more. Especially over here. What a climate! Course I do want to bring you and Peg over here after the war cause it is really beautiful country when the sun shines and is worth seeing. By the way, the sun is shining this morning for the first time since I arrived. I haven't been able to visit any of the towns yet but I sure hope I get to before we pull out. I would like to see the difference between our town back home and here. I'll write you all about it when and if I go. Another thing I don't like is the length of the days over here. The darn sun doesn't set until about 11 or 11:30 and it doesn't get dark till midnight or after and it gets light again about 4:30 in the morning. It is really hard to get a long nights sleep. I guess its all in getting used to it.

- - - - cut out - - - -

Our camp here is surrounded by, I think they are blue bells and holly bushes that are really beautiful. I'm sending a bloom and a leaf in this letter for you to see. I hope they come through. I will say that the setting here is really beautiful. I've never seen such a picturesque countryside as around here. The old farm houses, sort of low and covered with ivy. You've seen pictures of them. They don't have plowed fields like you see back home. Its all grassland and they have cattle grazing. You know what I would like to do is after the war be able to come over here and have a car and about a month and drive over the whole island, seeing all the historic and old landmarks and stopping at these quaint inns in these small villages and really seeing the country. You would almost have to do that to see any thing cause you can't really see anything traveling by train. I would want to be able to drive over these little winding roads, through all these little villages and really

see the place. The thought of London or any of these larger cities just doesn't interest me at all, especially from what I've seen so far.

- - - - cut out - - - -

One other thing I noticed, which may be due to the war, I don't know, was the lack of people on the streets. You know how the people bustle around the streets down town at home. Well here the streets in the cities and towns we went through were empty for the most part. Except for the people hanging out the windows the places looked like ghost cities. I was amazed and sort of confused or something. The women, for the large part over here are doing all the mens work in factories and railroad which may be the cause of it.

I wish I would hurry up and get a new letter. I've read and reread the last letter I got so much its just about worn out. I'm so anxious to hear from you and hear about all the new things Peg is learning. I guess she jabbers a blue streak now and is walking. It makes me feel so darn bad when I think of missing all that, and being so far away from you. After not being apart for almost 8 years I just can't hardly stand it now. I love you and I miss you so much, Darling, I'm miserable all the time.

Well, darling, I've about run out of news for today so I guess I'll close. I'll be able to do a lot better after I start getting mail again. Say a big prayer for me cause I expect I'll need it before long. By the way, I am making out an allotment for $10.00 so that you should start getting it August 1st or there abouts. Bye-now, darling. Miss me and love me.

All my love, always.
Your Sweetheart,
    Jack

P.S. I found something I shouldn't have said so I censored it myself. It wasn't important anyway but I just wanted to let you know why it was cut like it is.

Monday
17 July 1944

Dearest Sweetheart:

Well, Darling, I feel a lot better this evening. I received 3 wonderful letters from my wonderful darling and wonderful letters they were, too. I have definitely decided, though, due to the way I have received my mail so far, that I shall stick to my rationing program and answer only one a night, so tonight I shall answer #31, written Thursday June 22.

I got a pass last night (Sun) and went to a little town called _____. Another fellow and I walked in and just walked around taking in all the sights. It is really a fascinating place. They have a very beautiful cathedral which was built back in the time of the Romans, I believe they said. It was really wonderful. As we walked by a soloist was singing a hymn and you just can't imagine how beautiful it was but how it made me feel. Yes, Darling, we are definitely going to have to make a trip to England sometime as it is really beautiful and you would just go crazy over it. Especially these little towns and villages like this _____. I would like to be able to tell you about what I'm doing and how long I'll be here about, but I'm afraid the censor wouldn't like it so I'll just say, don't worry about me, darling. I'll be all right and I'll be careful. The way it looks I might not even see combat before this over, over here. Its nice to hope for anyway.

By the way, darling, in your letter you mentioned something about your letters being censored. You can rest your mind, tho, as incoming mail isn't censored, just outgoing.

I'm really surprised at how cheap it was to come all the way from the station to your house by cab. (on furlough) I was always under the impression that it would cost a small fortune, didn't you?

That's a shame about Katherine's baby. I'm really sorry to hear it and feel so sorry for her and her husband. We know what its like, don't we, Darling.

By the way, honey, don't worry your beautiful little head about the women over here. You could blindfold me and let me pick the first 10 girls I bump into in the states and put them up against the most beautiful girls in England and the 10 from the states would have it all over those from here. Especially my girl back home. I get to wondering real often how come I could be so lucky to get such a wonderful beautiful person to marry me.

Oh, yes, by the way, while we were in town last time I heard the first American broadcast over the radio that I've heard for over a month. We had stopped by the American Red Cross for coffee and donuts and as we were eating the Guy Lombardo's Orchestra show came on. It sure sounded good but it really made me homesick and blue. I got to thinking about, how on Sunday afternoons we used to sit in the living room and listen to all the good programs and just relax. It was so wonderful being together, just being near each other in our cute little house. It was so peaceful. You had fixed the house so darling, honey, and I remember I thought you had bought too much stuff for too much money and then after you had it all fixed up I remember how cute it was and how proud I was of it, but I never would admit that. I was glad you had gone ahead and gotten all that stuff. Remember?

It's really funny how vividly memories come to me now of the least little detail of what we did and how much fun we had together the different places we lived. I believe Heights Blvd {Houston} was the most vivid even though it wasn't the nicest place we stayed. Our night jaunts to the drug store and shopping on Saturday night and going by for the laundry. I remember the little back porch and the little kitchen and how our refrigerator wouldn't fit into it. I was so disappointed with our place on Chenevert when we first moved in, but then after we had been there a while I really was crazy about it. We had such swell friends there. I remember when we bought little Audrey. She was the sweetest little thing. Then when all the neighbors came out to the airport at 7 o'clock in the morning to see us off and they wouldn't let us take Audrey with us so we had to send her by train and she took the distemper. You know, I'll say that I believe we could have gotten by with taking her right on the plane with us if we would have said nothing about it and just stalked on with her. Then remember staying at the Tutwiler for three weeks, and then you found the place in Green Acres.

It's really nice to think back like that, sweet, but it just about brings tears to my eyes. We were so happy and then it all went up in smoke. Well, lets both just hope and pray that before many more

On June 25 one of the B 17 Bombers returning, completely shot up, from a raid in France crashed near Yeovil. Sadly there were no survivors. Later the people from the town put up a memorial stone.

45

Barwick House. Headquarters - 70th Replacement Battalion.

Barwick House and Park.

months pass we will be together and be able to start all over again.

Well, sweetheart, I guess I've given the censor a big enough job for one evening so I guess Id better close for now, darling. I love you and miss you more than anything in the world. I'll be seeing you, honey, and until then I'll get by.

All my love, always.
Your Sweetheart,
Jack

Friday,
28 July 44

Dearest Darling:

Well, honey, I guess you will think I have forgotten all about you as it has been three days since I last wrote you, but I have put it off for a reason. I have been up for assignment for the last three days and I didn't want to write and say anything about it till I heard, fearing it might break my luck, or something, but word came through tonight that they can't assign me here, which has really taken the wind out of my sails as things looked pretty good for me up till today. The adjutant here had everything planned as far as the job I was to take and even to the rating and was just waiting for the Headquarters to give him the go signal, so I really missed out on something good. Well, the old saying is "everything happens for the best," so maybe the next place I go I'll get a better offer. However, I wasn't particularly interested in the rating, but more the job, as it was really swell working here and I like it a lot, and too, I am so darned tired of bouncing from one outfit to another without settling down. Everyone seems to like my work and want to keep me but for some darn

reason they aren't able to. The same thing happened back in Texas. Remember? I'll never get anywhere unless I become assigned as they just don't give ratings or any other advantages to a free replacement. When I was in the states, it was the story that they couldn't assign a class 1 man and I was given the idea that after I got overseas, the first place that wanted me could get me, but I find now that even over here its the same old story. The way it looks I'll have to be behind the enemy lines before I'm eligible for assignment.

I haven't had a letter from you now for two weeks or a little better and needless to say has made me very blue and down in the dumps. I am looking forward so to those pictures I hardly know what to do. I expect I'll get a whole batch of them at once, but, gosh I hope I get them soon cause if I happen to move again it will be another month or two before I hear from you. Well, darling, I just happened to think, I have been in England a _____ today. The last month has gone by fast, I only hope that the rest of the time I'm over here goes as fast. I don't expect it will be too much longer before I'll be taking another boat trip.

How is Peggy, honey? Just think, tomorrow she'll be a year old. I just can't believe it. It hardly seems possible that we would have a daughter that old. Just think, if J. K. Jr. had lived he would be going on 3 years old. I would give anything in the world to be able to be home tomorrow. I'm so anxious to be with the two of you and to watch Peg grow up. It makes me awfully blue when I think of what I've missed this last year. Is Peggy walking now, without any help? From the way you talked in your last letter she was right on the verge of taking off on her own. You said she was standing and walking all around as long as she had something to hold on to so I imagine by now she is walking. How are the pups getting along? Does she play with them? I'll bet that is really cute to see the four pups gang up on her.

By the way, sweet, have you sold any of them yet? You know, thats the one big draw back over here, the news you get is all three weeks or a month old by the time you get it and it keeps you wondering what is happening now. Have you decided yet, whether you are going to keep any of the pups? I kind of hope you do keep one any way as I'm curious as the devil to see how they turn out.

I went to town last night, the first time in about two weeks, and I did something to make you jealous. I met a WREN. An English sailorette, and was invited to the YWCA of all places, for tea. No kidding, tho, she was a very nice girl and it was such a relief to talk to someone besides soldiers, or men. She and I compared pictures of our wife and husband and children and had a nice long talk. By the way she is from a little town just six miles from where Aunt Winnie's sister lives and thinks she knows her. She was just in town for that night, waiting for transportation to take her to a camp or something. When I told her that my wife had relatives living in Ilford, Essex, she nearly died. I believe that she was as lonesome and homesick as I was. After we left the YWCA then I took her up to the American Red Cross for Coffee and doughnuts. So we had a very continental or something evening. Having tea and crumpets one place, the English version of Coffee and, and then having Coffee and Doughnuts, the American version of Tea and. Pretty nice looking, by the way. No girl over here can compare to an American girl, however, in looks, personality, or as a conversationalist. They're a very peculiar people, these English. I asked her what she thought of the Yanks as a whole, and she told me that when they first came over she thought them to be the most rowdy, impolite and crude people that she had ever seen, but after she got to know them she found that they were really fine. She especially talked of how generous and friendly they were. All in all I had one of the most enjoyable evenings I have had for quite some time. I guess I spent about 2 hours with her before she had to catch her bus and I had to get back to camp.

Gosh, darling, I miss you so much and want to see you and Peg so bad I hardly know what to do. I love you so, even more now, than I ever dreamed I could love anyone, but I guess that is the way it is. When you get away far away from someone you begin to realize more than ever just how much they mean to you. You know, I'm an awfully lucky fellow to have such a wonderful sweetheart and little girl waiting for me to come home again. I'm so anxious to get home and start a home for my two sweethearts again. We were so happy before this happened, I can hardly wait till we can be together again. Well maybe it won't be long. I look for it to be over well before Christmas.

By the way, we have a date that I'll have to keep, too, remember? So its got to be over and I've got to be home by then cause I don't believe in breaking dates, especially with a beautiful woman, even if she is married. Well, sweetheart, I guess I'll close for now as it is getting rather late. Write real often, sweet, and give me all the news. Love me and miss me honey, and say a big prayer for me. I'll be Seeing you - -

All my love, for always and always,
Your sweetheart,
    Jack
P.S. Give Peg a big kiss for me and tell her happy birthday from her old man, too.

Bye now sweet,
Me

7 August 44
Monday

Dearest Sweetheart:

As you have most likely noticed, honey, I missed writing you yesterday, but for the first time since I have been here, I was able to get a pass for all day Sunday off so I took off to see some of the country-side around here, and as it was without a doubt the most beautiful day we have had since I've been here and so I got a bicycle from the Red Cross here in town and rode from about noon till about eleven o'clock. I really enjoyed myself, too, and was I tired when I got home. I went all by myself and just did everything I wanted to and stopped whenever I felt like it and saw everything there was to see. I want to at least have something to tell you about the country when I get home.

I'm getting a late start and I have some more work to do before I can really get down to letter writing in earnest. I feel exceptionally lonely and blue tonight which should help to make a nice long letter. I don't know why, but when I feel low and blue like this it always helps to write you and kind of talk my troubles over with you. I do wish that my mail would catch up with me a little though, cause I hate not knowing what happened in between letters, and your letters mean so much to me and help to get me through the day. When I don't get a new one each day I read the old ones over again and

pretend that I just received them and it really helps a lot. Honey, I miss you so and love you so I just don't know how to express it to you. I know how I feel and I get all swelled up inside to where I think I'm going to bust, I love you so much, but when it comes to getting it down on paper, I just don't know what to write, I can't get it out.

I was kind of wondering how my mail to you was being delivered but I really expected that by the 15th of July you would have received more than one letter. I expect you will get a bunch of them at once like I receive yours. Let me know how they start coming, as I write you almost every night, with very few exceptions and you should begin to receive them quite regularly before long. By the way, honey, before I forget, if, for any reason you have to get in touch with me hurriedly, you can reach me by cablegram, and the best and easiest way is to send it through the Red Cross. The best thing to remember is that you should go to the Red Cross for anything that comes up that you might need help on.

By the way, honey, would you rather I typed or wrote my letters by hand? Course, I don't know how much longer I'll be blessed with the use of a typewriter, but I believe that you get a much longer letter when I type. Let me know, will you, cause I aim to please.

That is awfully cute, about the pups. I'll bet they are really a lot of fun to watch. I can just see old Buff, trying to act so big and gruff. The darn old fool wouldn't harm a hair on anyone, and most likely the pups know he is nothing but a big bluff. We sure got a wonderful dog when we bought him, honey. I have never seen a dog with as fine a disposition and as gentle and sweet as he is. When I get home, I'm going to buy Peg a really good puppy, registered in her name all her own. I would like to see her become interested in dogs and love them like we do, especially cockers. Wouldn't you?

Peggy is really and truly growing up, now. She must be darling, honey. I'm so anxious to receive some pictures of her, to see how she has changed since I was home. They grow up so darn fast you can hardly realize it. I'll bet she just raises all kinds of cain around there, especially in the morning. I remember, how she was when I was home. She always felt so good in the morning when she woke up and just laughed and played. I would give anything in the world to be able to be with her now. I want to see her, and hold her and play with her so bad, and have her get to know her old man. I just got to know her and got to where she was familiar with me while I was home, when I had to leave again, and now when I get back it will be the same thing all over again. Only this time I'll be gone longer, a lot longer and I'll really be a complete stranger when I finally get home. She is especially learning to know people around her now, and it will be harder for her to get used to me. Lord, I wish this thing was over and I could get home.

I'll say this much, honey, you really have a full and busy day. It looks like Peg keeps you going all day long, without much of a let up. Just wait till she starts walking and getting around by herself, you'll really be kept hopping.

By the way, honey, before I close, I want to hound you again to please hurry and send me pictures. All that you can, as it really helps to be able to see what your family is looking like. It kind of gets dim after a while, being away so long.

Well, darling, I'm afraid I must close and get to work, and besides I've just about run out of something to gripe about. Don't pay any attention to this letter, honey, cause I'll feel better in the morning. I really shouldn't even mail this cause I know it won't do your morale any good, but just think of it as giving me a chance to let off steam without getting into trouble doing it, and really it has done me a lot of good to blow off like this just once. I'm really usually in a pretty good frame of mind and a pretty cheerful sort of fellow, and can take what they dish out as well as the next guy, and really, we aren't being treated half as bad as I have let on, in fact it has been pretty nice over here considering everything. I was really surprised. It is an awfully lot like a camp in the states. We have just about everything here we had back home. Of course we are rationed a little more but not enough to hurt, and it does keep you from spending a lot of money foolishly which is good. All in all, we have plenty to be thankful for, and our lot isn't half bad, so I am ashamed for griping like I did. Well, darling, I must close now so I'll say goodnight, sweetheart, sleep tight, and sweet dreams. Love me a lot and miss me a little bit. Say a big prayer for me every night and pray that this mess will be over very soon. Say hello to all the folks and give Peg a big kiss for me, will you?

All my love for always.
Your Sweetheart,
    Jack
P. S. I love you. - (No letter is complete without a P.S., Remember, so I just have to add one)

Tuesday Morn
8th

Morning Sweetheart:

How are you this morning? I had mailed this letter last night, honey, but found this morning that the mail clerk hadn't picked it up so decided to add a few lines before I finally send it off. I don't have time now but will write a short note by noon and then get the letter off. I'll be back, hon. Bye for now.

Here I am again, honey, for just a few minutes. I just want to tell you about what I did last night after I finished writing you and then I'll have to close and get this in the mail.

Two other fellows and I had to take a trip of about 30 miles in a jeep about 9:30 last night and we got lost out in the English countryside. It was more fun. We saw some really beautiful country and the weather was really wonderful. I'll tell you more about it later. I gotta go now. Bye. Well, honey, I'm back but I guess I'd better get finished as fast as I can and get to work. I wanted to tell you though, that on the way back we picked up three American soldiers and one of them was from Houston. It really felt good to talk to someone from the hometown. Gosh, Darling, the moon was so beautiful last night and it made me so lonesome for you.

Well, Darling, I must close now and get this in the mail. I'll write a nice long letter again tonight or tomorrow. By the way, Honey, I'm sending you a few more coins. I hope you receive them. Bye now, Darling. I love you.

Your Sweetheart
    Jack

Thursday
10 Aug 44

Dearest Darling:

Well, honey, I'm going to start a letter now, its lunch time, and finish it tonight as I received 5 letters from you and 2 from Dad today and it will take plenty of time to answer them. I want to write you a really long letter for a change, so I intend to answer all five of them today. I won't be able to answer your letters till tonight but I can write a few lines now, just to tell you how much I love you and miss you. I was sure looking forward to receiving some pictures in those letters today, honey, but no such luck. I wish you would hurry and write or rather send me them cause I'm about to die waiting to see how Peg looks and to get some new pictures of you and see what those pups look like.

Now I have all my letters from you up to the 17th (July) with the exception of the 7th, 8th, and 9th, which isn't half bad. I've read them all about 4 times already. Aren't I silly? I'll tell you though, I get so hungry for news from home that when I read

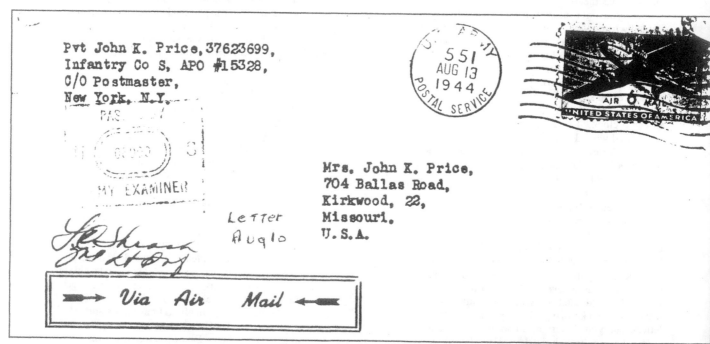

Envelope - Letter written August 10, 1944.

the letters I get, I read them too fast and have to go over them a few times. You would be surprised the things I find I have overlooked in them when I do read them over again, and besides I never get enough about how Peg is growing up and the cute things she does and I like to read about it again and again.

I noticed in the letter you wrote the 10th that you finally heard from me and know about where I am, as far as England is concerned. I wish I could tell you about where I was honey, cause I know you would know all about the place, and would be interested. In fact, I did tell you in one of my letters the town we were near enough to go to when on pass, but I learned after I wrote it that we weren't allowed to mention any town where we go so I guess they took it out of the letter, but we are too far away to visit Mrs. Wills and I don't expect I will be able to get there while I'm in England. I am in that part of England, but that part of England covers a lot of territory. I'll tell you something that might interest you and your folks honey, but I don't know just how strict they are on this censoring business, so if they cut it out, I'll just have to explain everything when I see you. You know the stuff you read about how the planes fly over and bomb Germany and all. Well those figures you read aren't prevarications. The planes start out from around here in the evening and for maybe an hour you hear a constant roar, and I'll swear, more planes go overhead than I have ever seen in my life. How they stand up against the pounding they are undoubtedly getting from the planes I'll never be able to understand. It looks to me like one raid would wipe out a city the size of St. Louis. The planes stretch out in the sky for miles, in width I mean, and you finally think they are never going to stop coming over. With the air power we now have and are using Germany can't last much longer. We have never had an air raid or seen any enemy planes since I have been here, but we have thought we saw a buzz bomb once in a while, but we aren't sure. The way things look, though, honey, I don't believe it will be too much longer before this will be over in Europe, and if I'm lucky I might be sent back to the states. Course, I'll still be in the army but at least I'll be nearer you and maybe you can come live in the town I will be near and we'll at least be together a little bit. Well, honey, I'm going to have to quit for a little while, and get out some work I have to do.

Here I am again, hon, but I don't know for how long. Things have quieted down around here for a while at least. Damn, honey, I've been trying to write for over an hour now, and every time I get started someone comes in and bothers me, (I'm by myself here this aft) so I guess I'll just quit for now and finish this tonight. Well, darling, here I am again, and as usual it is about 11 o'clock. I walked down to town with the Sergeant I work for and another fellow to the Red Cross and sat around and drank coffee till I thought I would bust and played ping pong. A very exciting evening. I had a very busy day today and I'm pretty darned tired.

I'll be back in a minute, honey. A fellow came up with a radio in his car and there is a program on from the states. Here I am again, just as I got out there the Officer he was driving came out to go somewhere so we didn't get to hear the program.

Well, darling, it is almost midnight, so I believe that I am going to close for now. I know this isn't the kind of letter I promised you but I promise I'll do better tomorrow. Love me and miss me. Say hello to the folks and give Peg a big kiss for me,

and take good care of her. Night, sweetheart, all my love always.

Your sweetheart
Jack

P.S. Of course, I am wearing both my medals on my dog chain, and wouldn't go anywhere without them. You would be surprised how much they do help. Bye for now darling.

Jack

By the way, honey, let me know if you received the English coins I sent. I'm sending a shilling piece tonight. Before I leave I'll try to send a ten shilling note and a pound note. Bye now for the last time. I love you.

Me

Sunday
13 August 1944

Dearest Sweetheart:
Well, darling, after all the griping I have done about not getting any letters to answer, now I have about 15 of them to answer and don't have time to do a darn thing. I haven't been able to write you for the last 3 days, and I'm not kidding or fibbing when I say that I absolutely haven't had a minute, from 6 o'clock in the morning till midnight every night to stop and write. It has been terrible around here, and even now I only have a few minutes, it is my supper hour, to write so I won't be able to answer any of your mail, just ramble a little bit. I will be working again tonight till all hours I expect and for the next few days, but by Wednesday I ought to be able to write you a real letter for a change and answer all these letters. I have been carrying them around with me for quite some time now thinking that at any time I could start answering them, but no luck. There are some changes being made around here that require a lot of work and won't be over till about Wednesday is why I'm so slow, honey, I can't tell you what it is of course, as I don't believe that it would go through, but it is nothing to affect me.

By the way, honey, before I forget, who told you that you couldn't send me chocolate over here? Whoever it is is nertz cause Sgt Carr, my boss, so to speak has been receiving a box of stuff like that with cookies and everything almost two times a week, so if you can find any chocolate bars or a box of chocolate candy or anything sweet like that, send them to me. And, honey, please don't worry about a Christmas present to me as it will be just that much more junk I have to lug around and now, every time I move, everything I own must be packed in a pack and carried on my back, so instead of buying me presents buy extra ones for Peg or else buy me something we can use for the house for when I come home. Please, please, honey, and I'm dead serious, don't send me anything except a lot of wonderful letters and whole lot of good food and sweets. Anything you send, make sure that it is something I don't have to carry cause I really don't know what I would do with it. I only hope I can get something over here to send to you and Peg for Christmas honey, but if I can't please understand. I'm afraid this won't be much of a Christmas this year, but it will be well worth it if by next Christmas we can all be home again for good. Pass this on to Mom will you honey, so she doesn't go to

Buff and Cookie's puppies, nine weeks old. "Little Buff, Sissy, Baby, Butch."

a lot of trouble for me, and please don't forget, - Don't send me anything I have to carry, anything that I can eat or use as soon as I get it, except pictures or something of that sort.

I think I received a letter from you the other day asking me a lot of questions and maybe this would be a good time to answer that one letter.

Well, honey, I finally found it after practically reading every one of this stack of letters over again and I won't be able to answer many of the questions you asked as they just won't let it go through. I'll answer the letter though, and maybe I can make an interesting short letter for you today.

I'm sure glad that you are donating blood honey, cause that is really important now. I hope it didn't bother you too much. Why don't you try to go real often as you have no idea how necessary that really is. I am really amazed, by the way, that it took so long for my first letter to get there, but I guess it is about right considering it was just regular mail. I'm glad you finally heard from me cause I know you were worried. As far as getting sick, seasick, I mean, it was just the other way round. I felt better and my appetite was something to behold. We had the most delicious meals and in such quantities; it was really wonderful. The food over here isn't bad but of course it is nothing like what we had back in the states. However, it is wholesome and we are well fed. The conditions aren't like they were back in the states either. Over here it is mostly field conditions under which we are living. Its really not bad though, and I don't have anything to complain about yet. Oh yes, for the love of pete, don't worry about bombs or anything. In the first place, the Luftwaffe is now nil, we haven't seen any enemy aircraft since I've been here. And in the second place, the only section of the country that the robots fall on is the vicinity of London, so you see, you don't have to worry at all. The only thing you do have to worry about for me, is how lonesome I am for you and how much I miss you.

I am doing clerical work now, honey, in a replacement headquarters but I'm just working here until my orders come though transferring me overseas and I'm not assigned. I told you, I believe, how they tried to assign me here and couldn't. I have worked for them now for two months almost, and now that they are leaving, I am going to work for the new headquarters that is coming in. Of course, I don't know how long it will be before I am ready to leave, but at least I am doing something

interesting and something to keep my mind off of home. Yes, the rest of the boys I came over with, that are still here, are training everyday, however, now I'm the only one left. As usual I leave a place last. Remember, in the states, how everyone of my outfit would leave before me? Well its the same old thing again, not that I mind a bit now. I would just as soon stay here for the duration. No kidding, this is as nice a camp as any other over here and I like the work so why not stay? I wish I could. Yes, things are pretty much the same here as they were at home, as far as administration of the camp, except, of course, this is a replacement camp where the one at home was a training camp.

Like I told you, sweet, the rating is definitely out until I become assigned to some outfit and the way it looks now, the war will be over before they decide to put me with any outfit. I told you I think, about how they had planned my rating for me and everything if I would have stayed with this headquarters, 70th Replacement Battalion, but no luck. I would have had a real job and really been lucky if I could have stayed with them and they tried every way they could, to get me, but the Depot headquarters wouldn't let them assign a general service man.

Well, honey, I've got to quit now, but I promise to finish this tonight and I also promise to write at least 5 pages and maybe more before I close.

Well, honey, here I am again for a while and I'll do my derndest to get a good letter off to you tonight. Its about 11 o'clock and I just finished and everyone has gone off so maybe I'll be able to write without interruption for a while.

Honey, You don't know what it means to me to read those wonderful descriptions of Peg that you put in your letters. I read them over and over again. She sounds so sweet and wonderful. It really hurts something terrible not to be able to see her and watch her grow. I want to be with you so bad, honey, you really have no idea what it is to be so far away from someone you love so terribly and of course its hard for you I expect but I've got two people to be away from and to want to see and one of them I hardly know, having only seen Peg for such a sort time before I came in the army, while you only have me to be lonesome for.

Of Course I won't change, what do you think? After all honey, it will naturally seem rather strange to me when I finally get home and I might act differently for a while until I get used to being a civilian again, but it will come back to me in time and I'll be the same as I always was. Don't you worry about that.

I believe that I told you that Bob Medley shipped out about a week or so after we got here and I haven't heard from him since. I expect he is in France now doing some fighting. Say hello to his wife for me in your next letter. You know I think that she was with Bob when we came up from Fannin on our furlough. She is really very nice.

By the way, did I tell you about the fellow we had who was bragging about all the blood he had given and then went in and gave his pint when we had the blood bank here and as he walked up the street after giving his blood he fainted dead away and had to be carried to bed? The funny part is that he was the only one who fainted out of the whole bunch and I mean there were thousands of them and he was close to being the biggest man there. He must have been 6 foot 5 inches and weighed about 230 pounds.

You know, sweet, it won't be any time till Peg is feeding herself and everything. She is really growing up fast now. It tickles me to hear how crazy she is about the water. We'll have to take her swimming real often when I get home. I would really like for her to be an expert swimmer. I want to see her so bad. Lets just hope and pray it isn't too far off. By the way, honey, I received a letter from Dad yesterday with the nicest prayer in it. I'll write it for you - "Oh my Jesus I supplicate thee through the precious blood of thy divine heart, the intercession of thy holy Mother and thy cruel death to assist me in this pressing necessity." You know, sweet, I just couldn't have asked for a sweeter family than I've got. I have the swellest Dad in the world. In fact, I never really appreciated him enough while I was home.

You know, I've come to the conclusion that your letters just aren't long enough. I'll go to another and after that one I think I'll go to bed. It's getting close on to midnight and I have a hard day ahead of me tomorrow.

I just can't get used to all that time for my letters to get to you. It takes almost a month for letters to get back and forth, do you realize that?

That is really cute about the pups sleeping in the hen house. They really sound cute, and old Buffie always getting into trouble by following Cookie around. That is just like a woman. The funniest though, was about the catbird chasing Buff. I thought I would die laughing, reading that.

I must close for now. Its way after 12 and I must get to bed. Take good care of Peg, sweetheart, and don't let her forget her old man. Be sure to say a big prayer for me every night. Sleep tight and sweet dreams. I just happened to think, that is silly cause right now you are just about to sit down to supper. Well, anyway, honey, goodnight. Say hello to everyone for me and give Peg a big kiss too.
        I love you,
Your sweetheart,
Jack

Friday
18 August 1944

Dearest Darling:
    How are you this evening, Darling? Personally I feel wonderful as I received 5 wonderful and real long letters from my sweetheart, and they have really made me feel good, although a little more lonesome and anxious to get home.

I got the pictures of the puppies honey, and they are the most darling pups and really, I was surprised at how good they look. Cookie really did herself proud. They have the most marvelous heads, so well shaped, etc. They have Buffs square muzzle and lips. I sure wish I could see them and play with them. You shouldn't have any trouble at all selling those dogs. They are exceptionally fine looking dogs, and the way Butch looks he should make a good show prospect.

Well, I guess I'd better get to answering your letters I received today. I really look forward to them cause they are so newsy and sweet and wonderful, just like you. They just make me feel so good and I read them over and over again.

I guess that will be or rather was a tough trip back home on the bus with the baby and those two kids. I have to hand it to you honey. I'd think twice, I believe, before I'd take that on with someone along to help. I never saw anyone with the energy and get up and go that you have.

I guess Ollie has gotten home by now. I kind of had a hunch he would open up his own business

now and get things going for when the war is over, as the news looks pretty good.

Well, honey, start planning for another Junior when I get home. I'm not scolding or anything sweet, but as sweet and wonderful as Peg is, I don't see how you can even think about anything but her. You're so silly, honey. It doesn't make any difference what color snow suit you get her to me. You'll get what looks best on her anyway. Course, you know me. I like blue and that is what I would get her but she might look better in some other color. Honey, don't worry about me not going to church every single Sunday. For some reason, you acquire quite a bit of religion over here and find that spiritual guidance really helps a lot. Lord knows, I've said my share of prayers and then some since I've been in England.

By the way, your birthday is almost here again and if I could get to town I could get you something but I just can't get out during the day to buy anything so I'll tell you what you do. You use that first $20 allotment check - that you'll get this pay day as a present from me and go down and use it for a down payment on a good fur coat and use the extra allotment, or part of it, each month to pay for it. You really need a coat and right now you have an opportunity and a little extra money so go ahead and get one, please, for me and from me. But be sure and get a good one. Pay a hundred and fifty or two hundred bucks for it. Now you go ahead and get one honey, please. Be sure to put a big birthday card in

Peggy, ten months old. Wooden stroller. Metal Taylor Tot strollers, gone to war.

it from me to you and wrap it up pretty, and then have a picture of you taken with it on and send it to me. Happy birthday, my Darling. Lets both pray that by the time another birthday of yours rolls around I'll be home to celebrate it with you and all in one piece.

How is Peg about riding? Is she good or does she cut up and act like some kids do? Does she like to ride in the car? Honey, of course sister's dog is good natured. Collies are noted for being swell with children. Course they can't compare with Cockers but they are nice dogs.

I am waiting anxiously for the package with my mouth watering like fury. I'm really hungry for some good candy and tidbits from home. We just can't get any real good stuff to mince on over here.

The last thing you asked me in this letter was about the sweater honey, don't send it to me. In the first place I won't be able to carry any extra stuff like that and in the second place I have two sweaters now that the Red Cross gave me. I just won't have room to put them anywhere and I don't want any more on my back than absolutely necessary.

Well, that finishes that one so I'll go to the next day and boy is it a nice long one. Three pages on both sides. I believe that this is the last one I'll answer tonight. I want to write Mom and Pop a line before I go to bed. I started this about 7:30 tonight for a change and its now about 9:30. Its surprising how long it takes to write a letter like this. It is really a lot of fun, though cause its just like talking to you except for being near you.

You start off your letter by saying you don't have a thing to write about and then proceed to write the longest letter I've gotten from you in a long time.

Hey, honey, I asked for paper but don't send me stacks of it cause I don't know what I would do with it. What I need, too, are envelopes as they are constantly sealing shut on me and I have to throw them away, but again don't send me large quantities of anything. Always remember when you send me anything, hon, that everything I have is carried on my back so don't load me down.

I started to write a letter to Peg on her birthday, like you mentioned in one of these letters I got today, but I got half way through and decided that it sounded too put on and corney sort of so I threw it away and besides that's just asking for trouble, in getting back, I mean. I'm getting real superstitious lately. Can't afford to take any chances you know.

Lord, I hope you're right about keeping that date for May 22nd honey, but I just have a hunch that around that time I'll most likely be in India or a reasonable facimile, thereof. As soon as this is over in France, I'll take another nice long sea voyage only I'm afraid in the opposite direction from the good old U.S. The way it looks, sweet, it will be another couple of years before I'll see home again.

Whoops, honey. Just got some wonderful news. Patton will be in Paris by morning according to the radio. The Germans are in full retreat and the battle of Normandy has been won. The gap was closed and the air corp is tearing the devil out of the Germans and their equipment who are trapped and are trying to retreat. Well, it looks like this part of the war won't last much longer.

I sure hated not being there for Peg's birthday sweet. I hope a good time was had by all and I hope, too, that those pictures you took come out cause I'll

bet they will be cute. I sure hope you are right about me being home for her next birthday. Its bad enough missing what I have of her, but missing two years, I just don't think I could take it. By the way, I got the piece of (wedding) cake you sent and I'm saving it. I tasted it and boy was it terrible. It was so stale it tasted just like fish food. You know how that is.

Well, dearest, I got writing and completely forgot myself and look at this letter. 10 pages almost and with the paper shortage as it is. Tsk Tsk. I guess I'd better close now and hit the hay as its about 10:30. Love me honey, like you always have or I think I'd die if you ever stopped. Give Peg a big kiss for me and don't forget the prayers. Night, honey. I love you more than anything in the whole world and miss you more than you'll ever know. "I'll be seeing you"

All my love, for always and always,

Your Sweetheart,
    Jack

(I had already bought Peggy a pink coat and hat and leggings. I promptly exchanged it for a blue one when I received this letter.)

Sunday
20 August 1944

Dearest Sweetheart:
    Well, darling, here is another dreary and lonesome Sunday rolled around. I feel so lonesome and blue today I hardly know what to do. I would give anything I know of to be with you all today. I guess right now you are at church as it is about 3:30 now here.

I haven't received any mail for the last 2 days but I have a couple of letters here left over that I can get busy and answer.

I feel a lot better. I just finished off a whole can of grapefruit sections all by myself that one of the fellows brought me. They were really good too, now I can get down to answering these letters. I have to write to the folks and want to write to Perry and Joe Barnes as I have heard from both of them and haven't answered them yet.

The letter I am going to answer now was written on Peg's birthday right after the party. It kind of makes me blue and sad to when I read it and think about missing her first birthday. I pray its the last one I miss. In fact you were writing this letter at the exact time that she was born. Lord, honey, how time flies. I can hardly realize that she is a year old already. Its almost impossible.

I hope you can read this, honey. I'm sitting in my tent, all by myself trying to write with this on my lap and its quite a job. Its raining cats and dogs out too, which isn't unusual. All the other fellows took off to town this aft but I didn't feel like it and besides I want to write you. Thank goodness I didn't go now.

How did Peg like the teddy bear and the Dumbo? I think she will be crazy about them. She just seems like the type that would like things like that, especially if she takes after her mother. I'll bet you are as crazy about them as she is. Gosh, honey, I sure hope the pictures you took of the party come out all right. I'm really anxious to see them. By the way, I received the invitation and I'm awfully sorry I couldn't make it. I wouldn't have missed it for the world but there was some unfinished business that I just couldn't break away from.

You know, honey, your Dad is a really swell person. That was pretty nice of him, what he did at the party. I think he thinks quite a bit of me and I only hope I can live up to it and be deserving of it. (He put the American flag on a chair.)

Of course, I get just as excited about what we will do and everything after the war as you. That's all I think about all the time and every night I talk it all over with you. You see, I am with you every single night. That is one reason why I go to bed so late, cause then I dream and I spend the whole night with you. Silly?

Well, honey, this is awfully short I know but you have no idea how lousy I feel so I think I'll go to bed a while. Maybe I'll feel better.

Hello, again, sweet. Well, I had a nice nap and ate and I feel better now so I will write for a while. I'm going to the show this evening at 7:30 here in camp. The Red Cross is having a picture, I don't know what it is, but they help to get my mind off home so I'll go. I'm going to try to finish this by then.

You know its funny how certain things affect you when you are away from home. I was sitting here writing and a fellow started playing some classical music on the piano in the rec hall, some really beautiful music and he was good, and it made me think so much of you and made me feel so all alone and blue.

I haven't gotten the package you said you were

sending yet but I expect it is on the way. I hope I get it quick cause I'm so hungry for something real good. By the way, I am friendly with the new mess sergeant in this new battalion we have so he and I were talking this evening and I mentioned that I wasn't going to chow this evening cause I didn't like corned beef hash (they had that today) and so he asked me over to his mess hall, which wasn't feeding any troops, and fried me 4 eggs, just right, and 2 big pieces of steak and we had coffee and pudding. Boy, was it wonderful. That is one reason why I feel so much better now than I did when I started this letter. Those were the first really good eggs I have had since I left the states.

I hope you have decided to buy that fur coat as my birthday present to you by now honey. Please go ahead, sweet, cause you have wanted one so long and you have never had a really nice coat.

I guess I'd better close and go take in that show. Goodnight my dearest. Love me and miss me. Say a big prayer for me every night. Give Peg a big hug and kiss for me and don't let her forget her Daddy. I love you and miss you more than anything in the world. Be a good girl and buy that coat too! I'll be seeing you.

All my love for always and forever,

Your Sweetheart,
Jack

Battle of Mortain, France

THE STARS AND STRIPES

Daily Newspaper of U.S. Armed Forces   in the European Theater of Operations

Vol. 4 No. 249   New York, N.Y.—London, England—France   Monday, Aug. 21, 1944

Yanks Across Seine, Nazis Say

Reds Start Thrust for Ploesti Oil

Nazis Reveal New Drive For Jassy; Russians Attack in 7 Sectors

Russia's powerful armies, attacking now on no fewer than seven main sectors from Estonia to the Vistula river, were reported by Berlin yesterday to have begun yet another "major offensive"—this time in the direction of the Rumanian rail junction of Jassy, battleground for last spring's fighting. The Red Army's new blow, intended to smash the gateway to the Danube gap and the Ploesti oilfields, was reported by German News Agency, whose Col. Ernst von Hammer broke through Nazi lines to a depth of about a mile and a half.

Von Hammer also admitted deep breaches in German lines northeast of Warsaw and on the Latvian front 80 miles east of Riga. He conceded "lesser penetrations" from the Soviet bridgehead across the Vistula 30 miles south of Warsaw.

The one area in which the Nazis apparently still held the initiative was near the main rail hub of Siauliai, about between Kaunas and Riga. Moscow said fierce tank battles there, with mans pouring in tanks and

The Saga of the Lost Battalion

Starved Yanks Fought On, Defied Demand for Surrender

By Earl Mazo
Stars and Stripes Staff Writer

MORTAIN, Aug. 20—The rumbling sound below was new but familiar. It wasn't the crashing grind of German tanks. There was a softer ring to the noise. For six days the Doughboys had waited for that sound, and now, as they looked down the hill, they saw Americans coming up.

The haggard, bearded remnants of World War II's lost battalion were saved.

For six days the men had held out without food or water and sometimes without ammunition, stubbornly fighting off repeated German attacks.

One evening a German officer, nattily uniformed with Iron Cross and trimmings, came up under a flag of truce.

"I demand that you honorably surrender to the German government," he said. "You will be treated well. If you do not surrender by 8 o'clock tonight you will be blown to pieces."

The answer, from an American who in 24 hours had eaten one K-ration biscuit and some raw potatoes, was:

"Go —— yourself. When the last round of our ammunition is fired and the last bayonet is broken in one of your bastard bellies, then we might talk surrender. But I doubt it. Now get the hell off this hill before I shoot you off."

The German dropped his dignity and forgot to salute in his haste to get off.

The battalion had gained the hill the easy way. The Germans had evacuated on Aug. 6 without firing a rearguard shot. Twenty-five German troopers on the hill gave up good-naturedly. The war was over for them, they said, and they were happy.

Headquarters was set up, road blocks of machine-guns and anti-tank guns were established and all was in readiness for a day or so of holding the line.

But the Germans struck sooner than expected. Shortly after midnight there was a movement of tanks below the hill and within a few hours the place was isolated.

German tank and infantry columns were making a last desperate bid to cut

the American armies below and above Avranches.

It was a full scale German offensive and the battalion on the hill was in the middle of it.

A tall, tanned, drawling Texas Lieutenant, Ralph Kerley, who commanded a company on the hill, said, " That first night they kept knocking out our road blocks and pouring around them, and we kept putting them back until we just didn't have anything else to put there. I knew when I heard Germans jabbering orders behind me that we were surrounded. I tried to get contact with battalion headquarters in the town, but there was no more headquarters; that is when I started worrying about contact with the other companies on the hill."

Small patrols were sent out to connect the battalion and by noon Monday that connection was established and Capt. Reynold Erickson, of Miles, Iowa, assumed command.

In the Mortain battalion headquarters the officer who was CO had reported to

(Continued on page 5)

Bridgehead Near Paris, Berlin States

Foe Tells of a Paratroop Landing; 'Gap' Carnage In 14 Divisions Grows

As some columns of the American Third Army stood on the threshold of Paris yesterday, others reached the west bank of the Seine northwest of the capital, and Berlin reported that tanks smashed across to the eastern bank under the protection afforded by Allied paratroops the Germans declared had been landed in that area.

While remnants of the German Seventh Army were being ground up in the Argentan pocket, a new double encircling threat was posed for those of the enemy who had escaped. With the U.S. Third Army already at the bridgeless Seine 30 miles northwest of Paris, the British stormed ahead in the east, reaching the Channel coast at Cabourg, about 13 miles from the mouth of the Seine.

Massed Allied artillery was ripping to shreds the last of 18 German divisions in the Argentan-Falaise death-trap.

An official disclosure that the "bulk of the combat elements of 14 divisions and parts of four other divisions" was caught, together with traffic jam of at least 1,000 vehicles, suggested that the final toll may be considerably heavier than that first announced.

Planes Attack In Toulon Area

Other Craft From South Russia Oil Refineries in

A Foxhole Flak Suit Saves a GI Occupant

WITH THE 2 INFANTRY DIVISION IN FRANCE, Aug. 20—They laughed when Pvt. Sam C. Gwin,

Toulon Facing Encirclement

Yanks, French Link Up

P.S. I woke you up this morning! Did you know that? About noon I was napping and I dreamt that the baby was throwing her toys out on the floor and jabbering and rattling the side of her crib and I got up and woke you up. Funny?

I love you honey,

Bye now,
Me

Tuesday
August 22, 1944

Dearest Lil Sweetheart:

I am going to start this now but don't know just how far I'll get before I have to get back to work. If I don't get a letter written now I won't get one off to you at all as I sure won't be in any condition to write when I get off tonight. Darn, I thought so. I'm going to have to quit.

Here I am again, Darling but not for long. As usual it is very late and I am very tired.

You started out by complaining about the climate. I'll say this, sweet, the worst climate St. Louis has to offer couldn't compare with this over here. Well, you won't have to worry about it after I get home cause we'll move on down to Houston, and bring our daughter up in a nice healthy place where it is warm all the time. I hope you can read this, hon, as I'm having one devil of a time trying to write by candlelight on my bunk. Darn pen ran out of ink so I had to borrow this and the fellow wants it back in a minute so I expect I'll not be able to finish this tonight after all. At least I want to tell you how much I love you and miss you. I've learned one thing since being in the army if nothing else and that is I just can't live without you, and I'll never be away from you again as long as I live. I am really an awfully lucky fellow to have such a wonderful wife and baby waiting for me. I just don't know what I would do if I didn't have you and know that you were there waiting.

I'm glad to hear that you are advertising the pups and I expect by now you have sold them. You can use what you get from the pups and my allotment on that fur coat. I'm going to keep harping on that subject, honey, till I get a picture from you showing you in the coat.

Remember that mail box we had at 1308? We really did have a nice little place. Course it was rather far out but considering B'ham it was the best place we could have lived. I never will forget how sweet you had the place fixed. I was so proud of it. All my beefing about the money you spent, remember, then I was ashamed of myself cause the place was so cute.

Well, honey, I'm going to have to quit now as the fellow wants his pen but I can write a few more lines tomorrow and it won't go out any later.

I've just got a second to write as I am on guard tonight. I'll do my best to write a few lines later when I get off.

Well, honey, here I am again. I just got off and it is about 11:30 but I want to finish this and get it off to you. Its a heck of a letter I know but I want to at least show you that I tried. There has been so much confusion, etc. around here the last couple of days that it is really a wonder that I have done this well. Course I can't tell you what has been going on or anything but what an uproar, and has it kept me busy.

I'm enclosing a copy of the newspaper we get over here as I thought you might be interested and I would kind of like it for a souvenier. I sure hope they let it come through. Did you get the coins I sent you? Let me know.

By the way, honey, did I tell you that this outfit is trying to get me assigned? I'll swear it looks like a lot of people want me but no one can get me. I sure wonder what is in store for me.

Well, Darling, Its late and I have a big day ahead of me so I guess I'd better close for now. Goodnight. Sweet dreams. Love me and miss me. Say a prayer for me and don't forget my kiss for Peg. I'll be seeing you.

All my love,
Your Sweetheart,
Jack
P.S. I love you. Say hello to the folks for me.

(The mailbox in Birmingham nearly became a Federal case. I painted it blue and the substitute mailman refused to deliver our mail because it was not "regulation." I won!)

ANDOVER
HAMPSHIRE
TIDWORTH GARRISON

Andover was also in Southern England, located a little over fifty miles northeast of Yeovil, England. The history of the town goes back to the tenth century.

In 1175 King Henry II gave Andover its first Charter. Because of its location on an important trading route, it was always a thriving market town. When the railways came, they contributed greatly to its growth.

The wool industry, both raising the sheep and trading wool, was very important for the whole area. Jack described it as very interesting country, more than the last camp, more historical with older buildings. He said the countryside was beautiful with hills galore and gorgeous sunsets.

Andover changed very little from its earlier years. The Guild Hall (originally known as the Town Hall) has remained the same except for the removal of the clock tower, and the general appearance of the buildings and stores in the town hardly changed at all. Some of the inns have been on one site for centuries.

In September, 1944, when Jack arrived, Andover, like the rest of England, was still filled with the Yanks. Although many had left at the time of the invasion, there was still a constant flow of American replacements, newly trained and very young, many of them coming in on troop trains. From Andover Junction Station, a short military rail line had been built through the village of Ludgershall ending at Tidworth. It was a distance of sixteen miles.

Ludgershall was a typical little picturesque English village. Being longer than it was wide, it gave the feeling of being larger than it actually was. Near the town were the ruins of an ancient castle and the depression of its moat. The castle's stones had been removed, little by little, for centuries to build the homes and buildings of the village. The village itself had changed very slightly through the years. Now, as it was everywhere, Ludgershall was filled with military vehicles and over-run with American soldiers. The Pubs, The Queens and the Crown, were favorite places as was the Prince of Wales Hotel, for everyone.

The entire area adjacent to the railway from Ludgershall to Tidworth was still filled with every sort of military vehicle from 1943 to 1945. Spread over the Salisbury Plain as far as the eye could see were the weapons and equipment needed to fight the war in Europe as long as it lasted. These weapons and equipment were continually being replaced.

Tidworth Garrison was a very old English army post. It had originally been an estate. The original house, Tedworth, was built about the year 1570. It had been one of the finest sporting estates in England. It was abounding in game, deer parks, and it even had its own foxhounds to hunt the 2600 acres.

In 1899 Tedworth House and the entire 2600 acre estate were bought by the British War Office to be used for an Army Training Ground. The house was used for some years as the Headquarters for the Commander-in-Chief, then later as an Officers' Club. This was the center of Polo in England and the world. The polo field still exists in the area south and west of the house.

In the early summer of 1942 Brig. General Theodore Roosevelt, Jr., Commander of the U. S. 1st Infantry Division, arrived at Tidworth with fifteen hundred men. This was the advance guard of the division. They were combat troops in training and would be followed by many more.

In the late summer of 1942, Tedworth House (which contained over 100 rooms) was taken over by the American Red Cross as a club for enlisted men. It was under the direction of Mrs. Theodore Roosevelt, Jr., General Roosevelt's wife. When General Eisenhower had given her permission to open the club, He told her it must be for the enlisted men. He said, "If my officers can't look after themselves, they're not fit to be my officers." The manor house, at this time, was generally referred to as Tidworth House, instead of Tedworth.

Mrs. Roosevelt moved into the house to prepare it as a club. No local help was available, (everyone was doing war work), but a corporal and nineteen men were detailed to help clean and refurbish. These were crack combat troops but were glad to be out of the training exercises. When the Club was ready to open, Mrs. Roosevelt was unable to find volunteers to run it; however, she was finally able to get some helpers from V.A.D. (Voluntary Aid Detachment), a part of the British Army. The club opened on September 3rd, 1943, and the dedicated girls from V.A.D. were allowed to stay until the end of the war. This was the Red Cross Club that Jack wrote about. He went there often, as it had everything in the way of relaxation for the soldiers' comfort. They even had a weekly dance. Two weeks after the club opened General Roosevelt with the 1st Division went to Scotland, and the 29th Division under the command of Major General Leonard T. Gerow moved to Tidworth. Later, the 29th Division then left also.

When Jack arrived, in September, 1944, the 12th Replacement Depot was located there. I learned later from official records the following: "Hq & Hq Detachment 12 Officers and 43 enlisted men left Camp 66 Barwick House England by motor convoy at 1500 hours 6 September 1944 and arrived Tidworth Barracks 1330 hours 6 September 1944." Jack was one of these 43 enlisted men. The units arriving there received further training and were then sent across the English Channel as replacements in the combat areas in the European Theater.

Saturday, September 9, 1944, was Jack's first letter from Tidworth. He was writing by the light from his fireplace as they had no lights. He said they were in a two-story brick building with real beds, a private bath, and a kitchen downstairs. (I later learned he was staying in the married quarters.) They were two men to a room and they even had a radio! His bunk mate was a Sergeant O'Toole. Jack said it was an old English post, quite large, nicer than any army post back home. He described the house and the surroundings, as much as was permitted, and sent a copy of the description of "a mansion I saw recently," cutting out the name Tidworth House.

Jack said there were no decent sized towns near, but he said they had everything they could ask for on the post. They had a PX (Post Exchange), but there were so many shortages it had hardly anything in it. He said they had a regular mess hall where the men ate and used

their own mess gear. It was always so cold and damp they slept wrapped in blankets; they had no sheets. Their uniforms were O.D.'s, which they wore the year round. That was what the standard uniforms were called; it stood for the color Olive Drab. When I asked, in my letter, how many men were there, he could only tell me they were coming and going all the time. The others trained every day until they shipped to France. He was not training since he was a clerk in the headquarters. He was still not assigned. He had a letter from Wallace Decker (the soldier with him in New York) from somewhere in France. Wallace was not assigned either.

On September 11th, 1944, Jack wrote, "Happy Birthday Darling" and wished he could send a card or present, but it was not possible. He started writing the letter while he was in the office; however; he had to stop, and he finished it that night in his "boudoir" (which was what he jokingly called his room). He wrote a lovely letter for my birthday and hoped I had bought that fur coat. I had! I asked him to tell me about his work. He said he did typing and reports and general office work. He worked most of the time. Day after day, his routine was exactly the same. He drew a picture of their room. He said O'Toole (his bunk mate) was sleeping and he was sitting on his bunk writing to me! The radio had Command Performance on with Bob Hope, the popular American entertainer. He said all they talked about was when they could go home, and the only people they talked to were GI's (other soldiers).

On Saturday the 16th of September, he and Sgt. O'Toole took a long bicycle ride. He said English bicycles have the hardest seats! They rode all over the country-side. He said the sunset was one of the most beautiful he had ever seen. They got home about 10:30 P.M. They gained an hour as summertime changed back to normal. Also, the blackout was officially over for England. There had been no lights at night since the beginning of the war in 1939, as a defense against German bombers.

He wrote, in his letter of September 16th, 1944, "It is a big day for the English. Just think, children here four or five years old have never seen a lighted city or village. Thank goodness Peg has a place to grow up where things are normal and they hardly know there is a war going on. Sometimes the going gets tough, you get mighty disgusted and wonder why you have to come way over here away from the ones you love and your home to fight on foreign soil. Then you stop and think if we weren't over here and hadn't been, maybe our families would be going through the same thing that these people have and you realize that it is well worth leaving home to fight for."

On September 29, 1944, Jack had a new job working as the personal clerk for a Lieutenant Colonel in charge of the Summary Court of the whole Depot. He had especially requested Jack; however, it was only temporary. He was still with the 107th Battalion but on Special Duty in the M.P. Detachment. It was 2 o'clock P.M.; he had cleaned the office and changed the furniture around. He said it seemed peculiar working for an officer of his rank by himself. They had a private office with a fireplace and a fellow to tend it. He said the work was hard, the hours long. He had more responsibility than he had ever had, but he enjoyed it. The Lt. Colonel was exceptionally nice to work for. He was from Houston, Texas, and had been wounded in France. He was going back to the front soon.

The next morning Jack received my letter with the pictures of me

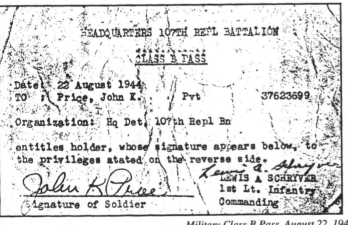

Military Class B Pass, August 22, 1944. Shows 107th Replacement Battalion.

in my Red Cross uniform and my new plaid dress. He treasured those pictures and was so proud when the Colonel admired them.

His room-mate, Sergeant O'Toole, shipped out (to France) October 6, 1944. He was Irish, red-headed, 29 years old, very short and single with lots of girlfriends! He had been a newspaper reporter in Pittsburg, Pennsylvania. Since Jack now had the room to himself, he placed the bed where he could sit on it in front of the fire, and the room was nice and cozy. He said he would hate to leave since he was living like a king almost. He was really getting spoiled. He drew a picture of his room with himself on the bed.

On October 14, 1944, he took a trip, by himself, to London, England, on a pass. He wrote that he got in line for the bus to take him to the town (Andover) where he would get the train to London and after waiting for 2 1/2 hours (at Tidworth), he finally hooked a ride in an ambulance to the station in Andover. He had lost much of his leave time so by the time he got to Waterloo Station, in London, it was getting dark. He took the subway to Picadilly and found Rainbow Corner (the Red Cross). They arranged for him to get a bed at the Hans Crescent Club — two buildings with 300 rooms for soldiers.

The next day he took a wonderful tour. Jack saw London! Returning Sunday night, he stood in line at Waterloo Station for three hours to get his 10:30 P.M. train to Andover. The next day, Monday, he wrote a wonderful 20-page letter to me describing every detail of wartime London. After 15 pages he said, "The censor isn't going to like this." In tiny letters the censor wrote, "He doesn't." That was the only time we had any indication the letters were censored.

On October 18, 1944, he wrote that the entire Battalion was taken to a town called (cut out by censor) for a concert by the London Symphony Orchestra. Jack wrote that they had a famous Cathedral there and hoped he would be able to see it. We thought it must Salisbury which indeed it was. He said he was really anxious for tomorrow to come as he had not heard any good music for so long. He wrote later that it was a wonderful concert and the Cathedral was very beautiful.

On October 21, 1944, Jack mentioned that Aachen, Germany, had been taken and the allies were moving ahead. He said maybe it wouldn't be too much longer before the war was over! He would hate to be in France or Germany as it had been raining steadily for a week and the fighting men would be bogged down in a sea of mud. They were!

It was so cold and damp that he had not been warm for a month, and his clothes never dried out. He wrote a saying he had heard: "England has three seasons: early winter, winter, and late winter!" He rearranged his furniture so the bed was in front of the fireplace. Now his front roasted and his back froze!

In his letter on October 30, 1944, he said he was working night and day. He had just started writing at 7 o'clock, was called out unexpectedly, and it was now 2:30 A.M. Something big had happened, but he couldn't tell me. It was big. The new Ninth Army had arrived in France and captured the Port of Brest on September 5, 1944. On October 23 the Ninth Army (including the 30th Division) was brought into the line in the Ardennes Sector and engaged in heavy fighting. The Americans were pushing into Germany. Replacements fresh from the U.S. were being pulled in and sent directly into combat. This was what he couldn't tell me!

Jack did not finish the letter until the next evening. He said he was holding down two jobs for the last two days, and he thought his letters might be coming from France very shortly!

On Saturday, November 4, 1944, Jack wrote that he was on a new job. It was only temporary while a fellow was on furlough. They were in the office with the M.P. Detachment. He was in the Staff Judge Advocate's Office handling all the cases of the whole Depot and the Captain-in-Charge had requested him. It was a lot of work and really interesting. He went back to his old job the next day. Also, he got a new bunk-mate, Pierce Lawrence (Larry). He was 28 years old, married, and had a little girl just Peggy's age. They were planning another trip to London.

On November 17, 1944, Jack wrote that he had worked every night and was so tired. He had gone out of town the day before and did not get in until 3 A.M. He could not tell where he had been or what he had done, but he really worked. It was very secret.

He said he didn't want to think of Christmas, but added "I don't really mean that cause I am going to Church (it would be St. Michael's Garrison Church on the post), have a Christmas tree and everything,

but honey it will be so lonely without you with me." He was glad the election was over and thanked the Good Lord that the President, Franklin Delano Roosevelt, had won. He was sweating out our nation's election. We all were! It was my first time to vote.

Jack and Pierce Lawrence went to London on a pass the next day. It was more enjoyable with someone and on the way back they had a most pleasant experience, which he talked about the rest of his life. On the return trip from London they met two girls about their age (both married). The girls invited them to the home of the friends they were visiting, the Gilbards, in the small town right outside of camp (Andover).

The boys accepted and were invited for tea. The girls with several other couples were going to a dance on an Army installation near town. The boys were going to walk them to the dance and then go on back to camp since they had to catch the last train into camp. On the way they all stopped in a pub. Later the others went on to the dance, but the girls decided to stay until train time at 10:15. P.M. Jack described it as a typical English pub, a place for the neighborhood with a big fireplace and all the people sitting around talking and singing. He said it was wonderful and the best time he had in England. I learned later the pub was probably the Junction Hotel. The Gilbard's were very hospitable, inviting them back. They also invited them for Christmas dinner.

November 22, 1944, was our fourth wedding anniversary. Jack wrote a beautiful, tender, nostalgic, eight-page letter — his Happy Anniversary Edition. He had just received the new photograph of Peggy at 14 months, for Christmas, for his folder. He could hardly believe how much she had changed, and he longed to see her. He thought she was looking more like me — wrong — she was always the image of her Daddy. He said we should have another one when he came home, as he was missing out on Peggy. (We had three more!)

The next day, November 23, 1944, was Thanksgiving Day. He wrote that they had a splendid turkey dinner with all the trimmings, then they all took the afternoon off for the football game at the Tidworth Oval (football field). It was the 12th Replacement Depot "Moore's Mauler's" versus Base Air Depot #1 "Bearcats", and the Maulers won.

During the half they set a turkey loose in the middle, with twenty fellows on each end of the field. The fellow who caught it got a turkey dinner at the Red Cross that night for himself and seven buddies!

The Lt. Colonel Jack was working for had left. Jack had worked for a Major, and he was now working for a Captain. He said he felt lucky to work under such good officers, but this Captain was the best since he had been in the U.S. Army.

There was no doubt that Jack was having a very pleasant war. The one thing he wanted, however, was to be assigned to a unit and get a rating. He was looking forward to the furlough he had coming January 1st, 1945. He planned to live in English hotels for the whole seven days and act like a civilian, but it was not to be.

In his letter on December 1st, 1944, he said the closer Christmas came, the worse he was feeling, especially with Peggy just old enough to enjoy it. This was a touching letter; he was very lonely and he poured his heart out. He wrote, "If I could only talk to you and hear your voice it would help. Be sure and keep Peggy as sweet as you say she is and try not to let her forget her Daddy." At the end of his letter he wrote, "Rumors, ugly ones, have been flying fast and thick the last couple of days that have everyone, including yours truly, in a sweat — something is brewing."

On December 5, 1944, Jack said he was all alone again. The 12th Replacement Depot had shipped all the fellows from the Battalion that he knew, and he was still there, as usual. It was hard to lose friends, but he was not complaining. He received another Christmas package, and he now had 25 bars of soap, 75 candy bars, and 3 fruit cakes. He wanted the family to please not send any more — anything, as he could not take it with him. He had a new job now with the M.P. Detachment of the Depot. He was typing, and he was learning a little. He said they were a swell bunch of guys. He was still not assigned. He was just on special duty. He said Sgt. O'Toole moved back with the 107th, just as he left.

December 10, 1944, Jack wrote that he had received the wool socks I had knitted for him. He had them on, and they were so warm. They fit just right, and the feet were so smooth. (Well, much more about those socks later!) He said the GI socks were not warm enough, but the English ones were, if you could get them.

In early December, 1944, the Allied High Command was planning a major offensive to be launched in midwinter of 1944. It was now midwinter! Because of the heavy fighting and enormous casualties in October and November, 1944, the replacements were so depleted, the high command decided to convert to troops the top heavy service and headquarters staffs — of which Jack was one. General George C. Marshall, United States Army Chief of Staff, ordered 65,000 Air Force and Service personnel to be trained as ground forces. The plans had already been laid for the offensive: The Rhineland Campaign. The 30th Division, to which Jack was later assigned, was already in Warden, Germany, awaiting the start of the offensive.

December 13, 1944, (Wednesday) Jack wrote that things were happening, but fast. He said to use the Hq. Det. 107th until I received another address, not the M.P. Section. He was so tired he did not know what he was saying and did not get to bed till after 2 o'clock in the morning. He had moved in with the M P's. He said he would try to get a letter to me, no matter how small, every night. He wrote, "Things will be uncertain for the next week, due to conditions beyond my control, so don't worry if you don't hear from me for awhile. It looks like I'm going to have a chance to visit Rusty after all, right soon too.

"I can't get to bed as it's so noisy in the barracks with the guys coming and going all night. I have a big day ahead of me tomorrow. I am going to sleep late in the morning. I have to rest up for the big weekend I am going to have." He was giving me clues — <u>Rusty</u> meant that Jack was going to Germany. This was the last letter from England.

The next letter was started in England on Thursday, December 14, 1944, at 11 PM. "I am looking forward to seeing Rusty. I hope to spend this Saturday and Sunday with him." (This told me where Jack was going, and when he was going.) "I won't be able to spend Christmas in England. I've given up all hope as far as the end of this whole mess is concerned. It has begun...." He finished the letter on December 24, 1944, Christmas Eve, in a foxhole "Somewhere in France."

THE LETTERS

To: Mrs. John K. Price   From: Pvt. John K. Price
704 Ballas Rd.   ASN 37623699
Kirkwood 22, Mo.   Hq. Det. 107th Repl. Bn.
U.S.A.   12th Replacement Depot
                         APO 551 c/o Postmaster
                         New York, N.Y.

Saturday
9 Sep 44

Dearest Sweetheart:

I received 3 very wonderful letters today and they made me feel so good to hear from you but so blue, too. I miss you. Sometimes I feel like this will never end and I'll never get back home to you and Peggy again. Those with the pictures I still haven't received. I'm so anxious to see the ones of you and particularly Peg as I want to see how she has grown. I haven't received the packages yet either. I guess I'll just answer one of your letters for tonight and then write you a nice long letter tomorrow. Darn, I don't know whether I'll be able to write or not. It's dark and we have no lights and I'm trying to write by a light from the fireplace. By the way I told you I had moved, but I haven't told you about the place. We are in regular two story brick buildings with fireplaces and real beds and everything. It is an old English post and is quite large. There are no decent size towns near but we have just about everything you could ask for on the post.

Tidworth House, American Red Cross Enlisted MensClub. WWII.

It is really a great deal nicer, with more recreational facilities than any post I was ever in back home. I wish I could tell you more about it and where I am but I'm afraid I can't. I can say this I believe, though, (censored). It is very interesting country by the way. Even more so than the last camp I was in. A lot more historical and older buildings, etc. For instance, the Red Cross on the post has been here since 1590. (censored) Quite a lot of hunting was done here as it was quite a large game preserve. The same family lived here for four generations. The house is really huge and one of the most impressive and beautiful places I have seen for quite some time. I only hope you will be able to read this writing. My kingdom (?) for a light bulb. I did want to answer it, too, cause they were such swell letters and so newsy and so much to talk about in them.

I only wish that I would be able to be with you on your birthday. Do you realize that this is the first birthday you have had in 9 years that I haven't given you a present. I only hope it is the last one.

I received a letter from Decker today and he is somewhere in France. Has been over there for the last couple of months but apparently has seen no action and hasn't been assigned to an outfit yet either, so I guess I'm not the only one in this unassigned fix.

I realize this is terribly short but I promise to do better in the daylight tomorrow. Give every one my love and be sure to say a big prayer for me and don't forget my kiss for Peg. Goodnight, darling. Sleep tight and sweet dreams.

All my love, always.
Your sweetheart,
Jack

P.S. I wasn't able to buy that Panda doll for Peg as I just didn't have the money so please get her something for me.

Bye now,
Me.

(Wallace Decker was the soldier with Jack at Camp Shanks N.Y.)

11 September 1944
Monday.

Happy Birthday Darling:
Needless to say, sweet, that I feel very low and mean and very bad about not being able to have sent you a present of some sort or at least a card but please understand, honey. I was going to write a special, in fact an extra special birthday letter to you a week or so ago, but then I thought it would be a lot better if I waited till your birthday and wrote a nice letter to you on the very day. I also still have hopes of being able to send you a nice present or souvenier as sort of a remembrance till I can get home and get you something really nice. Of course I still have hopes that you bought the fur coat I have been begging you to buy, but I have my doubts.

I hope, honey, that you are having as beautiful a day at home for your birthday as we are having here. It is one of those exceptional and very unusual sun shiny days, and reminds me a lot of spring at home. I just happened to think, I was home with you on your last birthday. Little did I expect to be where I am now then. Lets just hope and pray that next year this time I'll be with you and that I won't miss another one, ever, in fact, that I never have to be away from you and Peg like this again.

I wonder what you are doing today. Lets see, about now, you are just getting up I expect and eating breakfast, as it is about 2 o'clock here which would make it about 7 AM at home. Come to think of it, I guess you would still be snoozing in bed now, unless Peg woke you up early this morning. Let me know about what you did today and what presents you got, and be sure to let me know whether you got the coat or not, and if you did be sure to send me a picture of you wearing it.

Well, honey, I'm writing this on office time so I guess I'd better quit for now as I have some work I must get to. By the way, sweet, do you realize that I have passed my first year in the army and a whole year away from you? That 13 months seems like 13 years, honey. Maybe we should have been apart more than we were, the last nine years honey, as I might have been a little used to it and could have taken this separation better. As it was, we were always so close to each other and always together, and I relied upon you being there to help me over any rough spots, that now, when I'm away rom you it is doubly hard. I just don't think I could live without you darling. I need you and love you so much. You just don't realize how much you can depend on a person or how much you really love and need someone till you are away from them.

Well, honey, I am going to have to stop now, but I'll finish this tonight. Bye for now, sweet, I love you...

Here I am again honey, and as I said, I'm getting an early start as its about 6 o'clock. Please excuse the pencil but I'm still out of ink and I haven't a typewriter to use as I am writing in my boudoir or however you spell it. Anyway — bed room. I'll try to answer the letter you wrote on the 30th now.

I am really surprised, as I sure thought you would keep at least one pup. I guess that $60 was just too inviting, eh?

What do you mean make rash promises about going to church? It has been very few Sundays I have missed going to church since I've been in the army.

Another thing. We will definitely increase our family right away as I do not want Peg to grow up as an only child like I did. She should at least have a brother.

You had just gotten home from USO while you were writing this. You start out by telling me about you running around with those G.I.'s. Grrr - I'm jealous. You could at least pick on boys a little closer to your age. I can just imagine you as Martha Carr. I don't know what it is but all the time people come to you with their troubles.

I sure envy you, darling. How I would love to see one of the good old Muny Operas. I've never seen The Bohemian Girl but I understand there is some very beautiful music in it. Gosh, honey, Bing Crosby is singing "I'll be Seeing You." Gee, that song. It really makes me feel bad. You know all you have to do, honey, is read those words and you will know how I feel all the time.

I didn't tell you we had a radio, did I? Yes, we are truly living in luxury. It sure feels good for a change, too.

OK, honey, I'm going through and answer each one of the questions you asked me in this letter.

AN ENGLISH GIRL'S LAMENT

Dear old England's not the same,
We dreaded invasion - well, it came,
But no, it's not the beastly Hun
The bloody, damned Yankee Army's come.

You see them in the trams and bus,
there isn't room for all of us,
We walk to let them have our seats,
Then get run over by their jeeps.

They mean about our lukewarm beer,
and say it's like running water here,
But after drinking one or more,
You find them lying on the floor,

And you should see them try to dance,
They get a partner, start to prance,
when you're half dead they stop and smile,
"How's about it, Honey Chile?".

You'll see them try to jitterbug,
They twist and turn and pull and hug,
It's enough to make a monkey jealous,
The Yanks are civilized - so they tell us.

The Yankee officers make us smile,
with their light pants you can see a mile,
We wonder if they are mice or men,
Decide their values, so avoid their den.

In admiration we would stare,
at all the ribbons that they wear.
And think of deeds both bold and daring,
Which won the medals they are wearing.

The green ribbon alone denotes,
They crossed the Atlantic - brave men - in boats.
We speak to them, they just look hazy,
They think we're mad, we think they're crazy.

Yet to our Allies we must be nice,
We love them as the cats love mice.
They laugh at us for drinking tea,
Yet funnier sight you'll never see,
Than a gum chewing Yank with a dumb-looking face,
He'll raise a laugh most any place.

They say they can shoot - yes, and fight,
Sure they can fight, but when they're tight,
We must admit their shooting is fine,
Of course they can shoot, but what a line.

Page 2

They tell us we have teeth like pearls,
they like our hair the way it curls,
"Your eyes would dim the brightest star,
You're competition for Miss Lamar."

You are their life, their love, their all,
and for no other would they fall.
"And love you till death do us part,
and if you leave me dear, you'll break my heart

And then they leave, you're broken-hearted,
The camp has moved, your love departed,
You wait for mail that does not come,
then realize you're awful dumb.

In a different town, a different place,
It's a different girl, a different face.
"I love you, sweetheart, please be mine",
It's the same old Yank with the same old line.

An English Girl's Lament. Amusing tale, author unknown. (enclosed with letter, September 10, 1944.)

Happy birthday Peggy. One year old. Daddy not able to attend. Had some unfinished business.

Yes, we have a mess hall just like back in the states. However, in our last camp the mess hall was what they call a Nissen hut. They are the bldgs made of sheet metal or galvanized tin and shaped like this. (picture) You have seen pictures of them I am sure. No, we don't eat out of dishes. We use our mess gear all the time.

I don't know what you mean honey, about how many others are there. I couldn't tell you how many are in camp, but of course they just keep coming and going.

I'm doing quite a bit of typing and taking care of quite a bit of reports that we have to make and doing general office work. Of course, honey, I can't go into details you know. Generally, the work has (censored).

When I slept in a tent back in the other camp, honey, there were 8 other fellows in it with me. We all slept on cots. All there was in the tents were 8 cots. No we don't have sheets. We sleep wrapped up in our blankets.

There is no such thing as a summer uniform over here, sweet. In fact there is no such thing as a summer uniform. The only regulation uniform is the OD. However, Suntans are used in the states during the summer as an auxiliary uniform and I understand they are also used in tropical climates, too. It is much too cold to wear them over here, summer or winter.

When I'm not working I am usually writing to you. Once in a while I go to the show or something. Most of the time it is working, though.

About all we talk about is when we can get back home and usually the only people to talk to are GI's.

Yes there is a PX on each post but as everything is rationed and as there is nothing to drink or buy we don't hang out much there.

The food is about the same as back in the states except for more dehydrated foods which aren't too bad.

There, I answered every question you asked. And that is exactly what goes on day after day. There is no change. For instance, right now, I'm sitting on my bunk writing a letter to you. I have a table pulled up in front of me that I'm writing on. I write the same way in the same place every night. Here is a diagram of the room —
(picture)
There, now you know just what the place looks like. Or do you? For instance, O'Toole, the other fellow, is sleeping on his bunk now, a nice fire is burning in the fireplace and the radio has the Command Performance on with Bob Hope, Roy Rodgers, Frank

Sinatra and they are now singing "I'm an Old Cowhand." By the way, the Andrew Sisters are on too.

Well, Darling that just about finishes this epistle for tonight. I write again tomorrow. Goodnight darling. I love you more than any thing in the world and miss you. Happy birthday, sweetheart. Give everyone my love and say a prayer and be sure to give Peg a big kiss for me.

Goodnight, sweet dreams.

All my love, for always,

Your sweetheart,
Jack
P.S. I love you.

Monday
September 11th

Dear Mom and Dad:

Well, Folks, it has been quite some time since I have written and I am really sorry, but I've been so busy it honestly couldn't be helped.

I have moved again to a new camp but this time it is much for the better. We are finally out of tents and living two in a room in a real house. It is really swell. We have a fireplace in our room and a radio. All the comforts of home. It is really the nicest place I have lived since I have been in the army. I wouldn't mind staying here for the duration.

Well, the war news is looking good, isn't it? I don't expect it will be much longer before it will be over as far as Germany is concerned. The only trouble is that even when they are licked I still won't be getting home. I really don't expect to be home much before next year this time.

No, Mom, Babe didn't say any thing about your boat trip. Did you enjoy it? Is the old excursion still the same? Tell me all about it. How I envy you and what I wouldn't have given to have been with you.

I think Dot would be doing the right thing by going up to Farragut to be with Tommy. I wish now that Babe had come to Tyler with me. It would have been just that much longer we could have been together, and believe me every minute counts.

These Doggone Browns had to go and mess the business up right at the last. I sure was looking forward to having them play in the series against the Cards but I guess they are through now.

Well, Folks, I must close now as it is getting late. Write real soon and often and give me all the news from home and particularly everything there is to know about the cute things Peg does.

All my love to the sweetest
Mom and Dad in the world,
Your Son,
Jack

P.S. I'm sending you a copy of our paper we get over here. Thought you might be interested in it.

Goodnight,
Me

(Dot and Tom Gavin were Jack's cousins. Tom was in the Navy.)

Saturday
September 16th

Dearest Darling:

Well, honey, another week-end is here and another day without any mail from home. I have a hunch it is that address I have been using so be sure to use the new one I sent you as soon as you receive it.

I had a very wonderful time this evening. I borrowed a bicycle and O'Toole, a friend of mine, the one I bunk with, and I took a long ride. We just got back about 5 minutes ago. Its about 10:30 now. I can't take it any more though. We rode all over the country-side, which is up and down, hills galore, and I am all worn out. It was really swell, though, as the country-side is very beautiful around here and when the sun set it was one of the most beautiful sunsets I have ever seen I believe. Just like a picture. What I really would like to do is borrow and bike and get off tomorrow and really take a ride all over this section. There are some very interesting things to see and besides it makes you feel good to get out away from camp and soldiers for a change.

Well, I had a very busy day today and I'm just about ready to drop. Thank goodness we get a few hours extra sleep tomorrow. We also gain an hour tonight as the time here changes from summertime back to normal. Summertime is about the same as our daylight saving time. By the way, today the blackout was officially over in England for the first time in 4 or 5 years. Of course, it isn't completely over, as they have dim-out regulations, but automobiles are driving in the street with their lights on now, and you do see lights in houses, where it used to be pitch black, and I understand that street lights will be coming on as soon as they are serviced, etc. It is really a big day for the English. Just think, children over here four or five years old have never seen a lighted city or village, they don't know what it is like to be able to go out at night and see where they are going. Thank goodness Peg has a decent place to grow up in where things are normal and where they hardly know there is a war going on. Sometimes the going gets tough, and you get mighty disgusted and wonder why you have to come way over here away from the ones you love and your home to fight on foreign soil and then when you stop and think that if we weren't over here now and hadn't been over here, maybe our families would be going through the same thing that these people have been going through, you realize that it is well worth leaving home to fight for.

I'm so anxious to hear some news about Peg, honey. I just know she is walking now, and getting into everything, and doing so many cute things. I would give anything to be able to be with you all now as this is about when she will be the cutest. I think they are so cute and wonderful just about the time they start walking. Well, I guess she'll be doing some equally as cute things when I finally get home and I won't feel too bad about missing this part. Course we'll have to have another one right away so I can see just how they act and help him

Red Cross uniform, we made bandages.

New plaid dress. Jack's favorite picture.

61

grow up. All I'm thankful for is that we have a little girl cause they are much sweeter and cuter than little boys, but of course I want a little boy too. I was wanting a little girl all the time but beings our first one was a boy, nothing would do but we should have another boy to take his place. I knew you wanted a boy awful bad. And how and where we got the name Margaret Jeanne. I like it and don't believe that we could have done better. I think she fits the name perfectly. I like Peggy, too, its cute.

By the way, honey, did you get your coat? I wanted you to as a birthday present from me. Now, I want you to go down and pick out a real nice and expensive and good fur coat for yourself and buy it. With the money you have from the dogs and the extra money I'm sending you each month, you should be able to afford one very nicely. I couldn't send you anything for your birthday from here. I want you to give Mom ten dollars of the next $20.00 extra allotment you get from me so I can buy you a nice Christmas present. I am going to try very hard to get Peg a doll or something here and send it but I won't be able to get anything decent for you.

Ooh — that bicycle ride — I can hardly sit down now. These darn English bicycles have the littlest and hardest seats I have ever sat on. I really haven't been getting enough exercise, though, for the last three or four months. Sitting in an office every day and then either going up to my bunk and sitting down and writing you and going to bed or else sitting in a show for a few hours has been the extent of my exercise lately. I really ought to get out and walk and maybe start playing ball or something in the evenings.

By the way, you won't recognize me when I get home. I am down to about 140 or 145 pounds now. I got weighed tonight on an English scale and I weighed a little over ten stone, which is 14 pounds to the stone. I guess I'm just wasting away from loneliness. Just think, before we left Birmingham I weighed about 175 pounds too. I have really fallen off.

You have no idea how lonesome I am for you and how much I need you. I'll swear I'll never leave you again, even for an overnight fishing trip. I'm afraid you are just going to have to learn how to fish, cause you know how I am about fishing so you are just going to have to come with me.

Well, it is almost midnight, so I must head for my bunk. I have a continued dream of you and home coming up. Sleep tight and sweet dreams. Give Peg a big kiss for me. Pray for me, honey, and pray that this mess will be over soon so I can come back home to the most wonderful, beautiful and sweetest wife and little gal in the world.

All my love, darling, for always and always -

Your Sweetheart,
Jack
P.S. I LOVE YOU!

Tuesday
Sept 26th

Dearest Darling:
Well, honey, another day and no mail from you again, although I did receive a letter from Mom and

Headquarters Building, 107th Replacement Battalion, 12th Army Replacement Depot.

one from Dad today. I sure can't understand what is happening to your mail to me. I wish to the devil it would start coming as I am really getting anxious to hear from you, besides it is getting hard and harder to write a decent size letter to you without something to go on and answer.

Well, the news looks about the same and I am beginning to believe in what De Gaulle says — to wit — The war with Germany will end no sooner than next spring, or rather, the war will not be over by next spring and hardest fighting is still ahead. There is a lot of truth in what he says, as shown by the stiff resistance we are meeting now. Of course when Russia gets up on her border too, there is no telling what might happen. It sure can't end too soon to suit me but I do believe everyone is just a little too optimistic about the whole business. I'm afraid we are going to see quite a bit of rugged and rough going before Germany is finally beaten to her knees. Of course we could most likely end the war now, by giving in to some of her terms as to an armistice but then we would just have this whole thing to do again and it would be harder the next time so the best thing to do is be sure there is no next time, if possible. If we gave in now and offered Germany an Armistice, it would be the same as losing the war. No, regardless of how long it takes we had better see it through to where she is completely and absolutely beaten to where she can never rise again. When we are finished this time there shouldn't be any Germany left.

I understand from Mom and Dad that you have started having cold weather all ready. It is rather unusual as this is usually St. Louis' hottest part of the year. It has been plenty brisk over here the past few days and I expect summer is just about over. Gosh, how I dread to spend a winter over here. It doesn't get terribly cold but it is a damp cold that penetrates and with the heating facilities we have it will be next to impossible to keep warm. These buildings, especially headquarters bldg, aren't built like the old castle was, that we were in before we moved here. That was a little more air tight and I believe would have been a lot warmer. Oh well, I guess I shouldn't be complaining as we could be in tents trying to work, etc. In fact I understand that is how the (censored) the outfit I used to be with is operating now, and they are living in pup tents so I haven't any room to complain. Compared to them our quarters are luxurious, in fact they almost are as far as army quarters are concerned.

I guess you'd better just forget about any Christmas presents for me till I get back home. I would appreciate a couple of boxes of good things to eat however and a pair or three of wool socks or something like that, however. But remember what I told you sweet and don't send anything I have to carry. Nothing larger than a pair of socks and no more than 2 or 3 pair of them. Course send all the candy and cigs and that kind of stuff you want as I won't carry that. Good candy and home made cookies are whats best. If there is any way at all possible I am going to try to find you a little something in London, if I get there, or in one of these small towns around here, to send as sort of a souvenir.

How is that big gal of ours? According to Mom, she is really going to town on this walking business and it won't be long before she will be walking without any trouble at all. Mom said she walked from the coffee table in the living room to the dining room table the other day, all on her own hook. She said, she got as far as the table before she discovered what

Military pass 9 November, 1944. For Tidworth, Andover, and Salisbury, England.

she was doing, but when she realized she wasn't holding on to anything and that there wasn't anyone near her to help her she immediately sat down and crawled the rest of the way to where she was going. Even so that is a pretty good distance for her to walk and if she did that well three weeks ago, she is probably going like a house afire now.

I would sure give anything to be with her now and be able to watch her, learning to walk, especially. I can just see her toddling along and the expression on her and everyone else's face as she walks a little bit.

Gosh, honey, I miss you all so much and want to get this thing over with so bad so I can get back home, I don't know what to do. It wasn't too bad back in the states cause you could always find something to do on your free time and there were places to go and you could buy things that were familiar to you like ice cream sundaes or a chocolate milk shake or something of the sort and you could meet people you knew how to talk to, and you knew how to act and what was expected of you. Over here you have none of those things. You are among people who have no interest in you and if they did have, wouldn't have time to show it. There is just about nothing to do, no where to go. Then, of course, you always have that longing to be home and be with the ones you love. You never, I don't care how long you're here, get over that homesickness, not particularly for your home, but the whole blasted U.S.A. Every month I'm over here I realize just how much that country of ours means to me and I wonder what I would do if we didn't have it. There is just no place like it in the world.

Oh happy day — only 4 more days till payday. Then I'll be able to pay all my bills, and start borrowing again. No kidding, though, I've almost got it planned where I can maybe take a trip to London this payday. Now all I have to do is arrange for a pass. I do want to get to London though as there are a few things I want to see, like Westminster Abbey, Buckingham Palace, the Tower of London, and ever so many other things. By the way I am going to ask you a question I want you to be sure to answer — just to see how much you really do know about London. — What is Big Ben? Now be sure to write and answer that.

Well, Darling, this isn't as good as usual, but please excuse it. I must close now. My back is killing me from sitting here on my bunk writing without anything to lean on. I think I'll hit the hay early tonight for a change. Goodnight. Sweet dreams.

Love me and miss me, honey. Be sure and say a prayer for me and don't forget my kiss for Peg. All my love forever & ever.

Your sweetheart,
Jack
P.S. I love you.

Friday
Sep 29th

Dearest Darling Sweetheart:
Well, honey, I have a new job now, working as personal clerk for a Lieutenant Colonel in charge of the Summary Court of the whole depot. I don't know yet how I am going to like it however. It is still the same old thing of being attached unassigned again, and is not permanent. I only hope that when it ends I haven't lost my old job with the Battalion and can go back there. The colonel seems to be a very swell person and should be pretty nice to work for. We have a private office all to ourselves and a fire place at one end with a fire in it and a fellow who comes in every twenty or twenty-five minutes to see that it doesn't need wood or coal or anything. It seems very peculiar to be working for an officer of his rank all by my lonesome, especially after getting used to working in an office like the Battalion, with so many people in there and all the noise and confusion that goes on in an office like that. There won't be any change in my mailing address as I am still with the 107th Bn but just on Special Duty with this office. I have been here now since this morning, it is about 2 o'clock now, and all I have done is kind of clean the office a little and arrange the furniture the way I thought it would be best and then the rest of the time I have just piddled around. I would like to be answering your letters now, as I have nothing else to do, but I don't think it would be such a good idea, beings that this is just my first day and I really don't know this guy very well, so I'll just ramble along, as long as time permits too, of course. Needless to say, I feel very strange sitting here alone with so much brass. However, I would much rather be kept busy all day, as the time really passes quicker and I feel like I have accomplished something at the end of the day. I've always been that way, tho, to a certain extent. As long as I have to be somewhere, and put my time in at that place I want to be kept busy. Well, I finally have something to get busy on for a while so I'll quit for now.

Saturday 30

Hello, honey, it is a day later, as the job I have turned out to be a lulu. I worked through supper last night and got off about 10:30. Then I went to work this morning about 7:30 and worked through lunch and didn't get supper till 7 o'clock tonight and then went back for a few more hours.

I just got off and its about 10:30. I have to work all day tomorrow, too. I got chiseled out of my pass, too.

I received a letter from you today with some wonderful pictures in it. Honey, you get more and more beautiful with every picture you send. I love you so much and I just can't get my eyes off those pictures. They are so wonderful I just can't get over it. You look so cute in your uniform. You just make the most wonderful and sweetest little mother I have ever seen. Your new dress is really beautiful and it looks so good on you. You looked so sweet in that picture. Peg is awfully cute in the pictures, too, but she takes a back seat in them. You are the main attraction. The first thing everyone who has looked at the pictures noticed was how beautiful you are. The Colonel looked at them, too, and complimented me, in fact raved, about my beautiful wife, then all of a sudden he noticed Peg. Honey, I can hardly wait till the day I can be with you again and see you smiling that sweet little smile you have on in the pictures and love you and be with you to enjoy our big daughter together and start planning our future together again. I never want to ever be away from you again as I long as I live. When I look at the pictures, the love I have, and am storing up inside of me, for you almost bursts. You have no idea, darling, how I feel. Its worse now than it was when I just realized that I loved you and couldn't live without you and that you meant more to me than anything in the world. That was a long time ago, too, and instead of decreasing or even staying the same, it has grown by leaps and bounds. Just think, it will be 9 years the 11th of November since we first met. It seems like just yesterday that I called for you for that first date. We've had a wonderful time and a wonderful life since we first met. I wouldn't trade one day of the whole time for anything in the world. Even the days that we had some of the little spats we had, which were darn few and far between, by the way.

Gosh, honey, I have such a collection of pictures now I haven't any place or any thing to keep them in. I believe they are putting out some sort of folders or something, in the states now for Servicemen to carry their pictures in. I would appreciate it if you would pick one up for me and send it. And keep the pictures coming.

Doggone it, I'm mad at you (not really, though!). You shouldn't even mentioned fried chicken to me. I sure wish I would have been there. I think that when I get home I am going to sit down and eat at least three whole chickens all by myself and I can do it, too, I'll bet.

Peg sounds so cute, honey. She is at the age now where she is learning all these cute tricks and is showing them off. I'll bet she has the very devil twinkling in her eye all the time. She sure seems to be a cheerful little thing, from her pictures, honey, and Mom says that she is, without a doubt the sweetest natured and best little girl as far as minding you and being well mannered. Course I don't know whether she could be prejudiced but keep up the wonderful job, sweet. She is turning out just like we said our baby would be. Remember? I'm sure Buffie loves her just as much as we do, but you know how funny he is about really showing his affection. Peggy isn't really old enough to treat him like he is used to being treated so he just stays out of reach, but from what you say about him staying under her bed and being near her I don't believe he would let any thing ever happen to her. He knows I believe, that she is a part of the family now and will be just as faithful with her as he is with us. He is really a sweet old dog.

Did you get your coat yet? Now, honey, you'd better get it and right away, too.

How was the opera, honey? I hope you enjoyed it. There is quite a bit of beautiful music in the Bohemian Girl. Write and tell me all about it. (I expect you have by now though). Honey, you worry me, though. You know, you really should get out more to shows, etc. and kind of keep from feeling down in the dumps. We don't get anything but real old ones over here. For instance, last night they had Robert Taylor in Strange Interlude. I believe it was his first picture and as old as the hills.

I am still waiting anxiously for the new picture of Peg and you for my folder.

I know, darling, its awfully hard on you, and you just can't plan anything as far as when I will get home. When it does happen, it will happen when we least expect it. All of a sudden like. What I dream about most is taking a vacation somewhere with just you and Peg and about all the fun we will have, and I plan every little detail.

I guess I'd better get ready to close. By the way, this Colonel is from just 60 miles from Houston (the Colonel I am working for I mean) and we had a regular gab fest today. He is really a swell fellow and very unusual and different from the usual Colonel. He has been to France and was apparently wounded, but he is ready to go back now, and so very anxious to go. Although the work is hard, and terribly long hours, it is a lot more responsibility than I have ever had since I've been in the army, and I really am enjoying it.

Well, sweetheart, I must close now and go to bed as it is very late and besides — 10 pages — What more could you ask for unless it will be 12 pages. Sweet dreams. Love me and miss me and don't forget to say a prayer for me. Give Peg a big kiss for me, too, and say hello to everyone back home.

I'll be seeing you, and stay as sweet and beautiful as you are.

Night, honey,
Your sweetheart,
Jack
P.S. I love you!

Monday,
3 October

Dearest Darling:

Well, honey, I have a few minutes with nothing to do (very unusual, too) so I'll try to drop you a line or two. At least start a letter as I have never seen it fail that as soon as I start to write you something happens to get me busy again. I went out and saw a show yesterday evening and got back late and went straight to bed. I was off all afternoon yesterday too, but I went to a football game that was played here. Our Depot has a team that played an air force team over here. It was really a good game and the way everything looked and the guys acted you could almost have sworn you were back at good old Webster High watching them play. It was really swell. We won too. It is the first thing I've been to since I've been in the army that you could actually forget you had a uniform on and that you could completely forget all about the army and everything for a while. The players all have uniforms and the latest equipment and it really was swell. I was planning on going out for the team but being as busy as I've been the last month I never got around to it until it was too late. There were some mighty good ball players on the team, including several men who had played for a professional team, etc., back home, but I used to be a pretty good player myself and have no doubts that I could have made the team. I kinda wished that I had made the time and gone on out now.

I haven't received any mail from you now for the last two or three days. None today again. I haven't received any mail from you which you wrote in September and only half the mail you wrote during August. No packages yet either, although I have received quite a few of the pictures of Peg and you that you had mailed me. Gosh, honey, I just can't get over the wonderful pictures. I just look at them all the time. I guess the Colonel thinks I am nuts or something, but the first thing I do is pull the picture of you in your new plaid dress, the one where Peg is holding the zinnia, out and lay it on my desk next to the typewriter so I can see it all the time. I can't keep my eyes off you for a minute hardly. It will be so wonderful when we can be back together again, and have our own little house, and bring up our little girl together, and be able to do the things we like together again. That is all I ever dream of. In fact, it is always in my mind, I never stop thinking of it.

Well, I guess by the time you get this letter, Peggy will be walking and talking and everything. She is so sweet, honey. I would give anything to be able to see her, just for a little while. She is without a doubt, the cutest little thing I have ever seen. She takes after her momma, I guess and I hope. She will be a great big girl when I finally get to see her again. I wouldn't be surprised if she just wouldn't have anything to do with me at first, as she won't know me from Adam. We'll get friendly 'fore I am home very long though, although it is going to be kind of tough, not only on her but me too, as I am going to have to get used to being a civilian all over again and get used to having a family and all. It will all be rather strange to me at first, after being used to the army routine and discipline, all of a sudden to find that I am strictly on my own again, without anyone to tell me what to do or what not to do, except you of course.

I have the hardest darn time writing while I am supposed to be working. When I get up to the room I can think of a few subjects and write pages on them, but while I am down here I just can't think of a thing to say. I must spare the censor that much, anyway, as I guess I have made an enemy there anyway, with these 8 and 10 page letters I have been writing you, and almost every day too. I just thought of the reason why you haven't been getting my letters so regular lately. It takes the censor so long to read those long things that it naturally slows the delivery down a little. I can't stop writing cause I don't have anything to do and can't just sit here twiddling my thumbs, with the Colonel sitting right next to me. Gotta go now, business.

Here I am again, Darling, but not for too long as it is terribly late and I am tired. I wasn't kidding when I said business. I just got off and its now after 11.

I guess winter is on its way by now. It has been very cold here lately, and winter is definitely here. One thing I have heard is that it snows very little here. Thank goodness. I really dread spending a winter here as there are no heating facilities here at all and it will be twice as bad when I get to France.

I sure hope your new allotment started. It was $20.00, too, and not $10. As soon as I get a rating (if ever) I'll increase it some more. I get so worried about you not having enough money, with the baby and all, honey. I hope you are getting along ok, sweet.

Well, honey, I hate to mail a letter like this, but I want you to get a letter for today. Night, dearest. Love me and miss me. Sweet dreams, say and prayer and give Peg a big kiss for me.

All my love, for always and always,

Your sweetheart,
Jack
P.S. I love you.

Monday 9
Oct. 44

Dearest Darling Sweetheart:

Well, darling, no mail again. I am going to get this written to you this afternoon at work so that I'll be able to listen to the series this evening, it is really exciting. I wish I'd have been there to have seen a game or two. But I guess I should consider myself lucky to be able to hear the games.

How is that wonderful daughter of ours. It has been so long since I have received any late news of her I am at a loss trying to visualize how she has grown and what she is doing now. I have imagined that she is now walking good and her baby days are just about over. Mom says she is developing a little temper, too. Course that is only natural but don't let it go too far, honey. We want her to be a sweet little girl, and not like some of these kids you see. Mom also said that she was the most well-behaved and best natured little girl she had ever seen. That made me feel awful proud.

Well, I got what seems to be some good news this morning. I don't believe that it is definite yet, but it looks like they are going to keep me with the 107th after all and I won't be moving so you don't need to worry about any change of address again. I really like to work for the 107th and hope to return there in a day or so.

I think I told you that O'Toole has moved so I now have a room all to myself. I changed it all around and it is really nice and cozy. I go up and sit in my room in the evenings now and can dream of you without any interruptions. Here is the way it is arranged now.

(picture)

There now you can see one reason why I hate to leave. I am living like a king almost. It is really nice and I have a really cheery room which sure helps my morale. I am really getting spoiled and will I hate it when I have to move out into a tent again. I guess I'd better close. I love you and miss you more than anything in the world, honey. Take good care of Peg and give her a big kiss for me. Say hello to all the folks for me and take good care of yourself.

All my love for always,
Your sweetheart,
Jack

P.S. I Love you.

Did you get that coat yet? You'd better or I'll be mad —

Me.

Wednesday
18 Oct 44

Dearest Sweetheart:

I feel wonderful tonight. I received 4 wonderful letters today. I received one of the letters from you in 9 days, which is darn good service. I found some more notes on my trip to London so I can tell you some more of what I saw while I was there.

Well, I just got an invite to a show so I think I'll go and then by the time I get back I'll feel like writing. By the way, I picked up a real french 50 Franc note that was issued before the war that I'm sending on to you. Bye for now, Darling. See you later.

Hi, honey, here I am again. Its about 9 o'clock. We saw a dopey show that I'd seen before, but I should kick. After all, it was free. By the way, how did you like that 20 page one I wrote you yesterday. (London Trip)

So you and Peg had a big time at the birthday party. I'm sure glad. I think that is awfully cute, Bettie having a party for Butch — er, excuse me, Lynn I mean. Peg sounds so sweet, honey. I'll swear I just can't get over how she has grown. She is really a big little girl now. Good Lord, honey, Butch must really be a big rascal. That is sure tall for just 2 years. Is he still chubby, or is he getting thin like Joe? I'll say Peg was the Belle of the Ball. All those boys to one little girl. That is an eto man's dream — silly isn't it. By the way eto means European Theater of Operations in case you didn't know, but for your info, everything is abbreviated over here and the abbreviations are pronounced instead of saying the whole business. Now to get back to Peg and the party. That is sure wonderful about Peg being housebroken so well. Its very unusual that a child that young is that good about it. We have a very wonderful and unusual daughter. Gosh, I wish Peg could have as many nice toys and things as Butch has. Well, maybe when I get back home and begin to make a living for my family again we will be able to get her nice things like that.

Joe gets 16 bucks more a month or rather 18 more, than I do and is sending Bettie the same amount I send you. Well, maybe if someday I do get a rating, I'll be able to do the same as he. When I get home I'm going to see that Peggy just has everything she wants. I'll give her her way in everything and just love her and play with her all the time and just spoil the devil out of her so it will be up to you to be the boss and I don't care, either. I've got to make up for a lot of lost time when I get home. Honey, I want her to love me as much as I do my dad. We will be the most wonderful family you ever saw. I'm going to have to teach you how to fish, too, and teach you to like it like I do so we can go out a lot together, just the three of us. I want to be fixing Peg's dolls and stuff when they get broke and she wants me to fix them and I'm never going to be too busy.

Honey, I know it was and still is awfully hard for you bringing up Peg like you have all by yourself, but you have done a whiz of a job. We are going to have more children. We've got to have a boy for Peg.

I'm going out tomorrow night so I sure hope I get time during the day to write your letter. We are going to a town called - - censored - - to hear a concert by the London Symphony Orchestra. It should be real good. I'll write and tell you all about it. The whole Bn is going and we are being furnished transportation and are going to get in for free. While I'm there I would sure like to see the Cathedral as it is very famous and has quite a bit of history to it. If I can get the chance I'll go see it and tell you all about it. I haven't heard any good music for so long I'm really anxious for tomorrow to come. It should really be wonderful. (The town was Salisbury.)

Well, darling, I guess I'd better close now as I am very tired, its after 10 o'clock. I want to enclose a copy of the Stars & Stripes in this and a little folder of the R.C. Clubs in London.

Goodnight, darling. Sweet dreams, and remember that I love you more than anything in the world and couldn't live without you. Take good care of that wonderful daughter of ours honey, and give her a big kiss for me. Say a prayer for me. All my love.

Your Sweetheart,
Jack

Saturday AM
21 Oct 44

Dearest Sweetheart:
Well, sweet, I just got to work and figured it would be a good time to drop you a line, so I'll just ramble a little.

Well, the news is sounding a lot better today. Aachen has been taken and we are moving ahead. And the landings on the Philipines are really going good. May be it won't be too much longer fore its over. Another year or so. I would sure hate to be over in France and Germany right now — it has been raining here for a week steady now — and they'll be bogged down in a sea of mud. How is Peg? She sounds so darling from your descriptions. She is at the age now that she is really the cutest, learning all these new things and doing so many cute things.

Darn, honey, I wish now that I hadn't gone to London. I've got the bug now and I would really like to get back. I had such a wonderful time and there is so much still that I didn't get to see. Then, too, it is such a relief to get away from camp for a while and see that there are still civilians. I'd almost forgotten that there was anything but soldiers. Well, maybe I can go again next month some time. I would like to go on a day when the shops are open so that I could pick up a few souvenirs and things to send to you and Peg.

Oh, how I hate this darn weather. Its so cold and damp all the time. I'll swear I haven't been warm for a month and my clothes never dry out. When I think that I have to look forward to a whole winter and most likely spring of just this kind of weather it makes me shudder. I'll swear, I sometimes wonder how these people can live in a climate like this. Its a wonder they all don't have Rhumatism or come down with Pneumonia or something. Weather like this makes me feel so melancholy and blue and even more lonesome than I usually am. Sometimes it looks like this horrible mess will never end. All I hope and pray is that I'll have enough points when this is over to get back to the states for a while so I can see and be with you and Peg for a little bit.

Well, honey, I'll write a little more and then close this and get it off to you by noon. I'm kinda hoping a couple of those packages come through today, too. I'm sorry that you mailed some of them with my old address on them cause I won't get them for months. They have to make the rounds of France, you know, before they get here. Bye for now, darling. All my love, for always and always.

Your Sweetheart
Jack
P.S. I love you.

Tuesday
24 Oct 44

Dearest Darling:
Well, honey, I am writing under difficulties tonight, as it is very late, I just finished work, and I'm worn out and besides I lost my pen somewhere so must write with a pencil. Which reminds me, if you have a chance to pick me up a good cheap pen please do so at once, if not sooner, and send it to me as they are impossible to find over here and I really need one badly. I have changed my room around a little and now have my bed over where I can sit on it and be sitting right in front of the fireplace as it has been so cold here I want to be nearer the heat where I don't have to get up every time the fire needs fixing. I have a roaring fire going now and my front is burning up and my back is freezing.

I really hit the Jackpot on letters today. I received seven from you, two from Dad and one from Sister. They were dated Aug. and Sept. Tell Sister that the only reason I haven't answered her letter is that I just received it. You really have a wonderful, sweet sister, honey, almost as sweet and wonderful as you and I'm really crazy about her. Well, honey, I really hate to even try to answer a letter over 2 months old but I guess I'd better dive in and get this finished sometime tonight.

About the V-Mail letters. Well, darling don't fret any longer as I have ceased the V-Mail writing. As you have most likely noticed, you haven't received one now in over a month. Good Lord, I must have been feeling low that night I wrote that V-mail and poured my heart out to you. Its funny though, how much it helps when I'm feeling lonesome and blue and down in the dumps, to be able to pour my heart out and tell you all my troubles — just like I used to when I was back home. I think my trouble is that I feel that way too much, though. I must think about you civilians morale more!

You mentioned in your letter, honey, that the last time Earline heard from Rusty was the 31st of May. I sure hope she has heard later than that by now as, although this could be rumor, I hear, from a friend of mine who has a cousin in the same camp as Rusty, that they had a big attempt to escape and quite a few men were killed. An escaped prisoner told this fellow about it. It was really a big operation and over 1/3 of the camp was in on it, however, the largest part of the men were Canadians and British. Still and all I began worrying about Rusty, naturally.

About voting, honey, I would have been able to had I gotten my application off, but you know me — I put it off till it was too late so you'll have to do the voting for our family this time. Just vote the same way your Dad is going to and it will suit me fine. (We all voted for President Roosevelt.) Darn, there just isn't anything to answer in these letters — mainly cause they are so old. You finished it by writing the words to "Close to You," which is very beautiful and I like a lot, but it took a whole page up that you could have used to just talk. Well, I'll go on to the next letter and then I'll positively have to close as its about midnight now. You wrote exactly 37 words telling me you hadn't written me the night before. Tsk! Tsk! — remember my morale. You spoke of a letter you received from me that was real fat but when you opened it, it was a Stars & Stripes and just a few pages. I'll have you know all my letters to you for the last few months have been at least 8 pages and usually more. In fact, it is so bad the censor is complaining — he wants an extra man there just to censor my letters alone — you can believe that if you want to.

Honey, you think the clothing situation is bad in the states, you ought to see it over here. You are really very lucky, though as all clothing is rationed in England. That, by the way, is why I'm not able to buy you any kind of wearing apparel, etc. or for the baby either for that matter.

Your new coat really sounds wonderful, darling, and I'm sure tickled that you really got a good one. I am really anxious to get a picture of you with it on. Course I'm more anxious to see you wearing it, if you know what I mean.

I am going to have to stop now as I am about to fall asleep writing. Bye for now my honey. I love you and miss you more than you'll ever know. "I'll be seeing you" though "Some of these days" and you'll be "Close to me" again. Silly? Goodnight, honey. Sweet dreams and love me and miss me. Give Peg a big kiss for me and say a prayer.

All my love, for always.
Your Sweetheart,
Jack
P.S. I love you.

Friday
27 October 1944

Dearest Darling:

Well, honey, here I am again but I'm afraid this won't be a very long letter tonight as it is a little late and I've got to get to bed. I have the hardest darn time writing lately. I have all kinds of things to tell you and then when I get down to it I get all muddled just thinking about you and my mind goes blank except for that one thing. One thing that is the cause is that every thing over here is so monotonous. I do exactly the same thing day after day, with nothing new ever happening, and have nothing to definitely look forward to, as far as coming home, or you aren't able to see any end of this mess in sight and might go on like this indefinitely. It all seems so futile at times and it really gets me down. If there were some chance of promotion or something that I could work for it would really help. I really kind of wish I would get shipped. The only thing is that by staying around like this might mean they are keeping me till a specific job opens up and I might get a good assignment out of it, but I even have my doubts as to that. It looks almost like the only way you can really get anywhere or get something out of the darn Army is be being unfit for combat, a limited assignment man. Here I've been, working in the same depot now for six months. Two Battalions and a branch of the Depot Headquarters have tried to assign me but I'm not limited assignment, so they just keep me here to work anyway, regardless of whether I can get anything out of it or not. I've been in the Army almost 15 months, holding down one job right after another,

in I don't know how many different outfits, all of whom have tried to assign me and held jobs which are ordinarily held by non-coms and I'm still nothing but a buck private and have never been included in an outfit. I could have made a good rating by this time if, after I finished my basic, which by the way was over 8 months ago, I had been assigned to an outfit. I'd just as soon be in a combat outfit somewhere on the front lines as be here and under the strain I'm under of never knowing what was going to happen next. I guess what I need is to take another pass and get my mind off army for a few days. It looks like you are the only one I can blow my top to once in a while though, and you'd be surprised how much good it does. Kind of gets a load off my chest. Well, payday is next Tuesday so I guess I'll go to London again and forget my worries and besides I need the rest as I've been putting in some pretty long and hard hours lately. There is so much more there that I would like to see, too, before I leave here.

Honey, you just have no idea how it makes you feel to be so far from home and the ones you love. Instead of getting used to it, each month is just a little worse than the last one. Sometimes I wish I didn't love you so much, then it might not be so hard to be away from you. It is a very beautiful night tonight for a change and there is a beautiful moon shining down. I guess it is the same one you are looking at and that is shining in that upstairs window in your house. I remember how it used to shine in on me when I used to sleep in that middle room and keep me awake. Remember?

Well, I didn't get any mail today. I'm so darn anxious to hear all about that Newberry business and you might know the one letter that tells me all about it is late in getting here. Honey, the pictures you took of Peg really sound wonderful. I hope you got some good ones of you, too. Peg sounds so cute. She is really growing up now for sure. When they get to where they want to get out and play in the yard and don't want to be put in the pen anymore and walk around like she does, then she is almost over her baby days. Darn, but I hate to be missing all this in her life. I just hope she isn't too much older by the time I get home, so I don't miss too much of it.

Yes, honey, regardless of what anyone says, the Lord really looks after us. My Pop has proved that with his prayers and devoutness more than once. I just wish I could be half as good as Dad in that respect — and in every other respect to, for that matter.

Well, honey, I guess I'll close this the same way you closed your letter and for the same reason. I'm so darned tired tonight, and with this slight cold I'm getting I ache in every bone and from sitting here writing without anything to lean back on (I'm sitting on the edge of my bunk) my back is about broken. Oh by the way, honey, I sent you a description last night of an old mansion that I visited recently and I'm not sure whether the censor let it go through. I'd appreciate it if you would let me know. Its very interesting so I think I'll make a copy of it, censored by me as far as I can, and send it to you just in case you didn't receive the last one. Goodnight, Dearest. God bless you and look after both my wonderful sweethearts while I'm away. Sweet dreams. Don't forget my kiss for Peg. All my love to my beautiful and sweet darlings.

Your sweetheart,
Jack

P.S. I love you.
(The mansion was Tedworth House.)

Monday
30 October 1944

Dearest Sweetheart:

Well darling, happy Halloween — it is Halloween, isn't it? I didn't get to write you yesterday. I have been feeling plenty punk and all worn out so Sunday I stayed in bed all day, without even getting up for meals.

I feel a little better today, because of the rest I got, I expect. I have had a cold ever since I've been over here. I haven't received any mail since Saturday. When is this terrible mess ever going to end? I love you and miss you so darn much. You're a wonderful little sweetheart, honey, and I'm sure a lucky guy to have gotten you, although I don't know how I did it. I'm never going to be away from you again, after I finally get home. Won't it be wonderful when we can do all the things we've wanted to do, together and have a nice little place all our own again where we can raise our family and really enjoy ourselves like we used to. We'll have a car, too, and if we want, we'll be able to go out for a milk shake or a coke, or just take a nice long ride. I'll be able to play with Peg and maybe we can raise a couple of dogs like Buffie. I'll sit in my chair in the evenings, behind my paper, and pretend I don't hear you doing the dishes, and I'll most likely make you mad cause I wont cut the grass, or wash the dogs or something and it will be fun to listen to you gossip about what the neighbors did that day. Honey, you have no idea how much I miss all that. Its funny how well you can remember everything that has happened the last 7 or 8 years when you get away like this. When I get to feeling too blue and lonesome for you, I come up and lie on my bed and just dream about every little thing from the very first time I met you up to now. It helps to think of the wonderful times we have had together and how close we've always been. I just can't get over how lucky I was. It constantly amazes me. — Well, honey, its about 2:30 AM now. I got called out unexpectedly. Something big happened and I've been working ever since 7 o'clock when I left so I'll have to finish this tomorrow. I promise to get a nice long one off to you fore noon tomorrow, though. Goodnight, sweet dreams. See you tomorrow. I love you. —

Hello, honey. Well, its Tuesday evening now and I'm going to be able to finish this tonight I believe. Boy they have been working the very devil out of me the last few days. I have been holding down two jobs and working night and day practically. I don't imagine it will last a lot longer though and expect my letters to you will be coming from France very shortly now.

Maybe it won't be too long fore I get assigned to some outfit and get a chance at a rating and will be able to send you a little more. As far as having to enjoy O'Toole's description of London, you didn't have to do that, although I imagine you would have gotten a lot more out of his than mine. I guess by now you have received the letter I wrote telling you that O'Toole has shipped, but I'll tell you something about him. He was a Sergeant — Technician 4th grade to be exact. He is about 28 or 29 years old, and just a plain red-headed Irish mick. A little guy, though, smaller than me. He was single but was definitely attached to about 15 gals back in Pittsburg, Pa. He was a newspaper reporter. Swell guy, too. No, honey, a black cocker named O'Toole wouldn't do

at all, but a red one with that name would fit perfectly and be cute, too.

I'm sorry about my — uh — lack of interest shown in your and Peggy's new clothes, honey, and after this I promise to voice an opinion. Course when you send pictures, I can see and then tell you how I like them. Your plaid dress, for instance. I really liked that.

That is really wonderful about Newberry's, but I just can't understand whats going on back in the states. Do you know that this is the third offer for a job I have had now? I just don't get it. I'll swear they must think the war is over. Don't you get that way, honey, cause I don't want you to be disappointed. Take it from me, this is a rough fight over here and it will be quite some time fore it is done with. All I hope is that by next year this time we'll have them beaten to their knees. However, to get back to Newberry's, if I do dock in New York, I will definitely go up and see Mr. Friant. If the opening offer will give us a living I think I'll take it as I believe I will have the best future with them. It might be tough for a while, traveling around the country and all, but once you get settled to one store you've really got something.

Well, honey, its after 10 o'clock and I'm pretty tired so I guess I'll close for now. Take good care of Peg, darling, and give her a big kiss for me. Night, sweet, I love you and miss you
more than anything in the world. Pray for this mess to end in a hurry, honey, and love me and miss me. All my love. I love you.

Your Sweetheart,
Jack

Wednesday
1 Nov. 1944

Dearest Sweetheart:

Hi, darling. I feel pretty good today for a change. I received 2 wonderful, real long letters from you today. By the way, talking about letters, the officer who censors the mail for the M. P. Detachment where I am working, is in the same office with me and today he got a 60 page letter to censor — a fellow writing to his gal. Can you imagine? 60 pages. He just about passed out and I don't blame him. It took him almost 2 hours to get through it and surprisingly enough, he didn't have to take a thing out at all.

Well, I guess I'll get busy now and answer these letters. Its about 2 o'clock in the afternoon.

Yes, honey, you all with the Red Cross are doing a really wonderful job and if I were you I would definitely continue my work. That is a very little time to put in, considering all they are doing. I don't know what we over here would do if it weren't for the R.C. They are really taking care of us. They arrange entertainment for us, picture shows, etc, and there is always some where you can go for a cup of coffee and a couple of sinkers and have someone to talk to who is understanding. They are really doing a bang-up job and should be supported to the limit by everyone who can do anything to help. Just ask any man who has been overseas and he will tell you. Course, I don't know any thing about the part of the R.C. that you are in, but Lord knows, what you are doing is plenty important.

I'll bet Peg really is getting to be an all time job. Gosh, she is getting so big, honey. I don't like that temper though. Course they all go through that at her age, but it can be controlled. I sure wish I were there, honey, cause I could help a lot. In the first place, I could take care of her and play with her in the evenings and give you a chance to rest a little, after taking care of her all day. The way it is now, you never get a minutes peace, to yourself. Then, too I don't think it is good for her to be brought up among doting grandparents, etc. so to speak. If we were alone, in a place all our own, we could see to it that she minded and could teach her things. Its good that she can be outdoors so much. Its a shame there isn't some way you can let her play in the yard without having to be with her. Then she could stay out more and would give you a chance to get whatever you had to do done. I'll bet she looks just as cute as the deuce in her little overall outfit. I can almost picture her running around the yard in it, with you on her tail constantly. Course she is the most beautiful little gal in the world. It would be darn funny if she wasn't, considering how beautiful her Momma is. Just as long as she doesn't take after her old man. Honey, if I were you I just wouldn't put any stock at all in what you read about us coming home and being discharged, etc., cause if you do you are bound to be disappointed. I'll be home when it is over and not before, and so far there is no definite end in view so just pray that it isn't too much longer and hope.

No, I haven't received any of the Christmas Packges yet, honey. However, I am expecting to any time now. The mail is terribly slow now, due to the Christmas rush, so I expect they will be rather slow. Shucks, honey, I won't be able to have them laying around for two more months without opening them though. I'll just have to have my Christmas a little early this year and in installments.

No, honey, I haven't picked up any of those bad habits you mentioned — Lord forbid! But I'll most likely be a little careless around the house, with my ashes and clothes, etc. till you housebreak me again, but I'm not too bad so don't worry about it.

Well, honey, speaking of always getting everything you wanted and getting your way all the time, I think that is why I married you — so I could give you all those things. I only hope I have given you half of what you needed and wanted. You can just see me getting firm and putting my foot down and saying no in a big loud voice, cant you? Well, that just about finishes this letter. One thing though, the reason why I don't put kisses at the end of my letter is cause I'm not allowed to. You see, they could be worked into some sort of code, they figure, so no kisses. Aint you sorry?

I'll bet that really is a job, trying to get down to the folks house on the street car with the baby and all. She is getting so big, I'll bet she weighs a ton and then to have to carry all the paraphernalia you must have for her with you. You have a terrible time with our daughter, don't you. I know how it is, honey. They get an obstinate streak and won't mind and you just don't know what to do with them. She'll out grow this stage she is going through soon, though. The only thing for you to do is be patient and just be a firm as you can.

Well, darling, that finished up that letter so I guess I'll close for now. I want to drop Joe Barnes and the folks a letter today so I'd better get at it. Bye for now, honey. Love me and miss me a little and take good care of that wonderful big gal of ours and make her as sweet as her Mother. All my love, darling, for always and always.

Your Sweetheart,
Jack

P.S. I love you. I think I'm going to a dance tonight given for the 107th Bn. cadre only. Jealous? Its the first one I've been to since being in the army if I do.

2 Nov 44

Dearest Darling:
I received two wonderful letters from you today which made me feel a little better but I still feel awful lonesome and blue tonight. In fact, I felt so bad I just couldn't stay up in the room even to write so I'm now at one of the reading and writing rooms at the Red Cross writing this. I sure wish I could over come this terrible lonesomeness I have for you and home all the time. I love you so much that all I can do is dream about the day when this horrible mess is over and we can finally be together again and have our own home and bring up our family together. It all seems so far away and kind of hopeless sometimes, though. There just doesn't seem to be any end of this business in sight.

I'm glad you finally got the proofs of the pictures and that they turned out so well. Please hurry and get them to me as I'm so anxious to see how you and Peg look I can hardly wait. You have no idea, honey, how pictures from home help. Just send as many as you can as often as you can. You know, if I do, by any rare chance, happen to get home on a Saturday night, I believe I'll just not let you know I'm coming and walk in on you at the U.S.O. Wouldn't you be surprised, though. I believe you wouldn't even know me or believe it was me for a minute or two and then you'd just about faint. You all must be finally causing some talk around, to draw that many fellows at one time. Yes, I guess I would be rather worn out if I did decide to come home for next Saturday. That would be quite a swim.

That is wonderful how good Peg is about going to bed and going to sleep without any fuss. When I think of those sleepless nights we had in Birmingham with her it makes me shudder. Remember the night I sat up with her all night, rocking her so you could get some rest. We really had a time with that little gal for a while.

So you think you've been dreaming about when I come home. You don't know what dreaming is till you know how much I dream of the day they tell me I can go home for good. I wonder how civilian life will be after being in the Army so long. It will be kind of hard to get used to right at first I expect. Well, it is getting late so I'll close for tonight and hit the hay. Be sure and give Peg a big kiss for me and remember me in your prayers. All my love for always, to the most wonderful sweetheart in the whole world. Miss you, too. Night, honey.

Your Sweetheart,
Jack

P.S. I love you.
Excuse the paper but it was the best I could do tonight. Bye for now.

Me.

Saturday 4
Nov. 44
(and Sunday)

Dearest Sweetheart:
Well, honey, I missed writing you last night and I really should have missed tonight as I worked till

after Midnight last night and it is 11 o'clock now and I just got off and I have to work tomorrow and most likely tomorrow night. I am on a new job, temporarily though, as the fellow who usually has it, a T/4 is on furlough. I am handling all the cases of the whole Depot now in the Staff Judge Advocates Office and it is a man size job. However it did flatter me that out of all the clerks he had to chose from, the Captain in charge requested me for the job. Although there is quite a bit of work to it, it is really interesting and I have enjoyed it. It doesn't look like I'll be able to get a complete letter off to you tonight, honey, but I received a letter from you today and wanted to at least start answering it. I know how I hate for you to miss a day and I imagine you are the same way. One reason is cause it does me a lot of good to talk things over with you and makes me feel so much closer to you. For once I can say I haven't been lonesome or blue for the last couple of days. Course I've missed you something terrible but I haven't had time to think about it, I've been so busy, and believe it or not I am feeling much better than usual tonight, too. By the way, I got a new bunk or room mate. He is a married fellow about my age with a baby about 18 months old. Really a nice fellow. We, by the way, are planning another one or two day trip to London this weekend, as he hasn't been up there yet and also there are quite a few more things I would like to see and also I would like to try to get a few pictures, etc, to send to you. I'll write you all about it when I return. Well, darling, I was going to try to write a few pages tonight, but I'm so tired I can hardly keep my eyes open and besides, I am keeping Larry awake, so I think I'd better quit for tonight. I'll finish this tomorrow sometime and promise to make it a nice long one to make up for the last couple of days. Sweet dreams. I love you more than anything in the world.

Hi, honey. Well, I finally got back to this letter but it is Sunday night now, and about 10 o'clock or a little after and I just got off work, and I'm tuckered out, but I'm going to get a nice letter off to you tonight or die in the attempt. One consolation anyway, is that I go back to my old job tomorrow which should give me plenty of time to write again and I'll be able to keep up my correspondence. One thing I do want to mention, honey, fore I forget, though, is that if at any time you might go a few weeks or a month without hearing from me, don't worry, as it will be because of security reasons that I won't be able to write. One reason I'm mentioning this is that I met a fellow today whose wife had gotten all excited cause she hadn't heard from him for almost 2 months and had contacted the R.C. and Army, etc, to find out why, causing quite a bit of trouble all around, while all the time this fellow was on an assignment, which was very secretive and for security reasons hadn't been able to write or receive any mail for two months. I have no idea that this will happen to me but in case it should I want you to be able to figure out why you aren't hearing from me. You know, that if anything had happened to me you would hear from the government in a very short time just what is wrong. No news is good news.

As far as taking a vacation like I was talking about, to Washington, etc, I know that is out of the question, cause I have to get back to work, and it may be that I won't be able to take even a week off, but I get a heck of a big kick out of planning and talking and dreaming about taking trips. You'll just have to realize the position I'm in when I write. I'm lonesome for you and it helps to dream about being with you on things like that. I think of all the won-derful things I've seen and of how much you would enjoy them and how much fun it would be for me to be able to show them to you. To sum it all up, honey, after being over here for so long, the states look so wonderful (you really wake up to the fact of how much they mean to you and how much you love that big hunk of country over there). You dream about getting back and even catch yourself believing that everything will be peaches and cream when you come marching home and you will be as free as a bird, without thinking that you might need money to do all these wonderful things you have dreamt about. I could go on for pages telling you the things I miss and what I think about and all, but I think that covers it pretty well. About half the time, you live in sort of a dream world over here, to get away from reality, the realization that you are so far away from home and you finally believe that when you go back, it will be to a land of milk and honey. I guess all this I've written sounds kind of silly, and I expect it is just that, but it helps when you really get low and blue, to just forget everything around you and let your imagination run wild.

Sometimes you get the quakes when you think of the life ahead of you?!! Honey, how do you think I feel. It is quite a responsibility, raising a family, and I've got to be able to produce enough to give us everything we need, to have enough to give our child(ren) what they need, in the way of education, etc. It wasn't so bad; I didn't worry about it while I was home, still a civilian, working and making a good living, but when I think of coming back & being dumped out of the army, not having any thing, with a family thrown back on me to support and not even having a job and having to start over from the bottom again at my age, it really gives me the shakes. All I hope is, that I can make as decent a living for us when I come out as I was making when I went in the army, and that in the end we can be as secure and have what the folks have. It is really not going to be easy for us at first and I'm afraid we are destined to see some hard times. I intend to go with Newberry's and really shouldn't have any trouble getting on with them, after the interest they have shown. But even going with them right off, we won't have it too easy cause my salary will be rather small I imagine.

As far as how much money we will have when I do finally get home, honey, depends largely on just how far I go in the army and how much longer I stay in the army. After I become assigned, if ever, and get started bucking for ratings; and get one, why I intend to keep sending more money home as I can afford it and we will be able to save that. If I could finally get a decent rating out of this business, we could really save some dough. I figure if we could by some rare chance have 5 or 6 or 7 hundred bucks saved by the time I get home we would be ok. I would like to figure on getting a good car just as soon as possible after I do get home so we could use it right off to travel in to any city I am sent to with Newberry's.

I received the President's speech and really enjoyed it. I won't go into my political views here as I want to finish off this letter and close as I am so tired I hardly know what I'm saying and if I get started on politics I'd be good for a least another 3 pages on why I'd vote for you know who. I'm sure anxious to finally get those pictures and the wallet and all. I look forward to my mail every day in hopes but so far no luck.

Well, honey, I must close now and go to bed as I'm about to drop dead in my tracks. I'll write a nice long one tomorrow though. Night, honey.

Military Pass to visit London. 9 November 1944 to 11 November.

Sweet dreams and love me and miss me a little. Give Peg a big kiss for me and say a prayer.

All my love to my two sweet wonderful little gals. I love you and miss you more than you'll ever know.

Your Sweetheart,
Jack

P.S. I love you.
(Our entire family voted for President Roosevelt.)

6 Nov. 44
Monday

Dearest Darling:

Well, honey, I'm getting a little earlier start this evening, it being about 8:30 so may be I can get both you and the folks a nice long letter off. Course you come first and then if I have time I'll write them.

I am planning another trip to London and if nothing happens to change our plans I'll write you all about it Sunday. This fellow, Pierce Lawrence, who is bunking with me now, has never been up so I'm going to take a trip with him and try to see all the stuff I missed and also get a refresher on the stuff I have already seen but didn't write you about. By all rights I should have a better time this trip as it is always more fun to go with someone and you get around to more places than by yourself. I think I told you about Larry in one of my other letters, but in case I didn't, he is a clerk in the same boat as me, is married and has a little girl just a few months older than Peg and is about 28 years old. A really nice fellow, too.

So our daughter is old enough to have tea parties now. That is really cute. Gosh, honey, when you write and tell me things like that I just can hardly believe it possible that our little girl could grow so fast. I'll swear, honey, it seems like just last week or so that I was up all night with a red ugly looking little thing listening to her yell and feeling so sorry for her being covered with heat and impetigo and not knowing what to do.

I am looking forward to these [socks] you are working on now cause they are from you and made by you and every time I look at my feet I'll think of — no I don't mean that, my goodness, what was I about to say. Seriously, though, they will really be wonderful these cold wintry days. So nice and warm. And, too, over here your feet are always cold cause the ground is always damp and cold and the floors of the buildings never do warm up because of the inadequate heating facilities. Boy, they'll really be swell for these cold nights, too, cause I will most likely start sleeping with something on my feet at night as they are always so cold.

About my glasses, honey. In the first place I am just a little afraid to get new lenses for them over here and in the second place I can't afford them so I'm afraid my GI's will have to do till I can get home to have the others fixed. Tell you what, though, when I come home I just won't wear any till I get my civies fixed, how will that be?

Gosh, sweet, you don't dream about me coming home and what we will do and where we will go and everything any more than I do. Yes, I think the very first thing we had better do when I do finally get there is buy a car as we will very definitely need one to go wherever Newberry's might send me. I dread to think of doing anything in the way of traveling without a car. For the first year or two we are going to have to save every extra cent we can lay our hands on toward the day when we finally settle down in some city permanently, then we will maybe have enough to go ahead and buy our own house. I'm not sure but I think we will still be able to take advantage of this G.I. bill of rights on buying the house then. As I said, I think the only thing we need and should get is a car, to move from place to place more economically. That way, by the time Peg is five or six years old we will be able to have a nice house and place for her to grow up in. What we will do, is have our last little fling when I come home, by taking our few days at Montauk. Then we will knuckle down and get busy building for the future. Here endeth the lesson — Price's Five Year plan.

Honey, I really think that knitting just one sock big enough for both feet would be very impractical for me. You must remember, honey, that I'm in the Infantry and it would be hard as hell, considering all the marching I have to do, to have to hop all the time, and besides I don't think I could get a shoe big enough for both feet to fit into.

Well, honey, it is now after 11 and I am tired and have a big day ahead of me tomorrow so I guess I'd better close for now. Besides, 7 pages should make fairly good reading and I have finished answering your letter. Goodnight, darling. Love me and miss me. Give Peg a big kiss for me and take good care of our wonderful gal. Say a prayer, too, honey. All the love in the world to the most wonderful sweetheart there is from your "Daddy whats in the war"!! Sweet dreams.

Your Sweetheart,
Jack

P.S. I love you.

Friday
17 Nov. 1944

Dearest Darling:

Well, sweet, I am getting a fairly early start tonight so maybe I'll be able to get off a nice long letter. Its only about 9 o'clock now which gives me quite a bit of time. I'm not kidding, honey, I'm so tired out from working every night I don't know what to do. I didn't get to write you last night again cause I went out of town yesterday and didn't get in till after 3 o'clock this morning. I can't tell you where I went or what I did but I sure worked. Then I had to get up at 7 o'clock this morning and start all over again. I've worked now, every night this week and tonight is the earliest I have gotten off. All I hope is that all this work I'm putting in does me some good.

I haven't received any mail from my sweetheart for the last two days either which doesn't make me feel any better. You know, though, the only thing I like about working like I have been, is that since it started I haven't been so all fired homesick like I was. It helps a lot to be too busy to think about it. Just think, by the time you get this we will have four very wonderful years together behind us. How I wish I could be there with you on that day. Lets both just hope and pray that there aren't any more that we have to spend apart. And as far as Christmas, I don't even think about it. I'm just going to pretend this year didn't even have a Christmas in it. Course, I don't really mean that cause I am going to Church and I am going to have a Christmas tree and decorations and everything, but honey, it will be so lonely and unlike Christmas without you with me. I wish this horrible mess was over and we could all come back home and live like human beings again.

Gosh, honey, my socks sound wonderful and I can hardly wait to get them. It has turned real cold over here the last week and I'll swear my feet are never warm. It is always so damp and wet all the time your feet never do get warm. I'll really be able to put them to good use. I was sort of worrying about the knots and everything that would have to be in them, honey. Be very careful as you know I'm in the Infantry and have a lot of hoofing to do, and you have no idea what havoc even a wrinkle in your sock can play with your feet.

Well, everyone can be friendly again now as the election is over. All I can say is Thank the Good Lord he won. I was really sweating that election out. I don't know what would have happened to the country had Henry Aldrich won it.

It sure makes me happy, honey, to hear about Ollie. It would have been a darn shame if they had put him in the army. I am really happy for him. I guess he is plenty relieved, too. Well, honey, I've got to quit now and go hunt up some coal to steal. Be back shortly. Bye now. I love you.—

Hi, honey. Here I am again to finish this up and hit the hay. We got our load of coal so we will at least be warm for another week.

Honey, that daughter of ours is without a doubt the sweetest most wonderful little gal I've ever seen. I'll swear I have seen and heard of a lot of kids but from what you say she is the best natured, well behaved little thing. What amazes me most is how she can be awakened anytime and always has a smile, and never cries. Gosh, sweet, you have really done a wonderful job. I don't expect there is a more wonderful wife or Momma in the whole world. I am constantly amazed at how I happened to be so darn lucky.

What do you mean I used to think anything you made was so wonderful? I still do and everything you made was wonderful, too. Thats why I'm so anxious to get those socks.

I will be so glad when this is over and we can come back home. It will be so wonderful to be able to live normal lives again and bring up our family and have each other. I never want to be away from you again and I'm not going to be either. There is one thing I have been wondering and worrying a little about though when I get home, whether I'll be able to settle down again. Naturally, I'll have changed some (not much though). The one big thing that will help get me back to normal though, will be Peg, and knowing and realizing what a responsibility I have, making you and Peg at least a comfortable living as I was making fore I left home.

My goodness, honey, you are really taking your politics seriously. I sure get a kick out of your little talks, speeches, almost, on this election. I sure was relieved to see the election come out as it did, anyway.

Yes, honey, I think my favorite season is the fall too — as long as it is in the States. Over here it is miserable. It has been raining for so long I've forgotten what the sun looks like. You know, England has only three seasons — early winter, winter, and late winter, or else rainy season, wet season, and damp season. You know the old saying that the sun never sets on the British Empire. Well it never rises on England.

I just can't seem to get enough news about that wonderful daughter of ours. She does so many darn cute things. You don't know how I envy you, sweet,

Andover Junction Station. Signal box from 1890's, in use until 1973.

A Junction Hotel Pub, Andover Hotel named after railway station.

being with her every day watching her grow up. When I finally do get home, she'll be a big girl all grown up. I received the new pictures of Peg — the snaps I mean — and gosh I could hardly believe that was the same child as what the last pics showed. You weren't in enough of them. I like pictures of Peg but I want some of you, too, so after this how about having someone else take the pictures of both you and Peg together. Yes, darling, I definitely believe, if you have her vaccinated, you should have it done on her leg, as it sometimes leaves such an ugly scar. Too, having it on her leg, it isn't as apt to attract her attention as much while it is healing.

The only reason I knew your Dad had written that poem, hon, is because I have read some of his stuff before and recognized his style right away. You know, he is very good.

Well, that finishes up all the letters I have from you and catches me up to date again. I guess I'd better quit now, and get to bed as it is almost midnight again and I'm dead tired. Goodnight, sweet dreams, honey, love me and miss me. I love you more than any thing and am just counting the days, hours and minutes, as close as I can figure, till this Johnny can come marching home to his sweetheart. Give Peg a big kiss for me darling and say a prayer.

All my love, for always. I love you.

Your Sweetheart,
Jack

Sunday
19 Nov. 44

Dearest Darling:

Well, honey, another weekend is almost over and it has ended a week of a lot of plenty hard work and very little mail from home. Course I haven't been able to keep my end up, as far as writing is concerned, this last week. It all started by me taking that darn pass last week. It seemed like I never did get caught up from it and then with that new job I got, it really kept me busy. By the way, honey, speaking of passes reminds me I discontinued that $20 allotment to you today which means you won't get that extra check in January, but I will start it up again so February or March you will start receiving it. The reason is that the 1st of January or there abouts I am going on a short furlough I believe and I'll need that extra dough, plus any you can spare me. I had to discontinue it before the 20th of November in order to draw the $20, Dec 31st payday. I expect to take an extended tour of the U.K. and see all the sights I can — that is — if nothing happens to where I won't get it. I'd like to go to all the coastal towns and Oxford and Cambridge and see the Cliffs of Dover and just make a regular sightseeing tour of it. You can tell the folks that if they want to give me a nice Christmas present, they can just send me a Money Order instead of any presents. The way I figure is that this will be the only chance I'll get to see England as we'll never be able to come over, so I might as well get out and enjoy myself.

You know, when Pierce and I were in London the other day we got there so we could see the changing of the guard and I'll be derned if it didn't go and rain and they call the whole thing off when it rains so we missed it again. However we did see them practicing the next day and I've never seen such a snappy bunch of soldiers. They really looked wonderful. Course, as I told you before, they don't wear their fancy uniforms during wartime which takes away a lot of the beauty of the thing. But it would still be well worth seeing. We did get to see Madame Tussuads (?) and it was really interesting. I'll swear the wax figures look like you could almost talk to them. In fact, they had a wax figure dressed in the uniform of the attendant and you would be surprised at the amount of people who stopped and talked to him, some of them for quite a while, before they finally realized it was just a wax figure. We really had a good time this trip, though, as we went into pubs all over London and traveled in to the slums, like Lambeth, etc. and I'll swear it is like something out of a book. The most miraculous thing of all, though, is the spirit of the people, even after the bombings they have had and are still getting, which has and is terrific. They still laugh and make cracks about it and go right on with their every day life. You really have to hand it to these people over here after all they've been through.

How is Peggy? Has she finally gotten all those new teeth in or is she still cutting them? Poor little gal(s) — you, too, cause when she is fretful, it makes quite a job for you. Its a shame that they have to go through so much when cutting teeth. They are always so upset from it. Well it won't be much longer before it will all be over anyway, as she has just about all of them now. At least, all of them that will cause so much trouble.

Well, I got a half a day off today for a change and so I spent my afternoon at the football field watching a real old-fashioned American football game. Our Depot team played a Navy team and we won, too, 15 to 0. I really enjoyed it though. You'd be surprised how that helps. For two hours I was able to forget completely about the Army and being away from home and thoroughly enjoy myself. We really do have a swell team and they play some good ball. The most of the fellows on the team are ex-college or ex-pro players so really it is just as good, or better really, than a college game as there is quite a rivalry between the ground forces and air forces or navy and they really do fight.

Well, honey, next Thursday is Thanksgiving and also the day after our anniversary. I'll be thinking about you poor civilians and hoping you have a nice Thanksgiving dinner, too, while I'm eating my Turkey. Yep, we will have Turkey and all the trimmings, and from what I hear, that is a lot more than what a lot of folks back home will be having.

I've just stopped thinking about coming home. I've sort of acclimated myself to what I have and you would be surprised how much better I have been feeling. I've been going out more to shows and with the fellows of an evening to the local pub for a few beers and just getting my mind off things. In fact it even worried you, cause you mentioned it in one of your letters.

Every time I think of the 22nd being our fourth anniversary I can hardly believe it. It just doesn't seem possible that 4 years could go by in such a short time. Just think honey, it has been 9 years since we first met, too. The last four years have been the most wonderful years of my life and every day has made me that much more convinced that I'm the luckiest rascal in the world to have married such a wonderful gal. At the day in 1940 I didn't think it was possible to love any one as much as I did you, let alone that my love could increase. Honey, I can hardly wait till this is all over and I can come back home and we can start bringing up our daughter together and thinking about increasing our family a little, too, cause Peg definitely needs a brother.

I guess I'll close for now as I would like to drop the folks a little line. Good night darling. Remember me in your prayers and love me and miss me. Give Peg a big kiss for me, too. Night, honey. Sweet dreams,

Your Sweetheart,
Jack

P.S. I love you,

Monday 20
November 1944

Dearest sweetheart:

Well, darling, the ice was finally broken today, and I received a letter from you at long last. You wrote it Saturday the 28th of Oct. I expect with this Christmas rush and all, it is about the best you can get.

Honey, I understand when you miss writing me you can't help it and if you possibly can you'll write me every day. I know you understand about me missing a few days writing you. There are things that come up and you just can't help but miss once in a while.

My trouble now with writing is that I've written on about every subject I can think of so many times that I'm just about writ out. At least you have something new to write about every day. Cause you know I never get tired of hearing about Peg and the cute things she does and am always dying for news about her so you shouldn't and apparently don't have any trouble writing a wonderful reading letter every time.

I am very down in the dumps. It has been very nasty and cold over here and raining for the last two weeks without let up and I'm so sick of this horrible weather I don't know what to do. Oh to have the sunshine just once in a while, what a relief it would be. I think one of my trouble is, although I wouldn't tell anyone but you about it, that I am itching to get moving again. I'm getting so I can't stay in one spot more than a few months before I've got the itch to be on the move again.

I'm looking forward so much to that furlough I have coming up I don't know what to do. I believe I'm going to try to live in Hotels instead of Red Cross for the whole seven days and just act like a civilian again and forget all about the darn army. I'll swear I need a furlough.

I sure wish, honey, that those socks would hurry up and get here as you have no idea how bad I need them. With this cold damp weather my feet are constantly cold.

Every letter I get from you, telling me about Peg just makes me more amazed. I'll swear I just can't get over how she has grown. She is a regular little girl now. I'm sure tickled that she is so crazy about outdoors as that really makes for a healthy child you know. I'll bet she is cute as a bug running around the yard in her little overalls and all bundled up and playing in the leaves and everything. Gosh, honey, I would give a million dollars (If I had any more than an American dime and an English penny right now) to be able to see her and play with her and everything that a Daddy is supposed to do with his big daughter. Well, lets just hope this mess doesn't last too much longer so that I'll soon be able to do all those things. I still haven't received those new pictures of you and the baby or any of the Christmas packages except that one I told you about.

When I stop and think that just 2 days from today we will be celebrating 4 years of married life I can hardly believe it. It seems like just the other day, we were standing in front of the Minister at Grace Church and then riding down to Webster in that Lincoln Zephyr to have our pictures taken and the reception and Charles and Letty taking us home and how Letty cried. She was so jealous cause it was us instead of them. Remember?

You know, honey, I'm almost sorry to hear that Charlie made it through primary training. He is going to have a plenty rough time of it. I wonder whether he will be a bomber or fighter pilot. By the way, he is very close to being over the age limit for a pilot isn't he? I imagine he is too old for fighter planes and they'll put him in bombers. By the way, what is Bobby Stueber doing now?

I sometimes wish I could apply for OCI honey, but I'm afraid that is out — especially over here. For one reason, I don't have the qualifications and besides I haven't the military experience, as, although I've been in the Army about 16 months now, I've never been assigned to any job so that I could work for something like that. I have absolutely nothing on my record which would indicate that I was OCI material so I guess you'll just have to be satisfied with a private husband honey, as it looks like the war is going to end before I ever get assigned to an outfit at the rate I'm going now.

Well, honey, this is rather short, but I am finished answering your letter and I worked tonight and didn't get off till around 10 and its about midnight now and I'm tired, so I expect I'd better hit the hay. Night Darling. Sweet dreams, and love

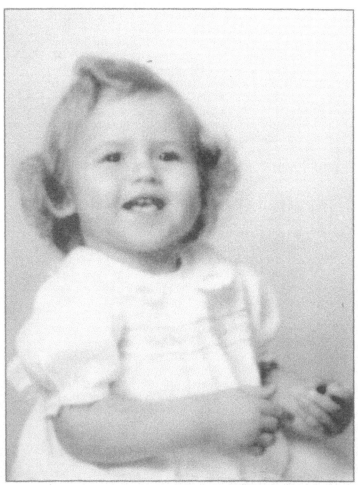

Peggy, October 2, 1944. Merry Christmas, Daddy.

me and miss me and don't forget me in your prayers. Give Peg a big kiss for me too.

All my love, honey, forever and ever.
Your sweetheart,
    Jack

P.S. I love you.
A million kisses, too!

(Charles and Letty Steuber were old friends.)

Monday
20 November 44

Dear Mom and Pop:

Well, folks, it has been quite some time since I last found a little time to drop you all a few lines. I've received quite a few letters from you and Dad, too, the last few days, but I have been so darned busy the last couple of weeks, I have even had to let Babes letters slip. I have a new job now, that has been keeping me busy day and night. Another thing is that I have an opportunity of taking a furlough the end of December and I am bucking like the very devil so that nothing happens to keep me from taking it as it would really give me a chance to get out and see some of England. By the way, instead of buying me any thing for Christmas, if you want to give me a real Christmas present you can just send a Money Order to sort of help my furlough fund along a little. I have discontinued Babes allotment for the month of December so that I can draw $30 the end of December, but I'm afraid that won't go very far with 7 days to spend. I plan on using my credit a little too, however, and should be able to increase that $30 to about $50 by making a touch here and there, but I'll still have to pay that back the next month which would put me right back in the hole again, so anything you care to donate — but fast — will be duly appreciated. I sure wish to the devil I would ship as when I made that allotment I was figuring that I was on my way to France and wouldn't need it, but as long as I stay here I really do need more than $10 a month, as that hardly buys my necessities.

I guess Babe told you about my trip to London last week. We had something very unusual happen to us. On the way back to camp we met two girls about my age. We started a conversation with them and ended up by being invited to these friends home that they were visiting. They were both from London and were on their way to this small town right outside of camp to visit some people. Of course, we gladly accepted and we really met a wonderful family. We had tea with them — they even made coffee for us — and then the girls who we met were going to a dance on an army installation near town so we were going to walk them to the dance and then go on back to camp. The reason for us not going to the dance was that we, the other fellow with me and myself, were both flat broke, and besides the dance was located at a place where we wouldn't have been able to get back to town in time to catch the last train into camp. Well, on the way to the dance we passed a pub and everyone, there were a few more couples with us, decided to go in for a beer. Well, we told the girls we were broke but to no avail. We went in and had a beer and the others left, but the girls we were with decided they would rather stay at the pub with us till train time, so we sat there from 7

till 10:15 drinking beer on them. The most unusual part of the whole business was, though, that they were both married and one of them was married November 22, 1940 — Babe and my anniversary and the other ones name was Peggy Price — in fact — her Christian name was Margaret Jeanne Price — can you imagine that? When I told them, they just about passed out.

I guess before I go any farther, I'd better explain what a pub in England is like so you won't get the wrong impression. It is a place usually run by a man and woman and is considered sort of a meeting place for the neighborhood for an evening of beer and conversation — they are all usually ultra respectable. The one we were in had a big fireplace with a fire burning and all these people sitting around talking and singing together. It was really wonderful and I believe I had a better time then than I have had since being over here.

Yes, Pop, I received another letter from Mr. Bunch today, which makes the second I have received. I have already answered the first one, as you most likely know by now.

Well, how did you folks like the way the election came out? As far as I'm concerned and the majority of the boys over here too, I'm as tickled as can be that the old man won again as I just couldn't see Dewey.

Well, folks, I hate to cut this so short but I must get on a letter to Babe tonight, too. By the way, I haven't received any of the Christmas packages yet but I have hopes of getting them sometime in the next couple of months. Goodnight. Take care of yourselves and kinda keep an eye out for Babe and Peg for me and write soon.

All my love,
Your Son,
Jack

Wednesday
22 Nov. 44

Dearest Sweetheart: — Happy Anniversary edition —

Well, darling, here I am but not for too long. I did receive the registered letter today with the M.O. for five bucks and the wonderful pictures. I don't see why you didn't put a little note, even a page would do, in with it, though. Thank you a lot for the dough, honey. I could really use it now as I'm flat, but I've put it away, instead, and am saving it for that furlough of mine. As long as I keep it in Money Order form I won't be tempted to spend it. I'll pay my bills out of my pay day and then just sit tight and not do anything to spend money till the end of December and that way maybe I'll have a few bucks for my trip. I haven't definitely made any plans as yet as to where I'm going, but am going to a few of the bigger cities of Scotland and the part of Ireland that isn't off limits to us, and all the bigger towns in England. I think I'll just travel from one place to the other so I can see everything possible that is really worth seeing. Course for that week you won't receive too many letters from me, I'm afraid, but I'll drop you post cards thru the Red Cross from every place I visit. I'm really looking forward to the trip, though and I hope I'm not counting my chickens before they are hatched.

Thank you, Darling, that is the most wonderful Christmas present I could wish for. I just can't keep from staring at them (the pictures). I can't get over Peg's teeth. She is so darling, honey and I'll swear, looking at her picture I just think I can't stand being away from her another minute. She has the cutest darn smile I've ever seen. You know, honey, she is developing an awful lot of your features and I was really surprised to see how much she looks like you. Her hair is really coming out nice, too, isn't it. It is getting nice and long. She is darn near a blondie like I used to be. I think I've showed them to almost every guy in this camp already and I guess the guys I bum with are sick of hearing me talk about my pictures and showing them to everyone. I don't care, though, cause you have no idea what a proud papa I am and so proud of having such a beautiful wife and daughter, Ive just got to show them off or I'll pop with pride. That is really a darling picture of you and Peg together honey. You both look so cute. It made me think, you know what would be cute is that after Peg gets a little older you and she should have dresses made alike — you know what I mean. I think that is awfully cute and I don't know, but for some reason, it would just go wonderful on you. I just looked again and I noticed what sparking and sharp eyes Peg is getting. I sure hope she takes after her mother in that respect cause I have never seen anyone with more beautiful eyes than you, honey. You know, not to change the subject, but I think that is one of the first things I noticed about you and the one thing that tied me up in knots like this, when we first started going together.

Just think, darling, four years ago today, if I was home, right this minute, I was still at the darn office on pins and needles while those guys at York, just for darn orneryness were keeping me there till the last minute giving me presents and kidding the daylights out of me, while I was trying to get away to get married. I finally got ready although, to this day, I can't remember how, in my slick new double breasted pin stripe suit — I was really sharp. We finally got to the church and everyone was running around like chickens with their heads cut off — and then you came. I never will forget that, honey. You were so beautiful and I was so much in love with you (still am, too). I just couldn't keep my eyes off you. I never, as long as I live, will forget waiting while you came down the aisle and how sweet you looked. Then, all of a sudden Betsy popped up with that "There's Jack." Then when it was all over we stood up in back of the church and shook hands and kissed all these people we had never seen before and tried to look glad because we saw them while all the time we were both wishing they would hurry up and get out and let us go. Then back to the reception for a hectic 2 hours. We finally did get away and Lettey and Charlie took us down to the apartment. The one thing I'm more thankful for than anything else is that you talked me in to having a nice church wedding. We really did have a wonderful wedding and I'll never forget it or how sweet you looked as long as I live. It is just like it happened yesterday, to me in my memory. I can remember every little detail of the whole day. It sure doesn't seem possible that it all happened 4 years ago. I'm just about the luckiest guy in the world, I guess. Honey, I loved you so much then that every time I looked at you I thought my heart would just pop and that love has just increased a little bit each day. I can't help but think of you every minute, and hope and pray about the day when this mess is all over and I can come back home to my sweetheart and my lil' gal, too. Honey, it is really agony to

love someone so much, especially being away from them, till you think that you've just got to see her someway.

Well, tomorrow is Thanksgiving, I have to get up bright and early cause we are having a big football game here tomorrow afternoon that I would like to see and I'll have a lot of work to do tomorrow morning if I try to get away for the game, so I need my beauty sleep. I would really like to go to church tomorrow but I'm afraid that is out so I guess I'll just rely on you saying a prayer for me.

Well, goodnight, sweet dreams. A happy Anniversary darling — and I'm brokenhearted (really, too) that I couldn't be with you today. Lets both just pray that next year this time we'll be together again and never have to be apart again.

Give Peg a big kiss for me, honey, and take good care of our big girl and her Momma, too. Say hello to the folks for me and don't forget the prayers.

Your sweetheart
Jack

P.S. I love you —   A million kisses, too—

Thanksgiving
23 November 44

Dearest Darling:
How are you on this Thanksgiving day? I guess you are just about to sit down to a great big Turkey dinner about now. Well, we finished ours and it was really a lulu, too. Then we all took the afternoon off and went to the football game. Man, we really saw a wonderful game. The winner of this game today, which was us, is playing for the ETO U.K. Championship in White City stadium in a week or so and I'm sure going to do every thing I can to be there. During the half of the game today they had a turkey-run on the field. The way they worked it was to issue 40 cards to various fellows who bought tickets at the gate. Then they put 20 of them on one side of the field and 20 on the other and then turned a big beautiful Turkey loose in the middle. The fellow who caught it got a turkey dinner at the Red Cross tonight with all the trimmings for he and 7 of his buddies. Man, you should have seen the scramble.

This has been a fairly nice day for me. I received 4 letters from you, a Christmas card from you and Peg and a letter from Dad. Not bad, eh?

Yes, honey, quite a few of the boys did vote over here, but it was far from what they expected and won't make a lot of difference one way or another in the way the election turns out. The fellows seemed to be not too interested for the most part in which way the thing turned out. You know, really, there is only one thing that any of us are thinking particularly about and that is getting this mess over with over here and getting back home. No, there was a definite lack of interest as a general rule, as far as the soldiers and the election were concerned.

About that poem, honey, the English Girls' Lament, it so happens I did send it to the Stars and Stripes and they did publish it. If you'll take particular note in the copies of the S&S you will most likely see it in there.

By now you know, I expect, that the Colonel has moved out and since then I have worked under a Major and now a Captain, but I have been darn lucky in getting really swell officers to work for. I

─ PROBABLE STARTING LINEUPS ─

NO.	12TH REPLACEMENT DEPOT	POS.	B. A. D. # 1 BEARCATS	NO.
15	Wooley	RE	Oltmanns	14
6	Dinwoodie	RT	Klimeck	17
4	H. Reed	RG	Mahoney	4
22	W. Reed	C	Kottomma	22
15	Loskowski	LT	Johnson	19
3	Roland	LG	Mailhos	5
11	Newton	LE	Rust	13
7	Spicer	QB	Filicotti	7
2	Trolio	RHB	Colo	10
1	Domino	LHB	Holt	2
9	Fortier	FB	Holtman	9

OFFICIALS
REFEREE---Sgt. Norman J. Doyle Jr.
UMPIRE----Major Gilbert L. Dailey
HEAD LINESMAN--Major Giles G. Batchelor
FIELD JUDGE---Sgt. Harry Skurnick

12TH REPLACEMENT ORCHESTRA

Music will be furnished before and during the game by the 12th Replacement Depot Orchestra under the direction of S/Sgt. George Bell.

12TH REPL. DEPOT "MOORES MAULERS" VS BASE AIR DEPOT #1 "BEARCATS"

FOOTBALL PROGRAM

Thanksgiving Day THURSDAY NOV. 23RD 2:00 P.M.

OVAL FIEL TIDWORTH

A Special Service Feature

12ᵗʰ Replacement Depot "Moores Maulers"

Col. George A. Moore
COMMANDING

NO.	NAME	POS.	NO.	NAME	POS.
1	T/5 Vincent Domino	B	21	1/Sgt William McCloskey	E
2	Cpl. Nicholas Trolio	B	22	Pvt Willard Reed	C
3	Cpl William Keller	B	23	Pfc Edwin Gnatman	G
4	Sgt Hubert Reed	B	24	Pvt Joseph Vilagi	G
5	S/Sgt Edward Capulli	B	25	Pvt James Enright	E
6	T/5 William Dinwiddie	C			
7	Pvt Russell Spicer	B		Black Jerseys	
8	Pvt Frank Busto	B	1	T/5 Charles Rulsscar	B
9	S/Sgt Orman Fortier	B	2	T/5 George Marquis	E
10	T/5 Frank Lanich	T	3	T/5 Russell Rice	E
11	T/5 Burnhon Newton	E	10	Sgt Edward Willins	B
12	Pvt Donald Coffey	G	11	Cpl Donald Pritchett	T
13	Pfc Arthur Rohlen	T	13	Sgt Clarence Paterick	T
14	Pfc Harold Rouse	T	14	Pvt John Sauzyo	T
15	Pvt David Wooley	E	15	Sgt Donald Edwards	B
16	Pvt Dominic Loskowski	G			
18	Pvt Robert Stefik	B		COACH---1st Lt. Jesse Clark	
19	Pvt Anthony Raffaelle	B		ASS'T COACH---Cpl Joseph Ropko	
20	T/4 Burt C. Page				

BASE AIR DEPOT No. 1 "BEARCATS"

NO.	NAME	POS.	NO.	NAME	POS
1	Gaffney	E	25	Timmrock	E
2	Hole	B	26	Braxton	G
3	Menke	B	27	Filicetti	B
4	Mahoney	G	28	Rodl	C
5	Mialhos	G	29	McGinness	B
6	Fish	G	30	Butler	T
7	Simons	B	31	Laramie	T
8	Saul	B	32	Wendel	B
9	Holtman	B	33	Rudo	T
10	Cole	P	34	Hoot	E
11	Hanna		35	Grecar	T
12	Hahn	T	36	Cardella	G
13	Hust	E	37	Kovacks	G
14	Oltmanns	E	38	Schwenger	B
15	Brown	E	39	Murphy	E
16	Mayer	G	40	McDonnell	
17	Klimect	G	41	Wetmore	G
18	Tafralian	T	42	Cleveland	
19	Johnson	T	43	Biondi	
20	Lafey	T	44	Troxell	
21	Kirwan	G	45	Longo	
22	Kattmann	C	46	Gallant	
23	Welburn	B	47	Tew	
24	Fooger	B			

really believe that this Captain is best of all. I think he is about the best officer I have yet seen since coming in the army, bar none.

Peg sounds so darned cute, honey. This letter was practically three pages of the cute descriptions you write of the things she does and everything and she must really be darling now, and a lot of fun, too. Gosh, honey, how I wish I were there with you now. I sure do hate to be missing all this. Well, we'll just have to get busy and have another when I get home so I can watch it grow up, being I missed Peggy.

No, honey, I won't forget Pop's birthday and I'll try to write him a nice letter or something. Thanks for reminding me, though, cause I hadn't thought anything about it up to now.

Yes, it really was a wonderful concert and I really did enjoy it. The Cathedral was very beautiful, too. You have most likely heard of the (censored) Cathedral, haven't you?

I promise that if I am here during Christmas and get a change to go to London I'll go visit Aunt Winnie's sister. You see, honey, the trouble is that it is really quite expensive to go to London and when I go then I'm broke for the rest of the month and it really makes it hard on me. It takes at least 3 pounds and I don't even draw that much a month.

I'm not going to get into answering any more letters for tonight. I can't seem to get my mind on what I'm writing and I'm tired out. I'll say goodnight for now. Sweet dreams, darling. Love me, honey and miss me.

All my love, for always to the sweetest most wonderful girl in the world.

Your Sweetheart,
Jack

P.S. Don't forget my kiss for Peg or the prayers.
I love you.

Sunday
26 November 1944

Dear Mom and Dad:

Well, folks I received a letter from both of you today. I guess Babe told you about the trip I'm planning to take, I guess I told you, too, so this fiver goes into the bank along with the one I got from Babe to help finance it. It will really come in handy.

Well, the weather over here has turned off real cold the last couple of days and you have no idea how thankful I am to have such swell living quarters. I only hope I stay here till warm weather sets in again. I'm sitting in front of my fireplace now with my feet propped up on the bed, writing this and keeping really nice and warm.

That is the first I had heard of them making a rehabilitation center out of Jeff Barracks. I don't imagine you see as many soldiers in town now as you used too. They have some pretty rough boys in camps like that so I guess every once in a while you do get some excitement in St. Louis from it.

Yes, Mom, I've been to London twice now and it was really wonderful. After spending so long a time in these small villages and army camps it is really a relief to get out to a really big city for a change and act like a human being again. It gives you a lift to where you can come back feeling fresh and get to work again.

I sure would give anything in the world to see Peg again. She sounds so darn cute and has grown so much. I can hardly realize it is possible to have a daughter that big.

I was sure sorry to hear about Tommy Harkey. You know, quite a few fellows in my class have been killed in action now. I was reading in that school paper you sent me, the names of all the fellows I knew and used to run around with and was really amazed.

No, Mom, I haven't received the Hershey's or the Christmas packages yet. It is strange, too, cause you folks mailed them very early and I have received a package from Sister already that was sent in October — about the 15th. I sure don't understand it, and wish they would hurry and come through before I move again. The ones you mailed to my old address, I can understand why they aren't here, as they are taking a tour of the continent but the ones mailed to this APO should have been here by now.

That is swell about the flowers, Mom, and thanks a lot. I was really wishing I could have sent Babe a little something for our anniversary but the best I could do was the cablegram.

Dad, when you try comparing the dampness and the climate of Florida with this climate over here, as you did, it is like trying to compare that Congregational Church that Mom goes to with Westminster Abbey. I guarantee you that you don't have any conception of what a damp, clammy climate is. And no, I'm afraid we aren't fortunate enough to have sheets. In fact we are damn lucky to have 4 blankets as the quota is only 3. You know I guess what the three seasons are in England, by the way, don't you? Well, in case you don't, they are Early winter, winter and late winter — or else, damp, rainy and wet.

Well folks that about winds it up for tonight, so I guess I'll close and hit the hay. Write soon and take care of your self and that family of mine.

All my love,
Jack

Friday
1 December 1944

Dearest Sweetheart:

Well, darling, another day with no mail from you and if I ever needed a letter, today was the day. I feel so blue and lonesome for you, and am so homesick for some reason. One reason, I guess is that every day closer Christmas gets the worse I feel. I get to thinking of the wonderful Christmas' we've had and thinking about home and how everything is all decorated and how the family all gets together and honey, its all I can do to stand it. When I think of being away, on this Christmas, especially with Peg just old enough to really enjoy it, it is really tough. I thought I could just make myself forget home and not write about it at all but if I don't tell you about it, I'll bust or something. I'll say this much, I'm definitely not cut out to be a soldier. I love my family too much. If I could only talk to you for a little bit and hear your voice it would help. That kept me going while I was in the states. There was always that thought that if any thing was wrong at home I could call up and talk to you. But here, I'm so darn far away from you, that if you did need me I could never get there and do anything at all.

How is Peggy, honey? I guess I wouldn't know her now as I expect she has grown so, she is like a real little girl instead of the little old baby she was before I left. How is the talking coming along? I expect she is saying quite a few words now and is learning new things to say all the time. Lord, honey, what I wouldn't give to see her and be able to play with her and everything for just a little while. You be sure to keep her as sweet as you say she is, honey, and try not to let her forget her Daddy. One thing, I shouldn't be too unfamiliar to her when I get home, cause of the way you have worked it with that picture of me.

Well, I was going to take a trip to London over the week-end but I expect I'll sit around camp here instead and enjoy it while I still have a little time to do so. All I hope is that I'm still here by Christmas. There is really not a lot to do in London after you have once seen the sights — unless, of course, you are interested in female companionship — which I'm definitely not. Can't get my mind off my two wonderful girls at home long enough to get interested or to interest any. Aren't you glad?!! Anyway, there is a football game here Sunday that I would like to see so I guess I'll just stay home and take it and a movie in and call it a big weekend.

I'll sure be glad when Christmas is over and our mail gets back to normal again. The Christmas rush has slowed it down something terrible.

Everything over here, honey, is just about the same as usual — including the lousy weather. Rumors, ugly ones have been flying fast and thick the last couple of days that have everyone, including yours truly, in a sweat — something is brewing. I haven't had an opportunity as yet to visit Aunt Winnie's sister, honey, and from all appearances, I won't get a chance to. I'm sorry. I've gotten to the point now where I don't give a damn about anything but getting home and seeing you and being with you and Peg again. Well, Darling, I've run out of words and besides I have a little washing I would like to do before going to bed so I I'll close this now. I'll try to do a little better tomorrow though, honey, if I get a letter from you. Goodnight. Sweet dreams honey and say a prayer for me. Love me and miss me like I do you, too.

All my love, for always,
Your sweetheart,
   Jack

P.S. I love you - a million kisses, too.

5 December 1944
Tuesday

Dearest Darling:

Well, honey, I have started a letter to you now every night since Sunday, just to find that I couldn't get more than a half page written fore I ran out of things to say. I haven't received a letter from you now for 2 weeks or more and I don't mind telling you it really has me down in the dumps. I hope I get one tomorrow for a change.

Well, I'm here all alone again. They shipped all the fellows from the Battalion that I was bumming with, including everyone else, but they must have forgotten I'm here. I don't mind staying as we are lucky to be stationed at such a nice place but it sure does get you down when you have to keep making new friends again and again — you just meet someone that you like and kind of click with and bingo — they ship him out. I can't understand, for the life of me, why I've been held here like this — but far be it from me to complain — at least I'm missing a lot of the mud and cold that the other boys are going through right now — the trouble is I don't know whether to feel good or bad about it.

I received another package today — from Aunt Stella — with more food and soap, etc, etc, etc. Please honey, don't send me any more anything. I have approximately 25 bars of soap, over 2 good size boxes full of candy bars of all descriptions — about 75 bars in all — 3 fruit cakes — crackers — and Lord knows what else. I don't know what to do with it all — and whats worse — if I ever ship I'll just have to leave it all behind as I won't be able to carry it with me.

Again I must say, darling, that I'm afraid that this will be a little short, but regardless I will mail it to you so you won't worry and will hear from me. It just seems like everything started popping around here at once and with the mail like it has been, I just couldn't get around to writing.

I now have sort of another job — a new one — I'm now working with the M.P's Detachment of the depot. I guess I shouldn't say working as I'm still pretty bewildered most of the time, but I am doing a little typing for them, enough to keep me busy and think I'm learning a little something. It really is a lot of fun though, and I am enjoying it. I have never worked with a bunch of fellows that get along so well together, and a crazier bunch of nuts — something new going on all the time. No, I'm still not assigned — still on special duty, but at least I do have a job, — something to do to keep me busy and keep my mind off home and you and Peggy a little bit. To be perfectly honest, I never really appreciated the MP's — but so far as I can see, it is totally unfounded — as they are really a swell bunch of guys. I think I'm going to like it here better than any place I have worked. Course its pretty confusing yet, but I'll get on to it before long. Well — I gotta go for a minute — I'm writing this at the office and something came up which requires my immediate attention — be back though. Here I am again for just a minute or two. Duty calls — and all that stuff.

Gosh, honey, I feel so lonesome and homesick — especially since all the fellows have left — it gives me time to think about you — being all alone in the evenings like I am now, I really do feel miserable though. Lord how I wish this whole horrible mess was over and I could get back home. In fact, I could take it ok if I could just get home for a few days over Christmas. That is the most horrible part of the whole business — being away from you and Peggy then. It is the one time in all the year that you want to be home with your family and all more than any other time. When I think of how I'll spend this Christmas it really gets me down. And whats worse, thinking about you and all the folks sitting around the tree having the usual glass or two of eggnog and watching Peg to see how she will react to her first Christmas — I am really envious, honey. Well, lets just hope and pray that this will end soon and we will all be together by next Christmas.

How is Peggy, honey? I haven't heard any news about her for so long I'm really anxious to hear all about her latest escapades and about all the new things she has learned. I'm also waiting for some new pictures of you and her. You know, I wish I could get a few pictures of you all at least once a month — cause by getting new pictures each month I can kind of keep up with how my family looks and how they are changing and all.

Well, honey, I told you this was going to be short and I wasn't kidding. I really have to close now, and get to work. I'll most likely get some mail from you tomorrow and will write you a nice long letter for a change — at least 10 pages — I hope.

Good night, darling, sweet dreams. Love me and miss me. I love you and miss you more than anything in the world. Give Peg a big kiss for me, honey, and say a prayer, too.

All my love, to the most wonderful gal in the whole world and lil' gal too.

Your sweetheart
Jack

P.S. I love you.

Wednesday,
6 December 1944

Dearest Darling:

Will wonders never cease — I got a letter — one letter — today. It is one of those kind of short ones but at least it was a letter, and will give me something to write about for a change. You wrote it Tuesday, 7 November, on election day, too.

You know, honey, I can't get over your Dad — voting for Roosevelt — I never thought I'd ever hear the day. And to build him up like he is doing — I don't get it. Your Mother had quite a job I expect, over election night. I'm really glad that you didn't take it honey, as with the baby and everything, it would have just been to much for you, especially with the little you get — it just isn't worth while as far as I'm concerned. By the way, this was your first time for voting wasn't it? I'm really glad you did go up — I really didn't expect you to.

I bet Peggy really looks darling in those little overalls and outfit you have for her. Gosh honey, I would give anything to be able to be with her a little bit. By the time I get home she'll be all grown up and we'll just have to have another real soon so I can help bring it up this time. It makes me so darned mad that I have to miss all that is going on around home now. I think of all the fun we could be having, with our own place again, and everything. Its a shame that you have to keep Peg in now, as I know how — from what you say — she loves to be outdoors, but till she is finished cutting those teeth or gets over the cold, whichever it is, you had better keep her in. I guess, she has about all her teeth now, doesn't she? That is, all of them till she gets to about 4 or 5 years old. From what you say about her feeling good and all, it must be those teeth, though as you know how a cold makes you feel.

Yes, honey, I wish now that I had gone out for the football team, but maybe it is just as well I didn't as I have been away from it for so long. It would have felt kind of good and been a lot of fun to play though. We have a really good team and they play some nice ball — I wish you could see a game — its really exciting and you'd swear it was some school game instead of Army, there is so much enthusiasm and all. It lets you forget all about being

away from home and the army, for an hour or so, when you go out to one of the games.

Hi, honey — I had to leave for a while and when I got back someone had taken the typewriter so I'll have to finish this by pen. Anyway, writing this way, it makes it look like you are getting more.

There was a stage show here in camp tonight which another fellow and I went to see is why I didn't finish this earlier. Its the first time I've gone anywhere in over a week now. It was a show something on the order of the U.S.O. shows back home, only British — sort of hammy but entertaining. So now its about 9 o'clock and I'm back at the office and will finish this now and get it off — so back to where I left off.

Remember how we used to go to all the games up at school after we were married? Remember the big games with Kirkwood? By the way, how did it come out this year?

I'm glad you are having such a wonderful Autumn this year. We could sure use some of that nice weather here. It has been miserable. Rain and mud all the time. Everything is damp all the time and it is almost impossible to get really warm. I have never in my life seen a place with such a horrible climate as England does. We average one day of sunshine a month — if we are lucky.

I'm still waiting anxiously for those socks and I really need them now. They'll sure feel good. These issue socks over here, unless you can get a pair of English ones, aren't worth a darn. Its like going barefoot in January at home.

Well, honey, tomorrow is December 7th. Three years now since we entered the war. Its been a long time, but I can hardly realize that we have been in it that long. Just think, JK Jr would be three years old. It just doesn't seem possible, does it? It would really have been swell if he would have lived — it would be swell for Peg to have had a brother about that age — we would really have a nice family now, wouldn't we? Well, we'll just have to work on that brother angle when I get home.

Well, its late and its beginning to rain again so I guess I'd better close for now and head for home. By the way, I'm living all by myself again and boy am I lonesome going up there in the evenings. Hope someone moves in with me soon.

Well, Darling, goodnight, Sweet dreams. I love you and miss you more than anything in the world. Love me and miss me. Give Peg a kiss and say a prayer for me.

All my love for always to my beautiful honey -

Your Sweetheart
Jack
P.S. I love you.

Sunday
10 December 1944

Dearest Sweetheart:

Hello, Darling — here it is, another miserable and lonesome Sunday. However, I received 4 very wonderful letters from you today which will help. They were dated the 9th, 19th, 20th, and 21st of November. I'll sure be glad when this doggone mail gets regulated and I get caught up a little bit.

Honey, I'm glad you enjoy the Stars and Stripes and I'll try to continue sending them to you every week. It does give you news thats going on over here that you don't get in the paper back home and kind of gives you the impression and ideas of the men over here and how we live and all. I know we sure enjoy them over here and don't know what we would do without it.

I guess your mother was worn out with her night at the polls, then taking off for her bridge club that morning. How does she do it?

By the way, I received the socks, honey and I have them on right now. Gosh, darling they are wonderful. They fit just right and are they warm. You really did a wonderful job — send me more. Its really wonderful the way you fixed the feet so smooth without any knots or anything. I don't know how you did it. I can't get over how warm they are. They are really swell for this weather, as the G.I. socks just aren't warm enough. Your knitting has definitely improved — I might as well admit, I was expecting something on the order of that sweater.

I think that is really cute, the way Peg plays with Buff. So she gets mad at him when he won't bring the ball back to her, eh? I would sure give anything to be home with you all now. Now is the time I should be there to help bring Peg up and besides now is the time that she will be the most fun. Well, lets just hope it doesn't last too much longer. I hope I don't have to miss another Christmas with you and Peg — one is definitely too much.

Well, honey, I've got to quit for a minute and see if any more mail has come in for me.

Hi, honey. Here I am again — no mail for me, although there is most likely some down there. They are so far behind due to the Christmas rush that they'll never get caught up so all I can do is wait.

By the way, honey, O'Toole moved back to the 107th just as I left. Yes, I left — I'm no longer with the 107th. It would help me to get my mail I believe if you would use this address now:

Hq. Co., 12th Replacement Depot
M.P. Section, APO 551
c/o P M, N.Y. N.Y.

I don't officially belong to that organization but my office is with them and I am quartered with them so I'll get my mail much faster. Officially I'm with the Summary Court, 12th Replacement Depot — on Special Duty with the Staff Judge Advocates Office. Complicated, isn't it?

By the way, I wanted to tell you I received that article from the American that you sent. Well, I really must go now, honey. See you later.

Hi, hon. Here I am again. It looks like this is sort of an installment affair. I just got back from the show — saw the most wonderful picture I've seen in a long time. Don't miss it, whatever you do. Its "Hearts were Young and Gay" by C.O. Skinner. It is really swell — and the scenes of England and Paris are really authentic — don't miss it.

Well, Darling, it is getting late and I have to move again before I go to bed so I guess I'd better close for now. At least I'll have something to write about for the next few days. Goodnight, honey. Love me and miss me. I love you and miss you more than any thing in the world. Say a prayer and give Peg a kiss for me. All my love for always to my two wonderful little gals —

Your Sweetheart,
Jack

P.S. I love you.

Wednesday
13 December 1944

Dearest Sweetheart:

I guess I'd better tell you, before I forget, not to use that address I wrote you about the other day — in other words don't use M. P. Sec, 12 Repl Depot — use HQ Det 107th till you receive a new address from me. Things are happening — but fast.

I'm so tired tonight I hardly know what to do — or what I'm saying so if this is a little incongruous — please excuse. I didn't get to bed till after two o'clock last night with all my good intentions. I am going to keep my promise, or try to any way, and see that you get a letter, no matter how small, every night. Things will be rather uncertain for the next week, due to conditions beyond my control, so don't worry if you don't hear from me for a while.

As a matter of record, I didn't receive any letters from you today again, but I do have a couple on hand to answer. By the way, honey, it looks like I'm going to get a chance to visit Rusty after all — right soon, too.

I'm glad to hear, honey, that your cold is better. I am glad to hear that you did take care of yourself this time. I really do worry about you honey.

I'll swear, I'm so darn tired I can hardly hold my eyes open, but there is no use trying to go to bed over in that barracks till 1 or 2 o'clock as I am bunking with the noisiest bunch of guys I have ever heard and they work different hours all through the night and consequently the lights are always on and there is noise all the time. I am going to sleep a little late in the morning, however, as I'd better rest up for the big week-end I'm going to have.

It just seems like this will never end. I can't remember anything but Army — civilian life and all the wonderful things and swell times we have had seem like a dream. I just can't imagine what civilian life will be like, or how I will feel when I finally do get to come home. If and when. It really gets me down sometimes. This business of being so uncertain for so long a time has definitely gotten on my nerves. Just think, I have been a replacement over here for better than seven months — in fact, I've never been anything else since coming in the Army.

We are lucky to have all that furniture honey, so we won't have to buy anything for a while, but we will have to go easy on that furniture business if I go with Newberry's as we will be traveling a good deal most likely. All those familiar things of ours mean as much to me as they do to you. The way it is over here, honey, you dream about things just like they were when you left home and you want to come home and find them just the same.

Yes, hon, I have no beautiful ideas about not spoiling Peg when I get home — you know how I am with kids any way, so I'll most likely spoil the devil out of her. I've got to make up for lost time with her so she'll undoubtedly be spoiled.

Well, honey, I know this is rather short but I

will have a big day tomorrow and I'm pretty worn out, so I guess I'd better close for tonight. Goodnight. Sweet dreams. Love me and miss me. I love you more than anything in the world, honey. Give Peg a big kiss for me and say a very special prayer for me now. All my love to the most wonderful sweetheart in the whole world.

Your Sweetheart,
Jack

P.S. I love you.
(This was the last letter from England. The next night he started a letter at 11:15 P M and ended it Dec.24 in France. Rusty was our code that he was going to Germany. He did not go to Germany; instead he was in the Battle of the Bulge!)

14 December 1944
Thursday

Dearest Darling:
How are you this evening, honey? I feel pretty good for a change. No, it's not from receiving any mail from you, as I drew a blank.

I am really looking forward to seeing Rusty again. I hope to be able to spend this Saturday and Sunday with him.

I still have a couple of letters to answer so I guess I'd better get on them. It's quarter after eleven so it looks like this is going to be a short one again. I sure have had a hard time writing lately. These evenings go too darn fast. Every time I think of Christmas it really puts me down in the dumps, and now that I won't be able to spend it in England it really makes me feel worse, if that is possible. Lord, I hope this is the last one I have to spend away from home. I've gotten very pessimistic about the whole thing, and have given up all hope as far as the end of this mess is concerned. It has begun ——

(December 24)

Well, honey, I started this exactly 10 days ago, and this is the first chance I have had since to write. I am now somewhere in France.

I'm not going to write any more on it as I have lost whatever train of thought I had. I'll close and write you a V-mail tonight. I'm afraid it will all have to be V-mail for the most part from now on.

Bye for now, honey, Love me and miss me a little and say a big prayer for me.

Give Peg a big kiss for me too.

All my love for always to the sweetest most wonderful wife in the whole world.
Your sweetheart,
Jack

P.S. I love you.

New address:
G.F.R.S. Pool, Det,102
493 Repl Co, Apo 131

(They were in foxholes near Givet, France. The letter was crumpled and the ink had run. They had just come down from Belgium.)

To Britons, 1940

God gave them strength to carry on undaunted
While 'round their isle the foe his hatred flaunted.
With bombs and fire their days and nights were haunted,
Yet stood they undismayed.

With bold defy that through the world resounded
And strength of will the tyrant's will confounded.
Battling for right, by cruel foes surrounded.
Still stood they unafraid.

by
Eugene Jerome Walser
from a book of his poetry

PART 3: COMBAT
BATTLE OF THE BULGE

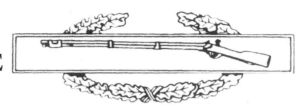

While Jack was writing that fateful letter on December 14, 1944, in the office, his orders came through. They were already on alert, but he had not expected to be leaving quite that soon. He had slept late that morning as they had worked until 2 A.M. the night before. The clue he gave me about expecting to see Rusty, his cousin, Saturday or Sunday meant that he was going to Germany. Later information indicated that he was slated to join the 30th Division which was at that time in Warden, Germany. Jack stopped writing in the middle of a sentence. It was 11:15 P.M.

He went to the barracks and finished packing his things. He had already gone through them, keeping only the bare essentials and the few things most dear to him. In the breast pocket of his shirt, he always carried his wallet, his prayer book, and the small folder with the baby's and my picture. Now, however, he would have to carry everything he owned on his back; for how far and for how long, he did not know.

Before dawn the next morning, the 15th of December, wearing the same clothes he had on, including the wool socks which I had knitted for him, he and another soldier left Tidworth, England. They waited in the early morning darkness, in Andover, England, for a troop train. They were headed for combat, as riflemen!

In a few short hours they were in Southampton, England. Southampton was the major embarkation port on the southern coast. A very large replacement depot was there. They were processed, given shots, issued their combat gear, assigned, and shipped overseas. They presumed it would be to the northern front where the Allied mid-winter offensive, the push into Germany, had already begun.

The German city of Aachen, on November 16, 1944, after bitter fighting, was finally in Allied hands. Aachen was precious to the German people, as Charlemagne had been crowned there. It was dear to the heart of every German soldier, and they were willing to fight for it to their death.

The 1st and 30th American Divisions, after their victory there, were now readying for their next objective, the capture of the Roer River Dams. These were a complex of heavy earthen dams. They had to be in Allied hands to keep the Germans from opening them, flooding our troops and the entire Roer Valley. All attempts to destroy them with daily bombing raids had failed, and now they had to be taken by ground forces.

The casualties in November, 1944, had been staggering. Two American divisions were totally decimated. The First Army had 8,000 casualties. The 1st Division alone had 4,000 casualties in the Huertgen Forest, due to combat exhaustion and exposure. The operation had cost 23,000 killed, wounded, or missing. Two American divisions had been sent back to France for rest and recuperation. There had to be replacements for these men.

Thus the decision to convert the top-heavy service personnel to ground forces. General George C. Marshall (Chief of Staff of the United States Forces) in early December ordered 65,000 service and air force personnel to be transferred to the infantry for the offensive which was to start December 13, 1944, but suddenly fate intervened.

On December 16, 1944, at Southampton, Jack and the others being processed were given their overseas shots, as shown on his medical record. They were also given K Rations, cigarettes, 200 francs, a booklet "A Pocket Guide to France," and the equipment they would need in combat. As was usual, they hurried up and waited for their orders, which soon came. That night they marched to the dock, were loaded into landing craft, and crossed the English Channel. It was raining, it was bitterly cold, the channel was rough, and the icy spray drenched them. They were cold, wet, and filled with apprehension not knowing what lay ahead, and many were very seasick. Thousands of thoughts ran through their minds. These were untested troops with no conception of what real combat would be like.

In the early morning darkness of December 17, they landed at Le Havre, France, and went over the sides of the boats using landing nets with full field packs (110 lbs), and then struggled ashore on steel landing ramps. The weather was not only cold, but it was heavy with clouds and thick fog.

Le Havre, France, had been a stubborn pocket of resistance which the Germans had defended to the last. It had been captured by American forces on September 4, 1944. The port had been heavily bombarded by the Allies, and then it had been completely destroyed by the Germans when they left. American engineers began reconstruction and had supplies and men moving by the first of November, 1944. By now, December 17, 1944, it was hard to imagine how bad it had been.

From the docks the men marched through Le Havre, France. People were on the street selling things, and Jack had time to buy a small bottle of perfume for me which he tucked in his pocket. To the east of Le Havre, France, is a range of very high wooded hills. After leaving the last houses, the road climbs upward for miles and miles until it levels out with farmland and small farm houses. They marched for miles up the road until they reached the large replacement depot (Camp Lucky Strike). There they were processed, attached to an outfit, and awaited further orders. This time it was almost immediately.

Rumors of a breakthrough by the Germans the day before, December 16, 1944, had filtered back. Communications were disrupted all along the front. The Germans could hear every radio message and our orders of troop movements. Orders were changing fast. No one in American Headquarters realized the magnitude of the German offensive being launched. There was even a news blackout for 48 hours at home.

The men were ordered to remove their overcoats, puzzling in such horrible weather, and also all insignia. Rumors had already spread that Germans in American uniforms, driving jeeps and speaking perfect English, had infiltrated the front lines. By the night of December 17th, 1944, Jack and the unit he was with were rumbling across France in open trucks. Every available vehicle had been commandeered. His unit was headed for the front wherever it might be.

On December 17, 1944, the First Army moved 60,000 men in 11,000 trucks to counter the German penetration. These were raw troops, 18-year-olds newly arrived from the United States, and service personnel, cooks, clerks, quartermaster, and others from England and the Continent.

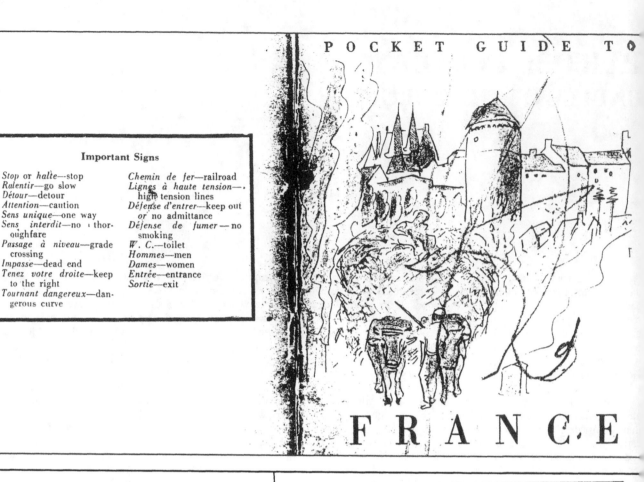

Important Signs

Stop or *halte*—stop
Ralentir—go slow
Détour—detour
Attention—caution
Sens unique—one way
Sens interdit—no thoroughfare
Passage à niveau—grade crossing
Impasse—dead end
Tenez votre droite—keep to the right
Tournant dangereux—dangerous curve

Chemin de fer—railroad
Lignes à haute tension—high tension lines
Défense d'entrer—keep out or no admittance
Défense de fumer—no smoking
W. C.—toilet
Hommes—men
Dames—women
Entrée—entrance
Sortie—exit

FRANCE

CONTENTS

I

WHY YOU'RE GOING TO FRANCE

YOU are about to play a personal part in the final stages of the war in Europe and the winning of the peace. Whatever part you take—rifleman, hospital orderly, mechanic, pilot, clerk, gunner, truck driver— you will be an essential factor in a great effort that has one objective—the destruction of a system and ideology abhorrent to all freedom loving men.

This great Allied effort you are taking part in is based upon a hard-boiled fact. It's this. We democracies haven't just been doing favors in fighting for each other when history got tough. We were all in the same boat. Take a look around you as you move into France and you'll see what the Nazis did to a democracy when they could get it down by itself.

In "Mein Kampf" Hitler stated that his plan was to destroy France first, then get England, after which he would have the United States cornered without a fight. The Allies have opened up conquered France and re-established the old Allied liberties. The job now is the destruction of Nazism for keeps.

5

Pocket Guide to France. Issued with equipment, Southhampton, England. December 16, 1944.

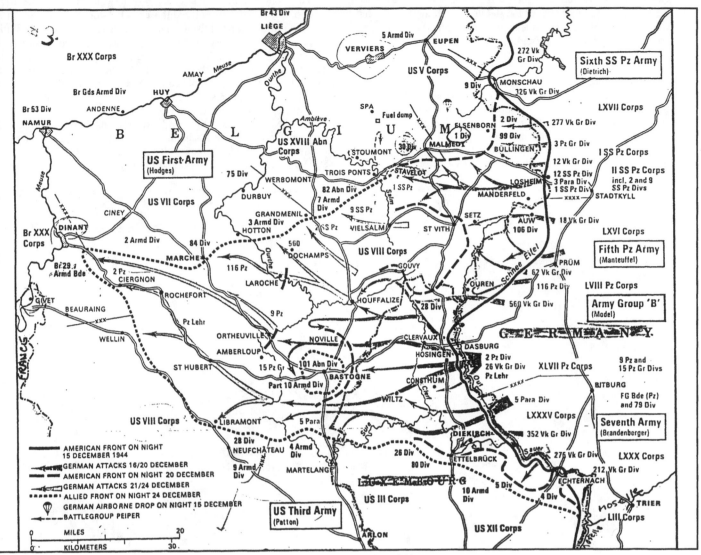

The Ardennes, 16 December, 1944.

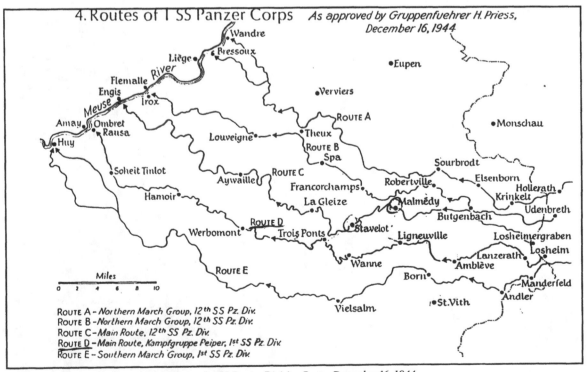

German 1st SS Panzer Division Route. December 16, 1944.

Jack was one of this number. Unit upon unit was piled behind the 30th Division on the northern front at Stavelot, Belgium, to strengthen its defensive position, as the American commanders felt confident the German push would drive northward toward Liege, Belgium.

***

In early December, 1944, the entire military, with a few exceptions, had been filled with optimism. While the Allied high command was making the decision to transfer troops to the ground forces, the fact was brought up among the discussions that, although the front along the Ardennes region was thinly held, there seemed to be no reason for an attack there. There were no military objectives in the region and American army units both north and south were heavily equipped.

The front was held by only three American divisions, the 106th Division which had just replaced the 2nd Division; the 28th Division, new to the Ardennes; and the 4th Division. After a trip to the 88 mile Ardennes front, the decision was made by the Allied commanders, to add the new 9th Armored Division and to go ahead with the winter offensive as planned. All thoughts were directed toward the Allied offensive which was to be launched on December 13, 1944, toward the Roer River Dams, and also the planned offensive on the southern front with General Patton's Third Army on December 19.

No one had appeared to consider the fact that in the middle of this thinly held front was the Losheim Gap, a valley five miles wide near the town of Losheim, Germany. It was a corridor from Germany to Belgium. The Germans had poured through there with their invading

French Money. 50 Franc Note.

armies in 1870 and 1914. In 1940 Hitler's hordes raced through all the way to the English Channel. Then came Dunkirk and the fall of France. Now the Germans had done it again!

The Ardennes region was once an extensive forest, but as time passed, the land was cleared for farms and grazing until only part of it was wooded. The most forested part was the eastern part along the Belgian-Luxembourg border with Germany. It consisted of tall firs, and although planted in very orderly rows, it was, actually, a dark and forbidding area.

The region on the east extends for 80 miles along the border with Germany, from the north near Aachen, Germany, to the south near Luxembourg City, Luxembourg. It is bordered on the east by the Our River which rises in Belgium, flows south, and makes the frontier between Luxembourg and Germany (it is the Sauer in Germany). There it joins the Moselle River and is roughly the end of the Ardennes. The rivers, except for the Meuse, are not wide or deep but are in deep gorges with very steep, forested sides. The Ardennes extends toward the west all the way to the Meuse River and a little beyond. The Meuse, a majestic river, winds its way through a beautiful valley. It begins in the hills of eastern France and flows north through Liege, Belgium, enters the Netherlands where it becomes the Maas, and empties into the North Sea.

In peaceful times the Ardennes had for centuries been a pleasant vacation area in the summer. It was very restful and quiet with its quaint villages and inns, castles, abbeys, and famed chateaus. The terrain is quite rugged, with valleys, deep gorges and twisting streams interspersed with areas of forested gentle rolling hills. The network of roads crisscrossing the region usually followed the valleys, and they twisted and turned along the streams and often passed through thick forests. Because this had always been a vacation area, there was an extensive network of roads.

In nearly every area where the roads crossed was a small town, village, or often just farm buildings. The roads usually narrowed to pass through these. The road junctions as well as their sturdy old stone bridges were critical to a military advance. Sadly, some of these towns would become famous in history because of this. All through September and October, 1944, the roads had been repaired, and bridges had been replaced after the fighting during the summer. Some of the railroads had been repaired and were being used by the military. They had been destroyed all over Europe by the Allies because the Germans had used them almost entirely for troop movements. The Allies were fully motorized and did not need the railroads.

Winter in the Ardennes comes early. The heaviest rains usually come in November. The days are short, gloomy, and often overcast. The predawn hours are dark and cold. At daylight thick fog rises from the rivers and does not burn off before noon. The fog then returns before nightfall. December brings freezing rain and light snow. The heavier snows do not usually come until late December or January. The snows can accumulate about a foot deep, but it is often much deeper in drifts.

Unseasonable and nearly constant rain had fallen in the Ardennes the last part of the summer and into the fall of 1944. They were torrential rains which turned the roads into quagmires. The entire area was knee-deep in mud. As December approached and the temperature dropped, the sodden ground would freeze at night and thaw again during the day. This made the situation much worse. There were patches of snow here and there.

As Christmas, 1944, approached things were quiet along the front. After the bloody battles of the summer and fall, some of the front line divisions had been pulled back for rest and recuperation. Many even had furloughs. It appeared as though the troops would sit out the winter there waiting for the spring offensive. It seemed as though it would also be the same for the enemy.

All the Allied armies were filled with optimism that the end of the war was in sight. They were sure the Germans were near collapse and would soon be surrendering, and everyone would be going home. They were sad about being away from home for another Christmas, but everywhere they were decorating trees and enjoying Christmas packages which were arriving from home. Many of the headquarters and hospitals were happily planning parties for the children in the towns, even having Santa Claus and Father Christmas. The night of December 15, 1944, they bedded down all over the Ardennes securely unaware of what dawn the next day would bring. Hitler's plan was ready!

That night three German armies began to move forward, unobserved, through ten miles of forest, which separated the front lines. The

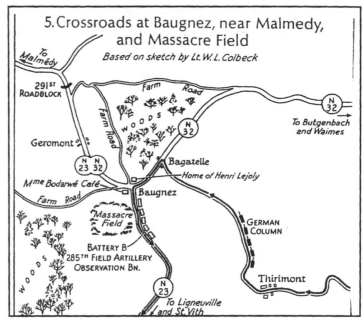

Malmedy Massacre Crossroads. December 17, 1944.

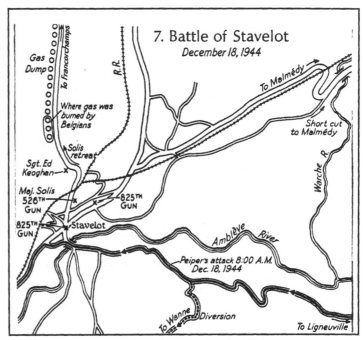

Battle of Stavelot. December 18, 1944.

last move brought them two and one half miles behind the front. The weather all week had been cold with drizzling rain and heavy overcast skies. As a result, American observation planes had been grounded for days.

The next morning, December 16, 1944, at 5:30 A.M. the Germans began the advance. Through the thick fog, pinpoints of light were observed all along the entire German lines by American sentries. These were the muzzle flashes of the German infantry. Seconds later shells were crashing into the American lines along the whole 85-mile front. Every type of weapon was fired—mortars, rockets, and cannons. The ground shook violently and snow showered down from the tall pines as their branches were shattered. The GI's grabbed their weapons and dived into their foxholes. Radios were suddenly jammed with German music. None of them had any conception of what was happening. German planes flew low to drown out the sound of the tanks and vehicles approaching.

After several hours of shelling it let up. Suddenly, the Germans turned on huge search lights, through the early morning fog, at the clouds to illuminate like day the American positions. Then their infantry moved forward through the fog in ghostly white camouflage. The tanks followed next, ready to roar through the gaps in the line made by their infantry.

Malmedy Massacre, Sunday, December 17, 1944. Indentifying the victims.

Every American unit on the front thought they were the only ones being attacked. No one realized the full scope of the German offensive that day. The commanders communicated by telephones the first day and used radios and runners to move troops and get reinforcements. The American command posts were complete chaos. They were crowded, everyone talking at once, and rumors were running wild. No one knew what the crisis really was yet. There had been a break through but no one knew exactly where. The units which had been overrun knew, but the Americans never dreamed it was twenty-two German divisions on their front.

The rumors about the Germans in American uniforms were facts, not rumors. In October, 1944, SS Major Otto Skorzeny was sent for by Hitler. He promoted him to Lt. Colonel, Waffen SS, and informed him of the plans he had for him and of the units which would be under his command in the planned offensive. They were to seize one or more bridges over the Meuse River wearing British and American uniforms. They were to create mass confusion by giving false orders, upset communications, and send American troops in the wrong direction. His unit (a whole brigade) would be assigned to the 6th Panzer Army. Most of these tasks they did accomplish in the first days of the attack.

In the north the German Sixth Panzer Army struck the U.S. 99th Division, nearly cutting off the American 2nd Division. The 2nd Division had already been attacking through the 99th Division toward the Roer River.

In command of the Germans was Nazi veteran SS General Sepp Dietrich. Under him were the 3rd Parachute Division, the 12th Hitler Youth Division, and the 1st SS Panzer Division. Both of the latter had reputations of cruelty and brutality.

The spearhead of the attack was the 1st Panzer Division under Lt. Colonel Joachim Peiper. He was 29 years old, a fanatic brutal leader, completely lacking any humanity. He had recently come from the Russian front. He had been told he was to show no mercy and to take no prisoners. This rule he followed. He started with 5,000 men and 120 tanks which included 42 Royal Tiger tanks. He expected to capture American tanks and obtain fuel on the way at Bullingen, Belgium, and the large supply dump near Spa, Belgium.

On December 16, 1944, Lt. Colonel Peiper moved out with his tanks and attached infantry. There was a light covering of snow on the ground. His assigned route was through the Losheim Gap to Stavelot, Belgium, where the massive stone bridge over the Ambleve River there would support tanks. His objective was Liege, Belgium, and the Meuse River. At first, the roads were jammed with the slower vehicles in front, and Peiper impatiently pushed his way through and stormed ahead. As the surprised and overwhelmed Americans fled before them, they were

attacked, and those who surrendered were mowed down with pistols and machine guns.

Racing ahead of his column, he reached Lanzarath, Belgium, around midnight and went into the cafe. Earlier that day a platoon of the American 99th Division reconnaissance detachment had been overrun by German infantry and, after a fierce battle, had been captured. Their action, however, had blocked one of the main roads and slowed the German advance. The wounded had been treated by German medics and brought to the cafe. Peiper observed none of it. He pinned a map to the wall with his bayonet and studied maps the rest of the night. The weather had worsened and blustery gale force winds had come up.

In the morning, the 17th of December, 1944, at 4 A.M. Peiper headed out again. They were running short of fuel as they had used so much idling the engines. The night before he had decided the paratroopers were holding him back and he would make the breakthrough himself. He decided to change from his assigned route which was to Stavelot, Belgium, and, instead, detour north to Bullingen. He could then refuel at the American supply dump there.

When they reached Buchholz, Belgium, about 4:30, the village was empty, but the American radio operator, hidden in a basement, had been able to send a message to his headquarters telling the size of the column. At the village of Honsfeld, Belgium, the small American garrison scattered. Peiper picked up their equipment, left the attached paratroopers there to mop up, and pushed forward. Nineteen American soldiers had surrendered, and they were disarmed and brutally shot down.

Traveling alone now, he detoured from his route turning north to Bullingen, Belgium. He overran that small garrison also, refueled his tanks, and picked up an extra 50,000 gallons of fuel. Fifty men surrendered. They were disarmed and killed, along with one civilian. He then turned southwest back to his assigned route. It was about 9:30 or 10:00 A.M..

Things were going well for him at this point. His breakthrough had been accomplished and, he had replenished his fuel. It was shortly before noon, and he was now approaching the crossroads at Baugnez (a hamlet three miles south of Malmedy) between Malmedy and Ligneuville, Belgium. There was a cafe, and there were several farm houses in the open fields and woods.

If Peiper had been a little earlier he would have met the Reconnaissance Detachment of the 7th Armored Division. They had just moved southward on a parallel road which went from Malmedy to St. Vith, and the history of the war would have been completely changed.

However, before the next unit of the 7th Armored Division (which was following) got on the road, a small unit had slipped into the gap in Malmedy. The unit was the American Battery B, 285th Field Artillery Observation Battalion. The small convoy consisted of 140 men with about thirty vehicles led by a jeep with two officers, of which the executive officer was 1st. Lt. Virgil T. Lary, Jr.

The last vehicle was an ambulance belonging to the American 1st Division. There was one driver with three medical officers all wearing red cross arm bands. The ambulance had just been repaired and freshly painted, clearly showing the red crosses. They had asked to join the convoy when it left Malmedy, Belgium. The entire column was unarmed except for machine guns. While they were waiting in Malmedy for a gap, Lt. Colonel David E. Pergrin who was in command of the 291st Combat Engineer Battalion there, told them there had been some sort of breakthrough and it might be wise to go by way of Stavelot, Belgium, instead; but the officers decided to stay on their assigned route, also the ambulance had to get to St. Vith, Belgium.

The little convoy slowly climbed the hill on the road leading south, then down hill toward the crossroad. They passed the road block where the M P, Pfc Homer D. Ford waved them on, and just as they reached the crossroad they were spied, through the woods, by the vanguard of Peiper's column. The Panzers were traveling on a parallel road heading north. It was 12:45 and what then occurred would forever be known as the Malmedy Massacre.

On the left, at the crossroad, was the farm house of Henri Lejoly, known to be a German sympathizer. Across from it on the right was the home and Cafe of Madame Bodarwe. Just as the convoy passed the cafe and turned south onto N 23, (the road to St Vith, Belgium) the German column opened fire with a canon and began shelling them. When the firing started, the Americans were so out-numbered Lieutenant Lary told them to surrender, to pass it on, and to obey all orders as the rules of war required.

The Germans then poured down from the tanks and across the field firing rifles and machine guns as they came. The convoy's vehicles slid across the road and into one another as the men piled out looking for shelter. The Lieutenant and several of the men hid behind the cafe, then ran to a barn where they could look out. Henri Lejoly and Madame Bodware stood by the road watching, and he pointed out their hiding place.

The German panzers raked Battery B's vehicles with machine gun fire and pushed them off the road where many burned. Then they mowed down the men, who by now were hitting the ditches, and also those who were trying to flee to the nearby woods. At this time a half track drove up with an officer who began giving orders. The GI's climbed out of the ditch with their hands in the air to surrender, and the Germans collected the rifles they had thrown down, had them empty their pockets taking what they wanted, smoked their American cigarettes, and were all in fine humor. When the column started again heading south on N 23, they and the officer moved on.

Then a command car with an officer drove up. It was the Commander of the tanks, Major Poetschke. The American prisoners were lined up now and moved back to the road intersection where there was an open field below the cafe. In the field they were made to line up shoulder to shoulder in eight rows. The Lieutenant, M P (who had been directing traffic at the roadblock), and men in the barn surrendered and were prodded into the field after Henri Lejoly had revealed their hiding place. They all thought they would be held until moved to a POW camp. They became very uneasy when an officer had two tanks moved around and placed at each end of the field facing them. Their hearts sank when they realized that this was the 1st SS Panzer Division which had the Deaths Head insignia on their caps.

Suddenly the officer stood up, drew his revolver, and aimed directly at a Medical Corps Major in the front row. The prisoner fell and the machine guns on both tanks then fired back and forth over and over. It took fifteen minutes before the screams and moans gradually stopped. It was now ten minutes past two on Sunday, December 17, 1944.

The panzer column finally began to move down the road again; and as it rolled by, the infantrymen on the tanks continued shooting at the crumpled figures lying in the snow-covered field. It took two hours for the entire column to pass. This was not enough, though. They had left a detail behind to walk through the piles of the massacred prisoners, some of whom had fallen upon one another, kick them in the groin, and, if they moved, shoot them in the head or use their rifle butts. A few had survived by playing dead. After the column passed they whispered to one another, and about fifteen or twenty made a dash for it across the field and into the woods toward Malmedy. The Germans shot at them and all but one American made it. Some had run into the cafe. The Germans then burned it and shot them; however, some escaped through the smoke and into the woods. There was a dreadful stillness then. Madame Bodarwe had watched it all with horror. Her fate is unknown; she disappeared and was never seen again.

In Malmedy, at 2:15 P.M. they had heard the sound of machine guns firing from the direction of the intersection, and at 2:30 P.M. Colonel Pergrin, who was in command, personally went on reconnaissance down there to see. Homer Ford with three men came screaming out of the woods and were taken to the aid station in Malmedy. Col. Pergrin made another reconnaissance just before dark. Gradually that night the few other men came straggling in, all telling the same facts. Some of the

American Fuel Dump on Francorchamps road. Over 400,000 jerry cans of gasoline stored. Set on fire to turn the Germans back, December 18, 1944.

wounded men had laid flat in the snow-covered field in freezing cold, twelve degrees above zero, for eleven hours. Several of the men in the woods had been helped by patriotic Belgian families. Of the 140 men who had unwarily come down the road from Malmedy that morning in that little convoy, only 43 were to survive. The rest lay in the field, as they had fallen, for three more weeks before they could be removed. Mercifully, on the night of December 21st, 1944, a heavy snow fell over the entire Ardennes, and a soft blanket of snow covered them!

Colonel Pergrin sent an urgent message with a full report of the massacre to General Hodges at the First Army Headquarters, where it was given wide publicity immediately. Colonel Pergrin was able to give information of the enormity of the breakthrough and that he was preparing the town's defense. General Hodges promptly started some reinforcements on their way. The report of this terrible deed stiffened the resistance of every G I in the Ardennes.

Malmedy was one of the most picturesque towns in the Ardennes and also the largest, with a population of 5,000 people. It was in the French-speaking area. The town was important to the first Army because of its location at an intersection of all the main roads. It had a Replacement Depot with 500 men, the 44th Field Evacuation Hospital, a tank maintenance and repair depot, and several large gas depots. It was very over-crowded.

View of ruined town during the terrible battle.

Innocent Civilians murdered by Peipers SS troops at Parfondruy. Discovered on December 21, 1944.

Lt. Col. David E. Pergrin was 26 years old, a very capable leader with an intense concern for his men. The battalion operated saw mills in the surrounding towns and did road maintenance. Company B was quartered in Malmedy and drove out to their work each day. On this day he had only a total of 180 men of Company B and the Headquarters Company. Although there were a number of units in Malmedy, he was only in command of his 291st Engineers. He had set up his Command Post on the fringe of the town.

Now, there was a steady stream of traffic passing through with everyone leaving, and in addition troops retreating from the front. Colonel Pergrin had immediately ordered road blocks to be set up on all roads leading into Malmedy. He was certain that it was the German army's objective. Shortly after the tragedy at Baugnez, Belgium, the rest of the 7th Armored Division Artillery Convoy entered the town. He plead with the commander to stay and help with their defense, but the convoy was under orders to get to St. Vith to aid the 106th Division, so he went on by way of Stavelot.

Panic had taken over. All the military units, the replacement depot, hospital, and ordinance began pulling out. In addition, there were the streams of frightened civilians fleeing in panic with bicycles, loaded carts, babies in carriages, and little children by the hand, all heading west away from the front. The day before at daybreak, four shells from the big railroad guns the Germans fired had fallen in Malmedy. They had done considerable damage and during the night the telephone lines had been cut.

Colonel Pergrin called in his Battalion. Co C was on a work detail in La Gleize, Belgium, and he ordered a Sergeant Hensel to promptly come to Malmedy. He was to drop off a squad at Trois Ponts, Belgium, and one at Stavelot, Belgium, to establish road blocks. Stavelot was on the direct route to Spa, Belgium. Also on that route, just north of Stavelot, was the huge American fuel dump with more than 400,000 five-gallon jerry cans of gasoline which must not fall into German hands. German artillery fire began falling after dark, and there was heavy bombardment in the whole area between Malmedy and Stavelot that night. The towns are approximately five miles apart in dense, wooded hills.

After Colonel Pergrin's call to First Army, the American 30th Division was ordered, at 3 P.M. on Sunday December 17, 1944, to move south from the Aachen, Germany, area. They had been resting in preparation for the coming Roer Offensive which was to have pushed off in two days. They moved out at 7 P.M. but could not possibly get to Malmedy before the next morning.

At this time, the only immediately available troops were serving as guards at the American First Army Headquarters at Spa, Belgium. They were two separate infantry units which were not part of any division. They were a 12th Army Group unit based at Spa, Belgium. One was the 526th Armored Infantry Battalion, commanded by Maj. Paul J. Solis. This was a new unit which had never been in combat. The other was the 99th Infantry Battalion. It was partially made up of Norwegian citizens and Norwegians who had escaped from occupied Norway. They had all volunteered to serve in the U.S. Army. The rest of the battalion was made up of Norwegian Americans, one of which was the commander Lt. Col. Harold D. Hansen. Attached to them was one company of the 825th Tank Destroyer Battalion with towed 3 inch guns, also based at Spa.

These units soon started on their way. They were to go separately to Malmedy, and upon arrival would be under the command of Colonel Hansen. They would be a stop gap until the 30th Division arrived.

Sergeant Hensel had dropped off the squad in Trois Ponts to set up the road block. The town was jammed with vehicles. By the time he arrived in Stavelot it was about 6:30 P.M., and completely dark. It was surprising to see the town square well lit and filled with vehicles of all sorts with lights blazing. The supply troops who were billeted there were pulling out. German buzz bombs were streaming overhead toward Liege. The huge American trucks were making so much noise they did not hear the German column approaching on the heights of the hill less than two miles away across the Ambleve River.

Stavelot, Belgium, a village of 3,000 people was nestled in a deep valley. It had been carved out by the Ambleve River which runs through it. It was a very old town dating back to the year 650 A.D. when St. Remacle had built two Monasteries, one at Stavelot and one at Malmedy. Over the centuries Stavelot had suffered through many wars and been rebuilt many times. It had always been a center of culture and music. In

Old stone bridge over Ambleve River, blown up with one charge of 1,000 pounds of dynamite, to stop German Tanks. Night of December 20, 1944.

World War I the Germans occupied the town until the Armistice in 1918. Then again, on May 10, 1940, the German Army invaded, and the town endured the occupation until their liberation by the American army on September 12, 1944.

On that day the American Army had come from Spa through Francorchamps, Belgium, to Stavelot. The American soldiers arrived at the top of the hill, overlooking the town of Stavelot, and paused to study the situation. The Resistance in the town asked their commander to wait until the Germans had completely gone before coming down, in order to protect their town. Finally a telephone call was made from the Belgian citizen to the American commander, and the column came on down the hill. When the first tanks and jeeps entered, the entire town was there to cheer the G I's, who were very surprised, but delighted, and immediately began giving them cigarettes, chocolate, and chewing gum. Troops were billeted there, and life was pleasant for the next few months. Suddenly there was the breakthrough. It was December 17, 1944, and Col. Joachim Peiper with his SS Panzers had reached Stavelot.

Sergeant Hensel and his men, arriving at the square in Stavelot, soon realized there was no one in charge and the town was totally undefended. They drove their truck across the old stone bridge past a few houses on the left and up the steep winding hill to the top. The road had been cut out of the rock and was very narrow, but toward the top it widened and flattened out a bit. They turned around there and drove

back to a sharp bend in the road with a rocky cliff on the right side and a deep drop on the left. Sergeant Hensel had them set up the roadblock there and placed mines across the road below it. He put machine guns on one side of the road and a bazooka team on the other. He sent Pvt. Bernard Goldstein up beyond the bend as a lookout by a small stone shed. It was now about 7:30 P.M. and completely dark. It was December 17, 1944.

Within minutes they heard the sound of German tanks feeling their way forward slowly in the darkness and German voices. Private Goldstein unbelievably stepped out in the road and demanded "Halt", pointing his M-1 rifle at the tank. The German paratroopers jumped off and opened up with machine guns and rifles. Sgt. Hensel and the other men fired. They tried to get up to Private Goldstein, but the German tank opened fire with its machine gun, so they hurriedly drew back around the bend where the bazooka team fired a rocket. By pure luck it damaged the tank. Private Goldstein scrambled up the hill to the west. Sergeant. Hensel and the men waited at the roadblock, but the German tanks made no effort to proceed. When they heard the tanks backing up, they coasted their truck down the hill so the Germans would not know they had left.

When Sgt. Hensel and his men reached the south end of the bridge, there was a platoon of engineers with a Lieutenant preparing it for demolition. They had it wired all ready to blow. Then all of them crossed over the bridge to the town side. The platoon of engineers attempted to

93

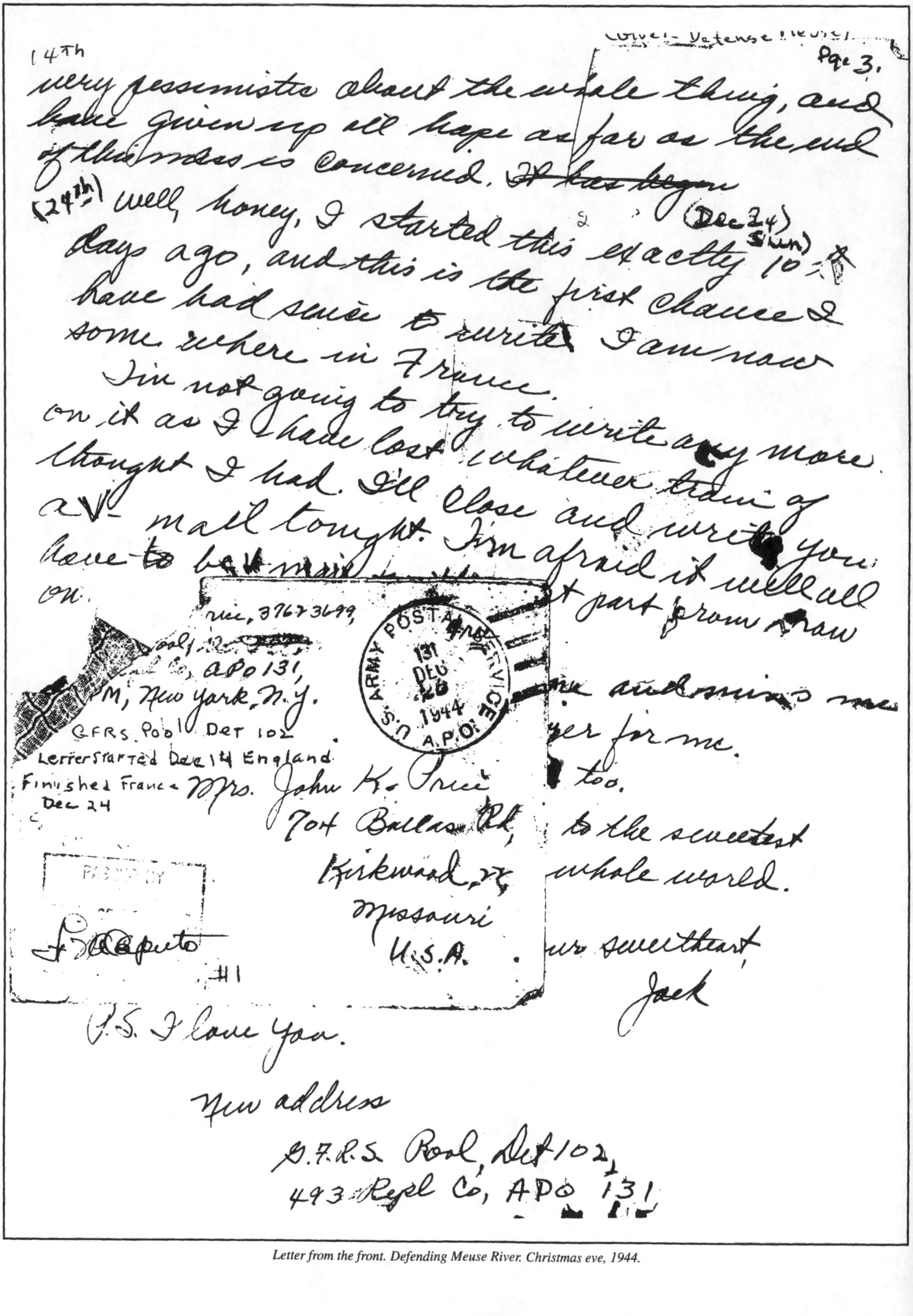

14th

very pessimistic about the whole thing, and
have given up all hope as far as the end
of this mess is concerned. It has begun

(24th) Well, honey, I started this exactly 10 (Dec 24) (Sun)
days ago, and this is the first chance I
have had since to write. I am now
somewhere in France.
 I'm not going to try to write any more
on it as I have lost whatever train of
thought I had. I'll close and write you
a V- mail tonight. I'm afraid it will all
have to be mail _____ part from now
on.

rue. 37673699

_____ APO 131,
M, New York, N.Y.
GFRS Pool Det 102
Letter Started Dec 14 England
Finished France Mrs. John K. Price

704 Ballas Rd,
Kirkwood,
Missouri
U.S.A.

PASSED BY

_____ #1

P.S. I love you.

New address

G.F.R.S. Pool, Det 102,
493 Repl Co, APO 131

_____ and miss me
_____ er for me.
_____ too.
to the sweetest
whole world.
ur sweetheart,
Jack

Letter from the front. Defending Meuse River. Christmas eve, 1944.

Print the complete address in plain letters in the panel below, and your return address in the space provided on the right. Use typewriter, dark ink, or dark pencil. Faint or small writing is not suitable for photographing.

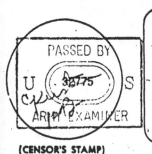

PASSED BY
U.S. 32775
ARMY EXAMINER

(CENSOR'S STAMP)

TO: Mrs. John K. Price
704 Dallas Road
Kirkwood, 22, Missouri
U.S.A.

SEE INSTRUCTION NO. 2

FROM
Pvt. John K. Price, 37622699
G.7.R.S. Pool, APO 131
% PM, New York, N.Y.

(Sender's complete address above)

26 Dec 44
(Tues)

Dearest Darling:

Well, honey, it has been quite a while since I was able to write you, but it really couldn't be helped. And I'll try to get a letter a day to you from now on, although it will have to be V-mail. I was going to write you a nice Christmas letter yesterday; but I drew guard duty so couldn't do any writing. As you see, Christmas was just another day around here and a darn lonesome and blue one to. I hope you and Peg had a big time. I would have given anything to have been with you, but I'm not even going to think about it.

France is not too bad, in fact, quite a lot like home; but we have no facilities for sleeping, etc, and its so darn cold that the water in our canteens freeze over night. I have never been so cold and miserable in all my life. I sure wish I could have waited till spring to come over here, though.

Well, honey, I see that I have to go now. I guess I'll close this for now. If I get time I'll write another tonight. By the way, I mailed you a bottle of perfume today and am going to try to get Peg one of those Belgian dolls which I'll mail. I have really seen some cute ones since arriving here. Well, darling, bye for now. Love me and miss me a little. Say a prayer for me honey. I love you. All my love for always and always, your sweetheart Jack

HAVE YOU FILLED IN COMPLETE ADDRESS AT TOP?

REPLY BY
V---MAIL

HAVE YOU FILLED IN COMPLETE ADDRESS AT TOP?

☆ U.S. GOVERNMENT PRINTING OFFICE 1943 16—28165-5

18

In tents like these! Unit off the line. 16th Replacement Depot, Compiegne, France. New Years eve, 1944.

blow the bridge but the charge did not go off. It was later learned that two of them were Skorzeny men (Germans) dressed in G I uniforms. Sergeant Hensel did not know them, but they appeared to be in charge so he and his men left to go back to Trois Ponts and join their outfit. It was about 9 o'clock in the evening.

Private Goldstein got back to the bridge about 10:30, after much difficulty wandering around the hillside. Sergeant Hensel was gone, but he had left Pfc. Lorenzo Liparulo there with a jeep. Shortly after midnight, December 18th, 1944, the Lieutenant in charge of the engineers who had wired the bridge, sent him and Liparulo up the hill in a jeep for reconnaissance. They were fired upon by some Germans; Liparulo was wounded and later died. Private Goldstein was badly wounded, but hours later was able to crawl painfully back to the bridge.

It was 3 A.M. on December 18th, and Company A of the 526th Armored Infantry Battalion had arrived in Stavelot and were guarding the bridge. They were setting up their defense and deploying their men. It was a very confused situation with infantrymen milling about trying to set up the towed anti-tank guns and the tank destroyers. Goldstein and Liparulo were taken to the 526th Battalion aid station in the town.

Because of Lt. Colonel Peiper's delays the Germans did not reach Stavelot until it was completely dark. His column was strung out behind him for twenty-five miles. Seeing the vehicles in the town, with lights blazing and so much activity, he thought troops were moving in, not moving out. This gave the American 7th Armored Artillery convoy time to complete their move forward. They wound their way through the streets of Stavelot and headed for St. Vith, Belgium, through Trois Ponts. In addition Lt. Colonel Peiper, seeing the road block, was convinced the town was heavily defended. He and his troops desperately needed rest so he decided to postpone his attack until morning. This was his fatal mistake, as during the night some of the reinforcements sent by First Army arrived.

When Colonel Hansen, the Norwegian commander, received the order to go to Malmedy, the American 99th Infantry Battalion was in Tilff, near Spa. He left immediately, ahead of his troops, in the late afternoon of December 17th, 1944. Going by way of Francorchamps he arrived at Malmedy around 10 o'clock that night. The rest of his troops arrived during the early hours of the 18th. He and Colonel Pergrin decided on the American defense using his troops to fill in the gaps. They soon realized Stavelot, Belgium, had to be defended, as the roadblock on the hill beyond the bridge was the only defense. Colonel Hansen did not know where the 526th Battalion was at that moment. He radioed First Army Headquarters requesting them to have the 526th Battalion divert one company plus a platoon of the 825th Tank Destroyer Battalion at Stavelot on their way through.

The American 526th had assembled at Remochamps west of Spa, Begium. After a delay they finally had moved out at 9 P.M. December 17, 1944. Company A of the 825th T D's, which was waiting for them, moved down from La Reid, joined their column, and they all moved southward through Stoumont, La Gleize and Trois Ponts. The roads

were terrible. They were iced over, and they slipped and slid in the blackout. When First Army received Colonel Hansen's message, they sent out a runner, with written orders, who found the column about midnight. The orders directed the 526th to detach one company of infantry plus one platoon of the Tank Destroyers (T D's) and take over the defense of Stavelot.

As the American column went through Stavelot, the small detachment, Company A of the 526th and the platoon of the T D's with Major Solis in command, were dropped off. It was 3 A M. on December 18, 1944. The rest of the 526th Battalion and Company A of the 825th T D Battalion proceeded to Malmedy.

Major Solis immediately began working out an American defense. The last of his units had arrived by 4 A M. In order to protect the Francorchamps road where the huge gas dump was, he put two rifle squads and an anti-tank gun near the branch railroad crossing north of town, a gun belonging to the 825th on the Malmedy Road, and the rest of the men belonging to the 526th Battalion and two T D's in Stavelot's main square. About 6:30 A.M. December 18, 1944, while it was still dark, he sent a detail of men across the stone bridge toward the hill to set up a heavy roadblock where Sergeant Hensel's men had been. He intended to blow the bridge as soon as they returned.

At that moment Lt. Col. Peiper opened fire with his German pre-dawn artillery barrage, using mortars and rockets to begin his attack. The whole valley rocked with the explosions. Of the detail of men sent across the bridge to set up the roadblock, two of the gun crew were killed, six were missing, and the rest dodged and ran back across the bridge. In the square both T D's and the half tracks which were towing them were knocked out when they attempted to turn around. Around 8 o'clock in the morning, when it was light (the artillery barrage continuing), the German Panzers began rolling down the hill. The gun on the Malmedy road disabled several of the tanks which delayed the rest of them. One of the citizens of Stavelot volunteered and was helping on the gun. Several of the houses on the Malmedy road burned when they were hit. The column now stretched all the way down the hill. It was about 8:30 A.M. when the lead tank rolled out onto the bridge. One after another crossed the bridge, in spite of meeting with heavy American machine gun fire from a street on their right. The bridge remained intact. The Panzers had crossed the Ambleve River! Turning to the left the lead tank bypassed the town square but had to turn on some twisting streets to reach the Trois Ponts road. As the tanks crossed the bridge to make the left turn, they were facing the last of the 825th T D's and they were blazing away.

At this point Major Solis ordered his troops to withdraw but instead of following him, the ones in the square headed east on the Malmedy road and were joined by the 825th gun and crew. They all went to Malmedy with no opposition. When the gun crew at the main intersection in the square saw the tanks by-passing them to the Trois Ponts road, they threw a grenade in the barrel of their gun, and withdrew to Malmedy with the others.

Major Solis withdrew up the Francorchamps road then, in a half track, with only his two rifle squads and the anti-tank gun and crew which had been by the railroad crossing north of the town. The Belgian 5th Fusiliers, under Lieutenant Detros, were guarding the gasoline dump. He and Major Solis agreed that the gasoline should be burned in order to stop the German tanks from coming up the road and to keep the entire 50,000 gallons from falling into their hands. The gasoline cans were then pushed into the ditch with vehicles and set afire. Not one German tank came up that road that day!

When the American First Army had alerted the 30th Division about noon on the 17th of December, 1944, the First Battalion of the 30th Division was in the Aachen area at Warden, Germany, spending a quiet Sunday. The battalion was under the command of Lieutenant Colonel Ernest Frankland. At 3 P.M. they received their orders; there had been a breakthrough and they were to move southward and bivouac in the Eupen area that night. They moved out in convoy at 7 P.M. December 17th. As they sped through Aachen, word of a large breakthrough filtered back. On the jeep radios they heard Axis Sally tell them there was an enormous German counter offensive which could not be stopped. She said, "The fanatical 30th Division, Roosevelt's S S troops, are enroute to rescue the First Army, but they will be completely annhilated!" (In August the 30th Division had fought Peiper in the terrible Battle of Mortain in France and beaten him thoroughly.)

The convoy was long, traffic was backed up; and as they proceeded, German planes were dropping flares in the area, exposing them. Eupen, ahead, was being heavily bombed. The 117th Regiment was routed through as their orders were to seize and defend Malmedy and Stavelot.

They finally arrived in Malmedy about dawn (18th) tired cold and miserable. Enemy troops were reported to be on the outskirts. They were ordered to set up defensive positions, and then the orders were quickly changed and they were ordered to go to Stavelot to relieve the 526th Armored Infantry Battalion. The highway to Stavelot was already cut off by enemy fire so, moving in trucks, they took the back road to Francorchamps, then south to Stavelot.

They piled out of the vehicles a few miles north of the town and waded through foot-deep snow. Ahead on the road was the huge gasoline dump which was being burned. Colonel Frankland ordered it stopped as he needed to have the road open. Major Solis then withdrew on up the Francorchamps road, arrived in Malmedy later in the day, and informed Colonel Pergrin of the arrival of the 117th Regiment in Stavelot. Some of the 526th Battalion men were filtered into the 30th Division's First Battalion, as the 526th Battalion was attached to the 30th Division.

When the leading troops had come down the Francorchamps road, about noon, two of the 526th Battalion's G I's were sitting on the ground eating K-rations. They informed them the Germans were in possession of the town. Colonel Frankland immediately began his plan, which now had changed from defense to offense. On the hill above the town, he put his attached 843rd T. D. Battalion and began shelling the German column passing through the town below. In addition, about 1 P.M., Airforce reconnaissance planes had spotted the head of Peipers long column near La Gleize. Although the weather was bad, they had been able to break through the low clouds. Fighter planes swooped down strafing and bombing the column, for several hours, as it stretched out and passed through Stavelot. They left when fog rose from the river about four o'clock in the afternoon.

Then, Colonel Frankland sent two companies of infantry into an attack on the center of the town, with Co. A to the right and Company B to the left of the road. As they headed down the hill they could see, on the streets below, huge Tiger Royal tanks. The riflemen infiltered slowly into the town center and, after a fight, they took the square. They could not go further as the streets were blocked by several of the huge tanks. After several attempts by the Germans to take it back, they were finally able to hold it; and at dusk Colonel Frankland ordered the battalion to hold and continue the next morning. After dark, on the 18th, the supporting tanks and T. D.'s came down and defenses were set up. During the night some of Colonel Skorzeny's men, soldiers dressed in G I uniforms, attempted to storm the square with two tanks and jeeps. They were disposed of promptly and the vehicles captured. The Germans then withdrew from the square during the night.

The next morning (19th) the attack was resumed. Company A and Company B led and by 10 A.M. they reached the river near the bridge. Germans in G I uniforms made one more futile attack across the bridge and all were killed. Company A fanned out to the right and Company B to the left part of the town. Company C, Company D, and Headquarters remained on top of the hill overlooking Stavelot.

The fighting continued all day. Seven enemy tanks approached the bridge on their side of the river. Mortars and artillery fire were trained on them and knocked out one of the huge tanks attempting to cross, and they all withdrew in the late afternoon. During this time, on top of the hill, a whole company of German infantry sneaked around the back of Company A toward Company C. From the right and in perfect battle formation they walked across a large open area. They were spotted and completely wiped out by the artillery.

That night, the 19th, sadly four G I's were tricked by the enemy. As two were standing guard by a house near the river, a voice in the dark asked in English if they wanted coffee. They said "yes," the voice said "Heil Hitler," and they were taken prisoner. The other two men were in a foxhole, one sleeping and the other on guard. Two persons speaking English spoke with them in the dark, then shot and killed them both.

All the next day December 20, 1944, the Germans made fanatical attacks to recapture Stavelot. Peiper had instructed them to take the town at all costs. The first attack was early in the morning in the vicinity of the bridge. Droves of SS infantrymen attempted an assault on the American Companies A and B by swimming the icy Ambleve River. The Germans (just boys) were completely slaughtered. During a lull,

shortly after, the German infantrymen at the bridge began another assault and again were slaughtered.

One after another the German attacks had been directed at Company A and had been thrown back. Thousands of rounds of artillery and mortars were fired by the Americans. After a lull, the Germans started again, just before dusk. After dark the G I's placed mines across the main highway. That night, the 20th of December, 1944, under a smokescreen and in sight of the Germans across the river, the American 30th Division engineers stole up to the bridge. In the darkness, they wired the bridge and placed a 1,000 pound charge of dynamite. The massive, old stone bridge was blown and not one German panzer

---

TEMPORARY

IMMUNIZATION REGISTER [1]

LAST NAME	FIRST NAME		ARMY SERIAL NO.
PRICE	JOHN R		3762 3699
GRADE	COMPANY	REGT. OR STAFF CORPS	AGE	RACE

SMALLPOX VACCINE

DATE	TYPE OF REACTION [6]	MED. OFFICER [1]

TRIPLE TYPHOID VACCINE

SERIES	DATES OF ADMINISTRATION			MED. OFFICER [1]
	1ST DOSE	2D DOSE	3D DOSE	
1st	11 Jan 45			
2d				
3d				

TETANUS TOXOID

	INITIAL VACCINATION		STIMULATING DOSES	
	DATE	MED. OFF. [1]	DATE	MED. OFF. [1]
1st dose	11 Jan 45			
2d dose				
3d dose				

YELLOW FEVER VACCINE

DATE	LOT NO.	AMOUNT	MED. OFF. [1]

OTHER VACCINES

DISEASE	DATE	TYPE OF VACCINE	DOSES	MED. OFF. [1]
Typhus	11 Jan 45			

------------------------------------, M. C., U. S. Army.

16—20202

Immunization, temporary, January 11, 1945. Back on line the next day.

would cross the Ambleve River at Stavelot. Later that night the snow began to fall.

The next day, December 21, 1944, only a few shots were fired and early the following morning (22nd), the American Company A pushed forward. After several scraps they recaptured the tiny settlement of Parfondruy, Belgium, near Stavelot, a community of less than 100 people. There the men of Company A were horrified to find one of the worst atrocities on the western front. They discovered twenty three Belgian civilians, mostly little children and old people, who had been murdered by the SS men. These were innocent people who had been hiding in a basement. They were ordered up into the garden. They were then lined up along a wall and shot, one after another. The German soldiers admitted their guilt, and they were hung later. A total of 138 civilian men, women, and children were murdered by Peiper's SS troops. This does not count the G I's, the American prisoners of war, the Germans massacred at Malmedy, Belgium.

December 22, 1944, was the last day of active fighting for the American First Battalion in Stavelot; however, they stayed there until they were relieved on January 11, 1945. There would still be terrible days for little Stavelot, Belgium, since entire blocks of the streets were burned by the shells and bombing. Their town was a pile of rubble.

***

When Jack and the other fellow from Tidworth, England, left Le Havre, France, with their replacement unit, they were headed for the front, wherever it might be. That front was Stavelot, Belgium. They were among the troops First Army piled behind the 30th Division there. They were loaded into vehicles of any kind which could be commandeered, including cattle trucks. Some were just open trucks. The weather was bitter, rainy and foggy. They were cold, wet, miserable and without overcoats. The convoy wound its way over back roads with frequent stopping and starting.

When they reached Belgium they got off of the trucks and walked the rest of the way. Jack was still wearing the same clothes he had on when he left the office that night at Tidworth, England. He also still had on those wonderful wool socks I had knitted for him. He later wrote, "They were so warm and really swell, but I also had a full field pack on my back and by the time we got to Belgium I was crippled by the looseness of the knit. Walking so much, one thread out of place can feel like a rope". (More about those wonderful socks later). He was finally able to stop and take them off!

Jack was slated for the 30th Division in Warden, Germany; however, that changed as the 30th Division was now in Stavelot, Belgium, and that is where he and the other soldier from Tidworth went. He later wrote and said that he had been on the line since December 19, 1944, and the first place they went was Stavelot, Belgium. He also wrote later that he was doing things he had no idea how to do. Obviously not! Due to the circumstances, there are no letters from there. He could not know, at the time, that in five weeks he would be officially assigned to the 1st Battalion of the 30th Division.

When the situation in Stavelot had become stabilized, his unit was sent to Malmedy, Belgium, and moved out about December 22, 1944. They then made a fast move around the combat area to Dinant, Belgium, for the defence of the Meuse River. The first heavy snow of the winter began falling the night of the December 21 and morning of December 22, 1944. It covered the entire front and would be the most bitter winter in the Ardennes Forest in fifty years.

At the meeting of the Allied High Command on December 19, 1944, the decision was made that, due to the complete disruption of communications, it would be necessary to split the battlefield. The split would extend from the Meuse River at Givet, France, on a line east to Prum, Germany, in the West Wall. General Bradley's headquarters would remain in Luxembourg City in the south, with General Patton's Third Army under him. The American First and Ninth Army in the north was under General Hodges. It would be temporarily under the command of British Field Marshall Bernard Montgomery, Commander of British ground forces. The change of command would officially begin at 1:30 P.M. on December 20, 1944.

Montgomery's first task was to form a defense line between Monchau and Malmedy, Belgium, and to take over the defense of the Meuse River bridges at Namur, Dinant and Givet and to make contact with the U.S.

VII Corps as defense. The Meuse River was vital for Belgium's protection; the only bridges were at Liege, Huy, Namur, and Dinant. On December 21, 1944, during the day, the British 29th Armored Brigade with 50 tanks, which were west of the Meuse River, moved up and established patrols and were guarding these bridges.

On December 23, 1944, the spearhead of the German 2nd Panzer Division had forged ahead and was climbing the last ridge before Dinant, Belgium. They had pushed forward north of Bastogne. That night a jeep loaded with Germans in American uniforms appeared in Dinant and were captured by the British.

In Bastogne, the 101st Airborne Division (the Screaming Eagles) were completely surrounded by the enemy and, in the midst of a terrible battle, were having to hold out until General George Patton's Third Army was able to reach them. Patton accomplished the impossible by turning his army completely around. His troops had already started the December 19th push into Germany. It was 75 miles under the most horrible conditions.

General Eisenhower soon realized the German objective was not going to be Liege, but the Meuse River. On December 17, 1944, he contacted Maj. Gen. John C. Lee who was Commander of the Communications Zone (The Service Of Supply) to take over the defense of the Meuse. General Lee quickly assembled a force of individual units. Four Ninth Army units were rushed to the area. They were routed around the combat area. Jack was one of these. He and the other fellow from Tidworth were now in the 493rd Replacement Company, Detachment 102. (The 107th Replacement Battalion at Tidworth and the 493rd Replacement Company were Table of Operation and Equipment units). General Lee's forces were to prepare the bridges at Namur and Dinant, Belgium, and Givet, France, for demolition; but they were not to be blown except on specific order. General Lee also committed two separate infantry regiments, the 2nd battalion of the 118th Regiment and the 29th Infantry Regiment.

Jack's unit moved across Belgium, routed around the area of combat, under awful conditions. When they reached Dinant, Belgium, streams of Belgian civilians were fleeing across the Meuse River bridge to escape the Germans. The river at Dinant is wide with a very swift current. Jack's unit was part of a large force, spread for miles as a defensive line west of the Meuse River. The major strength was, however, concentrated from Givet, France, north to Liege, Belgium. They dug in and waited. The weather had cleared the morning of December 23rd, 1944, and the Allied planes were immediately out in force, strafing and shelling the enemy. Although it brought brilliant sunshine, the temperature dropped below zero and was bitterly cold.

Early the next morning Jack's Company moved out of Dinant, Belgium, walking on both sides of the snow covered, winding road which followed the river. They crossed the Belgian border then, to Givet, France a distance of about ten miles. The official records show that the 493rd Replacement Company arrived at Givet, France, on December 24, 1944, at 10:30 A.M.

Givet was a very pretty little village. The town had been liberated by the Americans on September 9th, 1944, and now it was threatened again. Givet itself was the most western part of the Ardennes. It was surrounded by woods and small farms; there were no close towns for shelter. A number of German patrols had been spotted in the woods on the outskirts of the town. The Meuse bridge at Givet had to be defended. The river there is somewhat level, but below the town the banks are quite steep with very high cliffs.

Jack was finally able, that morning, to write a few lines to let me know he was all right. He had the letter he had started in England folded in his pocket. It was wet and the ink had run. He quickly scratched a few words, "Well honey, I started this exactly 10 days ago and this is the first chance I've had to write. I am now somewhere in France. I'll write you a V-mail tonight. New address: G.F.R.S. Pool, Det. 102 493 Repl. Co, APO 131."

He did not write a V-mail that night. That night was Christmas Eve. He was not able to write again for two days. They were dug in protecting the Meuse River bridge at Givet and watching for Germans dressed in American uniforms. They had been fortunate to find shelter in a bombed out barn. The dirt floor was frozen and covered with snow. It was so cold the water in their canteens had frozen. They were sitting around a small fire trying to keep a little warm when some of the fellows formed a choir and began to sing Christmas carols. He said, "All of us had tears in our eyes and if I had been alone, I would have busted out crying. You have no idea how miserable and lonely for you and home I was."

Christmas morning he and another fellow walked across the snowy field where they were bivouaced, to the little French Catholic church nearby. They had planned on going to the midnight service on Christmas Eve, but it had been called off due to "unusual circumstances!" Jack was on guard the rest of the day and all of that night. Dinner on Christmas Day was K-rations and coffee. They were too late for the turkey dinner the troops had. Hot meals are not sent beyond the perimeter. The night was bright and clear, and the moon shone brilliantly against the snow covered countryside. The temperature, below zero, made guard duty absolutely unbearable.

On December 23 the spearhead of the German 2nd Panzer, which had forged ahead, was now within three miles of the Meuse River between Dinant, Begium, and Givet, France. These were General Von Manteufel's Panzers. They were strung out for 12 miles, nearly out of food and fuel. They had gained more ground than any other German division and were traveling alone.

That evening an American patrol had been fired upon by some of the panzers Lt. Everett T. Jones was wounded and had come staggering into the headquarters of Maj. Gen. Ernest N. Harmon, commander of the U.S. 2nd Armored (Hell on Wheels) Division. The division had just arrived from a 70 mile forced march from the Aachen, Germany, area and were headquartered in a chateau near Havalange, 16 miles north of Celles, Belgium. General Harmon realized the Germans were within artillery range of the Meuse River and must be stopped. He got his tanks started. Within five minutes they were heading south.

Before daylight (24th), through the fog, the American 2nd Armored Division struck. A patrol riding ahead heard the rumble of the Panzers approaching and warned the rest of the column, which gave them time to get off of the road and into a grove of trees. They soon opened fire and completely destroyed the German column. That was, however, just the start.

Later that morning the leading tank of the entire German 2nd Panzer Division advanced and reached Celles. Here the column was ordered to leave the road and pull into the surrounding forest for the night. They were completely exhausted as was their fuel supply. Before dawn that morning the officers had stopped at an inn to ask directions. The innkeeper, Madame Marthe Monrique, earlier had only seen several G I engineers laying mines across the road and departing in haste in a jeep. She told the Germans, however, that the Americans had mined the road for miles and there were thousands of them just over the hill. This was alarming news, thus the decision to stay there for the night. This was their fatal mistake!

During the afternoon, one of the American 2nd Armored patrols spotted them coiled up there. (The Belgians said they were out of gas.) General Harmon was notified, and after much dialogue with the VII Corps, he was authorized to attack.

The all-out attack began at 8:00 on the 25th, Christmas morning. The Germans were taken completely by surprise. The light clouds had dispersed and the sun was shining brightly. Fighter bombers and rockets destroyed the huge Tiger and Panther tanks. The British 29th Armored Brigade stationed near Dinant (whose aid had been requested) blasted them with rockets. There being no way for the American tanks to communicate with the planes to guide them, the Piper Cubs artillery observers sent them to where the tanks were located. The Typhoons swooped down leaving a trail of burning, exploding panzers. The rest of the German 2nd Panzers which were following made several attempts to break through, but it was futile. This was the battle and aerial show which Jack and the others in Givet, France, were hearing and watching on Christmas day and which he described in his letter.

The terrible fighting lasted three days. On December 27th the Germans sent their reserves in. The battle raged all day before the village of Celles fell to the Americans. The total German losses that day were: 1,200 taken prisoner; 2,500 killed or wounded; 82 panzers, 83 field guns, and 441 vehicles captured or destroyed. The German offensive had been halted at the tip of the bulge. Not one panzer crossed the Meuse River. Sadly there was much more fighting before it was over.

On the morning of the 26th Jack wrote a short V-Mail to tell me he was all right. He said they had been up in Belgium the week before. He also sent, that morning, a package containing the bottle of perfume he had bought in Le Havre and enclosed the dollar bill which I had sent him in a wallet for Christmas. It was signed by all the fellows he worked with at Tidworth in the 12th Depot. He said he did not have good facilities for mailing it. This was true as I never received it!

On the 28th in the late afternoon he wrote that they were waiting to move again and he had a few minutes. He said he was no longer a clerk, and he was doing something he had absolutely no training for. He told about Christmas. He had not received any mail for three weeks. He said the war seemed so hopeless, and worse the closer to the front he got. It had been three weeks since he had a bath and the same length of time since taking off anything but his shoes. He was thankful for those wonderful socks I had sent him and he had received two pair of heavy woolen socks from his Aunt Stella. He knew I was worried not hearing for so long but he had been on the move all the time and could not write. He had to close as it was getting dark and they were without lights. They moved out that night.

While the 2nd Panzer Division was meeting their defeat at Celles, Belgium, Colonel Peiper and his 1st S S Panzer Division were meeting their doom against the American 30th Division at La Gleize, Belgium. After the terrible massacre at the little settlement of Parfondruy on December 22, 1944, Colonel Peiper and his panzers had continued on to Trois Ponts. The column was turned back when they reached the town as a unit of the 291st Engineers blew up the bridges upon their arrival. They then went on to La Gleize, a village of only fifty houses, and captured the town. Peiper pushed on to Chenault, Belgium, expecting to use that bridge, but American fighter bombers located him and alerted the 291st Engineers who promptly blew that bridge also. Furiously angry, Peiper went back to La Gleize. He was completely completely out of gas, trapped in the Ambleve River valley, and all hope was gone. He was surrounded and under attack. Under cover of darkness shortly before dawn on December 24, 1944, Peiper and all that was left of his Battle Group began their escape from La Gleize. He and 800 men (on foot) slipped through the American lines leaving their dead and wounded and all of their equipment. Before their final departure the 30th Division entered La Gleize and eliminated the pockets of resistance and occupied the town. Thus ended cruel and arrogant Colonel Joachim Peiper's dream of glory!

***

When Jack's unit moved out of Givet the night of December 28th, they were pulled off the line to a camp in the rear. He did not write for two days. They moved southwest across France in deep snow to Compiegne, a distance of approximately 120 miles, to the 16th Replacement Depot. They were housed in tents (sleeping on straw) in Compiegne Forest on the outskirts of the town. It was far better than sleeping on the ground as they had been. Compiegne had been greatly damaged when the Allied armies were pushing across France in August, and there was heavy fighting in the forest on August 29, 1944, when the town was liberated.

On December 30, 1944, in the afternoon, Jack wrote that he was sitting in a little cafe in a French town writing as they were in tents and it was impossible to write there. He said they had just come down from Belgium and mentioned the towns he had visited, or what was left of them: Stavelot, Malmedy, Dinant, and Givet. By writing "visit" it passed the censor as it did not suggest troop movement. He said he was in a well-known town, but he could not tell me the name of it. He then said he hoped he would be able to go to Paris before he had to go back up. (My father immediately knew the town was Compiegne, and he was correct.) They had a new address: G F R S Pool, APO 129. He said he wished he had not given me that first address as it would slow his mail. They were sitting there comparing pictures of their wives, feeling so blue and homesick. They were hoping and trying to believe this was the beginning of the end. They went back to camp for chow. He had planned to come back to the cafe and finish the letter that night, but it had begun to sleet, was getting terribly dark, and he was afraid he would get lost. They stayed in and he was writing by the light of a very smoky fire. He said he knew I wanted to hear about all the countries he had been in and the things he had seen but I would have to wait until he could see me in person!

The next night was New Year's Eve, December 31, 1944, and they were in the tent. He wrote that it was a year he would be glad to see end. He did not think much of France, the people were not at all friendly and seemed to have so much more. He said the people in Belgium had gone through as much, if not more, and were so congenial. He enclosed a very touching poem which he had written on a pieco of scratch paper while he was at the front in Stavelot.

On New Year's night, January 1, 1945, he was back in the cafe writing as it was too cold in the tent. The temperature had dropped way below zero. They were sitting around drinking beer, "the consistency of Missouri River water", he wrote. A little French boy was sitting in front of him playing Roll out the Barrel, and all our old songs on his accordion. They were all feeling weepy and sad. He had finally gotten a big turkey dinner that day but was very sick for the next two days! He had to close as they had a 9 P.M.curfew.

The next night, January 2, they stayed in the tent as it was snowing hard and too cold to go to town. They had rigged up a little stove and it was fairly comfortable. He had hung his flashlight from the front of his field jacket so he could see what he was writing. He was lying on his straw thinking of all the happy times we had together, how he would enjoy playing with the baby when he came home, and wanting her to know her daddy. He wanted to know whether his dad had been able to get the suitcase for my Christmas present. Things like that were nearly impossible to get, but he had. It was tan with multicolored stripes and bound in leather, very stylish just then.

They were finally moved from the tents into brick buildings. On January 5, 1945, he wrote that he was a garrison soldier again, but he said the tents with the straw were actually warmer. He hoped to buy Peggy a Belgian doll and a real French barette when he got paid, but he never did get paid. He said the G I food was good (Jack thought all food was good), but he was so hungry for coffee and doughnuts, cookies and two or three quarts of milk, or a milk shake. Weren't they all?

On January 9 he had nothing to write about but did not want to miss two days. It is remarkable that he was able to write at all when two months passed with no mail from home. He lived for my letters with every detail of Peggy's doings each day. He wrote regarding the socks I had knitted for him, "The other day my feet were so cold and the socks were so warm I put on a pair of G I cotton socks underneath first and now my feet really keep warm. Please make some more."

After that first letter he had scratched off on Christmas Eve in Givet, France, his letters were coming quite regularly to me. There had been a news blackout at first. We only knew the Germans had broken through and a terrible battle was going on in the Ardennes. After receiving Jack's letter that he would not spend Christmas in England and would see Rusty that weekend, we knew he was in it. It was a heavy-hearted Christmas, but we saw that Peggy had a happy one. At 18 months it was the first one she understood. I received the Givet letter about January 8, 1945, and answered it promptly. I am afraid I did not take his being there very well.

When he finally received the letter in Germany in February, 1945, he replied,"Honey there are a lot of other fellows over here in the same boat and I'm no better than any of them and Lord knows it is well worth fighting for. All we can do is pray that this is over soon and that I can get home whole.

"A person doesn't realize how religious he is till he gets up here." I was deeply concerned and prayed for all of them, but it did not keep me from feeling Jack was special.

Continuing his January 9, 1945, letter he wrote that it was still bitterly cold, had snowed all day, and was miserable to be out in. He was finally able to take a bath as he couldn't stand to live with himself any longer. He heated water and took a bath in his helmet. It felt good but how he longed for a bathtub. He planned to finish the letter the next morning, but it was two more days before he was able to do so.

On January 11 he finished it. He had been on guard duty. It had snowed for two days; there was a foot of snow on the ground and they had to be out in it all day. They were guarding German prisoners. It had cleared the night before and the temperature dropped way below zero. They had just received all new shots and his arm was so sore he could hardly write. It made 9 shots for the same thing since December 16, 1944. He said he had serum instead of blood in his veins! They would be going back on the line soon. He still had not received any mail, but the other fellow who had come from Tidworth had. He was sitting there listening to the Coca Cola program on the radio, making himself blue and miserable, bringing back memories he would like to keep in the back of his mind till he could come home again.

That letter was not mailed until January 17, 1945. With it he mailed a hastily written V-Mail just to let me know he was all right. These were the last letters from France. They went back on the line and I did not hear for ten days. The day he left France he received a Christmas package from my mother filled with cookies (still fresh) which had been mailed

in August. The railroads had been repaired, and they traveled to Belgium in 40 or 8 boxcars (40 men or 8 horses). They were French military rail cars. They all enjoyed the cookies and Jack read a wonderful book while traveling which he knew I would enjoy. The title was The Chicken Wagon Family by Barry Benefield. (Fifty years later my niece Phyllis obtained an out of print copy for me.)

Although the German advance had been halted, the battle was still far from over. On January 3, 1945, the Allied counter-offensive had begun, following General Montgomery's plan, with the First Army pressing forward toward the north to Houffalize, Belgium.

On January 8, 1945, Hitler authorized a troop withdrawal from the tip of the bulge, and the Panzer Divisions were moved to the Russian front. On January 12, 1945, the Russians began their long awaited winter offensive on the German front. The rest of the German army was to continue defending the towns in the Ardennes which they still held.

On January 16, 1945, the American First and Third Armies linked up in a pincers movement at Houffalize, Belgium, as planned, then the all-out advance turned eastward. Most of the German army managed to slip out of the trap, leaving their equipment behind. It became a disorganized retreat, long-winding columns back to Germany, on foot. They were pursued by American artillery and planes. Unfortunately, there were still some fanatical pockets of resistance and bitter fighting to clear them out. Also, prisoners had to be taken and guarded.

At midnight on January 17, 1945, the First Army reverted to the Twelfth Army Group. On the 17th Jack's unit went back on the line, and the fellow from Tidworth was still with them. The snow was waist deep and deeper in drifts. The weather was freezing and the advance was slow. The German soldiers had been prepared with plenty of heavy winter clothing, but the G I's were not. They sewed blankets together and stuffed newspapers in their jackets for warmth. They froze, their rifles froze, and what was worse their feet froze. Frostbite and frozen feet were the big casualty makers. They bivouaced in the snow; the towns where they could find shelter were far apart. The ground was frozen six inches deep and digging a foxhole was a nearly impossible task.

The Germans had been provided with white clothing for camouflage against the snow, but the G I's had none. They were a perfect target against the white snow. The Belgian women, out of the kindness of their hearts, donated their sheets and often their best tablecloths to cover the American soldiers.

I did not receive any mail from Jack for the next ten days. He wrote later, however, "The bulge was terrible. I have seen a lot of countries and a lot of interesting sights, but under the conditions I have seen them, they haven't meant a lot. For every wonderful and interesting thing I have seen, I've seen two that are too horrible to talk about." He wrote later in another letter, "I have been in almost continuous fighting on the line since December 19th. I have seen some funny things and some horrible things—guys falling all around me and me never getting hurt.

"When you are on the line you carry everything you own with you all the time. You fight day and night, eat whatever you can get your hands on whenever you can. You sleep whenever you can get a chance to sneak a nap. Never over an hour or two at a time. You move continuously. It's rough. You have to have stamina to stand it. I'm not exaggerating. It's impossible to describe. You wouldn't believe it. You would say no human could stand it. When you are up on the line you don't worry about getting killed. The only two things I worried about were you and Peg in case anything happened to me and about hurting, the pain if I got hit.

"I've had quite a few narrow squeaks too - I don't know whether the censor is supposed to let things like this go through but I'll try it once. One morning my buddy and I were lying in our foxhole while the Jerries laid a terrific artillery barrage down on us. This fellow was laying facing the wall of the hole and I was next to him with my arm over him, keeping our heads down as far in the mud as we could. When it finally lifted I raised up and started talking to him but he didn't answer or move so I turned him over and found that somehow a piece of shrapnel had hit him in the middle and he was dead. My arm hadn't been an inch away from where the piece hit and I can't for the life of me understand how he got it and I didn't—I being more exposed than he! Guess the Lord was just with me."

On the 27th Jack mailed the letter he had written on the 17th. He wrote that he was up in Belgium again, for good this time. He was lated for a regular outfit but could not give me any details or an address yet. He said if he had a decent place to write he could peel off 30 pages about the places he had been, the cities and things he had seen and countries visited. He said the most interesting towns he had visited were Compiegne, France, and Verviers in Belgium. He said Belgium was the best; the people were wonderful to them. Then he wrote, "I even had a steak dinner and an ice cream sundae here." This told me he was in Verviers! He was writing in pencil as his ink was frozen solid. It was Saturday and he and three other fellows were on a pass. He wrote, "We found a Belgian civilian who fixed us a steak with french fries and coffee for a dollar. It's a funny thing, but Belgium has about anything you want to buy. In all the shops they had candy of all kinds. It was pretty expensive, each piece was seven cents." What Jack did not know was that the Belgian Government took control as soon as they were liberated. The government immediately established a currency, also wage and price controls, and the country was soon on the way to recovery.

While he was in Verviers that day he went in a very old, beautiful Catholic church. (It was Notre - Dame Des Recollets.) The priest spoke fluent English and took him all over the church telling him the history of it. He spent two hours there.

Jack also wrote that they had a very modern department store here—J. Tytgadt-Arents—which they went through. (He enclosed their card). He wanted to buy Peggy one of the pretty little Belgian dolls which were only two dollars but he did not have any money. It was getting dark then, they were going to chow, and he would finish later. However, when they finished, it was so cold he had to get in his sleeping bag and said he would write again as soon as he could. This letter had a different APO (153) and a different censor. He had said he was slated for a regular outfit. He did not write again for three days. At about this time the socks I had knitted for him came to the end of their days. Gone were the toes and heels. He peeled them off and only the arch and top was left!!

On January 28, 1945, the Battle of the Bulge was declared officially over. The Allied losses totaled 77,000 men. 8,000 were killed, 48,000 were wounded, 21,000 were captured or missing. 733 tanks and tank-destroyers were lost.

The German losses totaled 21,000 casualties of troops, 600 tanks and assault guns, 1600 planes, and 6,000 other vehicles. The Allies could replace their equipment, but the Germans could not. Sir Winston Churchill said later, in a speech to the British House of Commons, "This will, I believe be regarded as an ever-famous American Victory." He spoke prophetically.

THE LETTERS

To: From:
Mrs. John K. Price   Pvt. John . Price
704 Ballas Rd.   ASN 37623699
Kirkwood 22, Mo.   G.F.R.S. Pool Det. 102
U.S.A.   493 Repl. Co. APO 131
                        (New Address Dec. 30:
                        APO 129)

A POEM FROM THE FRONT
When the evening shadows gather
  After all my work is through,
I can't keep my eyes from straying
  to that Photograph of you.

There it rests upon a nearby shelf
  The way you looked that day
Oh, it seems as it was but yesterday
  When I first heard you say
Words of love that made me happy,
  and made all my dreams come true,
But tonight I'm all alone, with
  just a photograph of you.

Then I wonder if you're lonely
  Yes, I guess you miss me too

While I sit here dreaming, gazing
  at that photograph of you.

Thus my heart is always with you,
  While I wait the long days through,
And the dearest of my treasures
  Is that Photograph of you.

When the years have told their story
  And the world is once more free,
I'll be home with you, my darling.
  There will still be you and me.

Then we'll build our dreams together
  Hand in hand the long years through,
And forever in my heart I'll hold,
  That Photograph of you."

(This poem — copied exactly as written — was "dreamed up" and written on a piece of scratch paper at the front in Stavelot, Belgium, in December, 1944, by Pvt. John K. Price to his wife Jeanne.)

14 December 1944
Thursday

Dearest Darling:
    How are you this evening, honey? I feel pretty good for a change. No, it's not from receiving any mail from you, as I drew a blank.
    I am really looking forward to seeing Rusty again. I hope to be able to spend this Saturday and Sunday with him. Well, I still have a couple of letters to answer so I guess I'd better get on them. Honey, I don't think you have to worry about me changing as far as temperment goes or my love for you. Course I will feel strange at first when I get home and be jumpy and restless but that's where your job will start, straightening me out and helping me forget all about the army and getting used to being my own boss again. It's quarter after eleven so it looks like this is going to be a short one again. Darn, every time I think of Christmas it really puts me down in the dumps, and now that I won't be able to spend it in England it really makes me feel worse, if that is possible. Lord, I hope this is the last one I have to spend away from home. I've gotten very pessimistic about the whole thing and have given up all hope as far as the end of this mess is concerned. It has begun —

Christmas Eve
Givet, France

    Well, honey, I started this exactly 10 days ago, and this is the first chance I have had since to write. I am now some where in France.
    I'm not going to try to write any more on it as I have lost whatever train of thought I had. I'll close and write you a V-mail tonight I'm afraid it will all have to be V-mail for the most part from now on.
    Bye for now, honey, Love me and miss me a little and say a big prayer for me.
    Give Peg a big kiss for me too.
    All my love, for always to the sweetest and most wonderful wife in the whole world.

Your sweetheart,
  Jack
P.S. I love you.

New address: G.F.R.S. Pool, Det 102
493 Repl Co, APO 131

Dearest Darling:

Well, honey, it has been quite a while since I was able to write you, but it really couldn't be helped and I'll try to get a letter a day to you from now on, although it will have to be V-mail. I was going to write you a nice Christmas letter yesterday, but I drew guard duty so couldn't do any writing. As you see, Christmas was just another day around here and a darn lonesome and blue one too. I hope you and Peg had a big time. I would have given anything to have been with you but I'm not even going to think about it.

France is not too bad, in fact, quite a lot like home, but we have no facilities for sleeping, etc, and it's so darn cold that the water in our canteens freeze overnight. I have never been so cold and miserable in all my life. I sure wish I could have waited till Spring to come over here, though.

Well, honey, I see that I see that I have to go now so I guess I'll close this for now. If I get time I'll write another tonight. By the way I mailed you a bottle of perfume today and am going to try to get Peg one of those Belgian dolls which I'll mail. I have really seen some cute ones since arriving here. Well, darling, Bye for now. Love me and miss me. Say a prayer for me, honey. I love you. All my love for always and always,

Your sweetheart, Jack

V-MAIL
Thursday
28 Dec 44

Dearest Honey:

Well, darling, this is the first chance I have had to write you and I hope I have time to write a half decent letter for a change. I am waiting to move again and have a few extra minutes — I hope. Well, from all appearances your husband is no longer a clerk. I'm kind of peeved about it but there is nothing I can do about it. They give you months of special training then come over here only to find you are going to do something you have had absolutely no training for. How was Christmas, sweet? Be sure and write and tell me all about it. Especially about Peg — what she got and how she acted and all. It was sure one miserable day for me. In fact it was worse than the usual day as far as days go. As far as the day being Christmas it could have just as well been the 4th of July or something for all the day meant. I did get to go to church though. Another fellow and I went to a little Catholic French Church in the little town near here Christmas morning. They had planned on having a midnight service that we were going to but due to unusual circumstances it was called off. Christmas eve we were sitting around the fire here trying to keep a little warm when a bunch of fellows who had formed a Choir began to sing Christmas carols and I guess all of us had tears in our eyes. I know I did, and if I'd been alone I'd have busted out crying. Honey, you have no idea how miserable and lonely for you and home that I was. I just had to keep my mind off of you or I think I'd have gone nuts. I wanted to write you and Peg a nice letter on Christmas but I didn't get a chance. Merry Christmas anyway. I wonder if you have received the bottle of perfume I sent you? The dollar bill I sent with it with all the names on it was the same one that was in the billfold

you sent me. I had all the fellows I was working with at the 12th sign it and I thought I would keep it as a souvenir. Also that 10 shilling note I thought you would like to keep. (Neither those nor the perfume were ever received.) I sure wish I could have stayed in Tidworth till after Christmas as I had an invitation in Andover for a nice Christmas day, and dinner. I sure hated to miss it. I haven't had any mail from home now for better than 3 weeks and I expect that it will be another month or two fore I do receive any. I sure could use a letter or two right about now. I am really anxious to hear some news about home and anxious to get some new pictures of Peg.

Lord, when is this horrible mess going to end. It all looks so darned hopeless, even worse the closer to the front you get. I,ll tell you this, if they would show the folks back home how these people here are living and how they look, etc, the war would definitely end a great deal sooner. And the boys over here haven't any picnic. Oh what I wouldn't do for a bath. It has been almost three weeks, maybe a little more, since I've had a bath and about the same length of time since I've taken off any clothes except my shoes. It has been so darn cold, below zero, that it's too cold to do anything. Thank goodness I've got those wonderful socks you sent me, they are really warm. Did I tell you that the package I received from Aunt Stella had 2 pair of heavy woolen socks, so I'm pretty well fixed as far as my feet go. One thing, honey, if several days go by that you don't receive any mail please don't worry. I'll write just as often as I can but it is kind of hard sometimes and most likely won't be able to write every night. I guess you were worried not hearing from me this last time but I was on the move all the time and couldn't write. Honey, I love you and miss you so darn much. When I get to thinking what home is like I just can't imagine how it was, way back when I was a civilian. All recollections of how it was before I came in the Army are so faint. It's just like I have never known anything but Army.

Well, it's getting dark and as we are without lights, I guess I'd better close while I can still see. Be sure and say your prayers for me cause I really need them now. Take good care of Peg, honey, and give her a big kiss for me. I love you, honey.

Your Sweetheart,
    Jack
P.S. I love you.

Saturday
30 Dec 44

Dearest Sweetheart:

I am sitting in a little cafe in a French town writing this as we are in tents and it is impossible to write in camp. My hands are so cold I can hardly manipulate this darn pen but it at least isn't as bad as it was last Wednesday (27th) and before. We just moved here from Belgium and I mean it was cold there. By the way I got to visit Malmedy, Dinant, and a little town of Givet last week, or rather what's left of the towns — ask Uncle Bob if he remembers them from when he was here. Also saw Soissons and Le Havre. Course I've been through a lot of towns but the ones I mentioned I actually got to visit. I am in a very well known town now but because of Censor regulations I can't tell you the name of it. I only hope I can go to Paris before I go back up. I sure would give anything to get some mail from you. It has been almost a month since I've heard from you. By the way — change of address again, write me G F R S

Pool APO 129 — I only wish I hadn't given you that old address now. It will just mean that much longer waiting for the mail to catch up. I think I'll be here at this APO long enough though for you to write me using it. I have been looking all over trying to find a doll or something nice for Peg but so far I haven't had any luck — anyway I only have about 100 Francs left so would have to wait till payday fore I would be able to buy anything. We are sitting here now comparing pictures of our wives and I'm really feeling blue and homesick. It just looks like this thing will never end and I'll never get back home. We all are hoping and trying to make ourselves believe that this break through and drive is the beginning of the end and maybe they'll quit by Easter. Lord, I hope so anyway. I love you and miss you so much, darling, I don't know what to do. If it weren't for you and Peg back home I'd really be in bad shape. Just the fact that I know you are there waiting for me and loving me keeps me going. Well, honey, I've got to quit now and get back to camp for chow. I'll finish this tonight if I can get back down hereto write. Bye now. Here I am again but it had begun to sleet and was terribly dark and as I was kind of afraid I'd get lost I decided to stay in so I'm writing this here in the tent by the light of a very smoky fire under extreme difficulties. I only hope you can read this. I know now why some fellows don't write after getting over here. It really is an effort under these conditions. I guess you have noticed how my letters have gotten shorter and shorter. 4 pages like this has gotten to be about my limit now. I know you are anxious to hear all about the countries I have been in and the things I've seen but I hope you don't mind waiting till I can tell you in person.

How is Peg , honey? I sure wish I could see her and was able to help bring her up and watch her grow. Send me some new pictures so I can see how much she has changed. I'd like some new ones of her momma too.

Well, honey, I guess I'll close for now, the light is getting bad and I can't see what I'm writing. Goodnight darling, sweet dreams say a prayer for me. All my love for always.

Your Sweetheart,
Jack
P.S. Give Peg a big kiss for me. I love you.
New address:
G.F.R.S. Pool, APO 129

(By writing visit, it passed the censor.)

Sunday
New Years Eve.

Dearest Darling,
Well, another year is almost over — and it is one that I'm tickled silly to see done with. It has been the most lonesome and miserable year I have ever spent. I sure hope I don't have to spend another like it. I've been sitting here trying to remember what we did last New Years Eve. I know you were in Tyler, but what did we do and where did we go? I wonder what you and Peg are doing tonight. What I wouldn't give to be with you.

Well, I don't think so much of France. As far as the climate and country are concerned I like it better than England, but the attitude of the people I don't like at all, they aren't to friendly to us. Course another thing that doesn't help matters is the fact that we don't speak the same language and have one hell of a time trying to talk to anyone. The women over here are much more beautiful than in England, as a general rule, but are much more aloof. The country though is very beautiful and worth seeing. I'm sure anxious to hear from home, about you and Peg, but I guess it will be a month or so fore any of your letters catch up to me. Tell the folks I'm having a terrible time writing.

Here is another poem, honey, I dreamed up while I was up at the front — I wasn't going to send it, but figured maybe you would enjoy it — I've got it on a piece of scratch paper so I'll just copy it.

Well, with that I'll close and hit the hay. Love me and miss me, say a prayer for me and give Peg a big kiss for me. All my love,

Your sweetheart,
Jack
P.S. Sweet dreams. I love you.

1 Jan 1945
Monday

Dearest Darling:
Happy New Year, sweet — lets just both hope and pray that this year will turn out to be a happy one and that fore many months of it have passed I'll be back home with you and Peg. Things do look a little better now and maybe this big drive going on now was Germanies last. The general opinion is that this is the beginning of the end and when this drive has been wiped out, they will collapse. Let's hope so anyway.

Well, honey, I'm back in town tonight writing this in a cafe as it was just too darn cold out in the tent. We are sitting around drinking beer (the consistency of Missouri River water) and listening to a little French kid play Roll out the Barrell on the Accordian and trying to write letters all at the same time. This darn kid is sitting here in front of me playing all our old songs and the old WW I songs too. It's making all of us feel weepy and sad. All I can do is think about you and Peg and how I want to be with you and wondering what you are doing now. When and if I do get home, honey, I want to be able to come to our own little place, with all our own familiar things around and everything just like I left it and be able to have you and Peg all to myself. What a day that will be. Honey, I don't want you and Peg to meet me though. I want to be able to come home all by myself and have you waiting for me at home where I can just let go of all these feelings and emotions I've been storing up all this time without worrying about what people are thinking and all. Guess kind of I'm counting my chickens fore they are hatched but it helps to dream and lately those dreams are about all I have to keep me going.

I guess I'd better close for now. I want to drop the folks a couple of lines and as there is a curfew law here at 9 PM I haven't a lot of time.

Say a prayer and give Peg a big kiss for me. All my love for always.

Your Sweetheart,
Jack
P.S. I love you.

2 Jan. 45
Tuesday

Dearest Sweetheart:
Well, Darling, I'm going to start this tonight but Lord knows what I'm going to write about or when I'll finish it.

I've been pretty lucky as far as writing goes for the last few days. I'm sitting in the tent tonight writing cause it is snowing out and was too cold to go to town. We rigged up a little stove here in the tent and it is pretty comfortable. The only bad thing is that I have to use my flashlight — got it hanging from the front of my field jacket — to see what I'm writing. Honey, I was laying here on my straw looking up at the ceiling thinking about you and all the wonderful times we have had together and got to thinking about our wonderful little house on Montview. You had it furnished so darn cute. That's what I want to come home to. I want to be able to come home and have you waiting there for me just like you used to. I want all our furniture there and everything just as it was when I left. I want to be able to spend a lot of time with Peg so she'll get to know her daddy a little. I have a lot of time to make up with her. I'm so anxious to see Peg and play with her and spoil the devil out of her, bringing her little presents when I come home from work and have her know she has a pop she can just wind about her little finger. I'm sure anxious to get some new pictures of her. I'll bet she has really grown up since the last ones I got. Is she talking much? I guess she jabbers like a blue streak but does she make any sense yet? Is her hair still blonde or has it begun getting dark yet? Is she still as pretty as she was when this last picture of her was taken? Be sure and write me a full description of her Christmas and all. I want to know every little detail of everything she got and how she acted and all. By the way, honey was Dad able to get that suitcase for you for my Christmas present to you? If he didn't, let me know what I gave you, will you? Well, darling, this is another short one, but it is getting late and I'd better quit and get to bed. It's only 9 o'clock but that's late here. Give my love to the folks, yours and mine, and give Peg a big kiss for me, too. Say a prayer for me, sweet. All my love for always.

Your sweetheart,
Jack
P.S. I love you.

5 January 1945
Friday
France

Dearest Sweetheart,

Will wonders never cease!! I'm a garrison soldier again — living in brick barracks, believe it or not — for a while anyway, although I'd a lot rather be back in the tent I was living in. It was a lot warmer in the tent. Only one thing I hope is that I'm here long enough for my mail to catch up to me. I was digging through a few letters from you I have and found one which I don't believe I've answered yet, so I'll get on it right now. By the way, I wore the socks you knitted for me while I was working in the office and they were so warm and really swell so when I left England I naturally had them on, but I also had a full field pack consisting of absolutely everything I owned, 110 lbs, on my back, and by the time we got to Belgium I was crippled by the looseness of the knitting in the feet and I was awfully afraid I wouldn't be able to wear them any more — those feet of mine are are really important now and with walking so much the least little thread out of place feels like a rope, but the other day my feet were so cold and the socks were so warm that I decided to try them again. I put a pair of G.I. cotton

socks on underneath first and by golly they were wonderful so now my feet really keep warm, so send me another pair, please mam. Also if you can, please send me a pair of really good leather fur lined gloves. I can get all the good G I gloves I want, but fur lined are particularly warm and desirable.

Darn, honey I wish I could see an end to this mess in the distant future somewhere. I want to be with you and Peg so much. You mentioned Peg curling up in the big chair looking at her picture book which reminds me, did you ever get those little books I sent her from London? I hope they were not too old for her. I looked that darn town over for something for her, and that was honestly the best I could do. (Booby Bear and Cyril Squirrel were received and much loved.) After I get paid this month I'm going to try to find a nice little doll and maybe a real French barette for her. I tried to get one in England but things like that were almost impossible to find there. Over here, though, things like that are more plentiful and cheaper too. Well, darling it's getting late and I'm plenty tired so I guess I'd better close for tonight. I love you and miss you more than you'll ever know. Say a prayer for me and give Peg a big kiss.

Your Sweetheart
Jack
P.S. I love you.

6 Jan 1945
Saturday

Dearest Darling:

Well, honey, another week is just about over and this has really been a long one and a lonesome one. I guess one reason is because I haven't heard from you for so long. You don't realize how much those letters from you help to keep you going until you have to do without them. I hope you have some new pictures of my wonderful family on the way too, cause I want to see how it is changing and growing. We just had a big discussion about dogs, which, of course I had to enter. I haven't had any news about how Buff is for a long time. Have you seen any of the pups since you sold them? I wonder how they turned out. We have really been having some rough weather here lately. It has been terribly cold, I don't know what the temperature was, but zero or below anyway and snow off and on all along. We haven't a great deal of snow on the ground as it is so cold it is blowing instead of packing on the ground. Doggone it, I'm so hungry for something good — something different than this G.I chow. It's good food but you need something nice once in a while. If we could even get a cup of Java and a couple of do-nuts once in a while it would help, but we don't even have a Red Cross where we can get it. Boy, what I couldn't do to some of those cookies of yours and 2 or 3 quarts of milk right now, or a milk shake. The first week or so I'm home I'm going to be sick from eating all the good things I've been missing for so long. Darn, the lights just went out so I'll have to finish by candle light. This is awfully short I know, honey, but I'll write again tomorrow. Give Peg a big kiss and say a prayer for me. All my love for always to my two wonderful Darlings.

Your Sweetheart,
Jack
P.S. I love You.

7 January 1945
Sunday

Dearest Darling:

Well, Honey, another very lonesome and blue weekend is just about over. It has really been a miserable one, even more so than usual. I just got through writing the folks a letter at long last, tonight. I was really beginning to feel ashamed as it's been so long since I last wrote them, but I really couldn't help it. I did get off a fairly decent letter to them so it should put me back in their good graces, I hope.

I got to digging in my old letters again this evening and I found another letter from you that I haven't answered yet, written the 19th of November. I never get tired of hearing about what you and Peg do each day to the smallest detail, and Peg will give you quite a bit to write about all the time. By the time I do get news she is altogether different again, it takes so long for the mail to get to me. I wonder just where we will go when I get home. I mean what city we will be living in if I go with Newberry, and where we will end up. Anywhere in the South, West, or Middle West will suit me fine. I wonder just what kind of offer they will give me. There is a certain excitement to settling in a new place and seeing new things and meeting new people. Remember how much fun it was when we went to Houston? All those things really give me a lot of wonderful memories to dream about, too. Well, it's getting late and I want to wash up a little fore I go to bed so I'd better close for tonight. Sweet dreams, darling, I love you and miss you more than you'll ever know.

Your Sweetheart,
Jack
P.S. I love you, kiss Peg for me.

7 Jan 1945
Sunday

Dear Mom and Dad:

I'm going to try to write you all a letter tonight. I feel awful guilty though about not writing you for so long. I'm still in France but have moved to a different camp, to the rear, since I last wrote you. (Jan.1) For a while we were in Belgium but had to come back to France. My new address is G F R S Pool, APO 129 now. I sure wish I would be settled long enough to get some mail from home. I'm hoping I stay here a few weeks. Mail and news from home is the thing that keeps me going. I definitely don't like France. I don't like the attitude of the general run of the French people. The people in Belgium have gone through as much, if not more, and they are at least congenial and give the average soldier a break. Course, there is absolutely nothing here for us to do on our off hours and we have had very poor living conditions, although they are better now, and have no Red Cross or anything here which does make it a little tougher. You know, it is funny, but as far as luxuries are concerned, it seems tome the French have a lot more than the English. It might be my imagination but that's the way it appears to me.

How was Christmas back home? I'm sure anxious to hear all about it. We sure spent one miserable Christmas. We were in a combat zone and I was on guard all day long. My Christmas dinner comprised a cup of coffee and a can of C ration cause I got off too late for the turkey they had. We were right in front of the point of that German spearhead — could hear the guns all day and planes and all. They finally moved us out two days after Christmas. Then New Years I had a big Turkey dinner and got terribly sick and was sick for two days from it, so all in all I had a very miserable holiday season this year. How did Peg act on her first Christmas? Be sure and give me all the details. Have you heard any more about Rusty? I wonder how he is getting along. I guess Babe told you all that I'm no longer a clerk, but an infantry rifleman now and it most likely won't be too long fore I'll be in a line outfit most likely up in the front. Well, maybe it will help get me home sooner — one way or another. Well, folks, I'd better close for now, I've got to write Babe yet this evening. Write soon and keep me posted on all the news. Look after Babe and Peg for me and remember me in your prayers. All my love to my extra special wonderful Mom and Dad.

Your Son,
Jack

9 January 1945
Tuesday

Dearest Darling:

I didn't write you last might, honey, Cause I just didn't have a thing to write about and tonight I'm not much better off, but I couldn't miss two days in a row. The weather, a good subject to start off on, has been cold as the deuce and it snowed all day today. It sure is miserable to have to get out in. I never could stand the darn cold anyway. I'm on the verge of wishing I was in the South Pacific where it's nice and warm. That reminds me I haven't heard from Joe Barnes (his friend in the S.P.) for a long time now. He usually answers my letters pretty regularly. The fact I moved around so much might be the reason. I finally got around to taking a bath tonight, at long last. I'm telling you I finally got to where I couldn't stand to live with myself so I heated some water and took a bath in my helmet. I sure feel good now — but, boy a bathtub would sure look good to me now.

I guess I'd better go to bed. I'll dig out an old letter or two of yours tomorrow evening and finish this and make a nice long one out of it. Good night, sweet dreams, I love you.

(He did not finish this letter for two days.)

(January 11.)

Well, honey, here I am again, but quite a few days later. I just got off a pull of guard and am I tired. It has been snowing for the last couple of days and we have about a foot of snow on the ground now and we have to be out in it all day. It is really miserable. Then to top it all off it turned off clear last night and the temperature went down to way below zero. They just gave us a new bunch of shots and is my arm ever sore. That is the reason for this very poor writing. I can hardly hold the pen. It makes 9 shots for the same thing I have had since Dec. 16th. I 've got serum instead of blood flowing through my veins.

I still haven't received any mail from you, over a month now since I last heard from home. The other fellow who came from Tidworth with me has received quite a few letters already. I wonder what is holding it up like that. Well, honey, I've got to go for awhile. I'll be back shortly. Here I am again and I'll try to finish this now. I'm sitting here listening to the Coca Cola program and making myself very blue and miserable. It brings back an awful

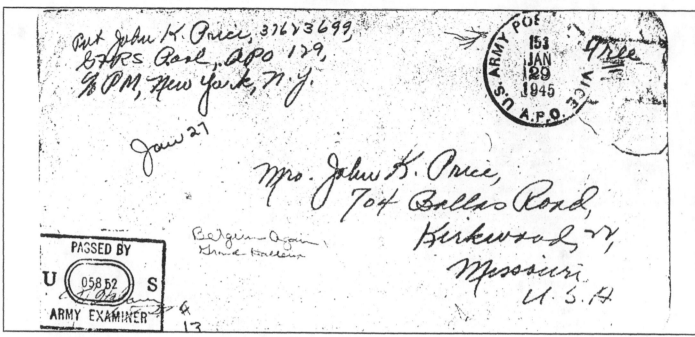

Envelope with diffrent APO, 1531. On pass, January 27, 1944.

lot of memories that I would just as soon keep in the back of my mind, at least till there is something definite as to when I can come back home to you again. Remember, in Birmingham on Sunday afternoons, laying around listening to all the beautiful music and relaxing after a big dinner? I sure wish I was there now, where I could look up at you, sitting in the chair reading or something, and thinking of how much I loved you and what a lucky guy I was. That was really a cute little house and you had it furnished so wonderful. I hope we can have as nice a place when I get back, although as long as you and Peg are there, any place will seem like heaven to me. I wonder, really, how I will feel when the news comes out that it is all over and they start sending us home for good. What a day that will be.

I haven't been paid yet, honey. I will only be paid a partial payment this month, $10, as they lost all my records when I shipped over here, so as soon as I am paid in full I'll shoot you as much as I can, keeping just what I need to get by on. Well, darling, I'm half sick, and feel so sore and stiff from those shots, I guess, so I'll close for now and hit the hay plenty early. Good night, sleep tight, sweet dreams. I love you and miss you more than anything in the world. Give Peg a big hug and kiss for me too.

Your sweetheart,
Jack
P.S. I love you - a million kisses, too.

(Medical records showed complete series of shots given Jan.11, They went back on the line Jan.12. This letter was not mailed until Jan 17)

(Censor)
To: From:
Mrs. John K. Price   Pvt. John K. Price37623699
704 Ballas Road   GFRS Pool APO 129,
Kirkwood, 22,   c/o P M, New York, N. Y.
Missouri, U.S.A.

17 January, 1945

Dearest Darling:
Well, Honey, Another V-Mail, much to your dismay, I imagine but it has been so long since I

have heard from you that I just don't have enough to say to fill a regular letter, so until my mail catches up I guess I'd better write V-Mail so I can at least drop you a few lines each night.

Things are going about the same as usual over here. The weather has been about the same, a little warmer, but still a lot of snow and cold enough.

I still haven't changed my opinion of France. I definitely don't like it at all. By the way, remember what Jim Keightly wrote about Holland? Well, according to all the reports I have received from the fellows here who are just back from Holland, he is all wrong. They say it is clean as a pin and that of all the places they have been the people there have treated them the best. Course, It could be that he was in a different part. I kind of hope that when I am shipped up again I go there.

How is Peg, honey? I am sure anxious to hear some news about her. I'll bet she is really growing up. Is she talking any better now? Doggone, I would sure give anything for a few letters from you.

Well, darling, this is an awful short note I know, but I really haven't anything else to say and mainly I just wanted to let you know I was thinking of you always and love you and was ok. All my love darling, for always to the sweetest gal in the world.

I love you, Jack
V-Mail

(This was the last letter from France. He was not able to write for 10 days as he was back on the line. They traveled to Belgium on 40 or 8 boxcars. The next letter, January 27th, (Belgium) said he was headed for a regular outfit.)

Saturday
27 Jan. 1945

My Dearest Darling:
Well, honey, I am going to start this now — the first for over a week — but Lord knows when I'll finish it. I'm afraid my letter writing will be a little poor from now on, honey, but I'll write just as often as I can and keep you posted. Please understand honey and don't worry, cause I'll be all right and will take care of myself.

The toughest part of this is the terrible cold weather and having to live in over a foot of snow — no heat or anything and the temperature is plenty low. I am up in Belgium again, for good now I guess. I am slated for a regular outfit but can't give you any details or the address as yet. By the way I haven't received a letter from you since December 12th, However, the day I left France I received the Christmas package your Mom sent me. You have no idea how wonderful it was, as we traveled on 40 or 8 box cars, (40 hommas — 8 cheveaux) and the cookies were really wonderful. Gosh, honey, if I only had a decent place to write I could peel off at least 30 pages to you about the places I've been, the cities and things I've seen, and all the countries, etc, I've visited since leaving England but under these conditions it's just impossible. It will just have to wait till I get home. I will say this much, the two most interesting towns I visited were Compiegne in France and Vervier in Belgium. Belgium is far the best though. The people are really wonderful to us and they have so much more than the other countries. I even had a steak dinner and a real nice cream sundae here. I'll tell you all about that when I can find a place to write you a full description of everything I've seen and done since arriving in France. The reason, by the way, for me writing in pencil, instead of ink is that my ink is frozen solid and it is just too cold to try to fool with it.

To go to a more pleasant subject. I just finished reading a wonderful book that I know you would enjoy. It's the "Chicken-Wagon Family" by Barry Benfield. I read it while traveling through the country. Try to get it, it's good. How is Peggy, honey? There is no use me telling you how If feel, but honey, you have no idea how I miss you and long to be with you and Peg — even for just a little while. I love you so much. You'll really never know how wonderful the few years we spent together were to me ,darling. I don't know what I would do if it weren't for the wonderful memories they have given me to dream about. That is all that has kept me going.

Well, honey, it is almost dark so I guess I'll have to close till after chow and try to write by flashlight when I finish eating. Bye for now, I love you. Well, I finished eating but it is so cold I believe I will just close this now and get in my sleeping bag to keep warm. I'll write again just as soon as I can so don't worry about me.

Love me, and miss me and remember that I love you more than anything in the world and you are always near in my mind and heart and I'll never be able to show you just what you mean to me and how I love you. Be sure to say your prayers for me more than ever now honey. Take good care of Peg honey and don't ever let her forget her Daddy. Give her a kiss for me too.

All my love to the dearest most wonderful girl in all the world.

Your sweetheart
Jack
P.S. I love you.

GERMANY

The American 30th division was relieved at Stavelot, Belgium, on January 11, 1945 by the 28th Division. The First Battalion moved north that night to Sart, Belgium, in trucks. They rested there for several days, being quartered with Belgian civilians. On January 14 they moved out in trucks through Francorchamps, Belgium, to an assembly point in Malmedy for the St. Vith offensive. When they left Malmedy and passed the crossroads at Baugnez, the bodies of the massacre victims were being removed. A sad sight, indeed, and a sad task for the soldiers removing them.

Near Lignueville, Belgium, they began coming under the German enemy artillery fire. The weather and roads were terrible. It had snowed heavily, and the snow was nearly two feet deep. During the following days the fighting was hard and there were heavy casualties. On January 22, 1945, they reached the heights overlooking St. Vith, and on the night of the 23rd they made contact with the American Seventh Armored Division there and were relieved. On the 24th of January they were pulled back into Rodt, Belgium.

On January 28, 1945, the Battle of the Bulge was officially over. 600,000 Americans had participated in the battle. The total casualties were 81,000 American soldiers killed, wounded, captured, or missing in action.

The 30th Division was then moved from Rodt, further back to Grand Halleux, Belgium. On January 29th, 1945, after leaving Verviers, Belgium, Jack joined them there. The entire 30th Division then rested in that area. The town had been greatly damaged in the earlier fighting there. The streets were full of rubble, but somehow they managed to find houses for shelter.

On January 30 Jack wrote, "I'm no longer a replacement after 9 long months. I have finally been assigned to a regular outfit, not as a clerk but I don't know but what I'm a lot happier because of it. I'm with what seems to be a pretty swell bunch of fellows and you have no idea how good it feels to feel that you belong and are one of an outfit. My new address from now on is Co C, 117th Inf, APO 30 so get busy sweet, and get those letters on the way. I am with the 30th Division so you might be able to follow in the newspapers. I believe this outfit has made one of the best shows of any over here and I'm glad I hit it. It's one of the roughest but they have really gotten things done and really have made a name for themselves." He said it was still snowing there and cold as the devil. "The worst thing to worry about is the cold — it's the big casualty maker."

The next day, January 31st, 1945, it turned warm. It was rainy, sloppy, and nasty, but it was still better than the bitter cold. That day they were issued cold weather equipment and special arctic boots and gloves. He wrote, " These boots are really the berries. (He meant they were wonderful!) They are rubber

Card from department store.

from the ankle down and leather on the other part, which reaches almost to your knee. Two extra pair of heavy wool socks come with each pair and also felt pads 1/4 inch thick to put in the bottoms. You don't wear any shoes with them. It's like wearing slippers to have them on. It sure would have saved many a pair of frozen feet and trench foot if they had been issued a couple of months ago."

He wrote that they were living in a town now — in evacuated houses. "From salvaging a few items we have made a home(?) We found a few beds to sleep on and have carpets on the floor, a desk to write on, and two stoves with coal so we are real cozy. We have 8 fellows living in one room, a little crowded but each morning we take the beds up. We have quite a few easy chairs. It's really something. Too good to last long though. We are having good meals, even had steak today for lunch. I'll write again tomorrow. Say a big prayer for me and all the fellows over here in this mess. Don't worry about me, I'll come back never fear."

He did not write the next day. They moved out on February 2, 1945, and the American 30th Division became a secret outfit to deceive the Germans. They had removed all unit insignia from their clothing and from all vehicles. They were absolutely forbidden to tell anyone, anywhere, their unit. They left at 10 P.M. in vehicles to Verlautenheide, Germany, north of Aachen, a distance of fifty miles. As the convoy moved secretly, their "friend" Axis Sally, told of their movement over the radio! (She was a turn-coat American broadcasting Nazi propaganda.) They arrived in Verlautenheide at 2 A.M. February 2, 1945. The bitter fighting there in September and October, 1944, had caused much damage; however, among the rubble they were finally able to find rooms and basements for everyone.

On February 4, 1945, Jack wrote a letter from there telling me they had moved and were now in Germany. He guessed it was the last country he would visit. He was hoping to get some letters that day, but it was not to be. He said the weather had been like spring, the snow had all melted, but that morning it had clouded up. "It started to rain and now the wind is blowing like the very devil and it's getting cold so I guess we are in for some more snow. I hate to think of it, cause it is miserable enough, but living in holes in the snow and cold — burrrr!" He had learned that either the battalion or the regiment had just received a Presidential Citation — a little blue ribbon bordered in gold to wear on their uniform. He drew a picture of the 30th Division shoulder patch and said Axis Sally referred to them as "F D R's personal SS troops." They were known as the Old Hickory Division, named for Andrew Jackson. They had originally been a very old Tennessee unit. He enclosed one of the patches which I still have!

On February 6 they left Verlautenheide, Germany, and the whole Battalion went to a monastery near Kerkrade, Holland, for a lovely two-day rest. Jack's letter from there was written on the morning of February 7. He said he guessed his two sweethearts were still snoozing in our beds. He said he was in Holland now. He asked about Rusty and said he was going to try to go see him soon. This was our code, to tell me he was going back into Germany.

He wrote two letters that day, full of personal thoughts about the war and his love for his family. He repeated something he had heard, "I am awfully glad Peg was a girl cause with girls you can love them and kiss them regardless of how grown up they are but little boys after a while you have to stop kissing them and start shaking hands with them. That's pretty good isn't it? Let's both pray, honey, for an end to this mess so our boys, all of us can come home and stay home for good. When you think of the death and destruction that has been caused by one man, it is appalling. I just thank God that you and Peg are safe and comfortable. It's bad enough missing you like I do, but if I was coming home not knowing whether you were dead or alive or where you were, I don't think I could take it."

On February 8, they left the monastery and returned to Verlautenheide for the night. The next afternoon they went on to Warden, Germany, where the Battalion had been before the Bulge. They stayed there for two weeks while training for the next operation, the crossing of the Roer River.

On February 12, 1945, at long last, Jack received his mail! It was two months to the day since he had heard a word from anyone. He got five letters and was beside himself; he could hardly wait to answer them. He mentioned what a terrible Christmas he had, but he couldn't tell me where he was or what he had been doing. He just said he had been in a very

precarious position. He had received my Christmas package the day before — in perfect condition. The enclosed note said not to open it before Christmas. Well, he didn't! He said he was grateful they were living in houses, and he was glad he was with a swell bunch of guys.

On February 14, he wrote that he had just gotten back from a little entertainment by Micky Rooney (the Hollywood actor). He said it was good, a lot of laughs and that he played a private in the army, which he was. They also had a movie for them that night, The Great Moment, with Joel McCrea, a very popular movie actor. He had received two more letters, and he chided me for worrying about snipers and booby traps and said he wished that was all he had to worry about. He said he would be careful, and if anything were to happen, it was in the books. I should just say a prayer for him every night, and he would be back before I knew it the same as before he left.

None of us at home ever stopped praying for him, day and night. I promised God anything and everything.

On the morning of February 18, 1945, Jack received eighteen letters. He finally began to get his mail which had been held up in an Army Post Office somewhere.

February 19, 1945, he received the pictures I had sent. At last could see how much Peggy had grown and what a pretty little girl she was becoming. He could hardly believe his eyes. He wrote, "I just can't imagine that daughter of ours is that big. She is really darling. It made me feel awful blue to look at the pictures though. I'm so proud of her, I keep bragging to the other fellows and showing them her pictures — I guess they get tired of hearing me go on about her." I had sent him the pictures of Peggy, taken in November. She was wearing the little red corduroy jacket and pants which I had made for her. I also sent the picture of Peggy with the Christmas tree, and the pictures of me in the much-talked-about fur coat! He was so happy to hear from me at last.

He agreed that I should let Peggy stay up until 8 o'clock! She was still brought up by every word in the Better Homes and Garden Baby Book which I had used from the beginning.

The American Military Commanders had begun to crack down on discipline at this time. The entire battalion began to drill for a ceremony planned on January 19, 1945, when the First Battalion was to be presented the Distinguished Unit Citation for their performance, 7 August 1944, in the Battle of Mortain near St. Barthelmy, France. It was presented by Major General Leland S. Hobbs, Division Commander. Jack mentioned it in his letter that day and remarked that he would be able to wear the ribbon even though he had not participated in the battle. He sent me a mimeographed copy of the Citation.

On February 21, Jack wrote that he had not had time to write that day, but he would begin and then finish it the next morning. He said although they had been fairly comfortable in houses, he still went to bed with his shirt and pants on so he could get up in a hurry if necessary. His records were still lost and he hadn't been paid since November 30, 1944. He owed considerable money to the other fellows. If he got paid in March, 1945, he would get $118.

He finished the letter the next morning so it would be censored that day, February 22, 1945. He had just received nine letters from me that morning, two of them had his new address, and he said he would answer them that night. He never did. Also, he never had a chance to read them. This was the last letter from Germany. The next morning the push into Germany, the Rhineland Campaign, began with the Roer River offensive and they left for the front!

THE LETTERS

To:
Mrs. John K. Price
704 Ballas Road
Kirkwood, 22, Mo.
U.S.A.

From:
Pvt. John K. Price 37623699
Co. C, 117th Inf. APO 30
c/o P M, New York, N. Y.

Belgium (Grand Halleux)
30 January, 1945

Dearest Darling:

Well, honey, I am no longer a Replacement after 9 long months. I have finally been assigned to a regular outfit, not as a clerk, but I don't know but what I'm not a lot happier because of it. I'm with what seems to be a pretty swell bunch of fellows and you have no idea how good it feels to feel that you belong and are one of an outfit. My new address from now on is Co.C, 117th Inf, APO 30 so get busy sweet, and get those letters on the way. The last letter I received from you was dated November 29th and the last letter I got was on the 12th of December so you see I really need some news from home. In case you aren't familiar with those APO's I am with the 30th Division, so you might be able to follow what we do and where we go in the newspapers. As far as divisions go, I believe this outfit has made one of the best shows of any over here and I'm glad I hit it. No need saying it's rough, one of the roughest but they have really gotten things done and really have made a name for themselves. How is Peg, honey? I'm sitting here looking at her and your pictures trying to imagine what she is like and how she has grown and all. I just can't imagine or believe it possible that she is 18 months old yesterday. Is she talking a lot yet? Darn I wish I would hear from you. Well, it's still snowing here and cold as the very devil. It sure makes it miserable when you have to be out in it any length of time. Well, maybe it will be over soon from the way those Russians have been moving lately. I don't mind telling you we have all been pulling for them over here. The last report we received was that they were only 91 miles from Berlin and still moving. Course the fact that they take Berlin doesn't mean that the war will be over by a long shot, at least it's that much closer to taking the damn country. I've slipped quite a bit with writing. You haven't a heck of a lot to write about and besides you just haven't any place to write at all in this weather. So, if, sometimes you go 8 or 10 days or so without hearing, don't worry about me as I'll be ok. You know that if anything does happen to me you will hear from the W. D. in very short order so just remember no news is good news. The worst thing to worry about is the cold - it is the big casualty maker, not bullets.

This is short, I know, but I'll have the opportunity to write every day for the next few days. All my love for always.

Your sweetheart,
Jack
P.S. I love you.

31 January 1945
(Grand Halleux)

Dearest Sweetheart:

Well, honey, another month is just about over and another month closer to coming home. Maybe it won't be too many more before this mess is over and we will all get home for good. What a feeling that will be — to have you with me every minute all the time and to know that in a few days or weeks I won't have to be leaving you again. Let's hope when we get through here we are completely finished and they don't shoot us out to the South Pacific.

Well, it turned off warm here after all that terrific cold weather we had and it has been raining all day today. It is pretty sloppy and nasty out but a lot better this way than with snow and cold. It's a funny darn thing but it looks like when we finally are issued good cold weather equipment it turns warm. Yesterday they issued us special arctic boots and today they are issuing gloves. I'll say this much, these boots are really the berries. They are rubber from about your ankle down and leather on the upper part, which reaches almost to your knee. Two extra heavy pair of wool socks come with each pair and also felt pads about 1/4 of an inch thick to put in the bottoms. You don't wear any shoes in them as they are shoes and overshoes combined. It sure would have saved many a pair of frozen feet and trench foot if they had been issued a couple of months ago. No kidding, it's like wearing house slippers to have them on.

I had to quit for awhile and go get a haircut and have some more equipment issued me and it is just about to get dark now so I'll have to finish this while I can still see, if I can think of anything to write about. Those long ones I used to write will have to wait till I hear from you. Letters are the only thing you have to look forward to over here. What burns me up is that if I had just stayed just one or two days longer at the last place I was I would have gotten some mail. As it was, about 30 minutes before we shipped I received that package from your folks and that's all the mail I have received since I left England. I'd have traded that package and anything else I had for just one letter from you. We have had it fairly nice and comfortable since we moved in here — a lot more comfortable than I've been in the Replacement Depots. We are in a town now, living in evacuated houses and from salvaging a few various and sundry items we have made a home(?). We found a few beds to sleep on and have carpets on the floor, a desk to write on and two stoves with coal so we are real cozy. We have 8 fellows living in the one room. It's a little crowded, but each morning we take the beds up to get them out of the way which helps. We have quite a few easy chairs about — it's really something. Too good to last long, though. We are having darn good meals — again better than I had in the Replacement Depots — even had steak today for lunch which is the first steak I've had since leaving the states — no, I take that back, while I was on pass in Verviers we found a Belgian civilian who fried us (3 other fellows and myself) a steak with French fries and coffee for a dollar. It sure was good. That's a funny thing but Belgium has just about anything you want to buy. Well, hon, I'm going to have to quit to go to chow but I'll finish this later — I think I'm going to a movie, too, but I'll finish it tonight and tell you some more about Belgium. Here I am again, darling, but I don't know how long I'll write. I might finish this tomorrow as we have just a coal oil lamp for light — hard as the devil to see what I'm writing. Oh yeah, I had just gone to chow. Well, I got back and then walked down to a movie Special Services put on. I saw "My Kingdom for a Cook" with Charles Coburn. It was real good — a comedy — which we need. If you get a chance it would be worth seeing.

I was telling you about my visit to Verviers so I'll finish that and then hit the hay. As I said, the Belgian people seem to have been hit the least as far as the war is concerned. What hit the spot most was going in and buying — or rather having bought for me, an ice cream sundae. Then in all the shops you could buy candy of all kinds. Course it was pretty expensive but it sure tasted good. Each piece, just a chocolate like comes in regular boxes of candy, was seven cents so it should have tasted good. I went in the Catholic church, or cathedral, while I was there and met the priest and much to my amazement he spoke very fluent English. He took me all over the church and told me a lot of the history of it. I spent better than two hours with him before I knew it. He was really a wonderful person and very interesting. These people are, or seem to be, very devout and each town, regardless of how small, has a beautiful church, which in every case I have seen, is the dominating piece of architecture in the town and is built on the most domineering position in the town. The Belgian people as a whole have been nicer to the American soldier than the people in any other country I've visited. It's hard to describe anything to you in a letter, but will I have the things to tell you when I finally get home. By the way, I meant to tell you. In Verviers they had a department store, one of the most modern I've seen anywhere, so I went through it. They had some dolls up there that I'd have given anything in the world to have been able to buy for Peg. They were only about $2.00 but I hadn't been paid and was flat broke. It sure made me feel bad, but maybe I'll get a chance later on to send something nice if I happen to get a chance to go back to the rear. One thing, I'll have plenty of dough when I finally do get paid. Honey, have you received that perfume and the dollar bill and the ten shilling note I sent you? I bought it in LeHavre while I was there. I didn't have very good facilities for mailing it. Was it any good? I paid a good price for it, but the way the French were diluting that sort of stuff I wasn't sure of how good it would be.

I'd better close and hit the hay. I'll write again tomorrow. Tell Mom and Dad I'll drop them a line tomorrow.

Goodnight, sweet dreams, and be sure to say a big prayer for me and all the fellows over here in this mess. Love me and miss me and don't worry about me. I'll be ok and I'll come back, never fear — can't help it cause I love you so much that I just couldn't let anything happen to me till I get a chance to see you again and show you. All my love to the most beautiful and wonderful family in the whole world.

Your Sweetheart,
    Jack
P.S.I love you.

(Curlew: Jan.28th the entire 30th Div. went into rest in vicinity of Grand Halleux. 117th Reg. stayed four days. Town battle scarred, but were able to stay in houses.)

4 February 45
Germany
(Verlautenheide)

Dearest Sweetheart:
    Well, Darling, as you can see, we have moved again. I guess this is about the last country I'll visit. I hope so as I've seen my share and then some the last few months. Just think, I left England, went to France then to Belgium, then Holland, back to Belgium, back to France, up to Belgium, and now Germany. I don't mind telling you I'm ready to see England again — but fast —or better still the states.
    How is Peg getting along, honey? It's been so darn long since I've heard from you or had any news from home, I've lost all track of how she is growing and I'm really anxious to hear all about her. I'm

hoping maybe a few letters will get to me today. Well, honey, I went to eat lunch and didn't get back to writing till after chow this evening. I'll finish this now though and get it off this evening.
    Darn, we have been having weather just like spring for the last few days and the snow (we had a foot or more on the ground) all melted and it was really nice, but this morning it clouded up and started to rain and now the wind is blowing like the very devil and it's getting cold so I guess we are in for some more snow. I sure hate to think of it too, cause it is miserable enough when it's wet and rainy, but living in holes in the snow and cold — brrrr!
    I just found out that the 30th Division or rather this battallion or regiment I don't know which has just received a presidential citation and they also expect to get a Belgian and French citation so when I come home I'll be lousy with medals — in fact the Belgian and French are ropes you have to wear over your shoulder and the presidential citation is that little blue ribbon something like the purple heart only bordered by gold and that is worn over the right pocket. I'll be some dude, won't I? By the way, in case you are interested the shoulder patch of the 30th looks something like this —
    It signifies an O for Old, an H for Hickory as the outfit is known as the Old Hickory Division. The three X's of course stand for 30.
    I don't know whether you have read anything about the division or not, but lately there's been a lot of bally hoo about a new patch they might authorize. It looks like this -
    They call us FDR's personal SS troops so as a result that new patch was dreamed up. It would be a flashy looking thing for back home but I'd hate to wear it in combat. Well, darling I'd better close for now. I know these have been terribly short, but as soon as I start hearing from you I'll try to do better. Say a prayer for me, darling, and love me and miss me and don't worry about me cause I'll be ok. I love you and miss you more than you'll ever know. Give Peg a big kiss for me and bring our little gal up to be a sweet wonderful person something like her momma. All my love for always.

Your Sweetheart,
    Jack
P.S. I love you.

7 February 1945
Holland
(Monastery, Kerkrade)

Dearest Sweetheart:
    How are my two sweethearts this morning? I guess you are still snoozing away in your beds — dreaming about me, I hope.
    Well, honey I've really been getting around lately, haven't I? Now I'm in Holland. You'll never know just how lonely I am when I'm away from you and it seems like each month is just a little worse than the last one. Just think, it has been almost nine months since I last talked to you even, and that was over the phone. The only thing I have to work for now, other than the end of the war, of course, is the completion of my first year overseas — only a little over three months to go — and then I'll be eligible for that 30 day furlough home. My only prayer is that the war is over and done with before that time though. I sure can't see where it will last much longer. The way those

UNITED STATES ARMY

you are interested the should patch of the
30th looks something like this —
It signifies an O for old, an H for Hickory as
the outfit is known as the old hickory Division.
The 3 X's of course stand for 30. I don't know
whether you have read any thing about the
division or not, but lately there has been a
lot of bally hoo about a new patch they might
authorize. It looks like this —
They call us Falk's personal SS troops
so as a result that new ... too ...
dreamed ...

Pvt. John K. Price, 37643699,
Co. C, 117th Inf, APO 30,
% PM, New York, N.Y.

30 FEB 1945
ARMY POSTAL SERVICE A.P.O.
Free

Feb 4 1945 Mrs. John K. Price,
704 Ballas Road,
Kirkwood, N,
Missouri,
U.S.A.

PASSED BY
44890

#162

Letter February 4, 1945, 30th Division. Verlautenheide, Germany.

Russians are going now it shouldn't be too much longer before the Germans realize they are doing worse by themselves for continuing this business. They are fighting a losing battle and should wake up to the fact soon.

Have the folks heard from Rusty lately? I am going to try to go see him soon, if my luck holds out. I'll have to see if I can't locate his A.P.O. and that way I can find out if he is near enough to where my C O will give me a pass or something. (Letting me know he was going back to Germany.) I still haven't gotten paid, but as soon as I do draw a full pay I'll send you a Money order. I should be able to send about $50 or $60 and then each month I'll send you $20 or $25 instead of making out an allotment. Also in another month or so I should be getting another $10 raise — combat infantryman's pay.

Well, darling, I'm still waiting for my mail to catch up with me. They should be finding me soon I hope. I'm about to go nuts waiting and looking. It should be a terrific pile when it finally gets here. With all the jumping around I've done the last couple of months it's a wonder if it ever catches up to me. Has Joe gotten home or is he on his way? I haven't heard from him for the longest time. Lord knows he has been over there long enough to get a furlough. Guess I'd better close this for now. Say a prayer for me and give Peg a big hug and kiss for me. All my love,

Your sweetheart,
    Jack
P.S. I love you.

I almost forgot — Happy Valentines Day. I hope I'm still your Valentine!

Holland
7 February 1945
Wednesday
(Monastery)

Dearest Sweetheart;

Two in one day — I'm really going to town. I just finished writing the folks, for a change, and was sitting here thinking about you and Peg and how much I love and miss you both so I decided to write and tell you instead of just think about it. Anyway, I'd better write all I can while I have the chance — there will be times when I'll have to go a week or two without writing. Darn, it's chow time already so I'll finish when I finish eating.

Here I am again, to try to finish this up. Honey, when I think of all the wonderful times we have had together, and all I'm missing being away, it makes me feel so darn miserable I don't know what to do. I especially hate being away and missing this part of Peg growing up. That reminds me of something I heard yesterday that expresses just how I feel about Peg being a girl. "I am awfully glad she was a girl cause with girls you can love them and kiss them regardless of how grown up they are but little boys after a while you have to stop kissing them and start shaking hands with them." That's pretty good isn't it? No kidding, I'm so glad we did have a little girl rather than a boy — that's what I wanted all along, although I wouldn't admit it to you at the time. Let's both pray, honey, for a quick end to this mess so our boys, all of us can come home and stay home for good. I'm ready to start learning all over again how a human being, supposedly civilized should live.

Monastery, Kerkrade, Holland. Rest for the entire 30th Division. February 7, 1945.

When you stop and think of the death and destruction that has been caused by one man, you might say, it is appalling; not withstanding the grief and unhappiness and hardships he has imposed upon us all. I just thank God that you and Peg are safe and comfortable and have everything you need. It's bad enough missing you like I do, but if I had to worry about whether I was coming home not knowing whether you were dead or alive or how or where you were living I don't think I could take it. How is old Buffie and Cookie getting along. Has Buff decided Peg is definitely one of the family yet or is he still the same old grouch? Any new pups expected yet? Well, I believe I'll say goodnight. Give your Mom and Dad my best and tell them to take care of my extra special sweetheart and gal for me while I'm gone. Sweet dreams, darling. All my love for always.

Your Sweetheart
    Jack
P.S. I love you. Don't forget your prayers for me.

(Curlew: Feb. 8, battalion returned to Verlautenheide, spent night. Next afternoon moved to Warden, Germany.)

Germany
11 February 45
(Warden, Sunday)

Dearest Darling:

Well, honey, I've been starting a letter to you every day for the last three days but never getting far enough with it to mail so I'll try again today.

I have been having the darndest luck with mail. I received a package from you this morning. That makes two packages the extent of my mail since December 12th. Something I don't understand is that this package was labeled Christmas parcel so it couldn't have been mailed before September 15th and yet you used my saltwater address. At that time you had my address in England at least three months. (APO 15328 was the address we had until he moved to Tidworth, APO 151. The first letter from there was September 9 which I did not receive for about 10 days.)

At least getting the package might mean that my mail is finally catching up with me. I got a bang out of the note & poem you had in this package asking me not to open till Christmas. As you can see, it was a considerable time after Christmas. It only took almost six months for the darn thing to finally get to me. Surprisingly enough it came through in perfect condition — not even dented. We have been having regular spring weather here. It has been raining quite a bit but nice and warm. Last night though it dropped down to just about freezing and we had a little snow. Not enough to amount to anything but thank goodness we are living in houses for the time being — warm and fairly comfortable, too. That's one thing about fighting over in this country — the towns are fairly close together and it gives us the opportunity of sleeping and staying out of the weather more than usual.

Well, darling, it looks like you are going to have to extend that day for our date a few months but from all appearances the end of this thing is in the not too distant future so maybe we will be able to keep the next one you set. It can't last too much longer, the way we are advancing — the Russians and all I mean. I can't see where it will run much longer than May or June at the most.

The only thing is that I'm afraid we're slated for the South Pacific and will be shot over there without a chance for a few days at home. I think I could take almost anything if they would see that I got a few days with my family first. It seems like I've been gone at least 2 or 3 years instead of since May. When you stop and think, though, I've darn near put in a year over here. That's an awful long time to be away from home, isn't it? I guess I'm lucky I spent all the time I did in England, although, at the time I griped an awful lot about it. I sure wouldn't mind being back there now. I was lucky, though, to get into what I consider a pretty darn good outfit and with a bunch of swell guys. That helps a lot any place you go. Well, honey, I think I'll close this for now and go wash up and shave. Bye for now. - - - Here I am again, honey, but just to finish this up and get it on it's way. How is Peg getting along, hon? Be sure to give her a big kiss for me I'll bet she is getting so big I wouldn't know she was the same little girl like in the last picture I got. I'll try to write a few lines again tomorrow. Love me and miss me and be sure to say a prayer for me. All my love for always to my two wonderful sweethearts.

Your Sweetheart,
    Jack
P.S. I love you.

(Curlew: The outfit stayed in Warden about two weeks training for its next operation, the crossing of the Roer River.)

Germany
12 February 1945
(Warden, Monday)

My Darling Sweetheart:

Happy Day! I received my first mail today — two months to the day since I last heard from home. I received two wonderful letters from you, one from Dad, a V Mail from Joe Barnes and a card with a note from Sister. The two I received from you were dated the 18th of December and the 8th of January. So — I'll get busy answering them right away. Gosh, honey, you have no idea how wonderful it is to finally be hearing from you again. I was getting desperate.

I guess the news was looking plenty bad at the time you wrote this letter the 18th. It was terrible, the bulge, I mean , but you know as well as I, that it was just what the people back home needed. They were definitely too optimistic. Well, we have straightened the line out now and things are looking pretty good so maybe it won't be too long fore it's over. I don't mind saying I've had enough of this business already and as far as being away from home — last May I was ready to come back to the states. (The next paragraph was cut out by the censor.)

As far as money is concerned, once I begin to get paid you will receive enough each month from me to be able to get along ok. I have absolutely no use whatever for any dough where I am now so I'll send you every extra penny I can which should amount to $30 or $35 a month.

Yes, sweet, I've seen a lot of countries and a lot of interesting sights but under the conditions I've seen them, they haven't meant a lot to me. And for every wonderful and interesting thing I've seen, I've seen 2 that are too horrible to talk about. No, I'd trade every minute I've spent over here for a day back home with you and would be getting the best of the bargain.

I expect you are just about right as far as me coming back home, honey, but I disagree on the time you set. I kind of feel that I'll see the states by this fall or early winter if I'm lucky. Course if I come through this over here ok there is still the possibility of me going to the South Pacific. Yes, honey, I was definitely feeling a lot better about being so far from home while there in England, mainly because of the nice job I had in the camp I was in with all the privileges and freedom I had all that time with the 12th. This next letter was written to one of my addresses I had in France, (He was in Givet.) and I must say, you were rather bitter about your husband being sent to France. Honey, there is only one way to look at this business and that is that there are a lot of other fellows over here in the same boat and I'm no better than any of them and Lord knows, it is well worth fighting for. All we can do is pray that this is over soon and I can get home whole. A person doesn't realize a religion or realize how religious he is till he gets up here then he (I was) is usually surprised how much spiritual guidance helps. The only reason I said I would have to write V-mail, honey, is that I was in a very precarious position when I wrote that letter and besides being kept plenty busy, was moving around quite a bit and about all the stationery I could get hold of was V-mail. I'll write as many regular letters as I can and as often as I can from now on though. Yes, I had a pretty terrible Christmas. You won't be able to imagine how bad a Christmas I did have till I can see you and tell you what I was doing and where I was.

I'm sorry, honey, but because of very strict security regulations I can't tell you anything at all about where I am, what I'm doing, or anything. I think by now you do know all about the shoulder patch I will wear as I explained it all to you in an earlier letter. As soon as I can, I'll send you one, if you like. No, I'm no longer a clerk and as far as fighting — read the papers, honey, as they'll keep you pretty well posted on where I am and what I'm doing.

As far as snow and cold weather is concerned don't even talk to me about it. At least it is and has been fairly warm here for the last week or so, even though we have had an awful lot of rain. I sure hope our snow is all over with. Well, honey, that finishes that one up. I told you I had heard from Joe — well he is in the Phillipines now. That boy really gets

General Hobbs Chats with Captain Spiker during unit citation ceremonies at Warden, Germany.

around. He seems to be in pretty fair spirits, so I don't imagine things are too rough for him. I'm going to drop him a line as soon as I finish this. From what you say about Peg she must really be getting big. I just can't imagine how she looks or anything. Be sure and send me some new pictures as soon as you can. Write and describe her to me in the most minute details, too, so I can kind of keep up with my big gal's progress.

I received a nice note from Sister today, too, which I want to answer tonight. I want to write to Mom and Dad, too, so I'd better end this. I don't imagine the Lt. who censors this will appreciate all this small writing and the length of this. I'll have to look him up and do some explaining and apologizing, I expect. I believe this is the first decent letter I have written to you in almost two months though, isn't it? Well, darling, I really must say goodnight. Sweet dreams, love me and miss me and give Peg a big hug and kiss.

Keep up those prayers for me too, honey, as I need them now as I never did before. All my love.

Your Sweetheart,
Jack
P.S. Love and kisses to both my sweet gals from their daddy!

(This was a seven page letter, censored by 1st Lt. Richard G. Graham.)

14 February 45
Germany
(Warden, Wed.)

My dearest Sweetheart:

Well, honey, I got a couple of more letters today so again I have some letter writing material. They were both pretty old, one dated the 16th of November and one the 19th of December but they were from my honey and were both wonderful to get. I'll try to get down to answering them now. By the way, I just got back from a little entertainment put on by Micky Rooney. It was pretty good — a lot of laughs. You know, I guess, that he is a Pvt in the Army. All he does is travel around the various fronts putting on these little shows. That boy's got it made. I won't be able to write a lot right now as there is a show tonight for us and I figured on going. I don't know what is showing but it's still a movie. I'll see you later.

Here I am again, honey, and I'll try to finish this up now. The show was ok but I had seen it before. It was the "The Great Moment" with Joel McCrea. Well, I enjoyed it anyway the second time. It sure does seem almost impossible that I have been away almost a year. In days it seems awfully long, each day seems to drag so, but added all up they have gone faster than the devil — does that make sense? Honey, Peg sounds so wonderful. She is really growing up for sure isn't she? I

guess by now she is really putting words together and talking a blue streak. What I wouldn't give to be there with you both. She really needs a daddy to kind of help her grow up. You'll really have your hands full now that she is climbing up and down the stairs. You'll have to watch her pretty closely.

I can't see that 8 o'clock is too late for Peg to stay up and it does make it a lot easier on you, having dinner so late and all, and besides you like to have a little time with her in the evening. Especially when I get home and come home from work I'll like to have a little time to spend with my big gal. I think that's pretty darn cute her having to have a shirt to hold before she'll go to sleep. That's a lot better than that thunb sucking or anything like that.

Don't torture me talking about chocolate cake. Oh boy, what I couldn't do to a piece of your cake about now. I'm afraid you will have a very sick husband the first couple of weeks I'm home cause all I'm going to want to do is eat stuff I've been dreaming about all this time till I'm sick. — ain't that awful!!

Now, honey don't you go worrying about me cause I'll be as careful as I can and besides you worrying isn't going to do any good. If anything is going to happen to me it is in the books, and all the worrying in the world won't stop it. As far as the snipers and booby traps you are worrying about — I wish that was all I had to worry about cause that is so minor it hardly amounts to a thing. Now just you say a big prayer for me every night and don't worry and I'll be back to you fore you know it, just the same as when I left.

Well, darling, that finishes both the letters I received today and I have nothing more to add. It would sure help if I could tell you something about what we are doing, etc, or if I would get a little more up to date mail from you. Good-night, dearest, take good care of yourself and Peg, and give Peg a big hug and kiss for me. Say a prayer, too, for me — all of us over here, in fact.

All my love, for always, from a guy what loves you more than you'll ever know and misses his two little gals sonething fierce.

Your Sweetheart
Jack
P.S. I love you.
Scuse the paper but it's the best I can do

Germany
14 February 1945

Dear Sister, Ollie, and kids:

I received your Christmas card with the swell note (a little late as you notice) yesterday so I'll get right down to answering.

No, I didn't have much of a Christmas this year — in fact as far as I was concerned there wasn't any December 25th in last year. I spent the whole day and half the night on Guard — I happened to have been right at the tip of that German bulge then so you can imagine the kind of holiday I had. You have no idea how hard it is to try to picture what that big gal of mine looks like. The last time I saw her she was only about 9 months and now she is running around. I sure hate to be missing all this. I sure do remember Kathy when she was about Peg's age — we used to come out to G. S. to visit and I believe I spent most of my time with her. She was sure a cute little gal. At least I will know just about what Peg will be like now.

GENERAL ORDER:

NUMBER 119:

APO #30
12 December 1944

BATTLE HONORS

Under the provisions of Section IV, Circular Number 333, War Department, 1943, and pursuant to authority granted by Commanding General, First United States Army, the following Battle Honors are announced:

The 1st Battalion, 117th Infantry, United States Army, is cited for outstanding performance of duty in action against the enemy on 7 August 1944, during the battle of Mortain, in the vicinity of St. Barthelmy, France. An aggressive enemy, making a desperate attempt to drive to the sea at Avranches and to split allied forces in France, launched a combined infantry-tank attack in strength. The brunt of the assault was borne by the 1st Battalion, 117th Infantry. The powerful enemy force followed closely behind intense artillery and mortar fire, and struck violently, causing many casualties among 1st Battalion front-line troops. In the face of numerically superior numbers, all available troops of the 1st Battalion, including clerks, messengers, and truck drivers were committed to action to fill gaps in the line. When the command post was overrun, the command group personally fought their way out. Throughout the entire battalion area, riflemen fought and outwitted hostile troops in fierce hand-to-hand fighting. Anti-tank gunners and rocket launcher teams, in the face of intense small arms fire, combined their attacks to annihilate numerous enemy tanks. Machine gunners remained steadfast and destroyed assaulting enemy foot troops. In the midst of incessant and withering fire, personnel of the 1st Battalion remained at their posts unhesitatingly and performed magnificently. Through the courageous performance of the men in the battalion, the attack launched by the enemy's finest troops was successfully repulsed, and the brilliant victory attained was climaxed by a general withdrawal of the enemy from the entire sector. The outstanding courage, unflinching devotion to duty, and marked perseverance demonstrated by members of the 1st Battalion, reflected the highest traditions of the Armed Forces and are worthy of high praise.

L. S. HOBBS
Major General - U. S. Army
Commanding

DISTRIBUTION - SPECIAL

This is not a classified document

Presidential Unit Citation. Ceremony, Warden, Germany, 19 February 1945.

HEADQUARTERS, 117TH INFANTRY
FORT JACKSON, S. C.

8 November 1945
(Date)

GENERAL ORDER)
                 :
NUMBER   54   )

9. Pursuant to authority contained in War Department Circular 408, dated 17 October 1944, the Combat Infantrymen's Badge is awarded to the following named Officers and Enlisted Men, 117th Infantry, for satisfactory performance of duty in ground combat against the enemy; effective as indicated.

COMPANY "C", 117TH INFANTRY

Pvt   John K. Price, 37522000   Effective 15 February 1945

By order of Colonel McHUGH:

LESTER D. ROYALTY
Capt., 117th Infantry
Adjutant

OFFICIAL:

Lester D. Royalty
LESTER D. ROYALTY
Capt., 117th Infantry
Adjutant

R E S T R I C T E D

COMBAT INFANTRY BADGE

Combat Infantry Badge. Effective 15 February, 1945.

I'm sorry about taking so long to write, Sister, but the way I've been traveling the last two or three months I haven't had a lot of time to do much of anything. In fact since the 12th of December I've been in England, France, Belgium, back to France, to Belgium, to Germany, to Holland and back to Germany again. I received my first mail from home since December 12th yesterday. Also please excuse this paper, but it seems to be all I can find to write on, so I figured it was better to use it than not to write. It looks like samples of wallpaper.

Well, Sister, this is terribly short I know but I have to get busy for now so I guess I'd better close. Say hello to the kids for me and everyone back home. A rather belated Merry Christmas and Happy New Year to you all.

Love,
Jack

P. S. I'm with the Old Hickory, 30th Division now so any time you wonder where I am or what I'm doing just look in the papers as this outfit keeps in the news quite a bit.

Germany
15 February 45

Dear Mom and Dad:

I finally have begun receiving a few letters. I received a letter from you the other day, Dad, that you wrote the 13th of December, I believe. Haven't gotten any of yours yet Mom, but expect them shortly. I guess you all do miss the baby and Babe when they leave after a visit. Well! they just passed out cokes so you'll just have to wait a second while I open it — aren't you jealous? Yes, we get cokes every once in a while when it's possible to get them to us, of course. I don't mind telling you it is a lot better in a regular outfit than it is sweating it out getting pushed around in those Replacement Depots.

So you've been having snow back home too? Man if I never see it snow again as long as I live it will be too soon. We have been having some really nice spring weather the last week or so, but it was sure miserable before that. Sleeping, eating, and living in snow a foot deep in bitter cold. I like to froze to death. Yes, I had a pretty miserable Christmas this year and would have given anything to have been with you all, or at least close enough to where I could have called you like I did last year. I hope you had a nice time this Christmas and I want you to be sure and write and tell me all about it — especially Peg's reactions and what she got and all.

I guess I'll close for now. Write soon and take care of yourselves. Look out for Babe and Peg for me and give everyone back home my love.

All my love,
Your Son,
Jack

Germany
18 February 45

Dearest Sweetheart:

Well, honey, I'm going to begin this now and hope by the time I write you a few lines I'll receive some mail from you.

How's that big wonderful daughter of ours getting along? I'm so anxious to get some up to date news about her from you. I'll bet she is growing up

so and talking a blue streak. I guess she keeps you plenty busy, tho, having to watch her almost constantly now that she is old enough to be running around and going up and down stairs. Gosh, honey, what I wouldn't give to be home with you and Peg now. We could have so much fun together, having our own place again and being together all the time watching and helping Peg grow up into a sweet young lady.

We had a movie last night so I went up to see it. It was "Rhapsody in Blue" — the portrayal of the life of George Gershwin. Did you see it? If you didn't please don't miss going when it comes to St. Louis. It was the most wonderful picture I have seen in a long time. The beautiful music alone was worth going to hear and the acting was very good. The darn thing ran 2 hours and 45 minutes but it seemed like I just sat down when it was over. I don't remember the name of the fellow who played the lead — he was new but he really was good. Of course Oscar Levant is always good and it had a darn good supporting cast. It was one of the best pictures this year with the exception of "Going My Way". I'll have to quit I see, but I'll finish this afternoon. Bye now.

Happy Day!! Will wonders never cease. I got 18 letters today — 11 of them from you dated from the 26th of November to the 24th of December (that very sweet and wonderful note you wrote me Christmas eve). I don't know how I'll ever get around to answering them. Something funny happened, too — remember that girl I told you I met coming back from London? Well, about 4 days before I left England another fellow and I were supposed to meet her and this Peggy Price to go to the Gilbards where we were invited for the evening. We went down to Andover and waited and waited but the two girls never showed up so we caught the train back to camp. They weren't the type people to just not show up so I figured something had happened. I didn't hear from them before I left, but today I got a wire telling me they couldn't make it — can you imagine? If I receive a letter from her (I dropped her a line today) I'll send it on to you. I received quite a few swell letters from Dad, in one of the letters he told me all about his and Mr. Friant's conversation and from all I can gather I'll have it made if I go with Newberry's, so unless things change considerably I definitely will accept that Newberry offer. Well, honey, I'm going to cut your letter a little short today so I can drop everyone a line before dark, but tomorrow I'll devote all my time writing you a real long letter — whether my Lt. likes it or not — he'll like that I'm sure! I really must close now. All my love for always to the sweetest most wonderful gal in the whole world. Don't forget to say a prayer for me.

Your Sweetheart,
Jack
P.S. I love you!

(His letter was censored by 1st Lt. Thomas E. Stanley Jr.)

Germany
19 February 45
(Monday)

My dearest Darling:

Another day, honey, and here I am again. I'll start right off by telling you I received those wonderful pictures of you and Peggy. Honey, I'll swear I just can't imagine that daughter of ours is that big. She is really darling. It made me feel awful blue and down in the dumps to look at the pictures though.

Peggy, in red corduroy playsuit. Quickly spotted in large yard.

Peggy, Cookie, and Raggedy Ann.

Honey, I want to be with you and Peg so bad, especially now, when she is at the age you can really enjoy her. She has such a cute little build, honey, and an awfully sweet face and that smile and laugh of hers is really something. I'm so darn proud of her, honey, I guess I appreciate her more than I should, cause I keep bragging to the other fellows about her and showing them her pictures — I guess they get awful darned tired hearing me go on about her all the time.

Before I forget, this battalion of the division was given a presidential citation the other day and they gave us a mimeographed copy of the citation which I'm sending you. The citation by the way is the highest award given a unit. I get to wear the ribbon as long as I'm with the Battalion although I didn't have anything to do with earning it. I'm kind of proud to be with an outfit like this and be able to wear it.

Yes, honey, from the looks of things we will move away from St. Louis a week or 10 days after I get home, as, if nothing unusual happens, I am definitely going with Newberry's. It seems that Mr. Kehrt talked to Mr. Friant about getting me for him in B'ham but Mr. Friant wants to start me off in small stores elsewhere and work me up. I will advance much more rapidly that way. By moving just as soon as my schooling was complete I would be in line for a store. The way things look, the only

thing we will need to start off with is a good car to travel in. I hope Peg liked the little books I sent her. It wasn't much I know, but it was the best I could do. Things in London were so darned expensive and with the little bit I was drawing each month then that's all I could afford.

You know, honey, this girl Peggy Price I was telling you about? She was married and that was her married name so I couldn't find out whether they were any relation or not. Her husband was from Wales and we have relatives there I know.

I received that cute little letter from Peg — you're silly but awfully sweet. I'll close this for today and answer more tomorrow. Remember me in your prayers, honey, and give Peg a big kiss for me. I love you.

Your Sweetheart,
    Jack

Germany
21 February 1945
(Wednesday)

Dearest Sweetheart:

Well honey I'm going to begin this tonight, but it won't be censored till tomorrow. I didn't get a chance to write during the day today, to get a letter off early enough to be censored so I guess I'll write one now and one tomorrow too so you'll get two for the same day.

I'll start off by answering the letter you wrote the 9th of December. This one is really filled with all the things Peg is doing now. There isn't a lot to answer in it but it sure was a wonderful letter. I was really hungry for some news of her. It looks like she takes after her old man in her taste for literature. I guess Mom told you about how crazy I was about Peter Rabbit when I was her age and how I used to worry grandma to death having her read it to me over and over again. That's really cute how she knows all the sounds the various animals make. Isn't it funny how a child will always take to the most battered up toys and books and things and the new ones don't interest them in the least. I know I was that way.

Lately we've been pretty comfortable as we are in houses, but I still go to bed with my pants and shirt on so I can get up in a hurry if necessary. By the way you're darn toot in I'm attached to those long johns of mine. Who wouldn't be? I really don't know what I'd do without them. I'll freeze to death if I have to wear that little short stuff during the winter time any more. If you have to do your own laundry when I get back, just think how pretty it will look to see all those long drawers hanging out on the line!!! Yes, I do have a completely nutty wife who can think of some of the screwiest things to write about, but she is awful sweet and wonderful and that is one of the things that made me fall in love with her and marry her. I just don't know what I'd do without you. I love you so darn much, honey. That just about finishes up that letter so I think I'll finish filling this page and quit for tonight. I was hoping to get paid this month so I could send you a few dollars, but according to our Lt, he doesn't think we will, and besides I believe my records are still among the missing so that lets me out regardless. I haven't been paid since November 30th so I'll be getting a nice amount. Course I owe considerable to the fellows who have been keeping me in rations, etc, as I've been broke since the middle of December. If I get paid in full by March, I should draw about $118 so I'll be able to send you at least a hundred of it, which no doubt you will be able to use. Well, honey, I'm going to quit now and hit the hay as I'm plenty tired tonight and it's getting late. Sweet dreams.

(Next day.
Thursday, February 22)

Here I am again ,honey but just to close this so I can get it off this evening. I don't know why but for some reason I feel so worn out today — no energy for anything I do feel good about something though. I received 9 letters from you and one from Mom today. Two of the letters from you had my brand new address on it and was written the 13th and 14th of February. That is really good time — it only took 22 days for my letter to get to you and yours back here. So tonight I'll start a nice long letter to you and try to catch up answering all the letters I have. Well, honey, it's about time for them to pick up the mail so I guess I'd better close for now I'll start another one tonight. Bye, honey, Love me and miss me and don't forget me in your prayers. Give Peg a big hug and kiss for me and take care of our big gal.

All my love for always to the sweetest most wonderful sweetheart in all the world.

Your Sweetheart,
Jack
P.S. I love you.

(Jack never got a chance to read those last letters he received. This was the last letter from Germany. The next morning February 23, at 2:45 A.M. they were awakened by an artillery barrage, the largest on the Western front, lasting 45 minutes. The next morning, February 24, at 10 A.M. they left Warden in trucks to the crossing site of the Roer River, and crossed late in the afternoon. On February 26 at 4:30 A.M. Jack was wounded in action in die Burge woods near Oberembt.)

GERMANY, ROER RIVER

The Roer River in Germany had been a small peaceful stream, until the flood gates were opened. The terrain was rolling plains consisting mostly of cultivated fields with the river winding and curving its way around. Its banks were bordered by trees and shrubs, with grass growing down to the water's edge. Not on this day, however! It was far above its banks — a raging, muddy, torrent — filled with every kind of debris as it flowed north to the sea.

The Roer Dams had finally been captured by the middle of February, 1945, and the German army had been driven back into the forests which stretched out behind them. Unfortunately, as feared, the flood gates had been opened by the Germans and torrents of water were flowing down the whole Roer Valley. The early thaw and rainy weather added that much more water, which complicated matters further; therefore, the Allied armies (United States, British, and Canadian), already poised for the attack, had to settle in and wait for it to subside. Two weeks passed, and then on February 22, 1945, the decision was made to start the attack the next morning. These were the two weeks Jack's unit had spent in Warden, Germany.

February 23, 1945, before dawn, they were all "rudely awakened" at 2:45 A.M., by the largest concentration of Allied artillery ever fired on the Western Front in the war. The Rhineland Campaign had begun with the assault on the Roer River, a 25 mile stretch of river from Duren in the south to Linnich in the north. The barrage lasted for 45 minutes and covered 8,000 yards of the German front line. Shells were bursting to the left and to the right as far as the eye could see and cannons in the rear had broken windows and shaken plaster loose in many buildings.

The Allied engineers had to carry heavy footbridges and boats down to the edge of the water. Corduroy roads — made of logs — were laid to the river bank through the wooded area approaching the river. The footbridges continued on, across the steel-covered rubber rafts, from one side of the river to the other. The thaw a few weeks earlier caused rushing streams to add to the flood, and this had made even the best roads quagmires. By 3:10 A.M. the bridge was in.

The engineers had performed a miracle by completing a bridge for vehicles in less than 24 hours. Early estimates had been for 30 hours. As a result the roads west of Schophoven, Germany, were lining up with tanks and tank destroyers. The equipment and men were all waiting to move. The infantry was also ahead of schedule, which added to the confusion.

The next day, February 24, 1945, Jack's outfit left Warden, Germany, at 10:15 A.M., moving toward Eschweiler, Germany. They crossed the Autobahn and arrived in Frenz, Germany, at an assembly point about 11 o'clock in the morning. They waited there several hours and then marched to Pier, Germany, and waited for commitment.

All of the First Battalion of the 30th Division crossed in assault boats. The assault regiments were the 119th and the 120th. Each made a bridgehead. The units following used the bridge. At this time the 117th Regiment (Jack's) was in reserve. The Battalion was to protect the right flank of the 30th Division in die Burge woods.

In the late afternoon of that same day (the 24th), Jack's unit, the 117th Regiment, moved on forward to Schophoven, Germany. There

At last, the "famous" fur coat! Peggy in her blue coat set.

Having fun in the snow.

they crossed the Roer River at the crossing site of the 119th Regiment which had made the bridgehead. Upon reaching the German side, they turned south to Krauthausen, Germany, to get back to their own zone of advance.

The day before the entire area west of the town, toward the river, had been heavily mined, and booby-traps (objects wired to explode when distrubed) were laid by the German defenders. The first troops going through in the darkness, just before dawn, had suffered many casualties, but by 10:30 A.M. Krauthausen, Germany, had fallen.

From Krauthausen Jack's unit went northeast to Niederzier, Germany, arriving at dusk. The First Battalion remained there for six hours as there was some delay ahead. Meanwhile they were under a heavy artillery barrage. The batallion stayed there until 1:45 A.M. February 25, 1945. The delay ahead was a roadblock being knocked out by the 120th Regiment. The night before the German 9th Panzer and the German 363rd Division had built a huge roadblock of logs, and they had set out 2,000 mines along the clearing by the road.

The American 30th Division objective for the day was Steinstrass, Germany, which lay ahead at the crossroad where the forest ended. The 30th Division was to take it and hold it. It would secure the main bridgehead. At 1:45 A.M. February 25, 1945, the 30th Division's First Battalion moved forward along the road in the darkness toward Steinstrass. Company B of the First Battalion was leading as they advanced slowly single file. As they drew near die Burge woods there was some question about tanks ahead. They stopped advancing and lay along the sides of the road for nearly an hour under persistent strafing by German planes and artillery fire. They learned the tanks were <u>Allied</u> and began advancing, spreading out into the woods. They spent the rest of the night walking around trying to find paths and locations in the darkness. When dawn of the 25th arrived, they were able to find their assigned positions and they dug in.

The First Battalion was to protect the right flank of its 117th Regiment which was advancing to the east. Company B dug in on the left; Company A dug in on the right, both facing east. Company C (Jack's unit) was in reserve, also dug in. They sat in their dug-in positions all day. There was very little rest, though, since the remainder of the regiment was busy reducing that roadblock on the Neiderzier - Steinstrass highway.

Shortly after midnight (26th) their orders were to take a part of Oberembt, Germany, the town 3,000 yards north of Steinstrasse. About 4:30 A.M., in the darkness, as they were preparing to move up for their attack, Company C ran into trouble.

The following is from <u>Curlew History - The Story of the First Battalion</u>, by William J. Lyman. "As Captain Stoffer was leading the Company from the edge of die Burge toward Steinstrasse he asked Colonel Frankland about supporting tanks. (The 793rd Tank Battalion was to send tanks which they were to ride, on the attack to Oberembt.) The Captain saw some armored vehicles approaching from the west and told the Colonel they were there. Two tanks and several halftracks were in the midst of Company C, however, before the G I's realized the vehicles were German, and the Jerries realized the infantrymen were American. All hell promptly broke loose and considerable confusion arose. Somehow C's soldiers managed to take care of the attached enemy foot soldiers while nearby 823rd TD's knocked out the Mark V's. Several casualties resulted from the fray, including Captain Stoffer, who was wounded in the arm. A few of the many smooth performances that day were those of Technician Fifth Grade Paul L. Christensen, Privates First Class Gert Humbert and Ronald L. Ward, and Privates Frank Baranowsky, Luther D. Curl, Sr., Sydney Kamler and <u>John K Price</u>."

Jack happened to be right in front of one of the tanks and started to climb up on it, thinking it was American. It was a German tank. These

Life Magazine - Soldier on the bridge fatally wounded. Magazine arrived, the day I received the telegram, that Jack had been seriously wounded.

were German Mark V tanks, huge monsters! A German infantry man riding on top of the tank shot Jack through the left shoulder with his machine gun.

Jack later described it thus in a letter from the hospital: "We moved up into this forest we were to take and dug holes while artillery was busting all around us. (25th) We had walked all that night, as well as the day before, to get up there, and just before daybreak got dug in and had fixed our fox hole up so that maybe we could get a little rest when the artillery started giving us the devil and very little sleep. We sat there till about 8 or 8:30 that evening without doing much except a patrol which went out occasionally.

"About 8:30 we pulled out and started to work clearing the woods. We made our way through to the far end and then dug in as an outpost more or less about 12 that night. We were supposed to sit there while another company went through us to take the next town. We had just gotten comfortable, as comfortable as you can get under those conditions, and settled down for maybe a few hours sleep when they called us out and told us something had happened to the other company and orders had come through that we were to mount tanks and ride in and take the next town.

"About 2:30 AM (26th) they had us all lined up along the road at the edge of the woods waiting for our tanks. Two tanks came from around the edge of the woods and started up the field toward the road where we were all standing. We figured it was our tanks and just stood there. The first tank got to the road and we all moved apart to give it room to come up crosswise on the road. It came up about 5 feet from me and then we noticed it was German instead of ours and that infantrymen were riding on it carrying machine guns.

"A fellow yelled Jerry and when he did the guy on the tank opened up with his M G. (machine gun). About the same time I turned and dived for a ditch next to the road. The tank moved on up across the road to a field and turned and kept on firing at us. When I dived in the ditch I had lost my helmet and glasses off my face and was afraid to show my head up over the edge of the ditch so started crawling down the edge of the road. When I did I noticed for the first time that my left arm was dead and that I was bleeding. That's the first time I knew of being hit.

"I crawled on down to where I could get up and then beat it back into the woods where the company was reforming. I told my squad leader I had been hit and tried to find our Medic to bandage me up a little but couldn't, so the Sgt told me to try to find the B Company C P as they would have a Medic. This was about 3 o'clock when I started back through the woods by myself looking for something I had no idea the exact location of, with no helmet or rifle. That is when I was really scared. I saw someone behind every tree and the trees were cracking all around from being hit by artillery."

Jack said later, at first he had tried to walk stealthily. Fearing he wasn't going to make it, he finally just crashed on through. Suddenly he heard, "HALT" in a very commanding voice. Halt is halt, so he did. He was sick with fear. They were speaking English — it was the B Company Command Post!!

It was 4:30 A.M. on February 26, 1945, and they were just about to change locations so the Medic cut his jacket and clothing away from the wound, sprinkled sulfa on it, and gave him some more sulfa pills (with water). He was still chewing the ones he had popped in his mouth without water! (Sulfa was a new miracle drug used by American troops.)

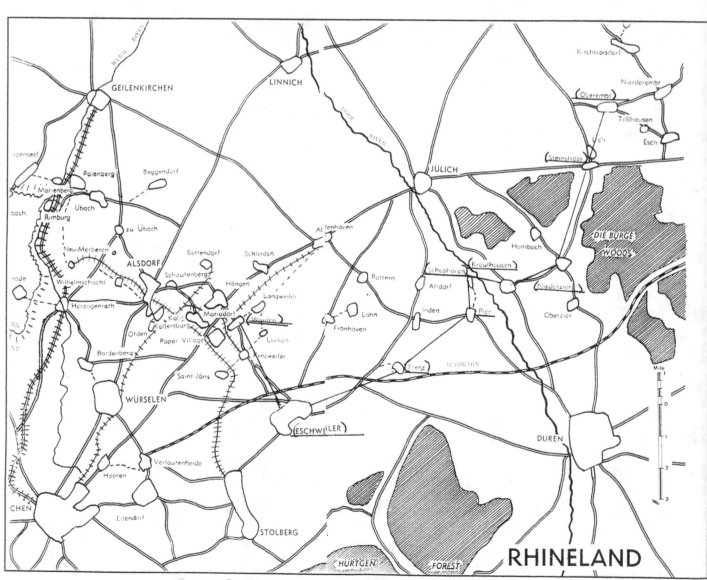

Germany - Roer River Crossing. From: Curlew history - Story of the first Battalion.

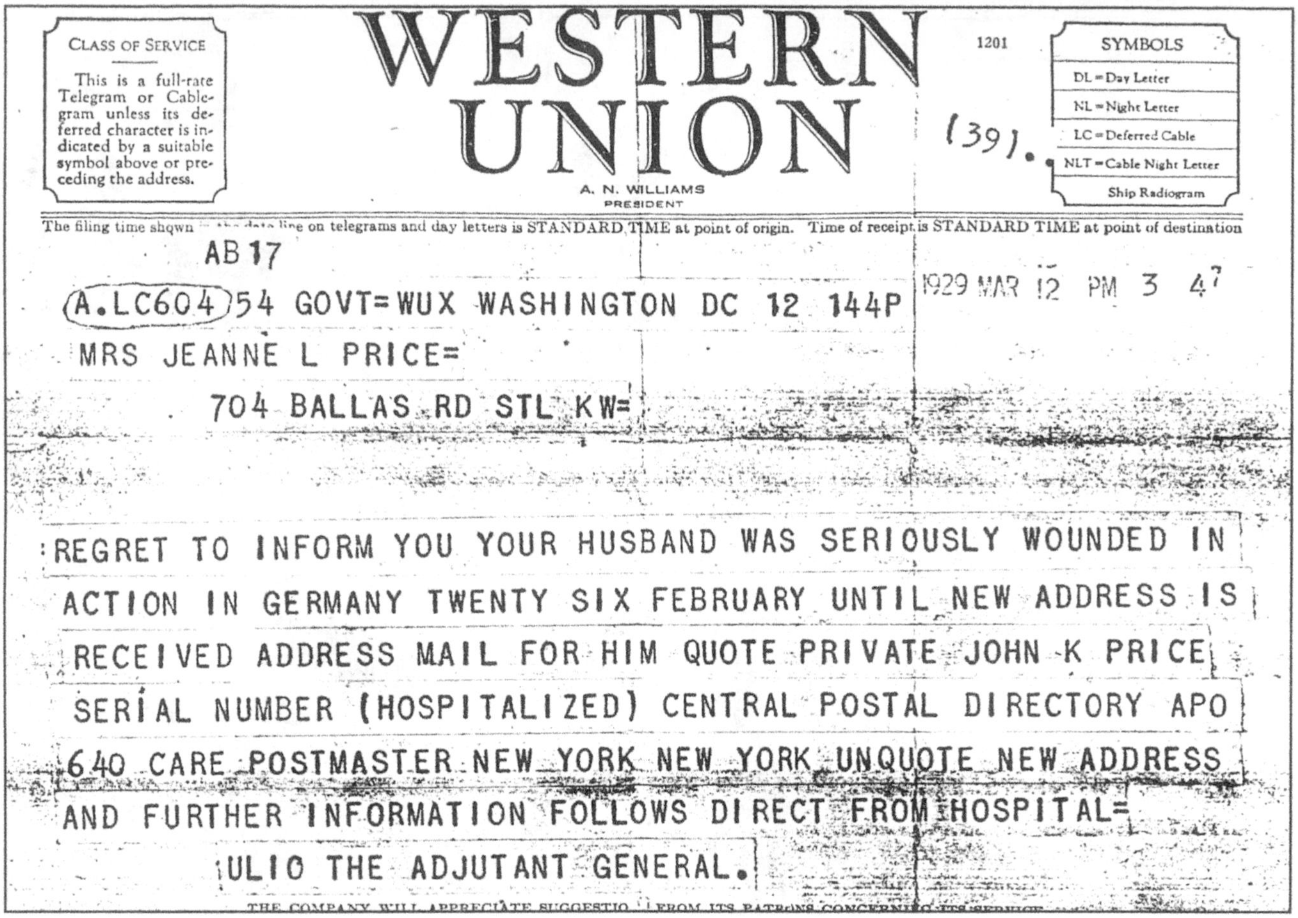

WESTERN UNION

CLASS OF SERVICE

This is a full-rate Telegram or Cablegram unless its deferred character is indicated by a suitable symbol above or preceding the address.

A. N. WILLIAMS
PRESIDENT

1201

(39).

SYMBOLS

DL = Day Letter
NL = Night Letter
LC = Deferred Cable
NLT = Cable Night Letter
Ship Radiogram

The filing time shown ... date line on telegrams and day letters is STANDARD TIME at point of origin. Time of receipt is STANDARD TIME at point of destination

AB 17

A.LC604 54 GOVT=WUX WASHINGTON DC 12 144P   1929 MAR 12 PM 3 47

MRS JEANNE L PRICE=

704 BALLAS RD STL KW=

REGRET TO INFORM YOU YOUR HUSBAND WAS SERIOUSLY WOUNDED IN ACTION IN GERMANY TWENTY SIX FEBRUARY UNTIL NEW ADDRESS IS RECEIVED ADDRESS MAIL FOR HIM QUOTE PRIVATE JOHN K PRICE SERIAL NUMBER (HOSPITALIZED) CENTRAL POSTAL DIRECTORY APO 640 CARE POSTMASTER NEW YORK NEW YORK UNQUOTE NEW ADDRESS AND FURTHER INFORMATION FOLLOWS DIRECT FROM HOSPITAL=

ULIO THE ADJUTANT GENERAL.

THE COMPANY WILL APPRECIATE SUGGESTIO ... FROM ITS PATRONS CONCERNING ITS SERVICE

Western Union Telegram. The dreaded message.

The Company Command Post had to leave but gave him directions to the 117th Regiment collecting station. It was now 5 A.M.

Jack headed out again. At least he knew he was going in the right direction, but he was still consumed with fear that they might have missed other Germans in those woods. His wound had bled profusely. He was soaked even into his boots; however, the cold weather had helped to control the bleeding.

He wrote later from the hospital and told about it: "I was lucky to be able to get out under my own power. Some of these guys had to lay up there for as long as 2 days without food, water or anything, and really hurt bad, too, because the medics couldn't get to them because of the heavy enemy fire. I don't imagine they would have found me had I been hit again or passed out or something going back. I believe the only thing that got me back at all was that I kept thinking of you and Peg and just made up my mind I had to get back and that was all there was to it. I believe that is the first thing I thought of when I got it, and it didn't leave my mind till I was in the hospital."

As the sky began to lighten in the east it became a little easier to find his way. No words can describe the feeling of relief when he finally reached the 117th Collecting station (the Army Field Hospital). It

was eight A.M. February 26, 1945. He had not had any sleep for over 48 hours, 25 of that had been walking, besides the seven hour walk after he was wounded. He was completely worn out. For two days all he had to eat was one small can of cheese and some water.

Some of the fellows at the Collecting Station were just coming back from chow and one of them gave him his coffee. He immediately passed out from exhaustion and loss of blood. They laid him on a litter; the medic then cut his clothes off and placed his personal items in a small bag.

His wallet, his prayer book, and his pictures of Peggy and me were all he had. He carried them in the upper pocket of his shirt. They were a little bloody! He had lost his gas mask which held three of my letters. He never did get to read them. He was carrying the medal his Dad had given him in his hand; his other medal was on his dog tag. They gave him a shot of morphine and he went to sleep instantly.

The next thing he remembered was being in an ambulance and sleeping in catnaps between shots. His medical record showed, "1. Army Field Hosp. — Germany, entered — February 26, 1945 — treatment for bullet wound in left shoulder — by enemy action." The ambulance was taking him to the Army hospital in Maastrich, Holland.

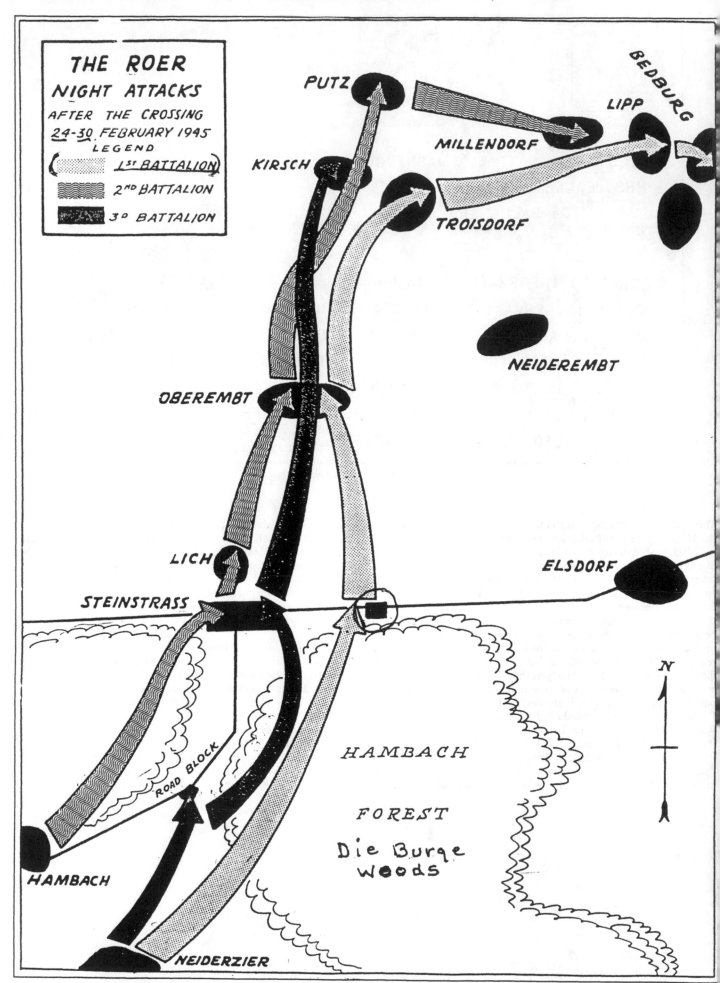

Germany - Die Burge Woods. From: Work Horse of the Western Front - The Story of the 30th Infantry Division.

PART 4: ARMY HOSPITALS
82nd GENERAL U.S. HOSPITAL
Whitchurch, England

ARMY FIELD HOSPITAL
Maastricht, Holland

When the ambulance reached Maastricht, Holland, approximately 35 miles to the rear, Jack was taken to the Army Field Hospital. He entered on February 27, 1945. They took X-rays and immediately prepared him for surgery. He was groggy, but awake enough to notice some of what happened there. He remembered it being a large operating area. The patients were wheeled in on operating tables arranged in a circle. The surgeons worked in teams, moving from one table to the next. As soon as one patient was operated on, he was moved out and another was immediately wheeled into his place. The American casualties had been very heavy.

When Jack had been prepared, the anesthetist told him to count to three, but before he reached two, he was out. They used Sodium Pentothal, which was so new we in the United States had never heard of it. They made an incision in the front and in the back of his shoulder which they left open to drain. It was fortunate the bullet had gone all the way through his shoulder. If it had come out one inch closer to his spine, he would have been paralyzed for life. The bullet had creased the lung so it was considered a chest wound.

His medical records showed: 2. Army Field Hosp. — Maastricht, Holland entered Feb 27, 1945 treated & operated on for bullet wound in left shoulder — result of enemy action."

ARMY EVACUATION HOSPITAL
Liege, Belgium

Later the same day, after his surgery in Holland, Jack was moved by ambulance to Liege, Belgium, a distance of approximately 16 miles. The report stated, "3. Army Evac Hosp. — Liege Belgium entered Feb. 27, 1945 — treated for Gunshot wound & awaiting evacuation to U.K."

Jack was deeply concerned about letting us know he was all right, before we received the telegram from the War Department. The nurse helped him write a V-mail telling me he had been wounded. "But don't worry, I'm OK," he wrote.

The next day he was taken by ambulance to another hospital in Liege. His medical record showed: "4. Army Evac. Hosp. # 54 — Liege Belgium entered Feb. 28, 1945 — Gun Shot Wound." This evacuation hospital was adjacent to an airfield where he and others were carried to a plane and flown to England.

The last letter Jack had written from Warden, Germany, was February 22, 1945. I did not receive it for about ten days. Having received no mail and reading the war news in the newspaper and knowing Jack was now with the 30th Division, we knew he was in the Roer River crossing.

Our family had received the March 12 issue of Life magazine, featuring the Roer offensive. The cover showed the picture of the lifeless body of a soldier on the foot bridge, and I was convinced it was Jack.

That same afternoon, February 2nd, 1945, I was out in the front yard of my parents' house taking pictures of Peggy when Jack's parents drove into the driveway. My heart nearly stopped! I knew why they had come. Jack's father never took off from work. His mother sat in the car rocking back and forth, sobbing. The floor of the car was full of wet kleenex! His father ran over to me, hugged me tight, and said over and over, "Jack's been wounded but he's all right. He's all right, you'll see!"

The War Department had my name, Jeanne Price, but Jack's parents' address, so they had delivered the telegram there.

A very caring lady, especially selected, brought it. She went next door first and asked their neighbor to please come over as soon as she left. She went right in, took Jack's mother to the sofa, sat beside her and read the telegram. It said:

"REGRET TO INFORM YOU YOUR HUSBAND WAS SERIOUSLY WOUNDED IN ACTION IN GERMANY TWENTY SIX FEBRUARY UNTIL NEW ADDRESS IS RECEIVED ADDRESS MAIL FOR HIM QUOTE PRIVATE JOHN K PRICE SERIAL NUMBER (HOSPITALIZED) CENTRAL POSTAL DIRECTORY APO 640 CARE POSTMASTER NEW YORK NEW YORK UNQUOTE NEW ADDRESS AND FURTHER INFORMATION FOLLOWS DIRECT FROM HOSPITAL = ULIO The ADJUTANT GENERAL."

Their neighbor kindly phoned Jack's father at work. When he arrived home, he and Jack's mother drove out to my house. My mother had been afraid for weeks to leave me alone, but that morning she had finally gone into St. Louis, Missouri, to shop. When she returned (the bus stopped in front of our house), she saw the Prices' car, and she too knew why they were there. Shortly after, my father came home and some of our neighbors had also come. Jack's poor mother was still crying her heart out.

I don't cry, I just freeze. I remember so well, standing in the dining room watching everyone and feeling as though I were watching a play. I felt as though I were someone else. When I went to bed that night, I finally wept. I sat and rocked Peggy with an aching heart, certain that she would never see her daddy again and would not even remember him. Then hope would return and I would believe he would be all right because I wanted to believe. Again I prayed and prayed, promising God any thing and everything.

The next days dragged like an eternity, but life goes on. Peggy had to be attended to. We heard nothing further from the War Department. Finally, one morning I received the V-Mail letter Jack had shakily written from the hospital in Belgium on February 27, 1945. I immediately called Jack's mother and practically screamed in the phone, "I got a letter; he's all right."

I had certainly made a lot of promises to God!!

Medical Report - 82nd General U.S. Hospital. Whitchurch, England.

When Jack's landed in England, he and the other wounded men were transferred to a hospital train which took them to a hospital on the border of Wales. Jack's medical record showed: "5. #4192 U.S.A. Hosp. Plant — 82 Gen Hosp. APO — 152 Whitchurch, England — entered Mar. 1st 1945 — treated for Gun Shot wound Dental work — teeth filled; also eyes treated and glasses prescribed & issued."

Jack's first letter from there written on March 4, 1945, arrived shortly after his letter from the hospital in Belgium. His letters came regularly after that, as did the progress reports, "making normal improvement," from the Casualty Branch of the War Department. In his first letter he told in detail about being wounded. He said he wasn't particularly scared the first time he went up to the front or while he was up there, but now he was petrified at the thought of going back there.

The next letter, March 6, 1945, to his parents said that he was up and around feeling fine. The doctors and nurses were exceptional. They kept him well medicated. It was such a relief to be in England, and he dreaded going back to the front. He said you get the best of medical care once you get back from the line. "I've been poked with so many needles of Penicillin, Tetanus, etc., I look like a sieve, but that stuff really works."

On March 7, 1945, Jack wrote that at first he had just a little round hole the size of his middle finger in front and a gash an inch long in back where the bullet came out. Now he had a big, long gash in front 3 inches long and 1 1/2 inches across and one in back 6 or 7 inches long. The shoulder bone aches like rheumatism. He described in detail what happened the night he got hit. (This was a seven page letter.)

On March 10, 1945, they sewed up the incision. The doctor told him it would be a couple of weeks and he would be completely healed up. (He was mistaken.)

Jack thought the war news looked good but that Germany was far from beaten. He was so anxious to get some news of Peggy. He had our pictures on his table next to his bed so he could look at them all the time.

March 15, 1945, he wrote they were having a lovely, warm sunshiny day. The weather in England had been wonderful lately, and he had been out nearly all day the past few days. He ripped a few of his stitches, and he got in trouble with the nurse! Jack said in his letter that he had been put in for PFC (Private First Class) before he left the outfit. The pay for a PFC would add $4.80 a month. The Combat Infantryman's Badge would add 10 dollars a month, so his total pay would be $74.80. His pay had been 60 dollars a month before. He had received 16 dollars (for March), a partial payment since his records were still lost.

He said the nurse removed all the stitches. They were festering and bothering him. She then taped the cuts closed. It was a lot more comfortable, but he had to give up his sling. He said he still had not received any mail.

He had lost all the fillings in his teeth from the vibration caused by terrific artillery barrages and was now getting started with the dentist. His arm and shoulder were still stiff, but he was using it more and more. The doctors found that the shoulder bone had not been parted, but it just had a hole through
it. He said the Army had him down for a rehabilitation hospital and then back to the front. He wrote out some instructions for me about my money from the government in case he went up to the front and anything happened to him.

On March 19, 1945, he received his Purple Heart. The nurse just laid them on their beds. They jokingly refered to them as their "German marksmanship medals." They were proud to have them though!

March 21, 1945, he wrote that he had still not received any mail, and it only had to be forwarded from Germany. He looked at his pictures over and over and he wrote, "I have pictures of Peg at almost every month, and I have them arranged so I can start when she is just a little thing and see how she has changed and grown up to the latest you sent at 16 months. I'm so homesick it's an obsession with me. I want to see Peg and play with her and have her know she has a father. If there only were some end in sight."

It was a comfort to have Jack safe in England for the present. Still the war dragged on and there was every possibility he would be back in it. We had no way of knowing that in a few more weeks the war with Germany would end!

In his March 24, 1945, letter he said the war news over there was looking good. They had a radio in the ward every other day. He had to stop writing as they were bringing lunch, and he had to help pass it out to the bed patients. Just then the mail was delivered and he got the first letter from me written March 18, 1945. It only took six days. He couldn't wait to answer it and he was full of questions. He said it would be a long letter — poor censor. It was seven pages.

He said his arm was bothering him as they had removed the clamps and bandages, and he was to start physical therapy. He could not lift his left arm over his head and could not lift it at all without using his other hand. He wrote some about his combat experience and told of his buddy in the foxhole with him being killed by a piece of schrapnel while they were under a terrific artillery barrage. Jack told me there was no possible chance of his being sent home. Unless the war in Europe was over soon, he would be back up at the front in another month or so.

I had mentioned that I had to use ration coupons now for Peggy's shoes. (Baby shoes were not rationed.) He asked if I could get ration-free sandals for her in the summer? That afternoon he finally got his glasses. He said it was so good to be able to see, he celebrated immediately by going to a movie they had.

In his letter March 29, 1945, he said the news over there was great, and they had been glued to the radio for the last day or two. He guessed we read that the American 30th Division spearheaded the attack crossing the Rhine yesterday. He said all of you back home only hear what Patton is doing, and he hated to think what the armor would do without the doughs (foot soldiers)!

He was a bit surprised at how long it took his wound to heal. He had not expected to be in England more than 30 days, and he thought that he would be back to the outfit by the end of April, 1945. He was to go to Physical Therapy that afternoon to learn to use his arm. He said that he had been helping in the ward kitchen because he could walk. Each hospital ward had 29 patients and their own kitchen.

Jack hoped his cousin Rusty had been liberated from the German POW camp by now. He said he would trade places any day if it would get Rusty home sooner. He said, having seen the poor condition of the Germans they had captured, how they lived and everything, you could have an idea of how our prisoners fared in their hands.

I had sent Peggy's little baby shoes so he was waiting and watching for the package. He wondered how I knew he would like to have them. Why wouldn't I know?

Jack wrote, "Peggy sounds so darling, she is really growing up. I'm glad she's talking so well. That is funny about the shirt. (She had to have a little baby shirt to hold when she went to bed, or else!!) I did want a girl, they are cuter and sweeter than little boys. Course, I want our next one to be a boy."

April 7, 1945, was the last letter Jack wrote from England. He said to stop writing to him or sending anything more until I heard from him. He said he was changing addresses again and not to send food as he would never be in a fox hole again. He wrote, "Don't send the pictures as I'll never get them. Wait till you hear from me. I'm not lonesome anymore, or blue!!!!. Bye now sweet. Love me. "I'll be seeing you." I knew exactly what he was telling me — that he was coming home. Undoubtedly the censor did also!

The next day Jack wrote a V-Mail to his dad and told him he was sure excited about the trout season opening there (he could not say where) and told him to go and get fishing licenses for both of them. He told his dad to start to practice casting and to plan to take a few days off soon.

His father had received the letter at his office. I was at their house that evening, and he came in with a big grin on his face and surprised me with it.

I had been receiving a card every other week from the War Department, stating that my husband was making normal improvement. The April 14, 1945, card read: "Evacuated to Zone of Interior — Final report." I had an idea what it meant, but I had to be sure. I called the Red Cross, and when I read the card to the very sweet lady who answered the telephone, she said, "My dear, he is coming home!" Now I knew it was really true. Jack was already on his way!

THE LETTERS

To: Mrs. John K. Price   From: Pfc John K. Price
704 Ballas Road   37623699
Kirkwood, 22, Mo.   Det of Pnts, 4192 U.S.A.
U.S.A.   Hosp. Plant APO 209
                                            c/o PM, New York, N.Y.

27 Feb 45
Belgium

Dearest Darling:
      Well, honey, I'm kind of having a hard time writing to you cause I'm in the hospital and am laying on my side with one arm all tied up to where I can't use it to hold the paper. I wanted to write you and tell you I have been wounded before you get the wire from the War Department and then be worried. I was shot through the shoulder, left one, and isn't too serious. I might have a bone or two broken but it hasn't bothered me hardly at all. So I'll have a couple of months or so of nice rest. Now don't go worrying and fretting about me cause I'm ok. Im a little too weak and uncomfortable to write much so I'll write you all about it as soon as I can.
      Don't mail my mail to me though till I write you and give you my new address. Tell Mom for me. I have to close for now, honey. I love you. Give Peg a kiss for me.

All my love, Jack

Sunday
4 March 1945
England

Dearest Darling:
      Well, honey, I've kind of let my writing slip, it being 5 or 6 days since I dropped you that note tell you I had been wounded but it was so darned hard to write the way I was all taped and bound up that I just gave up.
      I guess you all are all worrying and wondering what happened so Ill try to give you the whole story. I was shot through the shoulder by a German machine gun at 2:30 in the morning on the 26th. I made my way back to the collecting station from the front, arriving there about 8 AM. By the way, the bullet went in about an inch or may be two inches from the top of my shoulder and about 4 inches over and came out about 8 or 10 inches down my back on the left side. Well, they put me in an ambulance there and shot me back to Holland where they exrayed me and operated on me. then they put me in another ambulance and moved me back to an evacuation hospital in Belgium. There they put me on a plane and flew me to England. I got off the plane on to a train and ended up here. Now as far as the wound itself — it didn't hurt a bit, in fact I didn't know about it for quite a few minutes after I had been hit. Then I had to walk from 2:30 till 8 to get back to where I could get medical attention so it couldn't have been too bad. When I left the continent my records showed I had a compound fracture of a bone up in the shoulder but the doctor here says the bullet just chipped a little bone so I dont need a cast and other than having the holes sewed up where they operated on me (they left it open to drain) I'm just about well. I'm up and walking around the ward now and feel pretty good. I imagine I'll be heading back to the outfit in another month or so. The only ill effects I really suffered is the first day or so from loss of blood. So it was about 2 days from the time I left the front till I was back in England. They had diagnosed my wound as severe so most likely the wire you got will say I was seriously injured but that is a lot of poppy cock so ignore it — I never felt better — considering a couple holes in me — in my life.
      The one thing that made me madder than anything else is that I had 3 letters from you in my gas mask when I was hit and hadn't had time to read yet and I lost them. In fact, I lost everything I had except my wallet and your picture and my prayer book which I carried in my breast pockets. Well, honey, that's about all the dope I can give you on the whole business so I hope now your mind is at rest. Your guy is ok and doing fine — it will take more than a Kraut bullet to get me — I was born to hang. Course I don't mind telling you that I hope it is all over by the time I'm ready to go back — and there seems to be a pretty good possibility of that being so. You know, I wasn't particularly scared the first time I went up or while I was up there but now I'm almost petrified with fear of having to go back and that is really silly cause I went through a lot of really rough fighting and didn't get hit and then when I was hit it was on a fairly easy operation so I'd most likely go back and never get a scratch, but I'm still scared.
      I guess I'll have to go another couple of months now before I hear from you. — this will cause my

Progress Card. "Marking normal improvement."

mail to be all balled up again. Darn, I just get it straightened out to where I'm hearing from you quite regularly then I got to start all over again.

How is Peg, honey? You know, I keep looking at those new pictures you sent me over and over again and I just can't seem to realize she could be my big girl. She has gotten so big and is so darned cute. She has the most captivating smile I've ever seen. Gosh, what I wouldn't give to be there and see her and be able to play with her and kind of help her grow up.

Well, darling, this is all the paper I have and all the news I have to write about so I guess Id better close for now. Give Peg a big kiss for me and don't forget your prayers for me, honey, and thank God that I was injured so slight. Bye for now, honey. I love you and miss you more than anything in the whole world. Love me and miss me and say hello to the folks for me. By the way, I haven't written Mom and I'm sort of relying on you to break the news to her — don't let her worry about me, honey, and be sure to kind of look out for her. You know how she is and I'm afraid she might go all to pieces over it.

By now, darling. All my love to the sweetest most wonderful gal in the whole world.

Your sweetheart,
    Jack
P.S. I love you.

My address.
Ddt. of Pnt,
4192 USA Hosp. Plant,
APO 209
c/o PM, etc.

6 March 1945
England

Dearest Darling:
    Honey, I know how you dislike V-mail but please excuse this time cause I've hunted high and low for some writing paper, but no luck so this is better than not writing at all.

I'm feeling pretty good and although I have another operation to go through I'm up and around now. When I look at those others fellows here I realize how lucky I was to have been injured so slight in comparison. It really makes me ashamed of myself cause I actually find myself envious of them — some are going home and I would like to so much, but at least I have a chance to come home in one piece. At lease I will get a few days vacation here in England before I go back up.

The weather over here is still the same old typical English weather. Cold and damp and raining all the time. Its really hard to realize that just across the channel they are having nice warm spring weather.

By the way, did I tell you I lost all three pair of my glasses when I got hit? I'm just about blind now and sure wish they'd get around to making me another pair. I knew I should have sent that pair of civilian glasses home. Now I'll have to buy a new pair when I come home. Course I'd have had to get new lenses anyway but I hate the expense of new frames. (Page one — I hope they come together.)

I'll start on a new subject now, just in case you get this one fore page one so you'll be able to make some sense out of this.

I haven't written the folks yet but plan to do so today. How did Mom take the news, honey? I was really kind of worried about her. I knew you

wouldn't let your imagination run away with you, but you know how she is. I hope though, that you received that V-mail I wrote before you did the wire cause the darn wires leave so much unsaid that you would be bound to worry about me. Can you image me — a clerk!!! — with a poiple heart!! By the way, I haven't received it yet, but will send it to you as soon as I do.

Well, honey, I'm almost to the bottom so I guess I'd better start to close. Give Peg a big hug and kiss for me and take good care of that wonderful gal of ours. Say hello to all the folks, too, and don't let them worry to much about me. Remember I love you more than any thing in the whole world and miss you like every thing. Don't forget your prayers for me, honey, I need them more than anything. All my love to the sweetest most wonderful wife there is.

Your sweetheart,
    Jack
P.S. I love you.

6 March 1945
England

Dear Mom and Dad:
    I guess by now you've received the news and all the gruesome details from Babe, so I'll not go into it any more. I'm feeling fine and am up and around so you can judge for yourself how serious I was hurt. Course I've still got my shoulder bandaged up and have to have it sewed up, but that is minor. I'll have no ill results from it except for a couple of scars. I was really a lucky guy.

You have no idea what a relief it is to be back in England and I really dread to think of going back. The only consolation is that a couple of months will have passed before I get back and maybe it will be over by then. I don't think!! At least they should be across the Rhine by then and that's something.

One thing for certain you sure get the best of medical care once you get back from the line. They don't play around. I've been poked with so many needles of penicillin, Tetanus, etc. I look like a sieve but that stuff really works miracles. Well, folks, I'm out of room, I see, so I'll close for now. Write soon and look out for Babe and Peg for me. All my love to my wonderful Mom & Pop.

Your Son,
Jack

7 March 1945
England

Dearest Darling:
    Well, honey, I'm going to try to write — I finally found some writing paper — but I'll be darned if I know what to write about.

I'm getting along fine; feel pretty good and am up and around which really helps keep these days from getting too darn boring. I didn't tell you, but they operated on me and then left the cuts on both sides of my shoulder open to drain so I have one more operation to go through when they sew me up, then I'll be through. When I came in I had just a little round hole about the size of my middle finger in front and a sort of gash in the back about an inch long. Now I have a big long gash in front about 3 inches long and 1-1/2 inches across in front and one about 6 or 7 inches long in back. I'll sure have two beautiful scars up there, but I guess it was neces-

RESTRICTED

Purple Heart, Pg 2.
3/19/45
Hospitales

Private Paul J. Mulvihill, (Army Serial Number 42185310),
Infantry, U.S. Army, for wounds received as a result of enemy
action on 23 February 1945 in Germany. Entered military
service from New Jersey.

Private Gail W. Murry, (Army Serial Number 37746687), Infantry,
U.S. Army, for wounds received as a result of enemy action on
3 March 1945 in Germany. Entered military service from
Kansas.

Private John K. Price, (Army Serial Number 37623699), Infantry,
U.S. Army, for wounds received as a result of enemy action on
26 February 1945 in Germany. Entered military service from
Missouri.

Private Frank A. Renner, Jr., (Army Serial Number 33941538),
Infantry, U.S. Army, for wounds received as a result of enemy
action on 6 February 1945 in Luxembourg. Entered military
service from Pennsylvania.

Private William M. Rountree, (Army Serial Number 34837625),
Infantry, U.S. Army, for wounds received as a result of enemy
action on 5 March 1945 in Germany. Entered military service
from Florida.

2. By direction of the President, under the provisions of AR
600-45, 22 September 1943, as amended, and Section I, Circular 32,
Headquarters, European Theater of Operations U.S. Army, 20 March 1944,
an OAK LEAF CLUSTER for wear with the PURPLE HEART previously awarded
is awarded to:

Tec Sergeant Elmer P. Jeffery, (Army Serial Number 15058113),
Infantry, U.S. Army, for wounds received as a result of enemy
action on 26 January 1945 in Luxembourg. Entered military
service from West Virginia.

Staff Sergeant Paul J. Wiedorfer, (Army Serial Number 33729886),
Infantry, U.S. Army, for wounds received as a result of enemy
action on 10 February 1945 in Germany. Entered military
service from Maryland.

Sergeant Ovide (NMI) Trahan, (Army Serial Number 38652448),
Infantry, U.S. Army, for wounds received as a result of enemy
action on 9 February 1945 in Germany. Entered military
service from Louisiana.

Corporal William H. Baglan, (Army Serial Number 35476914),
Medical Department, U.S. Army, for wounds received as a result
of enemy action on 5 March 1945 in Germany. Entered military
service from Indiana.

Private First Class Charles H. Coffey, (Army Serial Number
34805188), Infantry, U.S. Army, for wounds received as a
result of enemy action on 6 March 1945 in Germany. Entered
military service from Alabama.

Private First Class Ira B. Dove, (Army Serial Number 39204448),
Infantry, U.S. Army, for wounds received as a result of enemy
action on 27 February 1945 in Germany. Entered military
service from Washington.

Private First Class Robert F. Kauffman, (Army Serial Number
33833313), Armored Force, U.S. Army, for wounds received as a
result of enemy action on 15 January 1945 in Belgium. Entered
military service from Pennsylvania.

RESTRICTED

(over)

sary so that it would heal inside me. I can feel it healing and it won't be too long fore I'll be out of here, if there aren't any complications as far as that broken bone in my shoulder is concerned. It has been giving me considerable trouble lately — aches and pains something like Rheumatism does. It's a funny thing, but my upper part of my arm bothers me more than anything.

You might be interested in what happened the night I got hit so I'll give you the whole story. We moved up into this forest we were to take and dug holes while artillery was busting all around us. We had walked all that night, as well as the day before, to get up there, and just before day break got dug in and had fixed our foxhole up so that we could maybe get a little rest when the artillery started giving us the devil and very little sleep. We sat there till about 8 or 8:30 that evening without doing much except a patrol which went out occasionally. About 8:30 we pulled out and started to work cleaning the woods. We made our way through to the far end and then dug in as an outpost more or less about 12 that night. We were supposed to sit there while another company went through us to take the next town. We had just gotten comfortable, as comfortable as you can get under those conditions, and settled down for maybe a few hours sleep when they called us out and told us something had happened to the other company and orders had come through that we were to mount tanks and ride in and take the town. About 2:30 they had us all lined up along the road at the edge of the woods waiting for our tanks. Two tanks came from around the edge of the woods and started up the field toward the road where we were all standing. We figured it was our tanks and just stood there. The first tank got to the road and we all moved apart to give it room to come up cross wise on the road. It came up about 5 feet from me and then we noticed it was German instead of ours and that infantry men were riding on it carrying machine guns. A fellow yelled Jerry and when he did the guy on the tank opened up with his M.G. About the same time I turned and dived for a ditch next to the road. The tank moved on up across the road to a field and turned and kept on firing at us. When I dived in the ditch I had lost my helmet and glasses off my face and was afraid to show my head up over the edge of the ditch so started crawling down the edge of the road. When I did I noticed for the first time that my left arm was dead and that I was bleeding. Thats the first I knew of being hit. I crawled on down to where I could get up and then beat it back into the woods where the company was reforming. I told my squad leader I had been hit and tried to find our Medic to bandage me up a little but couldn't, so the Sgt told me to try to find the B Company CP as they would have a Medic. This was about 3 oclock when I started back through the woods by myself looking for something I had no idea the exact location of, with no helmet or rifle. That is when I was really scared. I saw someone behind every tree and the trees were cracking all around from being hit by artillery. I finally found the CP about 4:30 but they were just about to move out so the medic cut my jacket and clothes away from the wound and sprinkled sulfa on it and gave me some pills and directed me back to the collecting station of the 117th. I left them about 5 oclock and walked back to the collecting station arriving there at 8 in the morning. They gave me a shot of Morphine and a cup of coffee and from then on I moved plenty fast from hospital to hospital till I arrived here in England two days later. Thats just about the whole story. I will say this, the only time I was really scared was coming through those woods with all that artillery and me by myself. That was the only time I was really worried about not making it. The funny thing is that I had been back to the collecting station 5 minutes before I passed out colder than a mackeral from loss of blood, they say. Thank goodness that didn't happen to me while I was in the woods.

Good Lord, I got to writing here and kind of forgot myself. 7 pages already about myself. I guess I'd better quit for a while and rest a minute or two. Be back. Bye now. I love you.

Its a funny thing, but you hate to have anything change while you are away. You dream about all these familiar things day after day and look forward to coming back and having them all the same — I guess it just never works out that way, though. People have to go ahead back home the same as we do here.

Well, honey, I guess I'd better begin to close for now and save a little to write about for tomorrow. Don't forget me in your prayers and give Peg a big hug and kiss for me.

All my love for always and always to the sweetest most wonderful little gal in the world what I am really in love with.

Your Sweetheart,
      Jack
P.S. I'm enclosing an article I ran across I thought you might be interested in. Also a couple of coins. I love you.

Bye now. Me

                              Sunday
                              11 March 45
                              England

Dearest Sweetheart:
      Well, honey, it has been a couple of days since I last wrote you, but I'll be darned if I could think of anything to write about. Its so darned hard when all you do is lie in bed all day or sit around the ward here. All we do is read or have bull sessions. It really gets boring sometime.

Well, they sewed me up day before yesterday so it won't be long now before I'm good as new with the exception of a couple of scars. The doctor said it would only be a couple of weeks before I would be completely healed up. Course I imagine it will be longer than that before the stiffness leaves my shoulder and I can use my arm like I used to. The arm is what bothers me most now. I have to wear a sling and I have no strength in it at all. I can't pull it away from my body cause it hurts like all get out when I do. I guess maybe that is caused by the bullet passing through my muscles and chipping the bone. They are going to work on my teeth, too, while I'm here. I don't know why, but for some reason, I lost all the fillings out of them. I just wonder if maybe I got too close to a shell going off and the concussion did it, cause when I went up to the front my teeth were in good shape. I also have to get two new pair of glasses, so all in all I guess I'll be here on to a couple of months. I don't mind telling you I'm going to do everything in my power to keep from going up again. I'd like to be a clerk a while now seeing that that is what they spent all their time teaching me to be. I don't know what it is going to take, but I'm willing to do almost anything to stay away from the front. Its a funny thing, but while I was up there it wasn't too bad — you get sort of acclimated to all the noise and dangers, etc.

and don't think much about it. It doesn't dawn on you that you will get hit, but since I've been hit and am back here and have seen these boys here in the hospital and all, I'm just about petrified with fear of having to go back. I'm really letting it get me down too much I guess, but I'm scared silly.

The news really looks good now doesn't it? I hope the folks back home don't go getting over optomistic about it though like they did the last time. The general opinion of the boys fighting over here is that we are going to have to completely over run Germany. There will most likely be no armistice. We will just fight till they are beaten and can fight no longer. I don't think they'll ever quit. If you could see the way they are fighting you would feel the same way. You folks hear all about how they are giving up but you don't hear that they kill quite a few of our boys before they do, and when they quit its usually because they are isolated and completely outnumbered and can fight no longer. When you even have to worry about kids 8 and 10 years old sniping at you and women fighting like the men, you begin to realize, that even though we are taking the country, the people are far from beaten.

They have been assigning quite a few wounded infantrymen to the Air Corp lately, I understand, as due to the transferring of Air Corp to the infantry a couple of months ago when they were so short of infantrymen which has left them in need of men, so maybe I'll be lucky.

How is Peg, honey? I'm so darned anxious to hear from you and get some new news about how she is growing and the cute things she does. Darn, I'd give anything in the world to be able to be there with you both now. I have your and Peg's picture on my table next to my bed so I can see you any time I look up. I have that old picture I have of you in the folder and the new one of Peg. Gosh, darling, I love you and miss you so much I don't know what to do. When I think of all the wonderful times we have had together and what fun it was being with you and babying you and think of all the time we have lost and are losing now it just about breaks my heart. I guess maybe we were always too close to each other. I know now that I relied on you too much cause now that I'm away from you I miss you so I can hardly take it. One thing, it wouldn't have been as bad had we not been as close as we were.

Well, darling, thats about all the paper so I guess I'd better close for now. Bye, honey. Love me and miss me and don't forget the prayers. Give Peg a big kiss for me. All my love for always to my sweet wonderful wife and lil gal.

Your Sweetheart,
   Jack
P.S. I love you.

Thursday
15 March 1945

Dearest Darling:
   Hi sweet — how are you this wonderful warm sunshiny day? We have been having the most wonderful weather here lately. I didn't think England could do it. I've been outside most all day the last couple of days just soaking up all the sun I could. I have been feeling pretty good — my shoulder is healing, although I did rip a few of the stitches out the other day which they weren't too pleased about and the wound in front was festering a little, but nothing serious. I still have my arm in a sling but I am get-

ting some strength back in it and can raise it a little and use my hand pretty good, too. It shouldn't be more than two weeks now before I'm all healed up and ready to go again. I figure another 6 weeks and I'll be back to the outfit again.

I still haven't received any mail but you know how long it takes for your mail to catch up when you move around. I could sure use a letter or two though. I want to get some news about that wonderful family of mine. How is Peg doing, honey? I'll bet she is really growing up fast now.

Just finished listening to the news and things look pretty good over here, but there is still a long, stiff fight ahead of us. Lord how I wish this was over and we were all on our way home for good. Its really getting me down.

What have the folks decided to do with Sissy? She has been a sweet little dog, just as good and faithful as any I've ever seen and I hate to think of them putting her to sleep. How old is she now anyway? I would say about 12 or 13 years old, but I don't remember, for sure. I guess she is getting pretty feeble and crippled up, but that is when we should be able to take care of her, now that she needs help.

Well, I finally got paid — but only a partial payment — 16 dollars, which will just about buy my rations, etc. for the next couple of months, so as soon as I can (as soon as they pay me in full) I'll send you anyway a hundred bucks. Just as soon as I get back into the Repl Depots I'll make out another $20 allotment so you'll be able to rely on some extra money each month.

I've got to quit for a few minute, honey. I'll be back, shortly. Bye now. I love you.

Here I am again honey and I'll try to finish this fore I have to go again.

How about your apartment, honey? You haven't mentioned it lately and I was wondering if you are still looking for a place. I definitely want you to have a place to yourself, and especially when I come home so we will have a place to ourselves where we can be alone a little. If things went right before I left the outfit I should be drawing $14.80 more a month now. I was put in for a Pfc which is $4.80 a month and also for a combat infantryman's badge which is ten bucks a month more so if they went through before I left I'm ok, but if something happened to hold it up till after I left I most likely won't get it. Hold your thumbs for me cause that extra will help. It will boost my pay to $74.80 which will let me send you a few more extra dollars. I'll let you know as soon as I find out, whether or not I got it.

Well, honey, thats just about all I have to write about for today. I waited to see if maybe I would get a letter but no luck so I'll close for today. Night darling. Sweet dreams to my most wonderful sweetheart. Love me and miss me a little and say a big prayer for me, too. Don't forget to give Peg a big hug and kiss, too, for me. All my love, always, to my two wonderful sweethearts. I love you!

Your Sweetheart,
   Jack

England
Friday
16 March 1945

Dearest Sweetheart:
   It's really a problem writing when you have to go so long without receiving any mail and especially

in a hospital — the same thing happens day after day and its very monotonous to say the least.

I'm feeling pretty good and seem to be getting along ok. I am now going to the mess hall for my meals and getting out in the fresh air again. So many of my stitches pulled out that yesterday the nurse just went ahead and pulled them all out and taped my cuts closed. Its a heck of a lot more comfortable and I believe I'll mend a lot faster this way. Those darn stitches pulled something terrible and bothered me a lot. She was still getting a little pus out of the one wound but doesn't amount to anything. I'm getting well too dog-gone fast! Ain't that awful?!!

They have movies here on the post every other day or so that I would sure like to go see, but there's absolutely no use for me to go — I couldn't see them anyway without my glasses. I'll sure be glad when they get around to fitting me out with a new pair.

I can't get over the beautiful weather we have been having since I arrived back here. Course I'm in a different part of the country than I was before which might have something to do with it. I guess just as soon as I get ready to leave it will start raining as usual and be nasty again.

Nothing much happened today. I layed around reading all day long. I did get the bad news that I have to go to the Dentist tomorrow. Boy, how I dread it. I think I told you I lost all the fillings out of my teeth. I don't know what caused it unless it was the concussion from a couple of terrific artil-lery barrages I went through on the last operation the outfit was on. I don't believe I have one filling left in my mouth.

How is that wonderful daughter of ours getting along? Gosh, honey, I feel so darned homesick and blue and lonesome for you tonight. I'd give anything in the world for this mess to be over and to be back home with you and Peg. Sometimes I wonder if I'll ever get back, it all looks so hopeless sometimes. I've been away so long this time I can hardly remember what you and a home is like. Its all so hazy. This darn Army life finally beats you out to where you haven't any recollection of being independent, it finally tries to take even memories away, too. I've come to the conclusion that it is really going to be quite a job adjusting myself to civilian life when I finally get home and I'm going to need a lot of understanding and help. I guess it will be strange for both of us for a while, to go back to being married and being a family. I'll do my best, but I know it will be trying as the devil for you sometimes, sweet, and you'll just have to jump on me and get me back in the harness like you used to do.

Have you all heard any news about Rusty lately? I sure hope he was in that bunch of POW's that were recently released by the Aussians and are on their way home now. Lets hope its not to long and that he is in good shape when they do reach him. He has really had it rough and deserves a few good breaks now. He has been captive for better than two years now, hasn't he?

Reading Daddy's letter.

A sweet kiss for Daddy.

Well, sweet, I'm just about out of news for tonight so I guess I'd better close for now. Night darling. Love me and miss me a little and be sure to remember me in your prayers each night. Give Peg a big hug and kiss for me and say hello to the folks, too. All my love to my wonderful darling. I love you more than you'll ever know.

Your Sweetheart,
Jack
P.S. I love you.

England
17 March 1945
(Sun)

Dearest Darling:

Well, darling, I made the ordeal of the dentist today without rouble. Don't know how many more I have to be worked on but he filled 5 of them today. Also got the sling taken away from me and have to take exercises now on my arm. Guess it won't be more than a couple of weeks fore I'll be heading back to the outfit. Wish I would go through the 12th Depot again. This time I believe I could work it so I would be assigned — or better still I wish this mess would end before I get back to the continent. My arm and shoulder are still pretty stiff and sore but I'm using them more and more each day and will be right before I know it — too soon, in fact.

I was hoping to receive some mail by now but no go. It sure seems that my mail should be here in the 17 days I've been here — it only had to be forwarded from Germany straight here. I sure need a letter or two from you — I'm so darned homesick and lonesome for you. Thats another thing that sure made me sick — when I first came to this hospital they thought I had a compound fracture of the shoulder and so the Colonel who made the preliminary examination recommended that I be returned to the Zone of the Interior or ZI'd as we say which would have meant I would be heading home but after my operation the doctor found that the bone hadn't parted but just had a chip out of it like this—just left a hole in the bone and so, even though it was still considered a compound fracture it didn't require a cast and would heal fairly rapidly so now they have me down for a rehabilitation hospital and then back to the front — my luck is still running true to form.

I haven't written the folks for over a week now, honey, but its so darn hard to find enough to write about — I'd appreciate it if you would sort of share your letters with them for a while and explain why and everything.

Well, darling this is awfully short but it really is the best I can do for today. I mostly wanted to let you know I was getting along ok and that I'm still thinking about you every minute and love you and miss you more than anything in the world. Night, honey. Sweet dreams and say a prayer for me. Love

Daddy's little soldier.

Mailing daddy's birthday present.

REPORT OF CONTACT

(6) Sta Hosp. Camp Patrick Henry — Newport News, Va

entered april 24, 1945 - treated for gun Shot

Office _____

Dated _____

Name _Wound — result of enemy action_____ No. _____
(Of ex-serviceman)   (C, XC, K, etc.)

Address _____

Person contacted _____

Address _____ Telephone No. _____

Personally _____ Telephone _____ Mail _____ Place of contact _____

Give brief statement of information requested and given:

(0.7) Baxter Gen. Hosp. — Spokane, Wash. — entered
May 1, 1945 ~~entered Hosp~~ treated —
Gun Shot Wound — result of enemy action.
also Dental Work

Medical Report - Station Hospital, Camp Patrick Henry, Newport News, Virginia.

ARMY SERVICE FORCES
Station Hospital
Camp Patrick Henry, Va.

APR 28 1945

6
4/28

Your Husband, Pvt. John K. Price

☐ Was admitted to this hospital on_____
He will remain here only until he can be transferred to a hospital
most suitable for his care and, if possible, the nearest to his home.
It is not advisable that you visit him here; you will be notified immediately upon his transfer. His present condition is satisfactory
and you will be advised at once of any change.

BAXTER GEN HOSP

☒ has been transferred to_____ Spokane, Wash.
for further observation and treatment.

JOHN D. NELSON
Captain, MAC
Registrar

SPTAK FORM 8225
REV 29 MAR 45

HRPE

Progress Card - "transferred to Baxter General Hospital, Spokane, Washington.

me and miss me a little and give Peg a big hug and kiss for me too. All my love for always to my two wonderful sweethearts.

Your Sweetheart,
Jack
P.S. I love you.

England
Monday 19 March

Dearest Sweetheart:

I must have started a letter to you at least three times yesterday fore I finally gave up; I just didn't have a darn thing to write about and as far as that goes, I still don't, but I can't go more than one day without writing my wonderful sweetheart.

By the way, honey, while I'm thinking of it, I want to give you some dope in case anything does happen to me when I go back up again. In the first place you know I have $10,000 Insurance which will pay you about $60 a month for the next 20 years. In addition to that you will receive a pension for you and Peg which I believe will come close to $80 a month as long as you don't remarry. Course as soon as you got married again the pension would stop, but the insurance will keep on for the full 20 years. Course, besides all this you will receive whatever pay and allowances I have coming so you should be fairly well taken care of. I believe, if any thing does happen, I would have Dad handle the whole business for you. That way, in case of any legal angle that might arise he'll know what to do. This is a hell of a morbid subject, I know, but it worries me quite a bit and I want you to know what little I know about it so you will be taken care of. That's my first concern — you and Peg.

You know, its a funny thing but while you are up on the line you don't worry about getting killed. The only two things I really worried about was you and Peg in case any thing did happen to me and about hurting—the pain—if I got hit. The funny thing being that there was no pain at all when I did get it. When I finally woke up to the fact that I was hit there was no pain—just a slight burning feeling in my shoulder and the blood making me uncomfortable. I guess this is enough of this kind of talk—I'll change the subject.

I got into another poker game the other day and darned if I didn't go back down to my original 4 pounds again. I should have sent that extra money home when I had a chance. Oh well, maybe I'll get it back. Anyway that's all the recreation we have around here so I might as well enjoy myself — You know me and Poker!

Dog gone I sure should be getting some mail from you soon. I've been in the hospital 20 days now and even though your new letters haven't had time to get here the old ones forwarded from the company should be getting here soon. Gosh, I hope so anyway — I'm getting desperate for some news from home. I'm anxious for some news about that big gal of ours. How's Peg getting along, hon? Gosh, I'll bet she is talking a blue streak now and really growing up. I wonder when this mess will be over and I can get back to that wonderful family of mine.

I'll finish this a little later. Bye for now. I love you.

Hi, honey, here I am again but not for long. I finally got my Purple Heart today and I'll mail it to you as soon as I get the chance. I must go now, honey, and get to bed as I am tired out. Goodnight dearest,

Love me and miss me like I do you. Give Peg a big hug and kiss for me and say hello to the folks, too. Sweet dreams darling. All my love to my two wonderful sweethearts.

Your sweetheart,
Jack
P.S. I love you.

England
21 March 1945
Wednesday

Dearest Darling:

Well, honey, I'll try to drop you a few lines tonight but I've still the same old trouble — no mail from you as yet and nothing to write about.

I'm getting well fast now. My cuts are healing nicely and although my arm and shoulder are still stiff, I don't use a sling and can put my arm in the sleeve of my PJ's and robe. Couple more weeks and all I'll have is a couple of scars and the memory. I guess I was really lucky as that bullet could have caused a lot of trouble had it been just an inch or two in any way from where it hit as it would have busted up quite a few bones. Kind of gripes me too, though, cause as long as I had to go through all the pain, etc, it could have been bad enough to get me sent home.

By the way, I haven't sent that Purple Heart home yet, but I'll go down to the Red Cross tomorrow and have them get it off to you, as I guess you all are anxious to see the thing.

I got out all my pictures today, I have quite a stack of them now, and looked at each one over and over again. It made me feel so sad and blue though. You know, I have pictures of Peg at almost every month and I have them arranged so I can start when she was just a little thing and see how she has changed and grown all the way up to the latest ones you sent of her at 16 mos. I'm so darn homesick, honey, I just don't know what to do. I want to go home so darn bad its become sort of an obsession with me. I want to see Peg and be able to play with her a little and have her know she has a father. I love you and miss you so darn much it almost makes me sick. If this damn mess would only end or at least if there only were some end in sight that we could look forward to.

Gosh darn, honey, I'm so darn hungry for news from home I don't know what to do. Have they heard from Rusty recently? I wonder how he is getting along and whats more important have the Russians reached his camp yet? Speaking of Rusty, I sure wish I could get with the air corp, especially as a clerk, when I leave here. What a break that would be. I sure dread to think of going back up on the line. I'm going to buck to stay here as long as I can, but after 128 days here they have to make some disposition with you; either back to duty or home. Maybe I can get a clerk job here for at least the 128 days, I hope.

Well, I got in another card game last night and ran my stake back up to Seven pounds. I think I'd better quit now that I'm ahead. I'm going to need all the dough I can get a hold of for this seven day furlough I'll get when I leave here. I'll most likely be able to get a 48 hour pass besides and that will take dough, too. What I'll have to do, I guess, especially if I don't get paid fore I leave, is make a loan, if possible from the Red Cross.

Well, darling that about unwinds me for tonight so guess I'd better close and hit the hat. Goodnight sweet, sweet dreams. Love me and miss me a little and remember me in your Prayers. Give Peg a big hug and kiss for me and say hello to the folks, too.

All my love to the sweetest most wonderful gal in the whole world.

Your Sweetheart,
Jack
P.S. I love you.

England
21 March 1945

Dear Mom and Pop:

Well, folks, its been quite a while since I last wrote you but life in a hospital is far from conducive to writing letters. I haven't a darn thing to write abou — the same thing happens — which is nothing, day after day. I lay here in bed and read or sleep or listen to the radio when we have it (we have a radio in the ward every other day). I'm feeling pretty good and am almost all healed up now. Still can't use my arm as normally as I used to (its still pretty stiff) but don't use a sling any more. I haven't any strength back yet in the upper part of my arm so I can't lift my arm away from my body and my elbow is still stiff from having my arm bound up so long, so I still can't straight it out completely, but its working loose and getting better every day. I received the Purple Heart yesterday which I'm sending to Babe tomorrow.

Say, Pop, I still haven't written Mr. Friant. I had a letter all composed, ready to write him, when we jumped off this last time and never got a chance to finish it fore I got hit and lost the draft. If you see him I wish you would mention to him that I was wounded and that I had intended writing him. You might tell him I told you I was very anxious to go with him and will go to work whenever he wants me. I would like about a month to acclimate myself to civy life, but its not necessary. I think going with them, with the reputation I seem to have with Friant, will be the best thing I could do, and with the proper handling, I should have a pretty good drag with the executive force.

Well, folks, this isn't much of a letter I know, but I haven't heard from anyone now for quite some time. Night folks, write soon and dont worry about me. Take care of Babe and Peg for me, too.
All my love.

Your Son,
Jack

24 March 1945
Saturday
Wales
Just found out I was in Wales, not England. Right on the border.

Dearest Darling:
Well, honey, another week is almost over — and a very lonesome and miserable week it has been for me. I don't know why, but I think I've been more lonesome for you and blue this past week than ever before. I'm so fed up with army I'm about to go nuts. I'd give absolutely any thing to be able to come home, even for just a few days and see you and Peg and be with you a little.

By the way, fore I forget, a fellow here that I've gotten fairly friendly with is leaving for home in the next couple of days and offered to call you up when he arrived. I didn't know how you would feel about it so I told him to call you collect — it will be from New York — and in the meantime I would write you and tell you that if you would rather not spend the dough just don't accept the call. You'll be able to ask him all the questions about it you want, etc. Now suit yourself about it. His name is Harold Thorpe. I'll send this Air mail so you will get it in time to know whats cooking.

Well, I still haven't received any mail, but have hopes. I'm due a couple of letters any day now as it has been plenty of time for my letter from here to get to you and your letter back to me. It sure would help a lot to get a few letters from home now. It would pep me up a little and Lord knows I need it.

I'm feeling pretty good now and seem to be healing up fairly rapidly. I figured I would be out of here in another month at the most, but yesterday I talked with a fellow who had been hit almost the same as I except for the fact that the bullet didn't go all the way through his shoulder and didn't hit a bone like mine did and he was here 4-1/2 months with it, so I don't know, now. That seems like an awfully long time for such an apparently minor wound compared to these other fellows here. I wouldn't mind it, though — the longer here the less chance of going back up there.

The war news over here does really look good now. I only hope it continues and is over before much longer as I'm just about at the end of my rope — this business really is getting me down.

Well, honey, they are bringing in lunch now, so I'll have to quit till this afternoon. I have to help pass it out to the bed patients. Bye now, honey. Be back. I love you.

Honey! I got a very wonderful letter from you just a few minutes ago. Oops, chow — be back in a sec. Here I am again — finished my chores for the day and ate. Gosh, honey, its so wonderful to start getting mail again. I expect I have quite a few more early than this one on the way. This was dated the 18th of March. Pretty fair service, eh? Darn though, some of the things I wanted to know weren't in it. Did you receive a wire from the War Department saying I was wounded? What did it say? Did you get that V-mail I wrote before you got the wire? How did Mom take it? Have the folks moved yet? etc etc etc. I'm really full of questions. Well, now I guess I'll get down to answering the letter and something tells me this will be quite a letter today — poor censor!

I'm not feeling too well tonight. Nothing serious — my shoulder is bothering me a little. Today they took all the clamps holding the wounds closed off and the bandages as both holes are almost healed up, but they bother me cause the clamps being off the skin pulls away from the cuts and hurts. As usual I'm getting better about three times faster than I should. From the looks of things I'll be lucky if I'm in here two months let alone 4. I start going to Physio Therapy in the next day or so for arm exercises to bring the use back to my arm and shoulder. I can lift my arm and move it around without any trouble, but can't lift it over my head yet and haven't enough strength to raise it without lifting it with my other hand. In fact I pick up my arm and raise it up away from my body and when I let go it just falls back. Don't worry, though, I'm going to do everything possible to keep from going back up there. I'm going to _____ to the high heavens. I'd like to be clerk a little now for a change, I've definitely had my fill of combat. No, honey, I can't for the life of me see how I came through all I did with such a little scratch. Since the 19th of December

I've been in nearly continuous fighting on the line and have seen some funny things and horrible things — guys falling all around me and never get hurt — then have to get it on a freak happening like I did. I've had quite a few narrow squeeks too. I don't know whether the censor is supposed to let things like this go through but I'll try it once. Here is one of the things that happened. — One morning my buddy and I were lying in our foxhole while the Jerry's laid a terrific Artillery barrage down on us. This fellow was laying facing the wall of the hole and I was next to him with my arm over him; keeping our heads down as far in the mud as we could. When it finally lifted I raised up and started talking to him but he didn't answer or move so I turned him over and found that somehow a piece of shrapnel had hit him in the middle and he was dead. My arm hadn't been an inch away from where the piece hit and I can't for the life of me understand how he got it and I didn't — I being more exposed than he. Guess the Lord was just with me or something.

No, honey, there is no possible chance of me being sent home. I'm sorry to deflate you so abrubt like, but there's no use beating around the bush. I'm not badly enough hurt to even make me limited assignment so unless I get a lucky break or unless this business is over with soon I'll be back up there in the next month or two.

About the Pfc, hon. I don't know that I am one. They told me before we jumped off the last time that they had submitted me for Pfc but the only way you find out if you get it is by waiting till you get paid and see how they list you on the payroll. After all, 4.80 more a month is $4.80. Fraid, honey, I won't be able to make it for our date. Its a sham, too, cause its the first time I've ever stood you up.

Gosh, honey, I've only finished answering one page of your letter and I've got 6 pages written already — guess it will have to take me two days instead of one to finish answering it.

What's cooking, honey? Is that big gal of ours getting spoiled and ornery? What ever you do, honey, don't ever let her get like Dianne used to be — remember? Remember, we said we would never have a child like that? Gosh, I'll bet she is really growing up. Sounds like she definitely has a mind of her own, too. I would sure give anything to see her. I imagine it is kind of rough on you now, having to use coupons for her shoes and all. You should be able to get her ration free sandals, etc, for summer though, hadn't you?

Well, honey that just about winds me up for tonight. I'll finish answering this tomorrow.

Goodnight, Darling. Say a prayer for me and love me and miss me a little. Give Peg a big kiss for me and say hello to the folks, too. Sweet dreams darling, I love you more than anything in the whole world. All my love forever from your bestest fellow

Your Sweetheart,
    Jack
P.S. I love you.

            26 March 1945
            Monday
            Wales

Dearest Sweetheart:

Hi, honey. I feel so good. I received two of the sweetest most wonderful letters from you last night. Its no wonder I'm so much in love with you,

no one could help themselves living with so sweet and wonderful gals. I also got a letter from Mom and one from Dad which were pretty swell, too.

I was going to write last night but I got in a big poker game and before I knew it, it was time for bed. No, I didn't lose, but I am exactly down to where I started from the first of the month. The two letters I received were dated the 16th of March, and the 19th of March. The air mail seems to be getting here faster than the V-mail. So, now I'll get busy answering them.

Shucks, honey, what I did and went through when I got hit wasn't anything compared to what the fellows usually go through. I was lucky to be able to get out under my own power. You take some of these guys that had to lay up there for as long as 2 days without food, water or anything, and really hurt bad, too, because the medics couldn't get to them because of the heavy enemy fire. One thing for sure, though, the person who loses his head is a dead one fore long. As long as you can keep your head and use some common sense you stand a pretty good chance of coming out alive. No, I don't imagine they would have found me had I been hit again or passed out or something going back. I believe the only thing that got me back at all was that I kept thinking of you and Peg and just made up my mind I had to get back and that was all there was to it. I believe that is the first thing I thought of when I got it, and it didn't leave my mind till I was in the hospital. You have no idea the feeling of relief I had when I finally did reach the aid station. I hadn't had any sleep for better than 48 hours and about 25 hours of that I had been walking, not counting the 7 hour walk after I was wounded and I was so completely worn out I couldnt see straight. I got back to the aid station where they cut my clothes off me and I layed down on the litter. It was just 8 oclock then and some of the fellows were just coming back from chow. I was about to die for a cup of coffee, I hadn't had anything but a very little water and one small can of cheese to eat for 2 days, so one of the guys gave me his coffee. I drank it and no sooner than I layed the cup down than I feel asleep. They gave me a Morphine shot then, and it just barely woke me up but went right back. When I woke up again I was in an ambulance heading for the hospital. I guess I had slept only an hour, but I had sort of gotten in the habit of catching what little sleep I got in naps of half hour or an hour that I couldn't do much better but it really helped. From then on I slept in cat naps between shots, etc. I got my first meal the second day after being hit and do you know I couldn't even eat it, after going so long without it? It took me quite a few days to get back to normal.

Heck, honey, I knew you would worry yourself to death if you had received the wire and no explanation from me so I had to write you as soon as possible. That was some letter though. Its a wonder you could read it. I was so darn weak, that by the time I finished just the V-mail I was so worn out.

About that clipping and those coins honey, no I didn't forget to enclose them — I'm positive I did put them in the letter so apparently they were lost during the process of censoring. All it was, was a few German coins with the swastika and all on them and the article was about a General Mosby in the Civil War. I believe his first name was John. I was wondering if he was any relation.

I still have all my personal stuff honey. You see I carried my wallet and prayer book and pictures and stuff like that in my upper breast pocket of my shirt so when they cut the shirt off at the aid station the medic emptied my pockets and put all my stuff in a little bag. Some of the stuff got a little bloody, but not bad. I mailed you some of the things recently and you'll notice some spots on them.

Gosh, honey, I sure won't be able to realize Peg is our big gal when I get home. I'd sure give a million dollars to be able to be there now. I'll say that is pretty good, how she is learning so fast.

Honey, I've got to go far a few minutes. Be back. Bye now. I love you.

Hi, sweet. Here I am again. I had to go pick up my glasses which they had finished. Sure feels good to be able to see again. I celebrated and went to the show this afternoon. Don't even know what it was but it was a pretty good show. Well, guess I'll get back to answering these letters.

There you go worrying about when I will come home. I promise honey, to let you know just as soon as I find out but really, honey, don't look for me till sometime after Germany quits. As much as I look forward to it and wish and hope they would send me home now, I know positively there is no chance for me to be sent home. They have me slated for a rehabilitation hospital and then back to the front. I just thank goodness I'm not with my outfit now. As you most likely have read, we spearheaded the attack and crossing of the Rhine yesterday.

Well honey, I want to write Mom and Dad and its getting close to mail time so I'll close for today. I'll write a nice long one again tomorrow. Bye Sweet. Love me and miss me a little. Say a prayer and give Peg a big kiss for me. All my love for always.

Your Sweetheart,
Jack
P.S. I love you.

26 March 1945
Wales

Dear Mom and Dad:
Well, folks I've finally gotten around to writing you a few lines. I received two letters from you, Mom, and one from Pop, and very wonderful letters they were too. A fellow just couldn't ask for a more wonderful Mom and Dad and no one could have any better than mine. I'm afraid I even had to let a couple of tears squeeze out after reading those letters — silly, aren't I?, but I just couldn't help it — you both are so darned sweet and are so swell to me. Kind of makes everything even and worth going through the hell I've been through the last few months when its for someone like you.

Well, I guess I'll get down to answering your letters and as ladies are first I start with yours, Mom, then to Dads, and back to your second one to finish up with. I'll start with yours of the 14th.

I'm sure sorry you received the wire before the V-mail I wrote you cause I knew they would say seriously wounded in the wire and I knew you would worry half to death over nothing. You can take my word for it, I'm not seriously injured, Its just a plain bullet wound and I'll be going back to duty in not too long a time. As I said before, the only reason

they sent me to England is because they thought the fracture I had (which was just a chip from the bone) would require a cast, which it didn't. A wound like mine which does break the bone requires approximately 120 days to heal, with no complications, and the hospitals over there don't make it a practice to keep men that long so there is why I'm in England, so for the love of pete don't worry, I'm doing fine — too good, in fact.

I'll say this, Mom, you don't hope I can stay in England for the duration any more than I do.

I'm right flattered from all the concern I've caused everyone. Be sure and thank them for me. Especially Mr. Florida, he is a right guy and has always been swell to me.

Gosh, Mom, I sure hope its true that Rusty is on his way home. After what that boy has been through he deserves a break. How long has he been a prisoner of Germany now, about 2 years isn't it?

Thanks for the candy, Mom, I'm really looking forward to it — my mouth has been watering ever since I read the letter. Mavrokos I hope! I thought I had received all the Xmas boxes Mom, but I can't remember how many I did get now. Didn't I ever tell you about the Hershey's? I received a box from you before I left England that had been torn to pieces and rewrapped. I opened it and in the box of 24 hershey's there were 49 hershey bars. The only thing I can think of is that 2 boxes broke and I got all of them.

No, Mom, I've never received the Money order, but it will catch up sooner or later. That was mighty sweet of you Mom.

Tell you what, instead of getting a bond for me for my birthday, get another one for Peg, instead. Will you do that for me?

Mom, I honestly believe that it was nothing but Dads and yours, and Babes prayers that did save me. It must have been to have gotten me back after I had been hit. Yes, I still have the medal dad gave me — in fact, I wouldn't take any thing in the world for it. Thats the first thing I was concerned about when they began cleaning my pockets out, and even carried it in my hand till I got to a hospital after my first operation to be sure I hadn't lost it. No, I didn't lose any personal belongings — one reason being that I never lost consciousness, except for just a very few minutes, all the time.

Well, Mom that finishes your first one so now I'll answer Pops. Yours was dated the 18th Dad.

Pop, you start off worrying about me the same as Mom. Now, don't worry. And about being hurt worse than I say I am, if any thing it might be less than what I say.

Yes, Pop, the trip back to the aid station was pretty rough, but not too bad or I expect I wouldn't be here. I'm sorry, Pop, but as far as your question about the amount of guys wounded when I was, its a military secret or something — if I wrote anything like that the Censor would cut it out. Take my word for it though, it was plenty rough.

Well, folks it's getting late so I guess I'd better close. I'll save your other letter till tomorrow, Mom.

Goodnight folks. Write soon and take care of yourself. Look after Babe and Peg for me and don't worry about me.

All my love to the sweetest swellest most wonderful Mom and Pop in the whole world.

Your Son,
Jack

Thursday
29 March 1945
Wales

Dearest Sweetheart:

The news has really been great, hasn't it? We have really been glued to the radio the last day or two. I hope, too, you noticed that the 30th division is spearheading the business. Course all you get back home is what Patton is doing — I'd hate to think what would happen to his precious armor without the doughs. As you most likely gather, I have no use for the man — I have to admit his military genius in handling armor but I still don't like him.

Well, I have about 5 of your letters to answer so I guess I'd better get busy. Besides yours, I received a letter from Mom I have to answer, one from Sister and one from Aunt Winnie who asks me to write her sister. You know, I really hate to write her — it seems such an imposition after all their trouble. They were sure mighty fortunate in getting out alive.

I am surprised though how long it takes for a little wound like that to heal. I didn't expect to be here much more than 30 days; I expect though, that by the end of this month (April) I'll be back to my outfit — if they are still here. I have to go to Physio-Therapy today to learn how to use my arm again.

Gosh, darling, I only hope its true about Rusty. At any rate, it shouldn't be long before he is reached by either the Russians or us if he hasn't been released already. You have no idea how I would feel to hear he is back home. I'd give my place up to him any day — I mean that, too, as bad as I want to get home, I believe I want him to get home more. You at home can't realize, can't even have the slightest conception of what that boy has been through the last couple of years. If you could see the condition of the Germans we have captured, how they live, etc, then you could have some idea of how our prisoners are faring in their hands.

As far as Bert is concerned, honey, I'd just as soon not discuss it. He deserved as good treatment as some of the Gerries I captured on the line.

Yes, honey, I knew I needed new glasses but I still hated to lose them. And where would they be if I didn't carry them with me? Honey, I carried everything I owned with me all the time. Don't get the impression so many other people have back home that you fight on an 8 hour day, honey. You fight for months at a time — I was on the line 30 days when I got hit, — you fight day and night, eat what ever you can get your hands on, whenever you can, sleep when you get a chance to sneak a nap — never over an hour or so at a stretch, and move continuously. Its rough, honey. Definitely no picnic and you have to have plenty of stamina to stand it. Its impossible to describe it adequately to you back there, and if I could you wouldn't believe me — for one reason you would say no human could stand it — I'm not exagerating either.

No, honey, I haven't received the box with Pegs shoes as yet, but I'm really anxiously awaiting them. How did you know? And I also haven't received the income tax refund check or pics yet. What about that income tax refund? How much was it, etc.?

First off, honey, please continue sending your mail via air as it is much the fastest — cuts from 3 to 6 or more days off the traveling time. In fact, I received a letter the other day from you in five days — the all time record — and I don't like v-mail so make it air mail please mam!

How do I know I'll get a Purple Heart! — Honey, every one who is wounded in action gets the German Marksmanship Medal! I have received it, by the way, and will send it on to you today.

I'll go on to the next dated March 20th. Boy, its a long one, too. 5 pages on both sides. Well, here goes—

Gosh, honey, the whole letter is about Peg practically so there won't be a lot to answer. She sounds so darling, honey. She is really growing up, isn't she. I'm awfully glad she is talking so well now. Man, she sounds smart as a whip and I'll bet she is a little devil — and spoiled, too! I can't get over that shirt business. Thats the funniest thing I've ever heard. Yes, honey, I must admit, although it really wouldn't have made any difference, I did want a little girl. They are so much cuter and sweeter than little boys. Course our next one I want to be a boy.

Now don't you go worrying about me coming home! When this is over, just as soon as I know myself, I'll let you know. Its just possible I won't be able to tell you till I get to the states but just as soon as I land I'll call you. As far as me coming home now, honey, just get it out of your mind cause I'm not being sent back to the states! It would be best if you could have a place of your own when I get there — however, with places as hard to get as they are, if you don't have a place, we'll just have to stay home I guess.

Well, honey, I guess I'll have to close — there is some work to do around here — I help in the kitchen (each ward — 29 pnts — has their own) and its almost lunch time. Love me darling and miss me a little and be sure to keep saying your prayers for me. Give Peg a big hug and kiss and say hello to the folks for me, too. I love you darling and miss you more than anything in the world. Bye now, hon, all my love to my only sweetheart forever and ever.

Your Sweetheart,
Jack
P.S. I love you.

29 March 1945
Thursday
Wales

Dear Mom and Dad:

I have one more letter of yours I haven't answered yet, Mom, so while I'm waiting for the mail today, I'll start this to you, and hope I get a couple more.

Darn, I'll sure be glad when I can finally get all the details of how I got hit to you — I imagine you all are getting mighty tired of hearing about it and I would just as soon try to forget it — its not a nice memory. I guess it was a pretty narrow escape I had going back thru the forest, but I wasn't thinking much about it at that time. Kind of get goose pimples when I think about it now though. I was very weak from loss of blood, in fact as soon as I knew I was ok, back at the aid station, I passed out for a few minutes. Guess I wasn't moving with my brain but instinct or something and when I relaxed — poof. Shucks, Mom, we were fighting up there and all the other fellows had enough on their hands without worrying about me getting back. If I had been hit to where I couldn't walk I'd most likely of had to lay up there a day or so fore they'd of had time to get me out. No, Mom, I'm afraid I'm patched up as good as new and as soon as I get my arm working normally again, which won't be too long, I'll be heading back up — if it is still going on up there. I have seen men here with the same trouble as the boy Mr. Florida knew had — what it is, is that the bullet or whatever hit and severed a nerve or several nerves when going into him. Luckily it missed mine.

Mail call just over with — I got two V-mail from you and one from Babe. Those V-mail are too short and there isn't room for any news at all. In fact, I get the Air mail 2 or 3 days sooner than V-mail believe it or not. Been getting air mail in 6 or 7 days and even got one from Babe in 5.

That was sure terrible about Lee Traske — I feel for him. In what theater was he stationed?

Envelope - Last letter, "I'll be seeing you."

Hq, 4192 U.S. Army Hospital Plant

APO ....209........, c/o POSTMASTER

...........New York, N.Y.

DEAR Mrs. Price:

I am pleased to inform you that on .... **APR 1 4 1945** .... your
(Date)

Husband **Pvt John K. Price, 37623699**
(Relationship), (Grade, name, Army serial number)

was * **evacuated to Zone of Interior. — Final report**

~~Diagnosis~~

* Enter present status as—
  Making normal improvement.
  Convalescing.

† Must be written in nontechnical language.

W. D., A. G. O. Form 234
9 November 1944

Very truly yours,

Thomas J. Pritchard

1st Lt. MAC.
Asst. Registrar

UKB. 2-45/887M/L-13899 (16/44/4 52079) 31815

Progress Card - "Evacuated to Zone of Interior. Final report." It was true!

Well, Mom, that finishes the one letter so I think I'll close for now. Write soon and take care of yourself. Look after Babe and Peg for me. All my love to my sweet wonderful Mom and Pop.

Your Son,
Jack

2 April 1945
Wales
Monday

Dearest Sweetheart:

Well, honey, its been three days since I last wrote you. I had a very good reason this time, though. Can't tell you what it is but its a good one. I wasn't going to write tonight either but I received an air mail and V-mail from you today and I just had to talk to you a little. I have a couple more to answer, too, that I received the last day or so. Guess I'll get busy and answer the one I received today. By the way, I also got one from your Mom, too. There isn't much sense me writing her now, though, so when you get this tell her I did receive her letter and thank her for me.

Honey, I knew you were counting on me coming home — I could read your thoughts — and thats why I wanted to set you straight — there is no sense in getting all hepped up like you do, just to be disappointed. This is still the army, and anything can happen! The way it would be honey, is that I'd no sooner get home than they'd ship me to the S.P. or CBI and it would be the same thing over again. So please honey, don't look forward to it at all.

Gosh, how I'd like to see that big gal of ours. She is sure growing up. I can't get over how well she is talking now and how smart she is. She sure seems to catch on to things fast.

Darn, honey, I sure wish you all hadn't sent many birthday presents — I hope you didn't spend a lot of dough.

Well, honey, this is awful short I know, but I'm so darn nervous and jittery I just can't sit still long enough to write a decent letter.

Night, honey. Love me and miss me. All my love for always to my wonderful Sweetheart. I'll be seeing you —

Jack

Wales
7 April 45
Saturday

Dearest Darling:

I received a letter from you tonight, honey, and although I wasn't going to write you this requires an answer.

First off, honey, stop writing me or sending me anything more till you hear from me as I am changing addresses again.

This is going to be short, honey, as I've got a good case of the jitters — sort of combat fatigue or something, I guess. I can't sit still a minute.

I got Phillie's letter, hon. Thanks. I also got that one of Dr. Beddow but you had sent that to me before and I had returned.

Now don't go bawling me out about my poker game — I won it all back and on my 4 pound investment I ran it up to 16 pounds. I have now in my wallet 62 dollars which I am hanging on to far dear life.

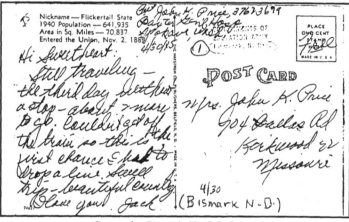

Postcards - Bismark, North Dakota.

About sending me any food honey, the only time I really need anything like that is when I'm in a fox hole — which won't be for some time — in fact never again I hope and anyway its silly to send me anything like that. Don't send the pictures either as I'll never get them if you do. Wait till You hear from me.

I'm getting along swell — up and around all the time. They are working me half to death though — I've been on steady KP for the past couple of weeks. This hospital life has really made me lazy though, so I need a little work to pop me out of it.

Well, honey, this is awfully short but the best I can do for now. I love you, honey, but I'm not lonesome anymore or blue!!!! And I don't miss you either! Worried? Bye now sweet. Love me.

"I'll be seeing you."

All my love,
for always,
Your Sweetheart
Jack

April 8, 1945

Dear Dad:

Just a note to tell you I received your letter today written Easter. You got me all excited telling me about the opening of the trout season up there so I had to write you about it. Tell you what you do — go down and get us both a fishing license right away and start practicing up on that cast of yours. If I remember right I was the one who caught all the fish so you'll need the practice if you intend to out catch me this time. You might make arrangements for a cabin at Montauk too, as we will take the women folks with us as I couldn't leave Babe behind. Been away from her too long now. You might try to arrange to get a few days off too. Now be sure and do that, hear. I want to spend a few days up there without fail. Well, Pop, thats about all for now. Be good and Mum's the word. Be seeing you.

Love,
Jack

BAXTER GENERAL HOSPITAL
Spokane, Washington

When Jack left England and crossed the Atlantic this time, he was on a hospital ship and there was no U-Boat menace now. On April 24th, 1945, the ship docked at Newport News, Virginia. The patients were then removed by ambulance to the Station Hospital at Camp Patrick Henry, Virginia.

Each returning patient was allowed one free phone call. Neither of us could believe it when we actually heard one another. How many times we had written, "If I could only hear your voice," and finally, at last, we did. It seemed like a dream! Of course, we expected to see one another within days.

The card which I received from the hospital stated that my husband would be transferred to a U.S. Army Hospital most suitable for his care and added, if possible the one nearest his home. This was the usual procedure for wounded soldiers when they returned to the United States; however, nothing for Jack had ever been the usual procedure.

Suitable care was what the Army had in mind. By the time I received the April 28th, 1945, card from Camp Patrick Henry Hospital, I thought Jack was well on his way home. When the hospital train left Virginia and headed northward, Jack thought they would change him in Chicago. Then he would go south to O'Reilly General Hospital in Springfield, Missouri, the hospital nearest home.

Not so! At Chicago the train continued on west. However, when they reached Miles City, North Dakota, he was able to get two postcards from the Salvation Army which they mailed for him. The first one was dated April 30, 1945, and said, "Still traveling, third day without a stop. Couldn't get off train. Address, Baxter General Hospital, Spokane, Washington." The next card was dated May 1st, 1945, and said, "Still traveling, getting tired. Will be 1,942 miles by train, in Spokane." They arrived in Spokane, Washington, May 2, 1945. The next day was Jack's birthday. He was 26 years old!

We simply could not understand why Jack had been sent to the very farthest part of the United States. His father wrote a letter to his State Representative to see if we could get him sent to Springfield, Missouri. The doctor in Spokane explained that his wound had been more serious than first diagnosed. It was considered a chest wound and had affected one of his lungs. There was scar tissue from the bullet passing so close to his lung. That hospital in Spokane specialized in such cases, and the climate was right for the proper treatment.

Spokane, Washington, was a very beautiful city, and Jack could hardly have been among more caring people. The patients had almost unlimited freedom and received invitations every time they left the hospital. He and Pete Martellero (another patient from Missouri) frequently went out together. They were taken to a barn dance at nearby Ft. Wright, Washington, one night, and he quickly learned his shoulder could not take "do si does." Another night a discharged Army Captain and his wife took them to dinner and a show.

One day while Jack and Pete were standing on a corner waiting for a bus, they began playing ball with some youngsters. The mother invited them in for supper and the evening. They had fried chicken and then played cards. Jack was even able to go shopping one day and bought me a lovely bracelet for Mother's Day.

On May 15, 1945, they had a three-day pass and took the bus to Tacoma, Washington, to visit Pete's brother. It was a wonderful trip. They saw the most beautiful scenery, and they went on a fishing trip that Jack never forgot.

It was distressing for Jack to be back in the country with no possibility of our being together. There was no way I could go to Spokane, because we had no idea when he would be leaving. Day after day dragged on! Finally, on May 22, 1945, he wrote that he had an appointment with the doctor at 1:30 P.M. to find out what they were going to do.

When he returned to the letter, he wrote in huge letters — "I'M FLYING HOME. WILL LEAVE FRI. AND ARRIVE SAT. NIGHT OR SUN. MORN. — Had to bluff my way through to get it, but it worked. Bye now, I love you, Jack."

THE LETTERS

To: Mrs. John K Price   From: Pfc John K. Price
704 Ballas Road   37623699
Kirkwood, 22, Mo.   Ward E-2 Baxter General
                         Hosp.
                         Spokane, Washington

Bismark, North Dakota
4/30/45

Hi Sweetheart:
    Still traveling — the third day without a stop — about 2 more to go. Couldn't get off the train so this is the first chance I had to drop a line. Swell trip — beautiful country. I love you.

Jack

Miles City, North Dakota
4/30/45

Lo honey:
    Rumor has it I'll be heading back on furlough shortly after I arrive — and a nice long one too. Will wire you. I'll write a nice long letter when I arrive. Love and kisses to my two sweet gals.

Jack

Butte, Montana
May 1st 45

Hi Sweet:
    Still traveling — getting kind of tired but seeing some really beautiful country. We are going to motor through here some vacation so you can see it. I still want to come home though. Found out yesterday I'll be 1942 miles from home by train when we arrive in Spokane. We have a priority, however, on Army planes so are going to try to fly home — only cost us a buck. Bye now. I love you. Jack

2 May 1945
(Wednesday morning)

Dearest Sweetheart:
    Hi, honey. Well, here we are in Spokane and a very beautiful city it is and such beautiful country I've never seen before. Well, I have a lot of news and plans so I guess I'd better get started.
    I sent you a wire this morning with a M.O. for $30 and I'm enclosing a M.O. in this for ten more. I hope that helps you out, honey. It leaves me with about $15 so I sure hope I get paid before my furlough comes around. Here is the dope on the furlough deal. I should get one in anywhere from a week to a month — depending on how my case is diagnosed. Apparently it will be 30 days with an opportunity (very liberal) for extensions and if I'm

ARMY SERVICE FORCES
Ninth Service Command
Baxter General Hospital
Spokane, Washington

Convalescent
Furlough

                                          23 May 1945
                                   _____
                                          (Date)

Certificate No. 1.

    1. It is hereby certified that   __John Price_____
                                            (Full Name)

__PVT_____ __37623699_____ has been confined at Baxter General
 (Rank)   (ASN)

Hospital, Spokane, Wash., from the time of initial entry into the
continental limits of the United States for the purpose of receiving
treatment for an ailment contracted, a wound or injury received in
line of duty outside the continental limits of the United States and
has been granted sick leave or convalescent furlough, beginning
__23 May 1945_____ and ending __28 June 1945_____ for the purpose of visiting his home to recuperate.

    2. It is further certified that travel by air will not be
detrimental to health or physical well-being of the individual
named in this certification and that such individual has been
notified that he may be removed en route, short of destination, for
a higher priority traffic.

    3. The individual named above has been informed that trans-
portation ticket will only be issued to that point, on regularly
operated routes, which is nearest to the final destination of the
individual requesting this transportation.

    4. This certificate becomes void __28 June 1945_____.

                                   Paul W. Ohl
                                   PAUL W. OHL
                                   Capt, CmC
                                   Adjutant

Convalescent
Furlough
Airplane priority

lucky I might be able to pull 60 or 90 days out of it. There is a large airfield here so a couple other fellows from St. Louis and I are going to try to fly home. If we can get any breaks it will only cost us about a buck (rent for a parachute) and as we are very high on the priority list we have a good chance.

I really think I got a good deal by coming up here, hon, so stop trying to do anything to get me transferred. I found out that this is a big discharge hospital — most cases are future discharges — they have facilities for occupational therapy, etc, so you see why I want to stay —I'm bucking!

Honey, this has to be short for now as they are examining us and I have to go. If they finish in time, I'll write again this evening and give you all the news about the trip etc. G'bye, sweet, I love you honey and I'll be seeing and just kissin' and lovin' my little gal to pieces fore very much longer. Bye now, I love you.

Your lonely anxious guy,
Me

2 May 1945
(Wednesday night)

Dearest Honey:

How's my sweet wonderful little gal tonight? I'm feeling swell. One reason is that I got some more news about coming home — most likely will be leaving here some time this week, I hope. I am worried about the dough for the trip now, but maybe I can get a partial pay or borrow some from the Red Cross. I did find out definitely that I'll get 60 days anyway. Pretty swell, eh? I got a letter from you today, too. Happy birthday me! Honey, I know how disappointed you are about me not coming home right off cause I am too. All the way across all I dreamed about was getting on a train and heading home as soon as we docked. However, after thinking about it I could see where they couldn't let me do that till we had been checked very carefully as we took a tremendous trip and anything could have happened. Course my reaction at first to being sent up here was of disgust but now I'm kind of glad. Here are some of the reasons. I will most likely be leaving for home very shortly now — and they are very lenient on giving furloughs. I'll get 30 days and the practice here has been to give extensions so I expect I'll be home for about 90 days all told.

About the money, I have coming to me in back salary through April $121.50 which will come in handy. I still don't know whether I'll get that Pfc and combat badge yet as they lost all my records so I didn't figure that in yet. That 121.50, I know I'll get it. Then for the 3 months I'm home I won't get paid so I'll have another 63.90 coming. You are so sweet, darling. No wonder I love you so much. I'm sure sorry we didn't come through St. Louis but that was the long way round. Here is the route we took. We left Newport went to Cincinnati, Indianapolis, Chicago, La Crosse Wis; Minneapolis & St. Paul; Brainerd; Fargo; Bismark; Billings; Butte; Missoula; and into Spokane. Bare midriff PJ's — wow — I can hardly wait. I'll bet they are cute though. Honey, I love you so darn much and I'm just about crazy to get home to you. I think I'll close for today, I'll write again tomorrow though.

Bye for now, all my love for always. See you soon — I hope!!!

Jack

P.S. Got a couple very lousy pictures taken but I'm sending them to you anyway. I really don't look as bad as they show me. Bye now

I love you.

Monday
7 May 1945
(War ended, Europe)

Dearest Honey:

How's my best lil' ol' darlin' tonight. I'd better apologize for not writing for the last few days. This furlough business has me all up in the air. I'm so darned excited about coming home and they keep putting it off. My nerves aren't much account anymore, anyway. I really need a few days at home to calm me down and get me on an even keel again. No kidding, I've started at least four letters to you and then get so darned jittery and nervous I have to quit. To night I'm going to write you a nice long one if it kills me. Received about 15 letters from you today from England which I read of course but I don't believe I'll answer and I have two or three new ones I'll answer tonight.

Well, honey, half of the war is over thank God. I knew it couldn't last a lot longer the way things were going but they sure fought to the last. Also, from all appearances my fighting days are over also. I guess Mom told you I called her. I was sure disappointed you weren't there. You had said you planned on staying down at the folks house and I figured you'd be there, is the reason I called. The doctor had told me I would be leaving some time this week, then, but there has been another delay. I've had to take some more tests and ex rays, etc, so now I don't know how much longer it will be. I'll wire you as soon as I leave and I plan on flying down. I have my priority and everything ready. If I have luck and get plane accomodations all the way through it won't cost me anything for the trip. Then I'll get ration money of 60 cents a day all the time I'm on furlough, and if I travel on orders — in other words am going back to duty instead of coming back here, I'll receive a nickle a mile for the trip. With my back pay this will make quite a tidy little sum for us to use while I'm home and when we get ready to leave.

I hope you are looking for an apartment as it would be much better if we had a place of our own while I'm home. Also, honey, how about staying at the Mayfair the first few nights? Would that be ok with you? Coming back to the army for a minute — I believe if I work it right I should be able to get out. They will most likely be very lax with their discharges as far as wounded limited assignment men are concerned so I should get out — my overseas time etc, included. By the way, honey, I have gotten a mothers day present for you but how would it be if I waited till I got there to give it to you? I have hunted high and low for it as you wanted one pretty bad. Anyway, I'd rather give it to you in person. (It was an identification bracelet like his, very popular). I think I'll have at least 51 days with my sweetheart. I love you so much, and want to see you so bad. It won't be long!

Now, sweet don't worry. I promise you just as soon as I find out when I'm leaving I'll let you know. Honest Injun. Which reminds me, I've come to the conclusion that maybe the best and easiest thing to do would be to stop by the folks and pick up the car before I come out to you. That way it would be a lot easier to manage, especially going to a hotel as I'll have my grip and you'll have yours and with Peg it would be quite a job to manage on the bus, especially with my shoulder — I'm still a little weak in that arm and am kind of shy of crowds. Whatcha think? Let me know.

I will be at home at least thirty days then I'll try for an extension then 21 day overseas furlough. The 30 day is a convalescent and doesn't count on my furlough time.

Well, darling, I'm afraid it's the best I can do for tonight. I'll write a nice one again tomorrow though. Night, All my love for always. Give Peg a big kiss for me too.

Your onliest,
Jack
P.S. Happy V.E. day. I love you.

Ward E-2
Sunday
13 May 1945

Dearest Sweet lil honey:

Happy Mothers day, darling. I guess you thought I had forgotten all about it and you too I guess, but really I haven't.

I have a real nice present for you but I haven't mailed it because I've been expecting to leave any time. That's the reason I haven't been writing cause I have been thinking every day will be the day. It's so hard to just sit here and wait like this.

I was so disappointed again today, honey, I thought sure you would be at the folks and I wanted to talk to you so bad and wish you happy mommas day and when I called you weren't there.

It really shouldn't be too long before I'm on my way. The first of the orders came out today so it should be any day now. Here is the deal. I'll receive 35 days from here. I'll get my day coach paid if I come by train or it will cost me a dollar if I come by plane so I won't need any money.

After the 35 days I'll report to Jeff Barracks and go through about the same processing as I did when I was inducted. Then when that's over I'll come back home for another 21 days. Just think darling 56 glorious wonderful days with you. I just don't see how I can wait. I love you, honey, and missed you so much. I guess I ought to be able to stand a few more days after all these months, but it's awful hard.

By the way, hon, I received that package with the baby shoes in it yesterday. My goodness, what a horrible mess it was. Of course nothing was worth eating but the shoes were so cute. (The package had been sent to the England Hospital.)

I guess you read about the point system by now and are curious to know how I stand so here is the dope —
Service —21 points
Overseas —11 points
Combat Service —10 points (2 campaign stars)
Purple Heart — 5 points
Peggy — 12 points
Total — 59 points
So you see, I haven't enough to get out but maybe I can work it with my shoulder.

Honey, I'll swear I've never been in a town like Spokane. It is really wonderful. The people are so swell to us. Pete, this fellow from St. Louis who I have been bumming with, and I have had more invitations than we know what to do with. We went to a barn dance Thursday night at Fort Wright, an air corp camp here, and had at least 8 or 10 invitations to homes, etc. We have accepted 2. One, last night for dinner and then the family and we went bowling. Really had a nice time. Tonight we have another date with a discharged Captain and his wife. They are taking us to a dinner and show — ahem!! What tops it all off though is the other day Pete and I were standing on a corner waiting on a bus. There were a couple of kids playing ball next to us so we started playing with them. All of a sudden their mother came out and invited us in for supper and the evening which we of course accepted. Had a fried chicken supper and played cards all evening. Swell, eh!

Well, honey, I guess I'd better go now and have my supper. I'm enclosing a piece of a letter I started Wednesday — no use wasting all those I love you's is there? Night, sweet dreams. I'm so excited — just a few days and I'll be home and just loving you to pieces and hugging and kissing you. I love you so much I just can't wait.

Bye now,
All my love (and boy
that's a lot, too. You'll see.)
Jack
P.S. I love you.

15 May 1945
Tuesday

Dearest Honey:

How is my wonderful sweetheart today? Your boy is just worn out almost. I didn't get in till the wee hours this A.M. — out appreciating the United States with Pete last night!

I usually don't do much drinking but I'm afraid I had about 8 or 10 beers too many last night. We went to town last night to buy our tickets to Tacoma — I guess Mom told you Pete has a brother in Tacoma and we are leaving this morning on a three day pass to visit up there. It's about 6:30 A.M. now and I thought I'd drop you a line fore we leave — we have to be in town by 8:30. I guess I'll be back here Thursday night. I'll write you all about it when I get back.

I'll see some beautiful country, I guess, like Mt Ranier and I'll be able to do some fishing. I'll say this though, if I had known I was going to be here this long, you and Peg would have been up here a long time ago.

Well, honey, I guess I'm going to have to close for now and get ready to go as it's getting late — 7:15 AM — and I still have to shower and shave. Bye for now darling. I love you, I love you, I love you.

All my love to my sweet lil' gals

Your guy,
Jack
P. S. I love you

(From a letter to his Mom and Dad, May 14.)

"When I arrived in the U S A three weeks ago, I arrived with no clothes or anything, so when my clothes were issued I had to have them altered, pressed, and all the ribbons etc, which are necessary put on —approximate cost $5.00. A new pair of shoes — $7.00, and 9 cartons of cigarettes for us — $11.00."

Railroad Ticket. Chicago to St. Louis.

Union Station, St. Louis, at night. The beautiful Carl Milles fountain is renowned.

Mother, the lost cause.

Tuesday
(May) 22nd

Darling:

Honey, I received two wonderful letters from you today and those wonderful darling pictures — and they were really magnificent — I love them so. I'm not going to try to answer the letters, honey, and I'm afraid this will be just a short note as I'm so darned nervous and jumpy I just can't write. I'm afraid my nerves are pretty well shot, hon, and this waiting isn't doing me any good either. I did want to kind of give you as much of the little I know of the situation though.

Here is the dope. Everyone I came in with has left — Pete left yesterday — with the exception of two other fellows and myself. I went down yesterday and blew my top znd finally got a little satisfaction. At least I know why now. You see, honey, I have what is almost considered a chest wound and it has affected one of my lungs. The way I understand it, my lung wasn't pierced but when I began to heal, the bullet had passed so close to the lung that the scar tissues have affected it some way — they have it diagnosed as a severe tenting of the left lung and a lot of other fancy names. So, they have been studying my case and as this climate is supposed to be right and because this hospital specializes in that sort of thing I'm staying here. The last ex ray also showed that the bone in my shoulder still hasn't grown together so I'm not in too good of shape yet, although I feel fine and my shoulder doesn't bother me a bit. I have also been having a little trouble with my frozen feet — they bother me a little — but nothing serious. I have an appointment at 1:30 today to find out just what they plan to do and how long it will take. I did feel rather hard at them for sending me up here at first, but after finding out what is wrong and finding the reputation they have up here for this type of thing I guess I'm really lucky to have come. You've got to stop and think that I am sick(?) and did need the care I received. I'm going to quit now and go down to see the Doc. I'll be back and tell you what I find out. I love you.
(over)
HONEY — I'M FLYING HOME — WILL LEAVE FRIDAY AND ARRIVE SATURDAY NITE OR SUNDAY MORN. HAVE A LOT TO DO SO HAVE TO GO. HAD TO BLUFF MY WAY THROUGH TO GET IT BUT IT WORKED. TELL YOU ALL ABOUT IT WHEN I GET THERE.

BYE NOW.

I LOVE YOU.
JACK

CONVALESCENT FURLOUGH
At Home

Near Spokane, Washington, was a large airfield. Jack had a priority pass (Special Orders Number 124) which enabled him to fly on a military plane, for the total cost of $1.00 for a parachute. It would take him some time to get home, as they put down at other bases. It was exausting since the planes were not designed for comfort. They took him as far as Chicago, Illinois, however. He then took the train to St. Louis, Missouri. His day coach fare was paid by the Army. The ticket shows: The Alton Railroad — Military Furlough. It is stamped May 27, 1945, but it does not show a price.

Jack had dreamed of surprising me, but it wasn't possible. He still had a long way to go before his strength was back to normal. His mother phoned me Sunday afternoon, saying he had called from Chicago and

Peggy learning to fish.

Sparta Country Club - resort. Jack, the fisherman.

said he would arrive at Union Station at 9'oclock. She felt she should tell me, and she asked me to come with them. I was nearly overcome with emotion, and I was afraid to believe that it was actually true this time.

Jack had written that he hoped we could stay at the Mayfair Hotel in St. Louis, Missouri, the first night he was home. My father called the Mayfair Sunday afternoon to try to get us a reservation.

Now, this was still wartime! Hotels in St. Louis had no vacancies, ever, and they had a waiting list besides. My father was a very romantic person. When he talked to the manager and he finished his sad tale of the returning "wounded-warrior" needing time alone with his sweet little wife, we had reservations for two nights!

Jack's parents with Peggy and I drove into St. Louis. We went to Union Station to meet the train. Jack had wanted me to be at home so he could just let go, as he said. Therefore, the baby and I stayed in the car and his parents went on into the station. It was nearly dark by this time, but they had parked in front of the station on Market Street along the curb by the fountains. We were able to get out of the car and walk around. Although there were only a few soldiers and other people walking around, we were perfectly safe during that time.

The fountains were very beautiful, and Peggy thoroughly enjoyed them. She was nearly two years old now. Jack had not seen her since she was ten months old when he went overseas. As I had done then, I was praying now that she would not reject him.

At last they came out the door of the station. His father was carrying his barracks bag, and Jack was holding his mother's arm. He was so thin. It had become dark by then, but I could see by the street lights how pale he was and what a toll the long trip home had taken.

He got into the back seat beside me, where I was holding Peggy on my lap. We sat in silence while he just soaked in the sight of us. We

kissed and he nearly crushed my hand. He feasted his eyes on Peggy, but made no attempt to hold her. He kept saying, "I just can't believe it," over and over. Finally he said, "Would you sit on Daddy's lap?" I held my breath. She had been studying him intently, and again I wondered if there was a little recognition of his uniform from his picture. She made no move to get on his lap, but made no protest when he lifted her over. She sat there studying him again and then settled down. After a while he pointed to his cheek and asked her if she would give Daddy a kiss. She obliged cheerfully and she completely accepted him.

When we arrived at Jack's parents house, they took Peggy in and put her to bed and we remained in the car.

We were finally alone! Then Jack broke down completely and shed the tears he had held back so long and said, with such relief, "Honey, you'll never, never know what I've been through." I held him close and wished with all my heart I could just make it all go away. We sat in the dark and wept our hearts out, and we thanked God over and over for bringing him home safely. It was Spring; it was May. The soft night air was sweet, and at that moment, for us, the war was over.

When we went into the house, Jack and his parents and I spent the next few hours at the kitchen table talking. I think Jack drank a gallon of milk. He was anxious to tell us all that had happened to him since he left, and we were anxious to hear. Was it only a year? It seemed a hundred years ago since he walked down that platform, turned and waved once, and boarded the train for overseas!

It never occurred to us to leave Peggy. We put the suitcases and the sleeping baby in the car at 2:00 A.M. and went to the Mayfair Hotel for our "Honeymoon." They had a crib in the room, and she didn't even stir when we put her in it. I finally got to wear my new Baby Doll Pajamas (the latest fashion) which I had bought when I thought Jack would be home in April.

Booklet for Returnees.

FOREWORD

ON behalf of the Eighth Service Command and of the Redistribution Station Command and Staff, I extend to you a welcome to this station. It is our intent to make your stay in Hot Springs a pleasant one.

This Redistribution Station has been established to study your physical condition and your qualifications so that you can be assigned where you will be most useful to the Army.

A certain routine for the study of your experience and records will be necessary. You can expect this processing to be thorough. It has been simplified as much as possible in order to give you the maximum amount of comfort, relaxation, and leisure time. However, it is essential that you meet all processing appointments promptly. Except for this processing you will find that you are completely free.

You are reminded that as soldiers you will be expected to conduct yourselves as gentlemen. As overseas veterans, your appearance and your conduct will be under close scrutiny, and the impressions you create on others will be strong and lasting ones. This fact constitutes a responsibility which you should shoulder with pride—pride in yourself, and pride in your Army. Accordingly, the very highest standards of military courtesy and bearing will be expected of you at all times.

Have a good time, enjoy your liberties, meet your schedules, and be considerate of the comfort and convenience of others.

RICHARD DONOVAN,
Major General, U.S.A.,
Commanding.

Foreword by Major General Richard Donovan.

Arlington Hotel. Luxurious Veranda.

In the mornings it was Peggy's routine to play quietly in her bed with her toys and then come and get in my bed. The baby book said, "Do not let the child sleep with you as this could create a problem when the father returns." Peggy was raised by the book, so this morning as usual she climbed out of the crib and into bed with me. Jack was facing the wall, completely covered up. When he suddenly turned over and sat up, Peggy screamed and wouldn't let go of me. Jack and I both laughed and I kept patting him and saying, "This is Daddy, we love him!" The problem soon ended. His shoulder still had bandages front and back and he could not use his arm very much, but she found it was great fun to sit on what used to be a nice fat tummy and play.

We left Peggy with Jack's parents that afternoon and visited my parents. We then went back to the Mayfair hotel for a night alone. That really was our honeymoon!

There had been volumes written on how to live with your returning soldier, especially if he had been in combat and if he had been wounded. Most of it was for things everyone would probably go through. I had read it all very carefully. By all means, I wanted to do everything right! Fortunately, most of it never occurred. Jack was a very pragmatic person and he had already sorted things out pretty well. The months in the hospitals had given him a chance to do a lot of talking with fellows in his same situation. Also, God bless the Army Nurses. Jack said they were wonderful, so tender and caring.

Jack's orders showed that his convalescent furlough was from 23 May 1945 to 28 June 1945. On June 28th he had to report to the Reception Station at Jefferson Barracks in St. Louis, Missouri, to receive his orders for the thirty days additional time for his overseas furlough. At the end of those thirty days he was to proceed on 1 August 1945 to the Redistribution Station at Hot Springs, Arkansas.

A little over two months was a rather long time without a place of our own. We stayed with my parents during the week and with his parents on the weekends. It was not very satisfactory, but an apartment was neither practical nor available. I had moved in with my parents for the duration, and it had been a long duration. Poor Mother and Daddy!

Finally, one day Jack announced that we were going away for a week alone. Some friends of his family owned a cottage on the lake at the Sparta Country Club in Sparta, Illinois, a drive of several hours. His Grandfather Evans had been the caretaker there for years, and Jack had spent many happy summers there when he was a boy. Alone, of course, included Peggy. It never crossed our minds not to take her.

The cottage was the usual living room, bedroom, and large screened porch across the front. It was nestled in the trees just a few feet from the water, with a nice sandy beach in front and shallow water. Jack had a boat which was rented, and he could fish to his heart's content. Sometimes the three of us went out in the boat, carried a lunch, and picnicked. I have never been a "fisherman," so Jack usually got up at dawn, went out by himself, and then got back in time for breakfast.

Being out on the lake gave Jack some time alone, and I'm sure it brought back memories which were dear to him. We couldn't have found a better place to heal both his body and soul although his shoulder was still far from completely healed.

Finally Jack's convalescent furlough was over, and it was time for him to leave. On August 1, 1945, his parents, Peggy, and I took him to

Jefferson Barracks, Missouri, where the U.S. Army bus would take them to Hot Springs, Arkansas. Pete Martellero was going also. Their being together again made it more pleasant for both. They boarded the bus with the others and soon left. Jack and I both had that empty feeling at parting, but we felt it would not be for long this time.

HOT SPRINGS, ARKANSAS
Arlington Hotel

It was the first day of August, 1945 (Wednesday). The heat on that summer afternoon was almost unbearable, so it was a long miserable trip to Arkansas and, of course, the bus was not air-conditioned. However, they could hardly have been sent to a more beautiful place.

Jack and Pete arrived in Hot Springs, Arkansas, about 7:30 that evening, and they ate dinner at a restaurant. They then looked up an M.P. (Military Police) who arranged transportation for them to the Administrative Office of the Station, at the Majestic Hotel, in Hot Springs. After they checked in, they were taken to the Arlington Hotel where they would stay.

The Arlington Hotel in Hot Springs, Arkansas, of course, was renowned the world over. It was elegant beyond description, and it was very expensive. The regular rates for the rooms were $9.00 a day single, and up. After they both registered, the bellboy brought them up to their room, number 1039. That same room today (1997) is $89.00 for a night. The rate is $48.00 and up! They went right to bed since it was late by then. The next day Jack wrote, "It's nice, in fact ultra, but is it hot!"

The next morning (Thursday) they got up at 7 A.M. After breakfast they went to a lecture, then to the P X (Post Exchange) to get their ration cards for cigarettes. At 10 A.M. they had an appointment for their Records Check. The Army had found that Jack was $100.00 overdrawn, so he would now only draw $10.00 a month. The Army had still not found his lost records from the Bulge. However, he was paid his ration money for the thirty-day furlough home, and he still had $20.00 coming for his transportation.

By now it was noon so they went back to the Arlington Hotel for lunch. To their amazement they were served in the main dining room. (The magnificent crystal chandelier had been safely packed away when the Army had taken over the hotel for the duration.) They had menus, tablecloths and napkins, waiters, and even an orchestra playing. Jack wrote, "This ain't the Army for sure!" They could even have liquor served to them in their rooms if they wished.

There was no charge for their room or meals. However, if the Returnees wife shared the same room she would pay only for her meals. For ten days her total would not exceed $25.

He and Pete were free for the afternoon. It was dreadfully hot so they went to a theater to cool off. The movie was "Tomorrow the World" with Frederic March. He said to be sure and see it.

At 4 o'clock they had a Welcoming Lecture which told them what they could do. There was very little they could not do! The purpose of their being there was for the U.S. Army to study their physical condition and qualifications and to reassign them where they would be of most benefit to the Army. That evening Jack and Pete went to a pool and swam, and that night to a dance on the roof garden of the hotel. He said they didn't dance, but the air was so cool they stayed until 11:00.

They were given a card with their schedules for appointments with Classification, Medical, and Personnel Sections. It was also used to show in the dining room for meals. When Jack had his appointment with the Classification Section, he learned that he would remain in the Ground Forces classified as a Clerk and would be on limited assignment. He would not go overseas again.

The returnees had been told that they would be surprised at the comforts there. (They were indeed.) The speaker told them the Army was not going soft, but the U.S. Army knew what they had been through and they deserved the best.

The Arlington Hotel had a barber shop in its Arcade. There was also a tap room (bar) there with their dates welcome. At another location was a Non Com Club (for Non-Commissioned Officers), and in addition there was a USO.

There were also Chaplains of Protestant, Catholic and Jewish faith who extended invitations to the servicemen to bring their personal problems to the Chaplains.

There was no end of equipment available to anyone who wished to play golf, tennis, baseball, basketball volleyball, or horseshoes, to name a few. There was also a miniature golf course and an archery range. In addition horseback riding and fishing could be arranged.

Jack and Pete expressed a desire to go fishing one day. On Tuesday August 7th (their free day), they were picked up at 5 A.M. in front of the hotel and taken to Lake Catherine, in Arkansas, where there was a boat with a motor for them. Also fishing tackle and a box lunch awaited them! Needless to say they had a perfectly wonderful day, both being ardent fishermen.

The next day (Wednesday) Jack went for his appointment with the Personnel Section. He was sent to the office of the officer, a Major, in charge of Classifications and Assignments for his interview. The Major had received a wire from the War Department about Jack regarding assignment to the Army Ground Forces Liason Department. It was a highly technical field. Jack would get a rating as soon as he joined the organization.

The Major said it would be better to not specify a preference to any section of the country, but to take whatever they offered. Jack followed his advice. The Major then wired Washington and highly recommended him. His orders would come from Washington in a few days.

Jack wrote that Pete was leaving Friday. Pete had gotten his orders on Wednesday and was going to Camp Crowder, Missouri.. He felt badly about Pete's leaving as they had been together for almost six months.

In Jack's letter he mentioned the news of Russia's entry into the war and the new bomb we were using against Japan. On August 11, 1945, he wrote, "We are all expecting to hear at any time now, today that the fighting is over. I sure wish I could be home with you and Peg when it happens. I do wonder just just how long it will take them to get around to discharging me?" He was still waiting for his orders. That was his last letter from Hot Springs, Arkansas.

Jack's orders finally came. They read, "Transferred to Hq. & Hq. Co. Army Ground Forces, Army War College, Washington D C. with station, Regional Station Hospital, Fort Ord, Calif. for duty with Army Ground Force Liason Office. Will proceed on or about 14 Aug, 45."

He left Hot Springs at 2:45 P.M. on August 14, 1945, for Little Rock to get his train. It was a date we would remember forever as V J Day. Victory over Japan. The end of World War II. God Bless America!

THE LETTERS

To: Mrs. John K. Price   From: Pvt. John K. Price
704 Ballas Road   37623699
Kirkwood, 22, Mo.   Returnee Co.2 AG & SF
                             Red.Sta.
                             Arlington Hotel Room 1039
                             Hot Springs, Ark.

2 Aug 1945
(Thurs)

Dearest Darling:

Well, honey, we arrived here late last night after an uneventful but hot trip and I do mean hot. Boy it was terrible. Pete and I went to bed as soon as we got here, heat or no heat, though, as we were completely worn out. What a hot box of a place.

Well, I guess first off, you are interested mostly in my exam. Well I haven't had my physical yet, but will get it tomorrow, but from all indications won't be discharged. However, I will get a fairly decent assignment out of it. In fact I am debating whether or not to stay here, I have the opportunity, or whether to take a chance in getting closer to home.

I think I'll give you a complete resume of what I have done since arriving. We got in last night about 7:30 and went in a restaurant and ate. Then we looked up an M.P. who arranged transportation to the Majestic Hotel here where we checked in. After that they brought us over here to the Arlington — the nicest hotel in town, rooms 9.00 a day (singles) and up. We registered and a bell boy brought us up to the room — nice, in fact ultra but boy is it hot. They really have done everything in the world to make us comfortable and have a good time. I sure wish now that you could have come with me though, as by myself it's not half so nice and there is really very little to do for a married man who doesn't like to run around. As soon as we get in the swing though on these tours, etc. it should be ok but as far as trying to find entertainment for yourself in town it's not worth a darn. However, when I got here I found they had cancelled all reservations for wives about two weeks ago because of all the men coming back from Europe.

Well, Pete and I got to bed about 9:00 last night. This morning we got up at 7 oclock and dressed and ate as we had an appointment for a lecture at 8 oclock. It was over at nine so we went to the PX and got our ration cards for cigs but no golf balls tell Pop. Then we had an appointment at 10 to get our records check, etc. I had mine straightened out — found I was overdrawn $100 approx. so I'll be on ten bucks a month for a while again. I got my ration money for 30 days of my 60 days which is all I'll collect here and signed a payroll for $10, partial pay and went to finance and collected $30.46 — rations and $10 I have about $20 more coming in

Arlington Hotel Entrance Army buses lined up.

151

A.

Maj Fabie – G-7

H7

8/9/45

XXXX JSH:AJU:hm/625

Orders To
Fort Ord from Hot Springs

CARD REPL SAG GNACR

HQ AGF WASHINGTON 25 D C Date 9 August 1945

CO
AG&SF REDSTA
HOT SPRINGS ARK

ATTN AGF LN O REUTT 5 AUG RSHS-L 370 REQUEST TRF PVT JOHN PRICE TO HQ AND HQ CO AGF AWC WASH D C W/STA AT REGIONAL STA HOSP FT ORD CALIF FOR DY W/AGF LN O PD SO SHOULD INDICATE ASC ARM CMA MOS CMA COS AND EXACT DEPARTURE DATE PD FURN CO GP TRPS AGF AWC WASH DC CY EXTRACT WD AGO FORM 24 PD FURN THIS HQ ATTN LN DIV 3 CYS SO END GNACR 8-337

CG AGF

OFFICIAL

JOSEPH D. HUTCHISON
Capt., A.G.D.
Asst. Ground Adj. Gen.

Copies furnished:

CO, Hq Sp Trps AGF AWC Washington D. C. (CWO Gustin)
AGF Ln O at Regional Sta Hosp, Ft Ord, Calif
RR GP
RR GP (Attn: WOJG Blair)
Ln Div (2) 1945 AUG 13 PM 11:03
Domestic Asgmt GP
(26576)

FORT ORD, CALIF
ASF REGIONAL HOSPITAL
RECEIVED

8-337

Assignment - Army War College, Washington D.C.

Order To go to Ft Ord Cal. R E S T R I C T E D 8/11/45 Aug 11, 1945

Par 72 SO 195 AG & SF Redist Sta Hot Springs Ark 11 Aug 45 contd.

73. Fol EM AGF reld atchd unasgd Co 2 1817 SCU this sta and trfd in gr atchd unasgd to Prcht Sch Fort Benning Ga rptg to Comdt thereof. WP 15 Aug 45

		AGNA SRAPEM	MCO	MOS	PPL
*Irwin, Clarence A Jr	Pfc	37691722	499	7745	C
Swaney, Lee H	Pfc	38439264	050	7745	C
Crutsinger, William T	Pvt	38413350	010	7835	E

PCS TOT TOMT RAPJ TDN 601-31 P 431-02 A 212/60425. Auth: Par 7a ltr Hq AGF File 220.3/34 (O/S Returnees) (3 Aug 45) GNACR, Subj: "Availability Reports of Certain EM fr AG & SF Redist Sta" dtd 3 Aug 45. EDCMR 18 Aug 45.

74. Pvt John K Price 37623699 MCO 052 Rec MOS 405 PPL-C SS Inf AGF reld atchd unasgd Co 2 1817 SCU this sta and trfd to Hq & Hq Co AGF AWC Washington DC w/sta Regional Sta Hosp Fort Ord Calif for dy w/AGF Liaison O. WP o/a 14 Aug 45 EDCMR 18 Aug 45 SRAPEM PCS TOT TOMT RAPJ TDN 601-31 P 431-02 A 212/60425. Auth: TWX GNACR 8-337 CG AGF AWC Washington DC dtd 9 Aug 45.

* * * *

BY ORDER OF COLONEL WHEELER:

ordered to go to Ft. Ord

ROBERT A BARR
1st Lt AUS
Adj

OFFICIAL:

Robert A. Barr

ROBERT A BARR
1st Lt AUS
Adj

DISTRIBUTION "A" plus
3 cys - ea orgn concerned
~~8 cys - ea Separation Ctr~~
2 cys - Hq 3rd SvC (Attn: SPHPE)

- 2 -

ASF REGIONAL HOSPITAL FORT ORD, CAL.
1945 AUG ... 03

R E S T R I C T E D

Orders - To Liaison Officer, Station Hospital, Fort Ord, California.

the next few days for transportation. It was about 11:30 when we got through so we came back to the Arlington for lunch. They serve us in the dining room — waiters, menu, and all — even an orchestra playing. Pretty snitzy — it ain't the army for sure. After we finished lunch we had nothing to do till 4 oclock so as we were so darn hot we were about to die we took in a show to cool off. We saw Tomorrow the World with Frederic March. Don't miss it if you can help it.

We got out of the show at about 10 to four and walked back to the hotel for another lecture. It was sort of a welcoming business and very nice. They explained the deal to us and kind of oriented us on what we could and couldn't do — and there isn't much we can't do. They even serve liquor to us in our rooms at reduced rates if we want.

We got out about 5:30 and so Pete and I hopped a bus out to a swimming pool here and took a swim till 8:30. Then we came back to the hotel and went to a dance they were having on the roof garden. I didn't feel much like dancing — kind of lonesome and blue for my family, but it was nice and cool up there so I sat and watched till 11 then came up here to write you. That about takes care of the day. I know about what we'll do tomorrow, too, but I think I'll just wait till tomorrow night to give you the dope.

Well, Darling, I guess I'll close for tonight and hit the hay. I'll write again tomorrow. Write, honey. Love me a little. I love you more than anything in the world and couldn't live without you.

All my love for always,
Your Sweetheart
Jack

P.S. Can't get any films but Pete has some for his camera so getting prints for us — will send. I love you.

Bye now.
Address:
Returnee Co. #2, Arlington Hotel, Room 1039
AG & SF Red. Sta.
Hot Springs, Ark.

6 Aug 1945
Monday

Dearest honey:
Hi, Momma. I've been waiting and waiting for a letter from you but so far no luck, so I guess I'd better not wait any longer for one fore I write.

Well, I guess first of all I'd better give you all the latest dope about me. I was classified the other day and found I will stay in the Ground Forces but as a clerk. Also due to being limited assignment I will most likely not have to worry about any more overseas service — besides the general procedure is to keep a man who has 6 months overseas duty here, or if he has 60 points or more to keep him here. So in view of all those, besides the fact that once assigned as a clerk you are fairly permanent, I don't believe I'll leave again.

I will most likely be leaving here in the next day or so. They have cut the time down due to the large amount of men returning. Tomorrow is the first free day I've had since arriving. From now till I ship out my time is my own. It's a very lovely and beautiful place and we have absolutely anything we want so I know you'd enjoy it. As it is, I'm not

having such a good time cause I miss you and am lonesome. Most of the entertainment is for couples and we could have had an awful nice time.

I'll give you an example of how they treat us. Pete and I expressed the desire to go fishing early some morning. So tomorrow morning at 5 AM a car is going to pick us up in front of the hotel. They will take us to a lake near here. There will be a boat with an outboard motor on it, fishing tackle and bait waiting for us to use. They have packed a box lunch for us to take for lunch and it won't cost us a red cent — nice?

It is still terribly hot here. I don't believe I have ever been in a warmer place in my life. The town sits down in a small valley it's pinned in on all sides by hills which blocks any breeze that might accidentally be blowing.

How is Peg, honey? Does she miss her Daddy or has she mentioned it at all? I felt so darn bad, hon, when I saw you leave the station. You looked so darn sweet when you came up to the bus window and sort of looked up at me. I could have just taken you in my arms then and kissed you and loved you to death. Honey, I love you so much it just makes me sick to be away from you like this. Why can't this thing end and let us live like normal humans again? And, honey be sure and write and tell me every little thing Peg does — how she talks and all will you?

Well, darling, I must close, this is my last piece of paper. I love you more than anything in the world. Give Peg a big kiss for me. All my love for always. Your Sweetheart,

P.S. I love you
Jack

8 August 1945

Dearest Darling:
How are you this evening, honey? I feel a lot better — I received a letter from you today. Sure did need it, too. I'll answer it in a minute. For now I'll give you some new developments on my assignment. I was called up to the Major's office in charge of classification and assignment today for an interview. It seems as though he received a T W X (wire to you) from the War Department the other day on me regarding an assignment in the Army Ground Force — Liaison Dept which is a very very good break for me. It is a highly technical field and therefore, as the Major told me the T.O. which regulates the number and types of ratings in an organization, doesn't call for anyone less than a Corporal. He told me it would be to my advantage not to give any preference as to the section of the country, as ratings have opened up quite a bit due to the screening of eligible overseas men from that type of outfit and my chances would be better if I took whatever they offered, which I did. He also told me it was about the best break a private in the army today could have, as did everyone else in his office that I talked to while waiting for him. Sounds awful good doesn't it? The way he talked I'll get a rating almost as soon as I join the organization I'm assigned to. That'll really be swell for us, won't it? Just think you'll be able to come wherever I am right away. No doubt, you all have received the news of Russia's entry into the war and also about the new bomb we are using against Japan. Well, hon, the way things look it won't be too long before it's all over but the shouting. For once since I arrived back in the states

I'm not worrying about going overseas again. In fact I doubt very much whether I'll even see six more months of service before it's all over.

Well, for the first time in almost 6 months, Pete and I are going to be busted up. I really kind of hate to see it. He got his orders tonight and is leaving Friday for Camp Crowder. I believe he is going in the Signal Corps or Service Forces, one. I guess it will be a few days yet before I get mine as the Major told me today that he would have to wire Washington (he said ,"to highly recommend me for the job," Ahem!) and then my orders would come from there, so no telling how long it will be. I'm sure anxious to get out of here and get going again. It's getting terribly monotonous and with Pete gone it will be more lonesome than it is. Well, I guess I'd better get back to answering your letter. I thought you were the gal who was going to let her hair grow! Darn it, I hope it grows out fast cause I like it long. You are so pretty! Peg sounds awful sweet, honey. Kind of makes me feel sort of good that she would remember and ask about me. Give her a big kiss for me, please mam.

Well, darling, that just about finishes this up for today. Write soon. Darn, honey, I wish you would start writing every day again. Will you? Don't write such long ones, but just a note cause it helps so darn much to even get a little letter from you. Goodnight, Give my love to the folks and tell Peggy her Daddy said hello.

All my love for always,

Your Sweetheart,
Jack
P.S. I love you.

Saturday
11 August 1945

Dearest Darling:

Well, honey, I received another letter today which I hope you notice I'm answering right off.

Well, it looks like maybe the whole thing is over with except for the shouting, doesn't it? I hope by the time you get this it will be all over and then let's get busy getting me home. We are all expecting to hear at any time now today that the fighting is over.— I expect there'll be a hot time in Hot Springs tonight if it does come through. I sure wish I could be home with you and Peg when it happens. It's just hard to realize that before many more weeks are past the army will be just a memory — I do wonder just how long it will take them to get around to discharging me?

Gosh, honey, I'm so darn miserable I don't know what to do. I can't take an interest in anything — I'm constantly wishing you were here with me and I'm so lonesome and blue. I wish to

hell I'd drawn enough money out of the bank and had you come with me now. I could have really enjoyed this stay then — and I know you would have.

I'm still waiting for my orders — Lord knows how long it will be as they are coming direct from the War Dept in Washington. I would like to see this mess over with before they come as it might get me out faster if I haven't been assigned yet — but in any event, I expect you and Peg to follow me wherever I go — and almost immediately after I get there and find a place for you to live, too! God knows where I'll end up. I'm so darn tired of loafing, I don't know what to do. I want to get to work again.

Won't it be fun when we can have our own little place again and be together all the time and work and look forward to the future again. I can hardly wait. You can get mad at me when I want to go fishing and nag at me for being sloppy — and of course I'll just ignore it! We will be able to bring Peg up like she should be and start thinking about another addition. Gosh, honey, we both need all that again so bad. Well, I'm just making myself feel worse, so I'll start answering your letter. I'm just about writ out. I'm so tired of having to write letters instead of being there with you — 2 years of letter writing is a long time — for you as well as me and I'll sure be glad when we don't have to do it anymore! Yes, hon, our outlook as far as the Army is concerned is better than it has ever been. In the first place I should be getting a rating very soon now and besides I've made up our minds that we can get along ok on what we have and will get, so it looks like we'll be together again soon for the rest of the time I'm in this thing. October my eye! You'll come to me just as soon as I find a place — I won't wait till October, so there! That's so cute about Peg calling you by your first name, but it isn't good as you're still Mamma! She is growing up now for sure. She wasn't getting bad or anything while I was home, it was just a change she is going through. She is getting independent and definitely knows her own mind.

Well darling that's about all I can get from your letter and that's about all the news I have for the present so I guess I'll close. I'll write again tomorrow. Write soon, honey. All my love to my wonderful sweetheart for always.

Love and kisses
Me!
P.S. I love you
X X X X X real ones, too.

(This was the last letter. His orders came through that night. He left Hot Springs the morning of August 14th for Fort Ord, California, his new assignment.)

PART 5: FORT ORD
California

Jack arrived in Little Rock, Arkansas, on August 14, 1945, after leaving Hot Springs. He found that he would have a 7 1/2 hour layover there before his train would leave for California. He was with another soldier, a Staff Sergeant who was taking the same train. Since they had plenty of time, they had a bite to eat, and they were getting ready to go to a movie. Suddenly the news broke that the war had ended!

On August 6, 1945, the first atomic bomb had been dropped on Hiroshima, Japan. When Japan refused to surrender, a second atomic bomb was dropped August 9, 1945, on Nagasaki, Japan. The Japanese government then agreed to surrender unconditionally. The Allies accepted the terms on August 14, 1945, Washington D.C. time, and the news was given to the world.

Jack and the Staff Sergeant just stood there on the corner. Both were perfectly speechless. Jack said he felt as though he were rooted to the ground. Although the surrender ending World War II had been expected, it was hard to actually comprehend. We had all prayed for this day for so many years.

Within minutes the news had spread all up and down the street. People began to gather, and soon the crowd went wild with joy. Jack and the Staff Sergeant continued to stand there, still watching. An open convertible with two girls in it pulled up along the curb. Over the din the girls shouted to them, "Come on soldiers, let's celebrate," and pulled the two of them into the back seat.

The girls both worked for a large and important newspaper in Little Rock, Arkansas. One of the girls was the fashion editor, and the other one was the society editor. They were obviously well known in Little Rock and took the two soldiers to one cocktail party after another all evening. Jack told the girls they had to be on that train. The war might be over, but he and the Staff Sergeant were still on Military orders. The girls saw that they had a good time and, as promised, at 12:15 A.M. they took them to the station. As Jack said, they poured them into their berths. At 12:30 A.M. the train left!

Their journey was full of mishaps. The two of them missed their connections at one point and had to be put on a troop train. These were still bad times for travel since the trains were very crowded and there were still food shortages in many areas of the United States. Regular trains were frequently pulled off onto railroad sidings to let troop trains go through; but in this case the two soldiers were on the troop train, and the troop train was running late! To make matters worse, after one and a half days the kitchen on the train ran out of food.

Jack and the Staff Sergeant finally arrived in Los Angeles, California, 12 hours late. They found they had missed their train up the coast of California, so they decided to spend the night in Hollywood. After finding a place to sleep, they went to several of the USO canteens, including the famous Hollywood Canteen. They both ate, drank, and were thoroughly entertained.

The next morning Jack and the Staff Sergeant boarded a beautiful streamlined train and enjoyed the magnificent scenery along the coast in luxury. They arrived at Fort Ord, California, the night of August 18, 1945.

Fort Ord was located on the Monterey Peninsula of California. In 1917 the United States Government acquired 15,324 acres. The terrain, plains and rugged hills, made it a perfect training ground for infantry, which was its main purpose. On October 9, 1933, it was named Camp Ord in honor of Major General Edward Ord who had been an Indian fighter, stationed at the Presidio, and later a Union General in the Civil War. In 1938 permanent buildings were constructed and the size of the post was increased to more than 20,000 acres. In the next two years more land was acquired by the Government. Also the people of Salinas and the Monterey Peninsula bought 274 acres of sand dunes and donated them to the Army for firing ranges.

On August 15, 1940, Camp Ord was designated a permanent Army installation and renamed Fort Ord. The 7th Infantry Division was reactivated and was the first major unit to occupy the post. During most of the war Fort Ord was used as a staging area for many combat divisions including the 3rd, 27th, 35th, 43rd, and some smaller units. At one time there were more than 50,000 troops on the post.

Fort Ord at the time of Jack's arrival was being used as a staging area for troops training for occupation duty in Japan. Jack was not involved in that part of the post since he was attached to the Medical Section, for duty with the Army Ground Force Liaison Officer.

THE LETTERS

To: Mrs John K. Price   From: Cpl John K. Price
704 Ballas Road   Med. Sec, 1962, S.C.U.
Kirkwood, 22, MO   Ft. Ord, Calif.

El Paso, Texas
8/16/45

Hi Hon:

Still on the way — running 8 hours late. Had a big V-J day in Little Rock. Will write when I arrive & tell you all about it, can't write on a train. In El Paso now — will arrive Cal. 18th or 19th. Kiss Peg for me. I love you,

Jack

Address:
Pvt John K. Price 37623699
Reg. Sta. Hosp.
Fort Ord, Cal.

Write Airmail

Post Card - Fort Ord, California, 1945.

Med. Sec. — 1962 SCU.
18 Aug 45
Fort Ord, Cal.
(Saturday)

Dearest Honey:

Well, sweet, I arrived in here tonight after one hell of a long and tiresome trip and I'm just about worn out so I'll not write too long tonight.

We left Hot Springs at 2:45 PM last Tuesday. We got into Little Rock for a 7 1/2 hour layover so we grabbed a bite to eat and were just about to go to a show when the news came out that the war was over. What a celebration that town put on. Maybe I shouldn't tell you this, but I will any way. I was with a S/Sgt and he and I were standing on a corner kind of dazed watching the goings on when a 1941 Nash pulled up and two girls said come on soldier, let's celebrate! So, we got in with them. It so happened they worked for a big newspaper in town, one fashion editor and the other society editor, both married. They must have known everyone in town cause we went to so many cocktail parties I couldn't keep track of them. About 12:15 they took us to the station and poured us into our berths. But what a time we did have. We pulled out of there about 12:30 and had trouble all the way, missing our connection, so were put on to a troop train to bring us in. We ran out of food after 1 1/2 days so just about starved to death, then were 12 hours late getting in to L.A. so missed our connections and had to lay over last night there. We spent the night in Hollywood at these Service Canteens. It's a very beautiful place. We caught a very beautiful train — streamlined — out this morning, however and this part of the trip was very nice. I, of course don't know anything new about what I've gotten into here, but will find out Monday and let you know.

Now for some discouraging news. I inquired about housing in Salinas and Monterrey — the two towns near here and there isn't an apartment to be had. Rooms are also very scarce but with a little effort I should be able to find one.

You'll have to bring winter clothes as it is very cold here. I about froze to death in my sun tans till they gave me some OD's which is all that is worn here. I just can't imagine it — yesterday we came through the Desert where the temp was 162 in the sun to here where it's really cold. Silly? This is terribly short, but I'm so tired. I'll write tomorrow and give you a play by play account. Give Peg a big kiss and pray that it won't be too long before I'm home with you for good. I love you with all my heart and more than anything in the world and I'm lonesome too.

Your Sweetheart,
    Jack
P.S. Happy V-J day!
I love you x x x

19 August 1945
Sunday

Dearest Darling:

Well, honey, I just arose after about a 14 hour sleep so now I feel a lot better and a whole lot more like writing.

Before I forget though, will you pack my blouse and a set of O.D.'s and send them to me please? I really need them as it's so darn cold here and I have had them altered to fit, etc, so I'd rather not draw new ones and have to have it done all over again. When you come you'll have to bring plenty of warm clothes for you and Peg.

Now for Fort Ord — I don't like it. It sits out in the middle of no where and how I'll ever find a place for you and Peg is beyond my comprehension. I began inquiring as soon as I got off the train — I asked the Travelers Aid, U.S.O. and everyone I met and they all told me the same thing — there isn't any. I went to the Red Cross this morning and they couldn't do any thing for me. However, they said I might find a room for 6 or 7 dollars a week. I don't mind telling you the way I feel anything would do, Just as long as you were here with me. I'll do everything I can.

I really dread to think of you having to make that trip — it is really terrible. When you come, be sure to take the Northern route — the Union Pacific. I believe you will go by way of the Eagle through Kansas City and also if at all possible try to get a compartment as you'll be more comfortable.

How is Peg, darling? Has she forgotton her Daddy yet? How I would love to be there with you or have you here so I could play with her and all. It's really harder for me being away now than it was when I first went in the army. All that time in the hospital and at home really ruined me. It's going to be tough to get back into the swing of things.

I received a letter from you just before I left Hot Springs. You talk about coming down the first of Oct. honey. Well that's ok with me. Course if I find a place before then you'll have to come down right away then.

By the way what kind of a celebration did they have in St. Louis? Did you have a good time? Be sure and write and tell me all about it. I'm telling you the truth, Little Rock just went crazy. We were really lucky to have gotten there at the time we did. I went to church, Catholic, Tuesday night, right after it was announced. Did you? I hope so, as if there was ever a time we all needed to thank God, that was it.

From what I can understand, honey, liaison work is — well, let me start differently. When a man is sent to the hospital he is away from any connection with his branch of the service. In my case now, I'm with the A G F or Army Ground Force Liaison dept. That means I'll keep contact with the men in the hospital whose branch is A G F — taking care of their personal wants — like allotments, insurance, wills, etc. In other words I'm the connecting link between them in the hospital, and their regular outfit. Is that clear? It's about the best I can put it over. The air

Ink Sketch of Jack by Louis Besser, newpaper's artist.

RECONDITIONING WEEKLY

Published weekly under the supervision of the Reconditioning Section by the patients and personnel of Fort Ord ASF Regional Station Hospital. Col. J.I. Sloat, CO.

Managing Editor.............................Dan Lomax
Reporters....................Bob Ickes and Bob Meisel
Typist .... Lloyd Baker
Printer .... David Watson
Artist.......................................Louis Besser
Adviser....................Miss Virginia Brainard, AR6

The RECONDITIONING WEEKLY receives material from Camp Newspaper Service, an official unit of the Information and Education Division, ASF. Republication of CNS material is prohibited without permission of CNS.

****

AGF LIAISON OFFICE OPEN FOR BUSINESS

An Army Ground Forces Liaison Office has recently been established in Building G-7 of the Hospital and the welfare of all Army Ground Forces Patients is of vital interest to the personnel of the Office. Three AGF men run the office; Major Carl Fuler, S/Sgt. Albert Mosely and Cpl. John Price.

Do not hesitate to contact their office in person, or by calling Ext. 667, if you are in need of advice concerning your personal problems; such as: insurance, allotments, family allowances, baggage and personal effects, pay (whole or partial), income tax, legal affairs, decorations, awards, additional pay for awards maternity & infant care, bonds, veterans benefits, etc. G7 is 2 buildings down from the Craft Shop at G5.

****

THE WOLF   by Sansone

"Who dealt this hand?"

Coming EVENTS

RED CROSS AUDITORIUM

Sat. 25th.		
Games and Recordings	2:00	
Rummy and Ping Pong	6:30	
Sun. 26th.		
Open House with GIRLS from Gilroy, Hollister and Morgan Hill	6:30	
Mon. 27th.		
Your Face is Your Fortune	2:00	
Al Tieder and Band	6:50	
Tues. 28th.		
MOVIE	2:15	
"Incendiary Blond"	5:30	
Betty Hutton	7:30	
Wed. 29th.		
Talk a Letter Home	2:00	
U S O SHOW		
"Swing Time Follies"	6:30	
Thur. 30th.		
Dancing Lessons	2:00	
Round Up Time	6:30	
Fri. 31st.		
MOVIE "These Endearing	2:15	
Young Charms" with	5:30	
Robert Young	7:30	

****

NURSES, WACS & RED CROSS WORKERS BOYCOT RECON GYM

At least it seems that the above mentioned Nurses Wacs and Red Cross Workers are 'boycotting' the Recon Gym judging from the attendance on the Monday nights reserved for them.

A recent survey of the candy sales to the gals here indicates that a nite of gymnastics should do wonders for someone. How about it, Gals? Don't you think you should pay a visit to the Recon Gym? The Instructors are happy to help you keep in trim.

Newspaper, Reconditioning Weekly, for newly established AGF Liaison Office. Three men run office, including Cpl. John Price. Artist, Louis Besser.

corps has the same thing — taking care of just air corps personnel, and each other branch has the same set-up. The TO is an abreviation for Table of Organization. That's the thing that tells you how many men and of what rank are needed to make up a certain type outfit.

Well, honey I should be able to write you every day. There really was so much going on in Hot Springs all the time I didn't get many opportunities to write but it is different here. It was nice at H. S. but it got tiresome at the last. I could really have enjoyed it had you been there.

I'm enclosing a little book which will show you what we had at H.S.

Bye, bye. Love me and miss me. Give Peg a big kiss for me and take good care of her. All my love for always. Write soon.

Your Sweetheart,
    Jack
P.S. I love you.

29 August 1945

Dearest honey:

Well, hon, just finished up my first day and what a deal I have got. In fact, it's really not a job at all, we don't do any work. I'm with a S/Sgt and a Major in charge. We sat around all day today gabbing and playing cards. By this time next month please address me as Corporal! Three months after that it will be Sgt. That's all planned out and I was informed of the fact today. Nice?!

I don't care a whole lot for the post, however. In the first place it's just too doggoned cold. (Send me some undershirts!) Another thing is that it's just impossible to find a place to live. I'll keep trying though and maybe I'll hit it lucky.

That was a very short letter. I've finished answering it already, so I will close and get my beauty sleep. Goodnight darling. Sweet dreams and love me and miss me. All my love to my two wonderful little gals.

Your Sweetheart,
    Jack
P.S. I love You
X X X X X — all for you!
x x x x x — for Peg cause she's littler.

25 August 1945
Saturday

Dearest Darling:

Well, honey at long last I received a letter from you and how wonderful it made me feel. You don't know what it is to be way down here like this and not hear from home. It's the one you wrote right after you received that card I mailed you from El Paso. Happy anniversary yourself! You are awful sweet, honey. Every 22nd whether it's the right month or not, it's our anniversary. Honey, I'd have written you on the trip down, but it is almost impossible to write on a darn train. I was traveling for 5 and a half days from Tuesday till Saturday night, so it was impossible to hear from me till I arrived.

I know you have my address by now. The one you used on the letter I got today took a day longer as this is a big place and they had to find me. That was the only address I knew when I mailed the card. I guess from the sound of your letter you are definitely coming down so I'm going to have to find a

place to live. You and Peg and I can stay at the guest house here on the post for the first few days, at least. If we had a car we could get out to these towns farther away from the post, but having to depend on bus service we would have to find a place reasonably close and there isn't anything to be had for love or money.

You shouldn't have too much trouble getting a pullman ticket now, as from the way the civilians I talked to on the train coming down here from Memphis, they didn't have any trouble, although the train was full — not crowded, but no vacant berths. However, honey, when you come, be sure to come the northern route, as the accomodations are much better. The Eagle to K. C. Then the Union Pacific. I would hate to think that you and the baby had to come down the way I did, as it was really miserable. I felt sorry for the people on that train with small children, and there were plenty, as half the time the civilians weren't served on the diner and those kids had to go hungry and all. It was really terrible. As far as the time to arrive, naturally the weekend would be best. However, I will be able to get off any time to meet you so don't worry about that. There isn't a chance under the sun of finding a place in Salinas or Monterey, honey, but we may be able to find a room in Pacific Grove or Carmel. A room will cost us approximately 10 dollars a week. Yes, I'll be able to draw rations and live off post when you come. I'll just draw a separate ration check of about 20 dollars a month for my food, which will help to keep us going. Naturally with conditions as they are down here, I feel a little uneasy about your coming, honey, but I wouldn't say anything in the world to keep you from it, as in the first place I need you something awful and in the second place I know how much you want to come. But let me warn you of one thing — be prepared to be disappointed and also to find that I haven't a place to live and that we'll have to stay in a hotel for a while. Of course, during the day you might be able to do more than I in finding a place. I hope by now you have sent my O.D's to me as I really need them. If you haven't, would you please also enclose that service cap of mine as they are authorized here and I will be able to get some good out of it. If you have already sent the stuff, just bring it with you.

Peg sure sounds cute, honey. I am so anxious to see her again. I wonder if she will remember me? I guess at first she will be strange again, but we will get over that. What is the big surprise for me? I'm amazed that she is putting sentences together so well, in such a short time. Course she was doing that to some extent before I left.

I sure would have given anything to have been in St. Louis when the news of the wars end came through. I was in an awful good town and had a good time, but nothing like I imagine St. Louis had and then too, I'd have been with you and we really could have celebrated. Did any soldiers grab and kiss you? I must confess, I kissed so many strange gals, especially after I got a few drinks in me, that I lost count. I really had a picnic, especially watching the expression on the girls faces when a perfect stranger walks up to them on the street and gives them a big smack. We really raised hell. That was one time though, when everyone could let themselves go, and for the large part did. Everyone seemed to be everyone elses friend for that one night. You should have gotten out of the car and walked around, if you didn't cause there is where you had the most fun. The only bad part was that this fellow

I was with and I were still suffering a little from combat fatigue and after about 15 minutes of all the noise (before we got drunk) everytime a car backfired or a firecracker went off we would just about dive into the gutter — it really got on our nerves for a while. That's one ofthe reasons we decided we had better get good and soused — so it wouldn't bother us any more.

As far as how the war will affect my prospects, honey, I don't know yet. There should be something coming out on it any time now. The Major I work for seems to feel that fellows like he and myself will be getting out before too much longer — he has seen a lot of combat in the S.P. You've got to remember, honey, this isn't my permanent station. I'm assigned to Army Ground Forces Liaison Division, Washington, D.C., and am only attached here for quarters and rations for the time being. My real mail address, for instance is AGF Liaison Officer, Agf Liaison Dept, Washington, but to expedite my mail, I have to use the medical detachment address of the hospital here. I'm liable to be moved anytime to any hospital or installation handling a variety of personnel. Just anywhere they take a notion to send me.

That should be a very pretty dress, hon. I really like that material. By the way, I liked that note you enclosed in the first letter about the definition of liaison — trouble is, that ain't what we are doing here, damn! Well, darling, that winds up your letter and winds up this one too. Three and a half typed pages, that's a little better, isn't it? Sweet dreams, honey. Give Peg a big kiss for me. All my love,

Your sweetheart,
Jack
P.S. No P.S.tonight — completely run down! I love you.
X X X X X
x x x x x
(Big ones for you, little ones for Peg)

31 August 1945

Dearest Honey:
Well, darling, I received another wonderful letter from you this evening. Just got back from the show, saw some second rate thing that wasn't worth a darn, but I was took so I shouldn't complain. Went to the early show so its only about 8:30 now. Doggone it, I'll sure be glad when we get together on our letters — I am so confused. All I am sure of is that you will be here by the 12th of October. I'm not going to write about it any more now, but just let you write and tell me exactly what you are going to do. It takes too long for your letters to get here and we sort of get our wires crossed. Honey, I'm sorry my letter made you feel sad and blue. I didn't mean for it to. It will be so swell when you get here. I won't be lonesome any more and it won't matter if I'm broke cause I won't need any money — I'll be able to come home to my sweet little family every night. You're darn right, we need to be together.

You get here in October. On the first of November I should be able to draw extra rations for living off post, and the first of December I will be drawing regular pay again and will get 37 dollars plus 20 or so for rations. It might be a little tough going till then, but we should be able to get by. If I get ration money, I'll have to pay for my noonday meal. I hope a hundred will be enough to get by on, for a month, it should be if we are careful. We should

have more than enough, don't you think? I think the best place for us to try to find a place is Pacific Grove — it is much the nicest of all the towns. The way things look now, it shouldn't be too long before I get a staff rating as this s/sgt we have now, is just about eligible for discharge, 81, points and I'll most likely get his rating. As I told you before, the only reason I haven't had a rating before this is because I was never assigned to an organization, and this sort of proves what I told you. Had I been assigned before, I'd have been S/Sgt by now. I know what I can do. This Major is an overseas man and is going to see that everyone working for him and himself get as much out of the army as they can. You'll meet him and see, we act no more like Officer and enlisted man in that office than Dad and I. Honey, I'll swear Peggy is so darn wonderful. I can hardly wait to see her. That is so cute when she said she wanted to fish and swim with Daddy. Hurry down, honey real fast cause I'm lonesome and can't wait much longer. All my love for always to the sweetest girl in the world. Your sweetheart,

Jack
P.S. I love you
XXXXXX xxxxxx

6 September 1945

Dearest Darling:
Well, honey, I received a letter from you at noon today, so I'm going to try to answer it before I go to town tonight. Remember I told you last night I was going to see about a job this evening, so I guess this will have to be a little short. Hope you aren't too disappointed!

Well, we had another big day today — a lot more stuff on discharges — however, you are right so come ahead — I'll be expecting you. Get your stuff packed and ready. If anything else does come up before then I can always wire you. How does that suit you? Arrange to arrive here either the 6th or the 13th of October — in other words on a Saturday. As soon as I hear definitely from you by wire that you are coming then I'll make reservations at the Hotel in town — better still I think I'd better make them about 2 weeks in advance so you are sure of a room.

I noticed in the papers today that the 5 day limit on reservations and all the other restrictions on travel are to be lifted as of the 16th of this month so if I were you, I'd make my reservations plenty in advance so you are assured of fairly good accomodations and then if anything does happen at the last minute you can always cancel them.

Yes, honey, as far as jobs go I got a much better deal by letting them send me wherever they wanted to. You'll see when you get down here — I have about all the free time I want — no restrictions or regulations to follow and am just about my own boss. That's good about not bringing anything with you. It would be foolish to load up with a lot of stuff. Lord knows how long we will be here.

Well, I covered all the high spots and must close and get to town. Wish me luck. Love, miss me, and hurry on down. All my love, honey — Only 5 more weeks.

Your sweetheart,
Jack
P.S. I love you.
X X X X X
x x x x x

7 September 1945

Dearest Darling:

Well, honey, here I am again for a while. I really had a busy day today and am plenty tired. I'm kinda anxious for you to take this trip and be able to see all that beautiful country from home here and also want you to see California as it really is different from any other place we've been. Course I know you'll get awful tired of this army life but it will be something different for a while and it shouldn't be too long before I'm heading home for good. Of course I mind if you still address me as Private. After all, I've only worked two years for this darn thing. It sure does help us out, doesn't it. If I'm here long enough I'll be Sgt. fore you know it. I told you I got a good deal as far as being sent down here and that proves it. I hadn't even been here two weeks when he told me to put in for a promotion. That's pretty good, I think. By the way, I still don't know about the job yet. I'll find out Monday whether or not they can use me. I'm trying to get on from about 6 pm till midnight or one AM. I received the five and thank you lots. It will run me a week or two now.

I guess you have received the letter I wrote telling you about the S/Sgt getting out. He'll be leaving in a few days or a week. I think if it is left up to the Major, I'll get it. Hope so anyway cause Staff Sergeant pay is 96 bucks a month and that will help a lot.

Oh yes, Gang plank fever is what fellows get just about the time they are to get on a boat to go overseas. As a result of this gang plank fever they start thinking up all kinds of ailments, etc, to keep from having to go up that gang plank on to a boat. Get it?

Well, darling, for the second night as short a letter as you would want to see, but I'll try to do better. I must close now and take a bath as I want to get to bed about 8 oclock tonight. I'm not feeling too good. Sweet dreams. Love me and miss me. I love you more than anything in the whole world.

Your sweetheart,
Jack
P.S. October — I can hardly wait.
I love you.

13 September 45

Deaarest Darling:

Well, honey, I'm going to try to get a letter off to you finally tonight. I have one half finished, but it's locked in the office. I'd better explain why I haven't written. Well, Tuesday night I went out to see about that job and didn't get back till too late to write. Wednesday night I went to work and didn't get off till midnight. Tonight I went down to work but they hadn't gotten any fish in so weren't working tonight, thank God. I'm so stiff and sore I can hardly move. I can't get my bad arm back to my hip pocket. I hate to admit it but I'm afraid I'm going to have to find something a little lighter to do. I hate to, cause I'm making 86 cents an hour and besides there is no set rule on working. If you don't feel like going in you don't have to. You can work any time the notion strikes you if they have the work to do. The way they work there is nice too, cause every two hours you get a break for coffee or something and every 4 hours you get an hour break. Now last night I worked 4 hours and made $3.50 which isn't bad. I guess I'd better tell you what I'm doing fore you have a fit.

I'm working for the Handen Canning Co. It's a canned fish outfit sardines and the like, and I'm doing plain labor. Pushing crates of cans around on carts — heavy, too. You see, Monterey is the largest sardine and fish canning port in the country. All the big companies have plants there like Del Monte, etc. but boy oh boy, I can't take it. Every muscle in my body is sore and my shoulder is killing me. The way I figure though after I get used to it, it'll be ok.

By the way, something new has come out which will help get us back home when the time comes for me to be discharged. It used to be that anyone here to be discharged would be shipped via military transportation to the separation center closest to his home and discharged and then be given 5 cents a mile travel money from there home. The talk now is that instead of doing that, they will discharge the men right here and then give them the nickle a mile from here home. If they do that it will give me about $125 to travel on. I'll be able to buy a special ticket for 1 1/4 cents a mile so we should both be able to get home on the $125. Nice? It sounds like Peg is really talking now, the way you write. Putting regular long sentences together and everything. I can hardly wait to see her. Well, honey, I really must go now. Love me and miss me and hurry down. Give Peg a big kiss for me. All my love, Your sweetheart

Jack
P.S. You will address me as Cpl from now on—! ! !
I love you

15 September 1945

Dearest Darling:

Well, honey, I would have written last night but felt so punk I just went to bed. That work I was doing was just a little too much for me I'm afraid, as my shoulder has really been bothering me so I think I better stop working down there. I have another job lined up though. As far as getting an apartment here, if we can, it would be the best thing. Most of them are furnished so we wouldn't need a lot of stuff. I'll tell you, the best deal here, are the tourist cabins if you can find one. They all have refrigs and little kitchens and bath and bedroom. I looked at a place in Pacific Grove, but as Pacific Grove is a summer resort kind of, they wanted 17.50 a week for the place.

I'm sure glad to hear that Joe is finally getting home and even getting out of the Army too. That's really swell, other than myself he is the one I'd like to see get out the most. Tell Bettie for me that I'm really glad for she and Joe. Maybe it won't be too much longer then before I get out of it too. I don't know why it should please me so much that Peg and Butch get along so well together, but it does. I really think quite a bit of those people though. They are nice people. You know, honey, if we are home for Christmas, I wish we could get Peg one of those tables like Butch has. They are really wonderful toys and I'll bet she does get a lot of fun out of playing with it. We'll have to get a little bicycle for her. She should be getting big enough before long to get a lot of enjoyment from one. I was just thinking, Joe will land in San Francisco and he will most likely stay there a few days. I sure wish we could maybe get together while he is here. The only trouble is that he doesn't know where I am. It would be easy for me to run up to Frisco. It's only 130 miles.

I feel the same way, honey, it might be best if I do stay in the army a few months longer. You'll be with me, and maybe we can get a little ahead. I do

Oct. 7, 1945

Hi honey:

Well, darling, I've looked and looked and looked for a place to live, but so far have had no luck at all, so this weekend took a trip up here to San Jose to see what cooks. It's really a beautiful little town

FROM *Cpl. John K. Price, Med Sec, 1962 SCU, Ft. Ord, Calif.*

MRS. JOHN K. PRICE,
704 BALLAS ROAD
KIRKWOOD, 22,
MISSOURI.

AIR MAIL
SPECIAL DELIVERY

SAN JOSE
OCT 7
430PM
1945
CALIF.

Our last WWII Letter!

have the job waiting so there is no huge rush. I really do have a snap of a job, and might as well take advantage of it especially with the ratings I have coming. I would be perfectly satisfied for the first time since I've been in the army. I couldn't have found better officers to work for. The Major is really one swell joe. Well, that just about finishes this up. Think I'll close now and get my clothes in shape take a bath and go to bed early. Love me and miss me and hurry down. Give Peg a big kiss for me and say hello to the folks. Night, sweet.

Your Sweetheart,
Jack
P.S. I love you.

28 September 45

Dearest Darling:

Well, honey, I feel a little better this evening so will try to answer some of these letters of yours. Went to work today for the first time since last Monday. I have really been one sick boy. Nothing serious — just a miserable head cold and cough. Bad enough, though, to make me stay in bed and take medicine.

Honey I'm so darn anxious to see you and Peg I don't know what to do. If what I'm working on materializes we will really be sitting pretty. It all depends now, I believe, on how soon the Major leaves — He has enough points to get out. The way things look I should be a Staff Sgt in about another month. — all the arrangements have been made already. That will mean that our income will go up to about $175 a month which is as much as I was making before I came in the army. It also means that I will be a first three grader (of the first three grades — 1st Sgt, Tech Sgt & S/Sgt) which entitles me to move my family once any where in the U.S. at Government expense. Which means that I'll not only collect a nickle a mile for my transportation home when I'm discharged but will also get paid for yours and Pegs. It really looks good, and to be perfectly honest, honey, under those conditions, I'm not in any too big a rush to get out of the Army. Maybe we can get a little ahead before my discharge comes through and will have a little to run on at first.

Peg sounds so cute and so grown up. I'm awfully anxious to see if she will remember me after 2 1/2 months, aren't you? From the way you write she hasn't forgotten me. Even if it is only a month or so before we head back again, it will be a nice trip for you and Peg — sort of a second honeymoon. Then you will be the first to see your new civilian husband when the time comes. Now, honey, stop worrying about my arm. I only worked down there one night and definitely decided not to any more cause I found out that I just couldn't take that kind of work. I was ok while I was working, but the next day that shoulder of mine really gave me fits, so I decided I was foolish to maybe injure myself just for a few pen-

Ralph Keedy, on the right.

Jack moving from barracks to our apartment.

Peggy at waters edge. Cove in the afternoon.

Our apartment, Peggy in front faces Monterey Bay, start of 17 Mile Drive.

nies. I have 2 more letters to answer, but I think I'll hit the hay now and go to bed early. Good night, Darling. Love me and miss me and hurry down.

All my love, for always,
Your Sweetheart,
    Jack
P.S. Kiss Peg for me. I love you.

3 October 1945

Dearest Honey;

I hope you forgive me for not writing, but for the last few days all I have been doing is run, run, run, — trying to find some sort of place for you to live in before you get here. So far I haven't had any luck at all. I have made reservations at a hotel, honey, but we aren't going to be able to afford that for more than a night, as the cheapest thing I could get, with baby bed and bath, was 4.50 a night. That is plenty high. The only thing is, I was thinking you would want a nice place to stay for that first night, so you could get cleaned up and all and you will be terribly tired after such a long trip. We will have to get out and find something the next day though, if I don't find something before then. The thing I'm depending on is thatyou won't have any trouble finding a place during the day. I have talked to fellows and they say the only way was by just walking up one street and down another. You can't do that cause of Peg. We will have to rely on these various agencies. The way it stands I'll meet you at 4.30 at the station in Salinas on the 13th, right? Some new poop has just come out regarding discharges. The latest is that all men with the purple heart will be next to be discharged, although nothing has come out yet as to when this will all come about. You never can tell I might decide to reinlist for three more years!! I sure hope I can find something before you get here. At least, honey, we will have a nice little vacation in California at one of the most ritzy sections, regardless of when I am to head for home. It will be really

nice to be together for a nice trip like that. Well, darling, I'm going to quit and get this off to you. 1 more week m m m m.

Jack
I love you!

Oct. 7, 1945

Hi honey:

Well, darling, I've looked and looked and looked for a place to live, but so far have had no luck at all, so this weekend took a trip up here to San Jose to see what cooks. It's really a beautiful little town and you would love it I know, but it's so inconvenient to camp. I want a place where I can come home every evening instead of just weekends. I wish we could have a car — I would like to be able to take you around and show you the beautiful spots in Cal.

Just think, only one week — next Saturday. I can hardly wait. By the way, sweet, just in case something should happen — I don't know what could — but no use taking chances. I have reservations at the Hotel Jeffrey (Jeffry) in town and it is within walking distance from the station. So if I'm not there when you arrive — in case something does come up — you can go right on up to the hotel.

I have arranged for a three day pass, Monday Tuesday, and Wednesday. I'll have to go out to camp Monday morning to get it — otherwise I'll be with you from Saturday afternoon till Thursday morning. I sure hope that in that time we can find a place. You and Peg can ride out to camp with me Monday if you like if the buses are running by then. The Fort is serviced by Greyhound and as they are on strike we don't have bus service. Course I never use them anyway but I don't imagine you would care a lot about hitch hiking with me. Well, honey, this is the last one I'll write you I guess. You be very careful and have a nice trip. I'll meet you Saturday at 4:30. Bye for now, darling. See you next week. I can hardly

Jack beside Army car.

Soldier by supply office, unknown.

wait — it will be the slowest week I have ever known. All my love for always.

Your Sweetheart,
P.S. I love you.
　　Jack

(This was our last Wartime letter.)

FORT ORD
After the war

The war being over made a difference in our plans. We were not sure now what the future held for us regarding the Army's plans for Jack.

Money, as always, was our greatest concern. I had $80.00 a month for Peggy and me which was my allotment from Jack's pay. His pay was very small since he was still only drawing partial pay until his records were straightened out. Finding a place to live was virtually impossible and rents for housing were exorbitant anywhere near Fort Ord..

However, in view of the fact that we could not live without one another, the only solution was for me to come in October on faith! This proved to be providential. By the time I arrived, men were being discharged from the Army daily and a few places were becoming available.

I had always lived a rather sheltered life and truly admired some of our friends who took all their children on buses or trains to be near their husband's military camps. However, Jack had never been in the United States long enough for me to do this. Now, taking the train alone, across the country, with our two-year-old child seemed an enormous undertaking to me. To all of us California was the end of the world. Finally October 12th, our day of departure, arrived, and Jack's and my parents took us to Union Station in St. Louis to see us off to "the end of the world!"

The train we were on was filled with soldiers headed for the west coast, many of whom had seen duty in the European Theater. They were now being sent to the Pacific Theater for occupation duty. The soldiers were all so friendly and helpful to us, and they thoroughly enjoyed Peggy. To their delight she was friendly and cute and very well-behaved. Another young lady and I were the only women in our coach so we had the restroom to ourselves. Peggy and I had the lower berth and the young lady had the upper berth. The seats on the Pullman coach were made into beds at night by the porter, and they had curtains which closed.

We took the Northern Pacific route as Jack had insisted. It was magnificent! Our pullman coach was switched to another train in Denver, Colorado. This was our only lengthy stop.

All went well until we reached Oakland, California, where we left the train and took the ferry to San Francisco. We were late arriving and we had missed our train to Salinas. I was overcome with panic, but kept reminding myself I was a mother and had to keep my composure.

At the train station Information Desk the lady suggested that we take the Del Monte Special, which was leaving shortly, and get off at Castroville California, "the artichoke capital of the world." There a bus would take us to Salinas.

Fortunately there were several other people who decided to do that. One was a very assertive lady who promptly took charge, to my great relief. Darkness had come. It was a foggy night, the train was speeding toward a destination unknown to me, and I knew Jack would be frantic when we didn't arrive as planned.

The train stopped finally at Castroville, and we stepped off of it into gravel. The train "station" was just a loading platform with a open shed in a field and one dim light in front. While on the train we had been told the buses were on strike, but a taxi would be there to take us to Salinas.

The Taxi was a very old car with a sign in the window proclaiming that it was a taxi. The driver barely spoke English. There were four of adults and one child. The two men were Oriental and they stood quietly while "Assertive Lady" bargained with the driver who had quoted us a ridiculous price. With all of the luggage we were quite packed in. However, in due time we arrived at the Jeffry Hotel in Salinas, California.

The young man at the hotel desk told me that my husband was frantic when I was not on the 4:30 P.M. train so he had gone back to the railroad station to meet the 11:15 P.M. train. The young man kindly phoned the station for me, but they said there was no Sgt. Price there. Then he he took us up to the room. I opened the closet door to hang up my coat, and there hanging neatly on the rod were Jack's uniforms. I just hugged his jacket and wept with relief. I was exhausted, I had reached the end of our long journey, and I was safe.

Jack was at the station, but he had been out on the platform all evening watching (he said) a crap game. When the 11:15 train arrived and we were not on it, he really was frantic. When he went into the station to find out whether there could possibly be another train, the station lady asked if he were Sgt. Price. She told him his wife had been calling and was already at the hotel. He ran the few blocks down the street to the hotel. What a joyous reunion!! Peggy had gone to sleep finally in the cab and was now sleeping soundly in the crib.

Because there was such a shortage of housing, we could only stay in the hotel for the weekend. However, Jack had a 3-day pass (Monday, Tuesday, and Wednesday) so we took the bus to Pacific Grove and got a room in a huge old Victorian-style hotel where we could stay three more days. The hotel was filled with servicemen's families and in spite of the "No children playing on stairs" signs, children were playing everywhere. The "No cooking in rooms" signs didn't deter anyone either.

Across the back of the hotel there were wide screened porches on all three floors which had once held big comfortable rocking chairs. The chairs were gone and now clothes lines stretched from end to end holding baby diapers. After three days there I found a room in an old home owned by a lovely elderly Swedish lady with — wonder of wonders — a hot plate. Now we could at least warm food and make coffee.

Every evening when Jack came in from Fort Ord, we would walk down to the little park on Lovers Point. We had noticed a very nice vacation-type apartment building facing the water and thought how lovely it would be to live there on Monterey Bay.

One day I decided to ask. The apartment manager (Mrs. Frazier) was so nice and to my surprise said that she would be having a vacancy very soon. The Lieutenant in one of the apartments was waiting for his orders. I would have to stop by every afternoon since she couldn't hold it. A few days later, as Mrs. Frazier walked down the sidewalk by our house on her way home from town, she tapped on the window of our room. She said to hurry down — the Lieutenant had moved.

I phoned Jack at the base immediately, and when he got home (he had brought a friend Ralph Keedy with him) they carried our entire possessions two blocks down the hill. Our entire possessions consisted of my trunk, our suitcases, a barracks bag, Peggy and ourselves. It was November 6, 1945.

The apartment was intended for summer people. It had a pull down bed and a wide window seat just right for Peggy to sleep on. The kitchen had a booth, a very small sink and stove, and a window box on the outside in place of an icebox. The window box kept cold things perfectly. Rents had been frozen by the government at winter rates. Even so, $75.00 a month rent was exorbitant for most people.

Some food was still in great shortage. The grocery stores all had signs in the windows — no eggs, no mayonnaise, no margarine, no butter. Well, dry toast and jelly for breakfast wasn't too bad, and there appeared to be plenty of milk. Jack got home every evening about 5 o'clock, having hitched a ride from the base. After supper he and Peggy

and I sat on the rocks at the park across the road and watched the sunset. We never got used to the splendor of the huge waves crashing against the rocks and then swirling back out. The weather was quite cool during the day and the nights were very cold. In the mornings Peggy and I wore warm coats and walked across the street, down to the little cove where it was warm enough to sit in the sand and play at the water's edge.

The food shortage was not our greatest problem; the money shortage was. Jack would now get Staff Sergeant's pay, and he was getting quarters and rations, but how would we pay the December rent of $75.00 for the apartment? It was due December 6th, and it would take most of our money. How would we buy Christmas presents for the baby? We needed a miracle.

The miracle came! Jack came home one evening elated with the

Peggy and little boy playing cards, very seriously!

Pacific Grove, California, beach and park at Lovers point.

news that a two-bedroom apartment on the base had become available and he was first on the waiting list. This was the answer to our prayer. The rent was 90 cents a day, to be deducted from his pay the end of December. We had to pay Mrs. Frazier $2.50 for one day's rent, and on December 7th, 1945, we moved out to Fort Ord. This was just regular military housing, but we were a family and we had a real home again!!

The military apartment was very attractively furnished with rental furniture for the living room, dining room, and bedroom. It even had lamps and carpet. The furniture rental was $15.00 a month total.

I had written my mother to send the box which I had packed with the barest essentials, and to please include one set of their Christmas

tree lights. They only had a few which still worked since the lights could not be replaced during the war. We absolutely had to have a lighted tree for Peggy's first Christmas with her daddy home!

The apartment had only wooden Venetian blinds at the windows which looked rather bare. When the box arrived, though, a pair of sheets became curtains in the living room. Tied back they were not too bad, and they made the room look warmer.

Upstairs were two bedrooms and the bathroom. We thought Peggy should have the other bedroom so with an old army footlocker for her clothes and my trunk with two seat pillows from the sofa at night, it was furnished. She thought it was fine! We were not too far from the ocean, and on a clear day we could get a glimpse of it from the upstairs windows.

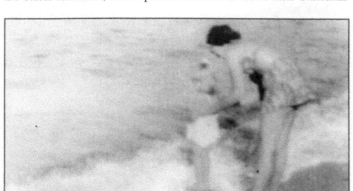

Mother and Peggy, feet only touching water. Pacific ocean never gets warm.

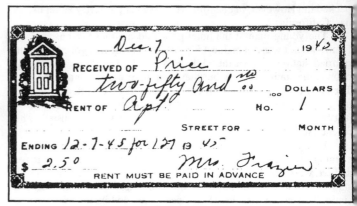

Rent receipt for last day in apartment.

Remote beach, Peggy covering Jack with coffee can sand pail. He has the latest beach attire, and the good old army blanket.

Jack and Peggy on our own back porch. 6E Fremont.

and could hear it quite plainly. The three of us often walked down to the beach, which was a long lonely uninhabited stretch of the Pacific Ocean. We had no social life and were quite content with simple pleasures. We spent one whole afternoon shoveling sand away from a huge log, finally rolling it out into the waves off shore. We took pictures, and we often remembered that day.

I loved living on the post; every one was so friendly. It was a comforting thing to know that Jack's office was within walking distance. Since we did not have a car, it was convenient having a bus which went all around the base.

Behind the apartment was a large field surrounded by a rail fence. Beyond that was a row of beautiful Monterey Cypress trees. We had a small porch at the back of the apartment. It was pleasant to sit there, and Peggy could play outside. I would never leave her alone, however. People frequently cut through the field and even on an army post it might not be safe. It was a pretty area with groves of Monterey Cypress (which only grow there) all about. The walk to the P X was along a wide shady path overhung with those beautiful trees.

Now I am an ardent shopper, so the Post Exchange was a place of wonder to me. We did our Christmas shopping mostly there. We bought Peggy a darling soft-eyed Panda Bear and a small wooden wagon with a rope handle, filled with blocks. The best thing of all, though, was a wonderful blue rocking horse with white dots and beautiful long eyelashes painted on it. It had been made by an older man on the post who also had made the wagon and blocks.

Peggy loved Dotty Horse which Santa had brought. Old Dotty was later loved by three more children and rocked many many miles!

A few days before Christmas Peggy and I went to town and bought a small tree. The price was incredibly high. She thought it very strange to ride on a bus with a tree, but these were all military people and no one seemed to notice. When we carried it in the house, she thought it stranger than ever to put a tree on a table.

Because of the war there were no Christmas decorations either so Peggy and I made our own. We pasted yellow typing paper to make chains, and we strung popcorn to drape around the tree. We made a manger scene from pictures cut out of "The Ladies Home Journal" and played Baby Jesus over and over.

On Christmas Eve after Peggy was in bed, we put the set of lights on the tree. However, we didn't dare leave the lights on because if one bulb went out, they all went out, and it was over. We had to have it lighted the next day for Daddy's first Christmas with Peggy.

Christmas morning Jack turned the lights on, and I brought Peggy downstairs. She was so excited with everything, and, of course, our joy was watching her as she played with her new toys. Neither of us could not get over the wonder of being there on this happy day.

Exactly one year ago Jack and the others had been in foxholes in Givet, France, defending the Meuse River. They were freezing in the cold, wet snow. He had stood guard all afternoon and that night, in bitter weather with frozen feet. They had begun to doubt whether any of them would ever see their homes again. It was over now. He was safe. We were a family again, and we had a home for the present at least. Our hearts were overflowing with thanks.

We had invited Ralph Keedy (Jack's friend) to have dinner with us. Ralph was from St. Louis, a very gentle person, on limited service because of a disabled hand. He brought Peggy a small fluffy black and white toy puppy. It had eyes which followed your eyes, very disconcerting! Peggy promptly named him Ralph Dog as good children always name a gift after the giver! He had brought us a large chicken which became our Christmas dinner. He also brought the unbelievable, some real butter. Of course, we never asked where he got it and he did not volunteer.

The lights on the little Christmas tree shone brightly all day, but finally that night one light went out and that was the end. No matter — they had done their job to the last. That would forever be the happiest Christmas of our whole lives.

In January Jack's orders came through for his discharge. This was the moment of decision. We never dreamed we would debate whether Jack should stay in the Army when the time came for his discharge. However, he was offered an excellent opportunity. If he stayed in the Army he would continue under the Army War College in Washington, D.C. After training he would receive the rank of 2nd Lieutenant. He would remain on limited service and would not be sent overseas. Jack had learned to enjoy military life and it's security.

On the other hand was the assurance of a career with J.J.Newberry Company in retail management. After much soul-searching he chose the latter. Thus on January 7, 1946, he took the bus to Camp Beale, California, the Separation Center, and was honorably discharged from the United States Army. He returned home the next day. On January 14, 1946, our belongings were packed and shipped by the Army to Jack's parent's home in Webster Groves, Missouri. Even Dotty Horse went in a large carton.

This was a very emotional time for us. We had been on a terrible journey through life for two and one half years. The Draft Notice on August 21, 1943, had changed our lives forever, and now his Honorable Discharge on January 7, 1946, would also change our lives forever. But together and with God's help we would make it to the end of our lives.

RESTRICTED

11/16/45

SPECIAL ORDERS)
:
NUMBER.....222)

HEADQUARTERS SPECIAL TROOPS, A.G.F.,
Army War College, Washington 25, DC.
16 November 1945.

1. Fol promotions, Hq & Hq Co, AGF, Liaison Pers, (Now on DS w/AGF Liaison Off at sta indicated after their respective names), are announced. Auth AR 615-5.

TO BE TECHNICAL SERGEANT (Temp)

S Sgt Michael E. Dufala, 13077694, AUS, Inf.
(US Army GH Cp.Pickett Va)
S Sgt George W. Morrow, 18126350, AUS, Inf.
(WDPC Ft Sam Houston Tex)
S Sgt Robert E. Stillwagon, 33104705, SS, Inf.
(WDPC Indiantown Gap Mil Reservation Pa)
Tec 3 Norman C. Tubbs, 31409552, SS, Inf.
(WDPC Ft McPherson Ga)
S Sgt Henry E. Van Raemdonk, 37540666, AUS, Inf.
(WDPC Cp Beale, Calif)

TO BE STAFF SERGEANT (Temp)

Sgt Harry V. Bonini, 39033234, SS, Inf.
(Regional Hosp, Oakland, Calif)
Sgt Ivan D. Bryant, 33090643, SS, Inf.
(Regional Hosp Ft Belvoir, Va)
Sgt Robert H. Miller, 37205060, SS, Inf.
(WDPC Ft Bliss, Tex)
Sgt Leslie D. Williams, 37426174, SS, Inf.
(LeGarde GH New Orleans, La)
Tec 4 John S. Broughton, 37244326, SS, Inf.
(Regional Hosp Ft Bragg NC)
Tec 4 Gilbert E. Winter, 36685801, SS, Inf.
(WDPC Indiantown Gap Pa)
Cpl John K. Price, 37623699, SS, Inf.
(Regional Hosp Ft Ord, Calif)
Cpl Robert L. Raimon, 12154932, ERC, Inf.
(Valley Forge GH, Phoenixville, Pa)

TO BE TECHNICIAN THIRD GRADE (Temp)

Tec 4 Edward D. Phelan, 30200018, SS, Inf.

TO BE SERGEANT (Temp)

Cpl William H. Schurk, 37603227, SS, Inf.
Tec 5 Edward F. Langevin, 39142330, SS, Inf.
(WDPC Ft Sam Houston, Tex)
Cpl Orvil W. Denny, 38479028, SS, Inf.
(Regional Hosp Cp J T Robinson Ark)

RESTRICTED

7 Pgs
Original

Promotion to Staff Sergeant. November 16, 1945.

ARMY SERVICE FORCES, NINTH SERVICE COMMAND
Headquarters, Fort Ord, California

12/27/45

27 December 1945

SPECIAL ORDER)

NUMBER   304)   E X T R A C T

55. The following EM, reld from organizations indicated, are trfd
in gr and WP to Sep Center, Cp. Beale, Calif., to arrive thereon 2 Jan 46,
for purpose of disch under the prov as indicated. EDCMR 2 Jan 46. RR 1-2
as amended will be complied with.

GRADE	NAME	ASN	ORGN	CIVILIAN ADDRESS
*	*	*	*	*

RR 1-1
ARW, NSC, HQ 1962 SCU, FORT ORD, CALIF.

| S Sgt | Price, John K. | 37625699 | Med Sec | 574 Providence,
Webster Groves, Missouri. |

* * * * *

BY ORDER OF COLONEL SULLIVAN:

K L POOL
WOJG USA
Asst Adj

OFFICIAL:
/s/ K. L. Pool
/t/ K. L. POOL
WOJG USA
Asst Adj

A TRUE EXTRACT COPY:

Willis R Irwin
WILLIS R. IRWIN
Captain, Infantry
AGWLO

Orders to Camp Beale, California for discharge from Army.

Q. M. C. Form No. 489
WAR DEPARTMENT
Revised June 20, 1938

TALLY SHEET
INCOMING

Tally-in No.______
Sheet No.______
Number of Sheets______

Station______ Warehouse No.______ Date received 1-14-46

Consignor______ Car No.______ Car Seals No.______

Via______ Requisition, Purchase Order, or Shipping Ticket______
(Rail, truck, boat, parcel post, mail)

No.______ Bill of lading No.______

Contents of packages { have / have not } been verified (strike out words not applicable)

U. S. Nos. on Packages	Number and Kind of Packages	CONTENTS	Gross Weight (Pounds) Unit	Total
	2 barracks bags			
	1 trunk			
	Rocking horse			
		Sgt. J. K. Price		

U. S. GOVERNMENT PRINTING OFFICE o16—20028

Checker Ray Stump

Tally Sheet - These were our total possessions at that moment.

Army of the United States

Honorable Discharge

This is to certify that

JOHN K PRICE 37 627 699 Staff Sergeant

117th Infantry Regiment

Army of the United States

is hereby Honorably Discharged from the military service of the United States of America.

This certificate is awarded as a testimonial of Honest and Faithful Service to this country.

Given at SEPARATION CENTER
CAMP BEALE CALIFORNIA

Date 7 January 1946

PAUL K DEAN
MAJOR   AC

8   605

(original)
(original)

WD AGO FORM 100
1 JUL 1945 100   This form supersedes WD AGO Form 100, 15 July 1944, which will not be used.   16—45815-1

222
7

Honorable Discharge - Army of the United States.

Afterword

Ralph (Rusty) Chapman.

The other person Jack wrote about was his friend Joe Barnes. They had known one another since they were teenagers

Joe was in the Pacific theater in the 32nd Infantry Engineers. His wife Bettie and I became close friends. She and their son, Butch, lived with her parents in St. Louis. We occasionally went shopping and had lunch together. Bettie had a party for Butch on his second birthday and invited Peggy. She was one year old and the only little girl. When I wrote and told Jack about it, he replied, "I'll say Peg was the Belle of the Ball. All those boys to one little girl. That is an ETO man's dream!"

In 1967, Butch (now Joe III) was in Vietnam. He was in the 25th Infantry Division, with rank of 1st Lieutenant. He had two children, a girl and a boy.

'Keep the faith,' says former POW

By ERIN BROTHERS
Managing Editor

A World War II prisoner of war tells families of Americans held in Iraq to "keep the faith."

Ralph Chapman of Harrisburg was held prisoner for 15 months, after his 407th Squadron B-17 was shot down over Germany on Jan. 30, 1944.

Chapman, a ball turret gunner, was one of two Army Air Corps men who survived after their aircraft was hit, collided with another B-17, and the two planes exploded.

"It is impossible to gauge how much you can take and come through with flying colors; the human ability to survive is incalculable," said Chapman, who retired from Scot Lad Foods' advertising department last year.

"The families of our men being held prisoner in the Gulf have my sympathy, but they must keep believing, and keep the faith that they'll come home," Chapman said. "The majority of POWs in Germany survived."

Most of the 15 months Chapman was held were spent in Stalag Luft III, near Sagan, Poland, the camp made familiar after it was featured in the movie "The Great Escape."

"Initially, they took us to an interrogation center, and after they couldn't extract any information from us, we were sent to a relocation camp in the heart of Frankfurt, Germany," he said.

But Chapman said he was one of the "lucky" ones.

ON JAN. 8, 1944, 22 days before his aircraft was shot down, Chapman learned that his son had been born.

"Some of those guys didn't hear about their children being born until months afterward," he said. "Mail was hard to come by while we were held. I probably received about four letters and a package during the time I was there."

The 138-pound member of the 92nd Bomb Group dropped to 100 pounds while he was held prisoner, but said the "hunger was tougher on the big, husky guys, than it was on us little shrimps."

"The food was poor, and in the wintertime, there wasn't much heat. We were moved west on a forced march in late January, early February 1945 in the middle of a blizzard, and there were a number of casualties in what we later called 'the blizzard march.'"

Chapman said that the U.S. government is "pretty powerless" to re-capture American prisoners until after the hostilities cease.

"There's not much you can do other than rant and rave; you can't go in and extract them. They're at the mercy of their captors," Chapman said. "They just have to have the desire, ability and determination to survive, whatever is thrown at them."

Chapman and other prisoners were re-captured by General Patton before WW II ended, and though they weren't used as human shields, as Hussein has threatened, they were held 2 ½ miles from an area where air raids occurred day and night, and they often threw blankets over their heads to protect themselves from 'falling flak.'"

Chapman said that in some ways, the POW is better off than his family back home.

"At least the POW knows he's alive, but the family doesn't know where he is, or how he's being treated."

"Somebody's got to stop this man (Hussein); a dictator's a dictator," Chapman said. "I haven't forgotten the lessons of World War II."

From the St. Louis Post Dispatch Newspaper.

There were two people Jack referred to quite often in his letters.
ne was his cousin Ralph (Rusty) Chapman. Rusty had lived with the
ices for several years when he was a small boy. Jack, being an only
ild, enjoyed having Rusty and developed a very warm affection for
m.

Later Rusty married his high school sweetheart, Earline. He also,
that time, enlisted in the Air Force. As I did, Earline and their baby
mmy lived with her mother. Rusty was stationed in England. On a
mbing run the plane crashed (see article). Rusty was captured and
came a German prisoner of war. In Jack's letter of December 14,
944, the last one from England he wrote, "I am really looking forward
seeing Rusty again. I hope to be able to spend this Saturday and
unday with him." That was our code that he was headed for the front.
e was!

Joe Barnes.

Bettie and Butch.

Sources

ENGLAND:
Andover Seen and Remembered. Edward Kendall & Derek Dine.

Crusade in Europe. Dwight D. Eisenhower, (Garden City, NY: Doubleday, 1948).

Day Before Yesterday. Mrs. Theodore Roosevelt, Jr., (Garden City, NY: Doubleday).

Information and Pictures, Tidworth, England. Anthony Pickernell.

Information and Pictures, Yeovil, England. Jack Sweet.

A Soldier's Story. Omar N. Bradley, (New York, NY: Henry Holt & Company, 1951).

South Somerset Official Guide. Somerset District Council.

BATTLE OF THE BULGE:
Battle of the Bulge. Danny S. Parker, (Combined Books, Inc.)

Battle. The Story of the Bulge. John Toland, (New York: Random House, 1957).

The Bitter Woods. John Eisenhower, (New York: G.P. Putnam's Sons, 1969).

Crusade in Europe. Dwight D. Eisenhower, (Garden City, NY: Doubleday, 1948).

The Damned Engineers. Janice Holt Giles, (Boston: Houghton Mifflin, 1970).

Dark December. Robert E. Merriam, (Chicago: Ziff-Davis, 1947).

A Soldier's Story. Omar N. Bradley, (New York: Henry Holt & Company, 1951).

A Time for Trumpets. Charles B. McDonald, (New York: William Morrow & Company, Inc., 1985).

GERMANY:
Curlew History. William J. Lyman, Jr., (Chapel Hill, NC: The Orange Printshop, 1948).

History of the 117th Infantry, 1944-1945. (Baton Rouge, LA: Army & Navy Publishing Co., 1946).

A Soldier's Story. Omar N. Bradley, (New York, NY: Henry Holt & Company, 1951).

Work Horse of the Western Front, 30th Div. Robert L. Hewitt, (Washington Infantry Journal Press).

FORT ORD:
Army Times-Guide to Army Posts. (Stockpole Books).

Encyclopedia of Historic Forts. Robert B. Roberts, (New York, NY: McMillan Publishing Company).

Printed in the USA
CPSIA information can be obtained
at www.ICGtesting.com
JSHW060045150824
68134JS00031B/2639

9 781681 622460